4477

*The
Beautiful,
Novel,
and
Strange*

Rec'd 4 *of*
five Shillings being the first Payment for a Short Tract in Quarto
call'd the Analysis of Beauty: wherein Forms are consider'd in a new
light, to which will be added two explanatory Prints Serious and
Comical, Engrav'd on large Copper Plates fit to frame for Furniture.

N.B. *The Price will be rais'd after the Subscription is over.*

W:ᵐ Hogarth

The Beautiful, Novel, and Strange

AESTHETICS AND
HETERODOXY

Ronald Paulson

The Johns Hopkins University Press
Baltimore and London

PR
858
.A74
P38
1996

© 1996 The Johns Hopkins University Press
All rights reserved. Published 1996
Printed in the United States of America on acid-free paper
05 04 03 02 01 00 99 98 97 96   5 4 3 2 1

The Johns Hopkins University Press
2715 North Charles Street
Baltimore, Maryland 21218-4319
The Johns Hopkins Press Ltd., London

32545829

To Andrew and Melissa

Superstition   p. 67ff

Contents

Preface

The aim of this book is to fill a lacuna in studies of aesthetics at its point of origin in England. The popular sense of "aesthetics" (as in the title of a recent collection of essays, *Aesthetics and Ideology*) is simply formalism.[1] The scholarly sense has tended to focus either on the refinement of taste or on the aspect of beauty that came to be known as the Sublime, excluding both the Beautiful itself and certainly Joseph Addison's third term, the Novel, New, or Uncommon (until it emerges much later in the Picturesque).

Taste derives from the aesthetics of Anthony Ashley Cooper, third earl of Shaftesbury, in which the Beautiful is a monolith, outside of which lies the deformed (low, mechanic, and ugly, a transgressive category as clearly social as aesthetic): all that matters is to define the perceptual apparatus that can enjoy the aesthetic experience of the Beautiful and to ask whether taste is relative or absolute.[2] The Sublime derives from Addison's aesthetics, which distinguishes kinds of aesthetic response in relation to its objects: not only the Beautiful but the Novel and the Great. Most studies, however, have followed from Longinus and Edmund Burke, who put their weight on the Sublime.[3] While Burke is careful to define the Beautiful, it is as a foil to the Sublime, in which he is primarily interested (self-preservation, pain, and power, as opposed to society, love, and passivity).

In the 1970s Martin Battestin could still begin a study of the role of art in the first half of the eighteenth century by positing in writers from Dryden to Fielding and Goldsmith "an assumption about the

interdependence of theology and aesthetics."[4] Those words in fact
comprise an oxymoron: English aesthetics began as an antitheology,
essentially deist. Its origins were in the philosophical twins of empiricism and heterodoxy. In Michael McKeon's terms, the discourse of
aesthetics replaced religious discourse, which had been put in question
by empirical discourse (in time it replaced empirical discourse as well).[5]
Even Neoplatonism, which had been used by priests to theologize the
Beautiful, provided Shaftesbury a model for the deist's merely transcendent god.

   This is not to deny that "deism" is a slippery term; that most
writers labeled "deist" (or Socinian or Arian) claimed to be orthodox
Anglicans. Robert Sullivan, for example, in his study of John Toland,
rightly describes deism, *sub specie aeternitatis,* as "a convenient term to
describe the revision of traditional Christian formulas which occupied
so many English writers between the Civil War and the French Revolution."[6] But in the 1700s "deist" was a term tossed back and forth in the
context of heterodoxy. It was used to mean certain things ranging from
freethinker to atheist, but the arch-heretic Bernard Mandeville defined
it thus: "He who believes, in the common acceptation, that there is a
GOD, and that the world is rul'd by providence, but has no faith in any
thing reveal'd to us, is a deist; and he, who believes neither the one nor
the other, is an atheist."[7] Mandeville meant that deists were essentially
disbelievers in miracles (in God's intervention in daily events once he
had created the world) and critics of the priests who enforced belief in
miracles by insisting on the divine authority of biblical texts.

   In fact, Shaftesburian deism supported the Protestant establishment and sanctioned religion as an acceptable expedient. Shaftesbury
dissociated himself from the name deist, referring it as a term of op-
probrium to his opponents.[8] The Shaftesburian heritage of Whiggery
and connoisseurship established a genealogy of heterodoxy, aesthetics,
and orthodoxy (of both church and state) shared by Addison, a pillar of
Whig orthodoxy, a severe critic of freethinkers, and an upholder of
"faith."[9] But Addison, in his most significant statement in the *Spectator*
on religion, based his "faith" on the creed of a rationalist. This essay (in
No. 465) could easily pass for deist, especially in its proof of God's existence in nature and its conclusion with Addison's hymn "The Spacious
Firmament on High."[10] Although the words of the hymn ("birth,"

"tidings," and "truth") invoke Christ, the reference is entirely to nature created by a transcendent god ("the Works of such a Being as we define God to be"). The essay series "Pleasures of the Imagination," which defines the parameters of aesthetic discourse for the century, is in this sense his response to the question of rationalist Christianity.

While not many historians would any longer equate art and divine providence, they do focus their attention on Shaftesbury, taste, and politeness, which comprise the orthodoxy of aesthetics—of so-called high art, aristocratic patronage, and various forms of idealization. This is also by and large true of historians of the Sublime. Before either Addison or Burke, "sublime" was an honorific adjective used to denote "high art."

However, an equally interesting aesthetics came into being, deriving from less respectable (less aristocratic) forms of deism. The philosophical progenitors in this case were Toland, Anthony Collins, and Thomas Woolston, whose critical deism, discrediting the Scriptures and the miracles of Christ, constituted an oppositional tradition, or countertradition, one that left its traces on art and literature. Most immediately it showed William Hogarth, the engraver's apprentice who was trying in the 1720s to adapt to the traditional assumptions of art academies, ways to counter Shaftesburian taste—a taste that was contingent upon the "disinterestedness" of the gentleman of property—with an aesthetics of the "common man."

Beginning with his *Harlot's Progress* (1732), deism was one source of the new graphic form Hogarth invented, which he called the "modern moral subject."[11] When he came to formulate his practice in *The Analysis of Beauty* (1753), in a paradigmatic act of aestheticizing, he revised the Christian symbol of the Trinity, a triangle inscribed with the Name of God, replacing the Name of God with his own Line of Beauty. He then made the triangle three-dimensional, changing a figure of the mind into one of the sensible world (figs. 21, 22). He retained the Shaftesburian monolith of the Beautiful (vs. the Ugly) but redefined its perception in the terms Addison used for his middle ground, the Novel (curiosity, surprise, discovery). He employed the Novel as an epistemology of Addisonian spectatorship in order to focus on the beautiful object, which was for him (in nature) the living, contemporary woman and (in art) the useful, everyday items of London life.

Accounts of aesthetics almost never mention, except in passing, *The Analysis of Beauty*,[12] and Hogarth himself has been seen either as "idiosyncratic," a maverick and eccentric, or as a simple, uneducated bloke, the "Cockney's Mirror" and man of the London street.[13] But in league with a few contemporary writers he created a realist aesthetics of the Novel, in his own case to correct Shaftesbury's idealist system; and in his engraved images he developed an alternative to the academic theory of painting, on which Shaftesbury had largely drawn in his writings. This sense of the Novel preempts the Beautiful and Great in the most forward-looking literature and art (as opposed, perhaps, to theory) of the period.

One example is the emergent form of prose fiction known as the novel (with a lower-case *n*). The proto-genre, which defined itself against romance, epic, tragedy, and other forms of "high" art, had roots not only in forms of journalism (novel/news) but also in the forms of rationalism which contributed to critical deism and its *deus absconditus*. As Irving Howe wrote in an essay called "History and the Novel":

> It was deism that taught us to accept the pain of historicity. By granting God powers of initiation and then putting him to sleep forever, deism freed the mind from the puzzle of origins and cleared the way for historical consciousness. Without such a tacit premise, the novel could not have gotten very far, since it really has no room for a will superior to natural law.[14]

Deism is a phenomenon that is not ordinarily related to the origins of the novel. Howe is probably remembering Georg Lukacs's formula that the novel is what has become of the epic in a world without gods.[15] Without an immanent deity, religion is replaced by manners and customs; the reality of Christ's miracles, the Last Supper, and the Trinity by stories of remarkable coincidences, cathected suppers, and romantic triangles. What makes these parodic is the strain of critical deism that filters through Hogarth to Fielding and others, even the "orthodox" clergyman Sterne—though of course with the usual mixed results of filtering. In Hogarth's satiric fables of art (1737–41) and the theory of the *Analysis* a decade later, as well as in Henry Fielding's preface to *Joseph Andrews* (1742) and his introductory chapters in *Tom Jones* (1749), an aesthetics of the Novel/novel begins to emerge, which in turn has its effect a decade later on Laurence Sterne's *Tristram Shandy* (1759–67).

In fits and starts in a number of books, I have gradually developed the idea of the Novel/Beautiful as a proto-Picturesque focused on human nature rather than on landscape.[16] I argued the case for Hogarth's role most fully in my biography *Hogarth* (1991–93), especially in volume 3, which laid out his theory of aesthetics. In the present study I outline a broader, less narrativized explanation, not limited to Hogarth. It has seemed necessary not only to spell out what I wrote there but to reformulate it in terms of its roots and its flowers, the novelists as well as the painters who developed its implications.

The central figure is Fielding, whose theory of the "comic epic in prose" mediated between Shaftesbury's "Divine Example" (the Platonic Idea) and Hogarth's theory of the Beautiful/Novel in the *Analysis*. Fielding's ties to heterodoxy have been denied by Battestin, his most recent biographer, but they cry out everywhere in his work for revaluation. My discussion necessarily contests the views of Battestin, Aubrey Williams, and J. Paul Hunter, who see the writers I deal with as still orthodox Church of Englanders immersed in sermons, devotional works, and belief in divine providence (which Melvyn New, after Smollett's Win Jenkins, has more accurately called the "grease of God").[17] I am suggesting that the tradition of the novel which Fielding founded— and which attempted to correct the Richardson version—was based partly at least on heterodox assumptions and a heterodox aesthetics.

Not only the "novel" but also, homologous with it, other innovative forms emerge in the wake of, and share the assumptions of, this neglected strand of aesthetics. The Picturesque is one immediate off-shoot (to make something *picturesque* is to aestheticize it), and Addison's other term, "the Strange," is only the far end of the Novel, New, or Uncommon. Addison uses "the Strange" to refer to those areas further off the map of the Beautiful and Great than the Novel; the Strange raises the stakes of all the claims that were first proposed by the Novel. For when the Novel turns Strange it only continues to perpetuate the counterdiscourse in another key. For example, *Tristram Shandy* produces an over-the-edge parody of civic humanist masculinity, *The Vicar of Wakefield* of equal providence, and the "children's book" *The History of Little Goody Two-Shoes* of the whole orthodox enterprise.

In the decades after 1750 we witness the simultaneous advent of sophisticated forms of erotica and of children's literature, which invent fantasy substitutes for (eroticized or childish versions of) inexplicable doctrines such as the Athanasian Trinity (in Fanny Hill, Charles, and her clients; in Two-Shoes, her animal familiars, and her children). *The Vicar of Wakefield* juxtaposes the childlike Primroses with Lovelace-like seducers, popular ballads, and the "sublime" Old Testament story of Job, recently reexamined in the biblical studies of Robert Lowth and others. And the contemporary *Goody Two-Shoes* rewrites the characters of the *Vicar* as literal children and its story as that of a child Redeemer (also incorporating the Job story). The Happy Valley as nursery, coinciding with the androgynous status of Uncle Toby, Tristram, and Yorick (and pointing to Harley in Mackenzie's *Man of Feeling* of 1771), also raises the question of whether it is a feminizing that takes place, or rather an infantilizing. The development of aesthetics in this period remains closely related to the demystifying of the Christian deity to a man, a woman—and now a child.

We might say that the Strange is an extension of the epistemology of the Novel into the range of the Sublime, but (in fact offering an alternative) without the awe and respect tendered the sublime object. After Joseph Warton and William Collins in the 1740s inaugurated the movement whereby the Sublime became the central aesthetic category of the later eighteenth century, Hogarth and others accommodated themselves to this initiative insofar as they worked to establish an alternative to the Sublime in the Strange, which might yet be true to the basic principles of the Addisonian Novel.

The Picturesque, however, as a term of aesthetics, gardening, and landscape painting, was named and theorized; whereas the Strange, like the Novel and Uncommon, had no theory to sustain it after Hogarth's absorption of it into his *Analysis of Beauty*. The works I categorize under the Novel and the Strange were given other names by their authors, working terms that corresponded to practical rather than aesthetic categories (e.g., "modern moral subject," "comic history-painting," "comic epic in prose"). These terms were outside (or beneath) aesthetic consideration. We may suppose that Hogarth appropriated the name Beautiful for the aesthetic dimension of works that in fact operated under the term Novel, works that no theorist after

Addison considered dignified enough to describe. The generic term "novel" applied to the form written by Fielding and Sterne, as well as Richardson, did not have more than occasional usage until the 1770s. So far as I know it has never been used in the way I use it to join Addison's aesthetics, Hogarth's theory, and the emerging forms of prose fiction.

The aesthetic tradition of the Novel can be more precisely situated by returning to its origin for Hogarth in the antiacademic discourse with which he reacted against art instruction as a young man. The "English School" of painting, which emerged from the conflicts within the St. Martin's Lane Academy (essentially an artists' club with a life class attached, which Hogarth founded in 1735), can be roughly divided into those who followed academic precepts (drawing based on canonical sculptures), often slavishly but sometimes imaginatively, and those whose paintings aimed at being antiacademic, "modern," and native "English." The first group included Joshua Reynolds, Richard Wilson, James Barry, and Benjamin West. In the second, Hogarth was followed by Johan Zoffany, Joseph Wright of Derby, George Stubbs, Thomas Gainsborough, and Thomas Rowlandson. I examined the latter group in *Emblem and Expression: Meaning in English Art of the Eighteenth Century* (1975),[18] regarding the period from Hogarth's point of view. A decade later John Barrell, in *The Political Theory of Painting from Reynolds to Hazlitt* (1986), recovered Reynolds's point of view, laid out in the *Discourses* he delivered as first president of the Royal Academy, arguing that antiacademic painters were merely academics *manqués*. Barrell, without mentioning the possibility of two traditions of painting, presented a tradition of academic theory—from Shaftesbury to Reynolds and beyond—which hypothesized an idealizing, heroic painting based on public spirit.[19] Drawing on the work of J.G.A. Pocock, he called it civic humanist;[20] and drawing on Michel Foucault's concept of "discourse," he argued that civic humanism was *the* discourse—artists could not think or conceive outside its terms. In Barrell's account the discourse of civic humanism suppressed all others, whether religious (Anglican, Dissenter, or deist), literary (satiric, pastoral, or georgic), aesthetic, or simply anti–civic humanist.

Andrew Hemingway's review of *The Political Theory of Painting* (in *Art History*) criticized it for being "The Political Theory of Painting without the Politics." Barrell idealized civic humanism, ignoring the politics of rule by a Whig oligarchy. My own review (in the *New Republic*) criticized it for omitting the painting, that is, any reference to the relationship between the theory and the works of art it was written to project. The reason for the omission was partly that Barrell was writing a history of theory, and partly that the paintings did not correspond to the theory, in most cases grotesquely so.[21]

Barrell also failed to distinguish between treatises written for the artist (such as Shaftesbury's *Judgment of Hercules* or Reynolds's *Discourses*) and treatises of taste or aesthetics written for the perceiver of works of art (such as Shaftesbury's *Characteristicks*, Addison's "Pleasures," Francis Hutcheson's *Inquiry*, Jonathan Richardson's various works on connoisseurship, or George Turnbull's *Treatise on Ancient Painting*); nor did he distinguish between the genres of philosophy and journalism as the purveyors of theory.[22] He posited a monist discourse, overlooking the possibility of both a strong directly contrary discourse and a host of other contending discourses that helped to shape the practice or theory of an artist or connoisseur. Foucault's model, which is monological and authoritarian, is less apposite than Bakhtin's for a period in which art—perhaps all experience—was notably "dialogical." Foucault's "discourse" provides a parody of what Pocock himself refers to as "tunnel history"—"selecting a single theme and pushing it through until it emerges in the daylight of a new country"—which does "not and cannot claim to have told all there is to tell."[23] One reason civic humanism has gotten far too much play in recent years is that Pocock empowered a rather precisely delimited tradition of conservative republicanism to include and to signify all expressions of political, social, ethical, and gender conviction with which it had any commonality. I emphasize Barrell's *Political Theory of Painting* because in the decade since its publication it has dominated art historical writing in the eighteenth century, which has idealized theory and the academic tradition as *the* English School of painting.[24] None of this writing acknowledges the possibility of a countertradition.

The civic humanist version of the English School of painting depends upon a confusion of tradition with canon, of countertradition with noncanonical works. A tradition (e.g., the one passed down from Hogarth to Zoffany, Wright, and the others) is a series of linked artists and their works held together by a kind of conscious filiation. Whereas a tradition involves choice from the inside by the artists themselves, a canon is established by outsiders, a community of readers or spectators who operate (by which we mean theorize) within an institutional setting. Insiders, however, can attempt to pass off their tradition as a canon, especially if, as was the case with the Royal Academy, they operate within the institutional setting of both school and academy.[25] It was Reynolds's purpose to create a canon of English art, and specifically one that was assimilated to the great canon of Continental art deriving from Italy. He declared noncanonical the art of Venice, the Netherlands, and Germany, and, in England, the art of painters such as Hogarth and Gainsborough.

Barrell and his followers reflect the present discourse of British art (and to some extent literary) history at its most sophisticated, but this should be recognized for what it is: Reynolds redux, a revival of the academic discourse of the later eighteenth century which raised the standing of Reynolds and marginalized Hogarth and the others in his tradition. It was specifically the discourse of Samuel Johnson, passed on to Reynolds because Johnson loved this young man who could paint and at the same time emulate the Johnsonian ethos.[26] This was a case of discourse, or theory, predominating over works of art in the words of someone who had little or no interest in paintings themselves. And while Hogarth consciously placed himself within a tradition of literary discourse, it was not the discourse of theory but of practice—of satire, of painting, and of politics. That discourse of theory, which Hogarth spent his career contesting and which was long ago succeeded in English art history by a discourse of taste, connoisseurship, and cataloging, has now returned with the credentials of both "theory" and (oddly, given its elitist subtext) "political correctness." And this discourse inherits from both academicians and cultural materialists a critical canon that studiedly excludes not only other discourses but other explanations, other narratives, and the scholarly works that proposed those narratives.

When I criticize this hegemonic and monistic history and argue for a countertradition, I mean to suggest not that there were only two traditions; but rather that, as opposed to the hegemonic idea of one tradition, there were several others, intertwined in complex ways, that shared certain characteristics—and, indeed, spoke the language of several different discourses, only one of which was specifically antiacademic and/or anti–civic humanist. Fielding, for example, while deviating sharply from Shaftesbury in certain particulars, and owing a strong allegiance to Hogarth, was primarily influenced by Shaftesbury, and certainly never deviated from an image of himself as an aristocrat. The antiacademic discourse is only one of several—one he probably picked up from Hogarth, while in important particulars retaining the stance of the civic humanist justice of the peace who was his father and eventually himself.

I do, however, mean to show that these particular discourses began by defining themselves against another discourse: deism against the authority of clergy, divine text, and other forms of mystification; aesthetics against religious belief, especially in its central doctrine of rewards/punishments; Addisonian tripartite aesthetics against the monolith of Shaftesbury's Beautiful; and, most particularly, the Hogarthian program against academic doctrines of painting.

In summary, the aim of the present study is to disclose at the moment of its origin a way of conceiving the modern category of the aesthetic which had strong support during the eighteenth century but has been obscured both by a more dominant contemporary discourse and by current trends in art and literary history. The official tradition was that which issued in the writings of Shaftesbury on taste and which flowered in the elaborate theorizing of the Sublime at the end of the century. The countertradition developed Addison's interest in the Beautiful, the Novel, and the Strange, and found its chief exponent in the practice of Hogarth. The Shaftesbury tradition inspired the academic discourse that was presided over by Reynolds and championed history painting as its supreme expression. Hogarth consistently articulated an antiacademic discourse that championed his graphic "modern moral subject."[27] But it is a central feature of this argument that the two traditions comprised not only painterly but also literary theory and practice, and much of this study is dedicated to retrieving the literary innovations that followed and complemented Hogarth's practice in the visual arts.

It will appear that the unique power of visual images (what W. J. T. Mitchell, referring to this period, has called "the tyranny of the picture") was the stimulus that prompted a countertradition to the stolidly literary discourse of the academy.[28] To be more precise, I should add: *popular* (concrete, particular, as distinct from idealizing) visual images. These images helped to define the limits and limitations of the theoretical discourse in the period. In fact, however, although Hogarth gathered together the mixed threads, he took them from the *writings* of Locke and Addison, Shaftesbury and Mandeville, Toland and Woolston, Swift and Gay; and, with the particular authority of his visual images, he passed them on—primarily, it would have to be admitted, though by no means exclusively, to writers.

With these images Hogarth reached the same audience—in size and composition—as did the writers, whether Addison or, later, Fielding and Sterne, and this audience was very different from that of any other contemporary painter. The discrepancy was summed up in the case of the tickets for the 1761 Society of Artists exhibition: It was precisely the large audience attracted by Hogarth's satiric etchings on the ticket (rather than the artists' paintings) which the artists wished to exclude, and did exclude the next year, as not prospective buyers of their paintings.

In short, this study attempts to conceive aesthetics as many contemporaries did—not as theory but as a poetics of practice; to show that the most popular of modern literary forms had a crucial relevance to those who contributed to the high-cultural pursuit of philosophical goals; and so both to coordinate the Novel and the novel and to distinguish one from the other.

It does, of course, represent only one history of the origin of aesthetics. Of necessity, the extrapolation from the art-historical context (and from the retrospective reduction of that context by modern scholars) to the more general history makes that history appear more polarized than it really was. Although the battle between two ideologically determinate opponents is, I believe, the approach called for in opening up the Hogarthian strain of aesthetics, it is my hope that this study will be followed by other treatments of the origin of aesthetics as a variegated field of possibility.[29]

The
Beautiful,
Novel,
and
Strange

Aesthetics and Deism

Shaftesbury: "The Divine Example"

The term "aesthetics" (first applied in the 1730s by Alexander Baumgarten) derived from the Greek *aisthetikos* ("of sense perception").[1] The branch of philosophy known as aesthetics emerged in England at the beginning of the eighteenth century—primarily in works published by Shaftesbury and Addison in 1711–12 (*Characteristicks,* and the "Pleasures of the Imagination" essays of the *Spectator*)— from the assumption of British empirical philosophy that all experience derives from the senses. But if the rise of aesthetics in England coincided with the rise of empiricism, so also did rational forms of religion, from latitudinarian orthodoxy to deist and atheist heterodoxy.[2]

A genealogy would begin with John Locke, who in his *Essay concerning Human Understanding* (1690) denied innate ideas (such as Do good, Believe in God), figuring the mind as a closed room with only a chink through which pictures of the outside world are passively received by the senses. Disturbed that Locke had left man morally neutral, Locke's student Shaftesbury recovered innate ideas in the form of a sixth sense, the moral sense, which perceives as immediately and accurately as the sense of sight. To the question of what leads a tabula rasa to act morally, Locke had answered: correct reasoning from the relations of things as perceived by the senses; the contracts and opinions of society; and (beyond reason) religion, which projects the fear of punishment and the hope of reward in a future life. Shaftesbury's primary moral insight was that an action is not virtuous if influenced by thoughts of rewards, whether earthly or heavenly. The same is true, in terms of desire and possession, of the beauty of a human form or a landscape. Thus virtue and beauty are as homologous as the moral and aesthetic senses. The one shifts the philosopher's attention back to motives as the other does to responses, and in both cases to the most disinterested, the furthest removed from personal gain.

Having effectively removed religion from his system, Shaftesbury permitted it to reenter in two ways. In an inferior way, the "divine example" of the god of the Christians can return as a belief in rewards and punishments in the afterlife. Although this religion cannot make a person virtuous, it can guide weak citizens to socially acceptable behavior.[3] Since this will be a cornerstone of our argument, it is worth quoting Shaftesbury. Of the different versions of a god, he writes, the essence of deity "must be either in the way of his power, as presupposing some disadvantage or benefit to accrue from him; or in the way of his excellency and worth, as thinking it the perfection of nature to imitate and resemble him." If, "through hope merely of reward, or fear of punishment, the creature be incited to do the good he hates, or restrained from doing the ill to which he is not otherwise in the least degree averse, there is in this case . . . no virtue or goodness whatsoever."[4] In the second case, the virtuous act is imitative, not prudential or pragmatic, and it supposes a deity as "an example" of beauty, virtue, and order that "must undoubtedly serve . . . to raise and increase the affection toward virtue, and help to submit and subdue all other affections to that alone" (1:268).

Nevertheless, Shaftesbury admits that "the fear of future punishment and hope of future reward, added to this belief," might contribute to the virtue of some people; "the principle of fear of future punishment, and hope of future reward, how mercenary or servile soever it may be accounted, is yet in many circumstances a great advantage, security, and support to virtue." And

> Thus in a civil state or public we see that a virtuous administration, and an equal and just distribution of rewards and punishments, is of the

highest service, not only by restraining the vicious, and forcing them to act usefully to society, but by making virtue to be apparently the interest of every one, so as to remove all prejudices against it, create a fair reception for it, and lead men into that path which, afterwards they cannot easily quit. (1:269, 270–72)

Finally, he extends the theme of punishments in the afterlife to public executions in this life, in which

we see generally that the infamy and odiousness of their crime, and the shame of it before mankind, contribute more to their misery than all besides; and that it is not the immediate pain of death itself which raises so much horror either in the sufferers or spectators, as that ignominious kind of death which is inflicted for public crimes and violations of justice and humanity. (1:273)

For Shaftesbury (and, more radically, another deist, Bernard Mandeville) religion was a myth created by priests and politicians to keep themselves in power, their society in order, and the oppressed vulgar happy. The key word "happiness" complements the concept of rewards and punishments: punishments here and now, rewards to look forward to in the afterlife (therefore no need of them in this).[5]

In Shaftesbury's system, however, there is also a superior type of "divine example," a benevolent deity who is loved and admired. In practice this deity is a Platonic abstraction, defined in mathematical terms of balance and harmony; among virtues, even benevolence can become a vice if it is disproportionate with the other affections of the mind: "This ... is certain," Shaftesbury writes in his *Inquiry concerning Virtue and Merit* (1699, 1711), "that the admiration and love of order, harmony, and proportion, in whatever kind, is naturally improving to the temper, advantageous to social affection, and highly assistant to virtue, which is itself no other than the love of order and beauty in society" (1:279).[6] The Shaftesburian divine creation is figured as order (beauty is to deformity as regularity is to irregularity) of both the world and of man's individual mind, which as an example can improve the already benevolent man. This example is hardly a religion, because it has no priests and dogmas; rather, it is a design (the *disegno* of Renaissance art treatises). "God" is the great artist, creator of an unfallen nature whose chief principle is the revelation of unity in apparent variety. When Shaftesbury adds to the passage about the "divine example" the statement that "if the order of the world itself appears just and beautiful, the admiration and esteem of order must run higher," he means order in itself, for its own sake: "and the elegant passion or love of beauty, which is so advantageous to virtue, must be the more improved by its exercise in so ample and magnificent a subject" (1:279). The magnificent subject, we infer, is aesthetics, the elite appreciation of beauty in itself, but as the passage shows, that beauty is at its highest equated with virtue.

This "order," in its perfection, has to be a mental substitute for the world as we have it. By denying innate ideas Locke had given up a central argument for defending divine revelation (or intervention in everyday events), and while Shaftesbury recovered innate ideas it was without revelation, as another of Locke's senses. The real world was inevitably marred by contingencies—by social contracts and by the doctrines of clergymen (or, worse, atheists) claiming that man is fallen, depraved, and in need of control by the belief in rewards and punishments. In a world that may require, but whose elite at any rate is better off without, a legalistic religion, Shaftesbury believed that a work of art is the only proper substitute for the real world, as the worship of beauty is for religion.

In short, Shaftesbury the deist replaced the immanence of the deity with what he designated as beauty—and specifically a god of rewards and punishments with what he called a "divine example" of (equated) beauty and virtue. In this way, in these terms, he invented and defined modern aesthetics. But if he replaced the deity with Beauty, he also shifted attention from God the governor (if not creator) to the men who can perceive and judge for themselves. In the same way, Shaftesbury the Whig (grandson of the great first earl) replaced a king and his priests with an oligarchy of nobles. He replaced the principle of the Many subordinated to the One, with the principle of unity in apparent variety, or politically the subordination of the many to the few. In terms of aesthetics, the civic humanist discourse that he expounded turned attention from the maker, the painter or architect, to the men of taste, the connoisseurs, and the collectors. Shaftesbury's politics and aesthetics join in his concept of disinterestedness: as a property owner, the civic humanist is above considerations of ambition, possession, consumption, and desire, and therefore is capable of a "rational and refined contemplation" of both morality and beauty—capable of both governing men and judging art.

As it happened, only in the case of architecture was it possible for Shaftesbury's aesthetic project to be realized—for the theory and the practice, the connoisseur and the architect, to coincide. Richard Boyle, third earl of Burlington, joined these roles in his function as patron, a patron who chose the designs of Palladio, commissioned architects to adapt those designs to England, published their plans, and executed a number of adaptations of his own. Indeed, Shaftesbury's roots were in Renaissance Neoplatonism and its particular manifestation in the academic theory of painting, sculpture, and architecture (that is, a theory based on the academy practice of hierarchy, authority, and copying from canonical sculptures).

Shaftesbury himself commissioned a painting after his program for an ideal history painting of the Choice of Hercules between Pleasure and Wisdom—but it was by an Italian (fig. 1), though English painters, from Thornhill and Hogarth to Reynolds and Benjamin West, responded in different ways to the paradigm.[7] In this paradigm the heroic man (not a god) chooses the difficult path up the steep ascent to the Temple of Wisdom, and while he is directed to this path by the rational arguments of a stern woman named Virtue, he rejects the blandishments of a recumbent, disheveled, and seductive woman named Pleasure. Painters bore in mind the academic and civic humanist model of Shaftesbury's system, which stood to correct the religious art associated with papal Rome and tyrannous France (haven for the Stuarts); but for Hogarth the classical associations were equally Roman-papist and French, as opposed to the native English tradition of Sir Christopher Wren in architecture, and Shakespeare, Spenser, and Milton in literature. (Shaftesbury's "Letter concerning Design," prefaced to his *Judgment of Hercules,* announced the program to eliminate the "gothic" disorder of Wren and his followers, which was effectively carried out by Burlington.)

There was, however, one brilliant literary adaptation of Shaftesbury's theory, by Fielding in *Tom Jones* (1749). Fielding followed Shaftesbury's description of the artist as surrogate of "the Creator," referring to *Tom Jones* as his "own Creation," compromised by those serpents the critics. "Such a poet," wrote Shaftesbury, "is indeed a second *Maker;* a just Prometheus under Jove. Like that sovereign artist or universal plastic nature, he forms a whole, coherent and proportioned in itself, with due subjection and subordinacy of constituent parts." This is the "moral artist who can thus imitate the Creator, and is thus knowing in the inward form and structure of his fellow-creatures" (1:136).

Toland and Hogarth: The "Common" Reader

Aesthetics is religion empirically challenged, belief turned into appreciation of beauty, good manners, superstition, a work of fiction, or some other provisional form. But the challenge, at the outset at least (in deism and other forms of freethinking), was in the name of either "morality" and/or "truth"—representing the two aspects of deism, ethical and critical. Morality invoked behavior that is no longer prescribed by a priestly caste; truth invoked history.

There were also high and low roads of deism, as there were of aesthetics, which derived from different versions of empiricism. The idealism of Shaftesbury, reacting against the realist strain of Locke, picked up its own counterreaction in Mandeville, some of the critical deists (those who submitted the Scriptures to analysis and demystification), and such fictional innovators and non-deists as Tom Brown and Daniel Defoe, not to mention Swift. The satiric engraver (and aspiring painter) Hogarth, instead of turning upward with Shaftesbury to a moral sense of benevolent virtue, turned downward with Mandeville to discover beneath Shaftesbury's idealism the sensations aroused by the human body.[8]

If Shaftesbury, an ethical deist, focused on human actions unmediated by corrupt biblical texts and clerical interpretation, the critical deists focused on the texts themselves. They relied not on the source of the doctrine but on its intrinsic intelligibility. Aesthetics and deism shared the assumption that the authority of belief is not in the doctrine but in the believer. Irving Howe (in the passage quoted in the preface, above) was referring to deism as a critical attitude, one with parallel sources in the Protestant Reformation and the English Enlightenment. As an extension of anti-popery, deists questioned any priestcraft; and as an extension of empiricist reason, they questioned the authority of readings imposed on Scripture by the clergy, and doctrines that flew in the face of reason. As John Toland wrote, "Popery in reality is nothing else, but the Clergy's assuming a right to think for the Laity."[9] While believing in God and his providential order, deists regarded the Bible and the church as purely human inventions; while subscribing to Christianity's moral principles in a pragmatic way, they could not believe that those principles were mysteriously revealed in Scripture. It was this version of deism that, in Oscar Kenshur's terms, "could be perceived as a threat to the political order, not only of society but more specifically because royal authority was commonly legitimated by an appeal to certain biblical passages [questioned by the critical deists]." This deism, more obviously than Shaftesbury's, "could be perceived not simply as heretical but also as seditious."[10]

Shaftesbury depended for disinterested virtue upon an elite: "the perfection and grace and comeliness in action and behaviour" cannot be found in "rustics," "plain artisans and people of lower rank," or even in those "happily formed by Nature herself," but "only among the people of a liberal education" (1:125). Hogarth's assumptions derived instead from Toland, author of *Christianity Not Mysterious* (1696), who claimed that ordinary human understanding is the only criterion of meaning and belief; that the common man is the authoritative interpreter. The terms Toland uses are "the Vulgar," "the Poor" (instructed by Christ, not by "the intricate ineffectual Declarations of the Scribes"), "the People," as well as "the disinterested common sort" (vs. "nonsensical Superstitions").[11] Toland focuses on the duping of the common man by clergymen and "experts." The key word is "priestcraft"; he argues that a clergy maintains itself by focusing on the mysterious activity of God and claiming that it alone understands the mysteries of religion.

Toland believed that laymen are the real measure of intelligibility, and he extended the concept, arguing that they were excluded equally from the mysteries of medicine, law, scholarship, and politics:

> The Learned will not, contrary to the Experience of their own Taste, take the Brewer's or the Baker's Word for the Goodness of Bread or Drink, tho ignorant of their Craft. And why may not the Vulgar like-

wise be Judges of the true Sense of things, tho they understand nothing of the Tongues from whence they are translated for their Use?[12]

Thus, while Shaftesbury used aesthetics to limit taste, moral capability, and political power to a select body of "disinterested" aristocrats, Toland projected a new polity of common men which lent itself to the needs (for example) of an upwardly mobile engraver.[13] They agreed that reason (essentially common sense) and not authority is the only basis for certitude, but Shaftesbury replaced clerical authority with his own Whig version of authority.

Hogarth's attacks on the clergy, like Toland's, extended accusations of "priestcraft" and "mysteries" to physicians and lawyers, but in particular to Shaftesburian connoisseurs, the "men of taste" who instructed artists how to paint and patrons what to buy. In the *Analysis of Beauty* he begins his aesthetics with the assumption that true theory, like religion, is reasonable, whereas academic theory is based on authority and Neoplatonic mystery. He introduces the notion (shared with Toland) that the less miseducation one has, and the less "overborn [one is] by pompous terms of art, hard names, and . . . dogmatic rules," the more one is able to enjoy the original aesthetic experience. His refrain is the advice "to *see with our own eyes*," "to learn to see objects truly"; his aim is to show "how much prejudice and self-opinion perverts our sight." The reason, he explains, why "gentlemen"

> have their eyes less qualified for our purpose, than others, is because their thoughts have been entirely and continually employ'd and incumber'd with considering and retaining the various *manners* in which pictures are painted, the histories, names, and characters of the masters, together with many other little circumstances belonging to the mechanical part of the art.

This, the study of "imitations," Hogarth opposes repeatedly to direct experience "of the objects themselves in nature."[14] While he utilizes both thinking and judging morally *for oneself* as the principle of interpretation in his "modern moral subjects," when he turns in the later 1730s—and increasingly in his *Analysis* and the prints of the 1750s—to the subject of art, he focuses upon aesthetic judgment.[15]

Deists as different as Shaftesbury, Anthony Collins, and Thomas Woolston initiated a particular kind of writing that, as defined by

Collins in *A Discourse concerning Ridicule and Irony in Writing* (1729), utilized buffoonery, banter, ridicule, irony, mockery, and raillery (5). Collins argued that "the solemn and grave [the orthodox] can bear a solemn and grave Attack," which "gives them a sort of Credit in the World," but "*Contempt* is what they, who commonly are the most contemptible and worthless of Men, cannot bear nor withstand, as setting them in their true Light, and being the most effectual Method to drive Imposture, the sole Foundation of their Credit, out of the World" (7). Like Shaftesbury, however, Collins distinguishes polite irony and ridicule ("as is fit for polite persons to use") from their grosser equivalents (77).

This ironic mode often paid lip service to an exoteric, nominally Christian doctrine while representing an existential world that is materialistic and rational. Toland's distinction between exoteric ("a set of politically necessary religious principles") and esoteric ("philosophical truths about physical and human nature") points to the two levels of readers (or readings) of allegory, the "double sense" of Scriptures first conventional among the church fathers but carried to the extreme of deflation by Woolston in his *Discourses on the Miracles of Our Saviour*, and picked up by Hogarth in *Boys Peeping at Nature* (fig. 2), introducing his *Harlot's Progress*, where the veil of allegory is being lifted from a sculpture of Nature or Truth.[16] The indirection of deists' discourse, largely intended to avoid censorship of the sort that sent Woolston to prison, was based on the assumption "that the priests and their preachings were fraudulent." The deists "felt justified . . . in using fraud to fight fraud."[17] "The Sacred Authors themselves complied with this Humour of *Parables* and *Fictions*," Toland wrote, "the Holy Scripture being altogether Mysterious, Allegorical and Enigmatical; and our *Saviour* himself gave his Precepts under this veil."[18] The parables of Christ, in particular, were read in this way.

Thus the writer addressed a censor and at the same time his deist friends; for Shaftesbury this meant *hoi poloi* and the Whig civic humanist; for Hogarth, a popular audience and a small elite, the deist or Masonic insider who replaces the artist's personal patron. Addison's distinction in the *Spectator* between an ordinary reader of allegory and a reader of "greater penetration,"[19] Fielding's preference for a reader of "greater sagacity," and even the dual points of view of such children's books as *Goody Two-Shoes* (the viewpoints of the child to whom the book is addressed and the adult who reads it to the child) carry on the same bifurcation. These are, of course, relatively crude and schematized versions of the major trope of the period, most subtle, sophisticated, and devastating in the hands of Swift, Pope, and Fielding: irony.

It should be stressed, however, that while Woolston or Collins (like Hogarth) brought to bear enough "esoteric" scholarly lore to satisfy readers of "greater penetration," the direct (or ostensible) appeal was to a particular sense of "esoteric"—the commonsense of the vulgar who can see with their own eyes that a virgin married to an elderly husband is going to need some human help to produce a baby. But this esoteric audience included both the subculture at the bottom and libertine aristocrats at the top of the social scale (ultimately Sir Francis Dashwood and the Medmenham Monks); while the exoteric consisted of the respectable church-going sorts who read Hogarth's "progresses" as stories of crime and punishment. The area between esoteric and exoteric, however, was blurred, except in the most blatant cases (such as Woolston's), by the fact that the area of agreement between deists and latitudinarian Anglicans (often themselves called deists by the more orthodox) was wide.

The basic shared assumption was that Jesus, whether or not a superhuman agent, was a profound moralist. Even Toland pays lip service to New Testament Christianity in *Christianity Not Mysterious,* referring to "the most blessed, pure and practicable Religion that Men could wish or enjoy," as opposed to the "Fooleries superadded" by priests. This means only that his source is "The Lord Jesus Christ, who alone is the Author and Finisher of my Faith" (as it was for Hogarth, in for example his St. Bartholomew's Hospital mural of Christ's miracle at the Pool of Bethesda).[20] Jesus, of course, concerned himself with the unprivileged, marginalized, and excluded elements of society—with such as publicans and prostitutes, women and children. When he read the lesson in the synagogue at Nazareth he chose the passage from Isaiah which includes: "The spirit of the Lord . . . hath anointed me to preach the gospel to the poor; he hath sent me to heal the broken hearted, to preach deliverance to the captives" (Luke 4:18, Isaiah 61:1–2). These transgressive elements (including the references to prison) were common to the teachings of Jesus and to Hogarth's morality and, later, his aesthetics.

The unique accomplishment of Hogarth, the inventor of popular graphic images, was to extend unprecedentedly the general (exoteric, as well as esoteric) audience, and this would not have been possible without the broad base shared by latitudinarian orthodoxy, deist dissent, and anticlericalism, not to mention nationalism.

Woolston and Hogarth: Demystification

Hogarth's first graphic "demystification" along the lines of critical deism, the six prints called *A Harlot's Progress* (1732; figs. 3–4, 6–8, 10–12), begins with Shaftesbury's recommendation to painters of the Choice of Hercules, his replacement of the New Testament Jesus with a classical hero, the embodiment of civic humanist "heroic virtue." But Hogarth takes his model not from the aristocratic Shaftesbury but from the plebeian Woolston, the follower of Toland and Collins, whose *Discourses on the Miracles of Our Saviour* (1727–30) had shocked respectable Londoners. Woolston's procedure was to test Jesus' miracles (i.e., the evidence of divine revelation) against historical fact and probability, demonstrating that Jesus did not perform miracles; rather, that his actions can only be interpreted as allegories, and invariably allegories not about Jesus' divinity but about the opposing corruption of the clergy, who out of self-interest censure his good works, while exploiting his miracles to their own ends. Woolston, for his pains, was prosecuted by the Anglican clergy and left to die in prison, while his books sold some thirty thousand copies.[21]

The complementary gestalts of plate 1—the parson, Harlot, and bawd; the Harlot, bawd, and gentleman rapist (figs. 4a, 4b)—indicate two contexts, both adversarial to the academic, civic humanist tradition of history painting; but one is classical and the other Christian. The first recalls the model for history painting presented in Shaftesbury's *Tablature of the Judgment of Hercules* (1713; see fig. 1), and the second the satiric deflation of New Testament miracles by Woolston in his *Discourses*. The Choice of Hercules can be inferred from the internal evidence of the three figures at the center of plate 1 (figs. 3, 4a); Woolston's portrait is on the wall in some versions of plate 2 (fig. 6).

From the first group and the visual-verbal references to the *Harlot* as a new art form in the subscription ticket *(Boys Peeping at Nature)*, we are led to conclude that Hogarth's first "modern moral subject" is a response to Shaftesbury's dictum that history painters should model their histories on the classical Choice of Hercules (Heroic Virtue choosing Virtue over Pleasure). Hogarth, however, substitutes a young woman— a protagonist neither heroic nor male—for Hercules. Shaftesbury's females, the upstanding Virtue and the whore Pleasure, served only as aspects of the male hero's choice. Hogarth makes a woman the center of anti-Shaftesbury statements about art, from the *Harlot* onward into the aesthetic theory of *The Analysis of Beauty,* where she is Venus herself (fig. 23).

Furthermore, he juxtaposes with Shaftesbury's classical gestalt a Christian one (or returns his pagan example to the Christian he suppressed), and not the Life of Jesus but of the Virgin. Focusing on the first and (with the Resurrection) least probable of the "historical" facts, the virgin birth, he produces a parody of the Visitation, probably based on Dürer's well-known woodcut (figs. 4b, 5). (N.B. Hogarth's engravings ordinarily reverse their graphic models. He began with paintings and never took into account the reversal that followed from engraving—as if to deny that he was any less than a painter.)

Then, in the historicizing mode of Woolston, he replaces the New Testament figures of Mary, Elizabeth, and Zacharias with recognizable living Londoners (Kate Hackabout, Elizabeth Needham, Colonel Francis Charteris)—the sort of contemporary portraits he had used in his conversation pieces. Like Woolston, he submits the Christian myth to reason, revealing the historical reality beneath, and then allegorizes the result as an attack on priestcraft (not only the clergy but constables, prison warders, physicians, and "Great Men" like Charteris).[22] For Hogarth this meant carrying skepticism to the edge of blasphemy and probably explains why he removed the portrait of Woolston in the subscription edition of the *Harlot.*[23] It was also blasphemy, in terms of art, to replace Shaftesbury's classical universals with contemporary particulars.

Another aspect of critical deism that is prominent in the *Harlot* (and Hogarth's later graphic series) is the deletion of the deity from the paintings on the walls and from the larger action of the "progress." In the second plate of the *Harlot* Hogarth (or the Harlot's Jewish keeper) replaces the Old Testament God striking Uzzah dead with an Anglican bishop stabbing him in the back (fig. 6). In *Marriage A-la-mode,* plate 1 (1745), he reproduces Domenichino's *Martyrdom of St. Agnes* but omits the upper level where Christ and his angels wait to receive the soul of the martyr. In *The Sleeping Congregation* (1736; fig. 13) he represents the inside of a church in which the *Dieu* of the royal motto is blocked out, leaving only *et mon droit,* the civil authority, manifested by two clergymen.[24]

The deletion of the deity was the most important stratagem Hogarth shared with the deists. This can be related to Protestant icon-oclasm, especially as it derived directly from the subject of art and its idolization; but the *deus absconditus* of the deists seems more consonant with what we see in Hogarth's work. At least in social terms, he portrays not the Protestant's iconoclasm but God's withdrawal from man.[25] What he shows, from the beginning of his career, is a world in which the deity—often in the form of the clergy—is absent when most needed; only to return when legal punishment is called for. Society's police are always present, whereas a benevolent God and social and civil mercy are absent.

But if God or Divine Providence, as an immanence, is being replaced by human agency, the specifically Shaftesburian form this takes in Hogarth's scenes is the works of art that hang on the walls. These substitutes for deity (which exclude the deity) are shown to be mere commodities, purchased, collected, and owned by his civic humanist "men of taste" (and their imitators such as the Jewish parvenu in plate 2, and even the Harlot herself in plate 3). They represent no more than a pseudo-religion, a system of manners that guides the actions of their owners and, supposedly, serves as a model for their inferiors.

Shaftesbury saw rewards and punishments as the chief feature that distinguishes interested from disinterested (true) virtue, or religion from morality. Hogarth responds by agreeing that rewards and punishments in religion exist only in artists' images of punishment in paintings, in which, moreover—he goes on to add—divine is replaced by human chastisement and there are certainly no rewards. The religion of rewards and punishments which makes it impossible to judge virtue becomes for Hogarth the active oppression by civil authority which punishes only the innocent and rewards the guilty (an insight perhaps based on his practical experience of confinement in the Fleet Prison for debtors with his father and family). He clearly gives no credence to Shaftesbury's alternative, the "divine example," which ought to appear in the "art" of the paintings on the walls; but they in fact represent (the practical consequence of Shaftesbury's own taste in art) Counter-Reformation images of sadomasochistic rewards and punishments displaced from a vengeful God to his surrogates.

In sum, there is internal and external evidence for Hogarth's employment of deist strategies and assumptions in the *Harlot:* Internally, there is the elision of God from the paintings and, as any sort of an effective presence, from the scene itself. There is no divine intervention in the lives of his harlots and rakes in a world dominated by self-interested clerics and magistrates. The scenes are informed by parodic echoes of New Testament stories; for example, in plate 3 the angel of the Annunciation is replaced by a London magistrate. Most often the surrogate is a clergyman: In plate 1 a parson turns his back on the girl to read the address of the bishop of London, the source of clerical patronage (Bishop Edmund Gibson himself); in plate 2 a bishop stabs Uzzah (above the portrait of Woolston; it was Bishop Gibson who prosecuted him for blasphemy); and in plate 6 a clergyman who should be officiating at the Harlot's funeral is making tipsy advances to the whore next to him. The most striking piece of external evidence is Hogarth's relieving himself on the steps of a church porch during the "Five-Day Peregrination" that celebrated the successful publication of the *Harlot* (as, in plate 3, Hackabout used one of Gibson's "Pastoral Letters" as a butter dish).[26] None of this, however, gives an adequate idea of the sheer, willful playfulness of Hogarth's *Harlot's Progress.*

If Woolston's attack was on the New Testament miracles, he merely applied Collins's attack on the Old Testament prophesies that were supposedly fulfilled in the New Testament, by which Collins had debunked typology.[27] In his *Discourse of the Grounds and Reasons of the Christian Religion* (1724) Collins begins with the assumption that the validity of the Christian religion depends on the validity of the Old Testament prophesies, and proves that only through an allegorical interpretation, carried to a satiric (or lunatic, depending on the point of view) extreme, can the argument be supported. Collins's very first example is the story of the virgin birth in Matthew, which he shows was not prophesied by the verses in Isaiah 7:14–16, which in fact, "in their obvious and literal sense, relate to a *young woman* in the days of AHAZ, King of *Judah*": "This is the plain drift and design of the Prophet, literally, obviously, and primarily understood" (41–42). Therefore, it has to be interpreted in "a secondary or typical, or mythical, or allegorical sense" (53), which he takes to be a "rabbinical way" of arguing—priests persuading their followers to believe in their doctrines (63). Thus the idea of a Messiah was ready to hand and was simply utilized for the historical Jesus when he came along, by Jesus himself and his disciples. Collins focuses on the prophesy concerning "the house of David" from which the Christ will descend: "the primary design of God [is] to preserve the house of DAVID, which God often evinces, by the promise of the MESSIAS" (66–70).

Woolston then, in his *Discourses,* focuses the allegory on the priestly interpreters, seen from the perspective of a literal interpretation of Jesus' New Testament teachings; and he uses a rabbi in his final *Discourse* as a mouthpiece to demystify the miracle of the Resurrection. Hence the presence of the Jew's Old Testament paintings in *Harlot* 2, where Hogarth puts M[ary?] Hackabout in the clutches of a Jew, with behind her on the wall a painting of David conducting the Ark of the Covenant (his gentile mistress) into Jerusalem. The types appear in the paintings of the Old Testament scenes on the walls; the antitypes in the New Testament story that unfolds in parody in the scenes beneath the paintings. The *Harlot* in this sense is about the "miraculous" birth of the Harlot's son—the true story under the type; which, allegorized, becomes another attack on priestcraft. Collins's replacement of typology with allegory supports the paintings' function as not typological (i.e., predictive) so much as allegorical representations of the present actuality of Hackabout's "progress."

Plate 3 (fig. 7) was, according to the contemporary report of George Vertue, the genesis of the series.[28] It is compositionally a parody of artists' representations of the Annunciation (fig. 9), but instead of the Angel Gabriel, the magistrate Sir John Gonson approaches to arrest Hackabout. In other words, the *Harlot's Progress* began as a clear parody of an Annunciation scene. The protagonist has a small medal of a calendar saint on her wall below her portraits of Captain Macheath and Dr. Henry Sacheverell (fig. 8).[29] This holy medal indicates that she keeps the portraits superstitiously as talismans, whose efficacy is contradicted by the intrusion of Justice Gonson and his constables. In the context of Collins's and Woolston's *Discourses,* the image on the holy medal in *Harlot* 3 could be Christ himself or the Virgin Mary. Either supports the reading of this plate as a demystified Annunciation, and given the well-known fact that both Macheath and Sacheverell were objects of female infatuation, indicates the sexual desire underlying the mystery. (Sacheverell was handsome, and women, infatuated with him, collected his portrait. Some of the portraits were small and sized for concealment in prayerbooks, others resembled holy medals.)[30] Displaying a holy image is the one point at which Hackabout herself makes the connection with New Testament typology which Hogarth implies throughout the series in his compositional analogies, identifying it (and priestcraft) at its extreme with papism.

As we have seen, the first plate is a parody of representations of the Visitation. Mary, doubtful of the miracle announced to her, comes to visit her "cousin" Elizabeth (the biblical commentators emphasize *cousin*), who herself "was filled with the Holy Ghost."[31] Hackabout brings with her a gift labeled "For my Lofing Cosen in Tems Stret," but instead of her cousin, here in 1730s London she is met by *Elizabeth* Needham, the most notorious London bawd of the day. The commentators go on to emphasize the miracle of the baby in a virgin's womb and conclude that "No considerate man will from hence conclude that . . . any thing is possible to God the contrary to which he hath willed, but God can do whatsoever he can will." And, *mirabile dictu,* by plate 5 there is a son, who reappears in the final, sixth plate, in a parody of a Last Supper, unmistakable with precisely twelve "disciples" and the Harlot's "Son" around a coffin holding the body of the dead Harlot, who shockingly replaces the Host—Christ's body (and blood—there is also a "chalice" on the coffin). The Last Supper suggests, in terms of Hogarth's satire on a corrupt society, an ideal against which to judge the present, degenerate scene. But, given the evidence we have examined, its logic leads to only one conclusion: The Harlot is the historical reality beneath the priestly mystery of the Eucharist, and, allegorized, such poor girls sacrifice themselves as atonement for our sins.[32]

The *Harlot's Progress*, then, is a demystification of the mystery of the Virgin Birth, with the Passion the Mother's rather than the Son's. Of the six plates, 1 and 3 parody scenes from the Life of the Virgin; 4 and 6, scenes from the Passion. Plate 4 is a "Christ Mocked" or "Flagellation," with the persecutors making faces that are echoed in the figures surrounding Hackabout (recalling such prints as Dürer's *Flagellation* in the "Albertina Passion"). Plate 5 is a combination of a "Death of the Virgin" and a "Casting of Lots" for Christ's garment. If the six pictures are hung two deep on a wall (plates 1, 2, 3 in the top row, and 4, 5, 6 beneath them), the symmetry is obvious. Plate 2, the top middle scene, can be read as the historical "truth" of the Son: The Jewish Joseph is cuckolded by the young man sneaking out behind his back (cuckold horns are discernible in the wallpaper behind his head), and this is followed in plate 3 by Hackabout's Annunciation. With its emphatic parallels between the Old Testament paintings and the action beneath, plate 2 serves to schematize the typological structure of the six (including the portraits of the contemporary "deists," Woolston and Samuel Clarke). The result tells us that the Mother has been given the Son's story of imprisonment, flagellation, and death; or the Son has simply been feminized (as was, in plate 1, the Hercules of the Choice).

In the context of these scenes, each with its *deus absconditus*, the overall text evoked is the Magnificat, Mary's song of praise to God for the Annunciation, itself an echo of 1 Samuel 2 (part of Luke's typologizing of the story of the birth [Luke 1: 26–53]). The Angel Gabriel comes to Mary and tells her, "thou hast found favour with God and will bring forth the Son of the Highest." Although Mary objects that this is impossible "seeing I know not a man," the angel sends her to her cousin Elizabeth for confirmation, after which Mary sings her praise to God for having "regarded the low estate of his handmaiden": "He hath put down the mighty from their seats, and exalted them of low degree. He hath filled the hungry with good things; and the rich he hath sent empty away." As the commentators note, Mary "celebrateth both the power and justice of God," which is precisely what does not take place here. The *Harlot's Progress* is a modernization of that scriptural song of praise, in which civic magistrates, in lieu of God, have put down those of low degree and raised the mighty, filled the rich with good things, and sent away empty the hungry. At the same time, Hogarth himself, the modern innovator of history painting, *has* fulfilled the project of the Magnificat, both morally and aesthetically: by his moral judgment and his art form he has "put down the mighty from their seats, and exalted them of low degree."[33] In its positive sense the Magnificat applies not to Hackabout but to the artist who draws our moral attention to the lowly and thus replaces the absent deity. Thus the last desideratum of the New Testament story, Jesus' resurrection, is rendered but by an artist in a work of art.

Critical deism also served as Hogarth's model for his transformation of morality into aesthetics in *The Analysis of Beauty*, where he materializes and historicizes religion (the theoretical and immaterial) and allegorizes the particulars as Beauty. In the subscription ticket, *Columbus Breaking the Egg* (frontispiece), he associates himself first with Columbus (jokingly equating the discovery of the New World, with the Line of Beauty); but second, by the compositional analogy to another Last Supper, he aestheticizes the Sacrament of the Eucharist; he replaces the Host with a plate of serpentine eels, showing his Line of Beauty as found in the lowly particulars of nature.

After using *Columbus* as subscription ticket for the *Analysis,* he inserted it as frontispiece. Opposite, on the title page, he replaces the Tetragrammaton in the triangle symbolizing the Trinity with his Line of Beauty—the most striking example of his aestheticization of religion. Not only does he replace the Name of God with the principle of Beauty (the word "Variety" is inscribed beneath the symbol), but he gives the Line itself the head of a serpent and places it beneath the lines from *Paradise Lost* describing Satan's seduction of Eve (figs. 21, 22).

The Doctrine of the Trinity:
From Parody to Demystification to Aesthetics

The other picture on the Harlot's wall near Woolston's in plate 2 (in Giles King's authorized copy) is of Samuel Clarke, who discredited the Athanasian doctrine of the Trinity, the mystery at the center of the most notorious religious controversy of the time. His argument was based on the biblical text but on common reason as well: "For the right apprehending of [this] Doctrine, men are (as in other matters of the greatest importance to them) sincerely to make use of their best Understanding; and, in order thereunto, to take in all the Helps they can find, either from living Instruction or antient Writers: But this, only as a Means to assist and clear up their own Understanding, not to over-rule it."[34] The Trinitarian controversy raged from the 1690s to the publication of Clarke's *Scripture Doctrine of the Trinity* in 1712, which effectively finished it off.[35] Clarke was disciplined by the Lower House of the Canterbury Convocation in 1714 as Woolston would be in 1729, though much less harshly (he promised to write no more on the Trinity).

Hogarth's first parody of the Trinity, in his engraved *Lottery* of 1724 (fig. 15), coincided with the first indication of his awareness of the High Renaissance tradition in art. He parodies the composition, well-known in engravings, of Raphael's *Dispute on the Blessed Sacrament* (Vatican, Stanze), the sacrament being the Eucharist, shown on a vertical axis that joins the altar and the Host to the Trinity. In *The Lottery*, Credit (the female figure of Fortune) has taken the place of God the Father; Britannia, that of the Son; and "Suspense," a Hercules figure turning between "Fear" and "Hope," that of the Holy Ghost. Divine Providence, in short, is replaced by chance. The print also twice parodies the Choice of Hercules, the classical equivalent of Providence: here choice is degraded to chance. The theatrical setting of a stage and a pantomime with Britannia, Apollo, and the usual cast of Rich's pantomimes, adds to the sense of pretense and the substitution of reality with illusion. As later in *Harlot* 1, the Christian and classical prototypes are both subverted, and the subversion is the work of an economically motivated society.

The Lottery was published as a pendant to an even earlier engraving, *The South Sea Scheme.* Here Hogarth showed the economic corruption of the City of London marginalizing the church (St. Paul's Cathedral), blocking it out with a huge monument to the South Sea scandal.[36] Clergymen replace the soldiers casting lots for Christ's garment in a Crucifixion, and in the pose of Christ in a Flagellation an allegorical figure of "Honor" is being whipped by "Villainy," again anticipating the *Harlot,* in this case plates 5 and 4, respectively.

What precedents had Hogarth for satire of this sort? John Dryden in *MacFlecknoe* (c. 1679), the model of mock epic, had shown a contemporary as a degenerate parody of both Christian and classical ideals, and in Pope's *Dunciad* (1728) this figure became specifically an anti-Christ, a Satanic parody of the true mystery. *The Dunciad,* of course, came too late to influence Hogarth; but Dryden's use of analogy may have influenced *The Lottery,* with its associations of high Renaissance art. The Trinity there is an anti-Trinity on the model of an anti-Christ. *The Lottery* is still based on conventions of Augustan satire. If Suspense, under the sway of chance, simply rotates between Hope and Fear, Good Luck (the contrasted version of Hercules) has the power to choose between Pleasure and Folly and is Hogarth's indication of the ideal surviving in a debased world of chance.

In the same way, the gambling clergymen and the warder whipping Honor in *The South Sea Scheme* are the 1720s reality beneath the ideal of the Christian Passion. But *The South Sea Scheme,* based on Northern European models of painting, comes closer to anticipating the breakthrough of the *Harlot.* It reflects the works of Bosch, Massys, Cranach, and Brueghel in which Christ is surrounded by contemporaries who fill the roles of mockers. Insofar as the clergymen and the warder anticipate Woolston's writings of four or five years later, they show the contemporary, historical reality beneath the mystery, and priestcraft is the allegory beneath the exploded mystery. Hogarth must have found in Woolston the theory behind his satiric practice. Woolston's demystifying he emblematizes in the unveiling of Nature in the *Harlot*'s subscription ticket. But then he increases the historical particularity, giving the bawd, rake, and constable recognizable likenesses; and he uses Woolston's allegorizing as an excuse for getting at a broader sense of priestcraft, a cover term (through the references to Bishop Gibson and the particular likenesses of the Walpolites Charteris and Gonson) for Walpolian politics. But he also adds the Virgin (and the Hercules) who in 1730s London is really a whore, Hercules' Virtue who is really a self-interested clergyman, and the angel of the Annunciation who is really a constable come to arrest Mary.

There is a progression in Hogarth's work from a satire that shows religion corrupted, replaced by priestcraft, Walpolian authority, and business interests, to a deist demystification, which posits the disappearance and replacement of God himself—the destruction of the myth of his immanence (and Christ's New Testament mysteries). *The Sleeping Congregation* of four years later (fig. 13) can be read both ways: *Dieu* is replaced by a family coat of arms which designates (as in the arms of the major landholders on maps of England) the church as private property, in tandem with the arms of the monarch. In this print Hogarth leaves open the question of whether God is a deist *deus absconditus* or has been reduced to parody or replaced by the representatives of priestcraft. Is he *absconditus* in the *Harlot*, or has the Jewish keeper had him replaced with a bishop? Has Lord Squander in *Marriage A-la-mode* had the Christ and angels painted out, and have the great property owners paid the clergy to have their arms replace *Dieu* in the royal motto in the local church? Hogarth's particular orientation— or his ambiguity—was one of the factors that kept him out of Woolston's sad plight.

In *The Sleeping Congregation* the triangle of the Trinity has been emptied of its Tetragrammaton and turned upside down (the old topos of "the world turned upside down"); God is absent from both the symbol of the monarch and the Trinity. But the empty triangle is also a Masonic symbol, surrounded by the same glory, with the Name of God replaced by an open eye, symbol of human reason. In this church, the eye is displaced to the closed eyes (all but one) of the sleeping congregation; there is neither god nor reason.[37] Moreover, the Masonic allusion points to the elements shared by Freemasonry and deism: You replace the Name of God with the eye of human reason—or on *this* model you replace it with the Line of Beauty. Indeed, we might speculate that Hogarth learned the technique first as a Freemason. In these terms the young woman, to whose bosom the priest's worship has been deflected, can be read as a positive, an aesthetic alternative to both *Dieu* and *mon Droit*, religion and power. The Christian myth, exploited by clerics and magistrates, will be replaced by the artist, whose alternative, first sketched here, will eventuate in the theory of the *Analysis*.[38]

First, then, religion is replaced by morality, as in the *Harlot's* and *Rake's Progress*, and then by aesthetics, as in *The Sleeping Congregation* and the artist satires that followed in the later 1730s (see the next chapter). The difference is evident moving from *Harlot 6* to *Columbus Breaking the Egg*, both parodic Last Suppers. In the first, the replacement of Christ's body with the Harlot's is a moral comment on this society (in Toland's sense of "priestcraft"); she has died for the sins of the men who enjoyed and exploited her, in a deeply ironic sense "atoning" for their sins. In *Columbus* the female body has been replaced by the two natural Lines of Beauty on Columbus's plate, and the moral comment by an analysis of beauty.

Throughout his oeuvre Hogarth shows contemporaries how to secularize, iconoclast, modernize, and aestheticize the major religious topoi—Christ's miracles and parables, unreasonable doctrines, Roman or Anglican High Church sacraments—into the building blocks of the new fictions of Fielding, Sterne, and Goldsmith. He may have begun with the classical parodies of the orthodox satirists Dryden, Swift, and Pope, but he found his primary model in the freethinking ridicule of Toland, Collins, and Woolston. The results in his works, however, are always more emphatic, more acerbic than in those of his followers. As late as 1751, in *The Four Stages of Cruelty*, a series portraying the brutal cruelty of an urchin, Tom Nero, Hogarth contextualizes him as he did the Harlot. When Nero (whose name, of course, connects small with great men) is apprehended in the act of murdering his sweetheart, Hogarth places him in a scene that parodies such paintings as van Dyck's *Taking of Christ in the Garden* (Prado, Madrid). The emphasis has shifted from Nero's "cruelty" to that of the society that enabled and now exorbitantly punishes him.

If, as we have suggested, deism led an author to write history as demystified religion, it also endowed the reader with a privileged status. The demystifications of Collins and Woolston, followed by those of Hogarth and, later, Fielding, began with an esoteric but created a skeptical reader who automatically reads spiritual autobiographies as histories or, more specifically, novels. The claims to divine intervention, divinely ordained rewards and punishments, and a divinely inspired text in the orthodox works of Defoe, Richardson, and others are reinterpreted by postdeist readers in the light of common sense and daily experience of the contemporary world as the claims of a Robinson Crusoe or a Pamela Andrews.

TWO

Shaftesburian Disinterestedness

Disinterestedness and Interestedness

"Disinterestedness" has become the term that most commonly distinguishes aesthetic perception. Something is *beautiful*, Jerome Stolnitz has noted, when it becomes the object of a "disinterested and sympathetic attention . . . and contemplation . . . for its own sake alone" as, for example, "the 'look of the rock,' the sound of the ocean, the colors in the painting."[1] But there is a strong sense of "disinterestedness" and a weak one: The strong defines aesthetics as an experience independent of all theoretical and practical value. This is the modern or Kantian or Nietzschean sense in which aesthetics is distinct from ethics as well as religion, and of course rhetoric; in which writers of bad faith "aestheticize" politics, and "aesthetic distance" is a disguise for bourgeois mystification (as moral sentiments are the internalizing by the individual sensibility of the police state). The weak version of "disinterestedness" defines aesthetics as independent only of personal or private interest or advantage.

This is the limited sense accepted by most of the eighteenth-century English theorists with the exception of Hutcheson, who held to the strong sense. For Shaftesbury, usually given credit for the concept of disinterestedness, the term has at least two contradictory aspects. On the one hand, reacting against Locke's systems of social

contracts, Shaftesbury draws attention to the impossibility of true virtue within a pragmatic system of rewards and punishments. Disinterestedness removes virtue from considerations of profit, thus in effect
(the deist aspect) dissociating it from Judeo-Christian religious beliefs.
On the other hand, disinterestedness makes virtue the province of an
elite, and distinguishes the lower orders—set off primarily on the basis
of education—as the people to whom a religion of rewards and punishments could be useful in order to keep them happy and society safe and
whole.

In response to Shaftesbury's equation of virtue, disinterestedness,
and civic humanist landowning, Hogarth might have remembered the
motto from Cicero which Steele used for his discussion of charity in
Spectator No. 294: "It is a hard matter to pay much regard to that virtue
which is dependent entirely on good fortune" (3:47). But following
Mandeville's critique of Shaftesbury, he shows in his "modern moral
subjects" that private interest (the interest of the Shaftesburian politi-
cian and collector) is in fact the hidden underside of Shaftesbury's
theory. His one reference to the word "disinterestedness" in the *Analysis*
is ironic: he notes "that the very worst painters sit as the most profound
judges, and are trusted only, I suppose, on account of their *disinterestedness*" (24, his emphasis). The truth under the irony supports
Toland's application of the word to "the People" in *Christianity Not
Mysterious:* "the disinterested common sort" are freed by their com-
monness from the conventional practices of tradition—and by their
deism from orthodox piety and the complacency of priestcraft's "nonsensical Superstitions" (xxii).

In particular, the potential for sensual enjoyment is rigorously
and consistently held in abeyance by Shaftesbury. But the common
man—of Toland or Hogarth—is unwilling to dissociate the senses from
sensuality, as Shaftesbury the Platonist is so eager to do. This involves ultimately Hogarth's most radical response, the substitution for
Shaftesbury's anti-Venus of a living woman.

The central Shaftesburian text is *The Moralists,* in which the
perception of beauty in an object is divorced from any personal utility
to be obtained from it. Shaftesbury's two terms, "pursuit" and "pleasure," will also be Hogarth's, but his "pursuit" is of "order and perfection" and soon becomes a "search," "pursue" alternating with "seek."

The second term, the dangerous "pleasure," has to be valorized by an "unbiassed" perspective.[2] "Pleasure" is the key word, but Shaftesbury refines it out of a physical into a mental state, distinguishing pleasures qualitatively, "one indifferent, sorry, mean; another valuable and worthy." One is a pleasure "which may be very great and yet very contemptible," and the difference lies in the "situation" or "that point of sight whence probably we may best discern" the object, "and how to place ourselves in that unbiassed state in which we are fittest to pronounce" on it (2:31).

The argument is conveyed in Shaftesbury's usual dialogue form, between a teacher, Theocles, and his somewhat less orthodox friend Philocles. In the central discussion of the disinterested perception of the object of pleasure (2:126 ff.), Theocles speaks against "the absurd enjoyment which reaches the sense alone," whereas "our reason has taught us" that "whatever in Nature is beautiful or charming is only the faint shadow of that first beauty" (2:126). Philocles' mistake is in believing that Theocles advocates "seeking the enjoyment elsewhere than in the subject loved," when in fact the question is only the way in which the subject is regarded.

Theocles starts with the ocean and the desire to command it, "like some mighty admiral," rather than simply contemplate its beauty; then, drawing "nearer home": "Suppose (my Philocles) that, viewing such a tract of country as this *delicious* vale we see beneath us, you should, for the enjoyment of the prospect, require *the property or possession of the land*." Thus a "covetous fancy"; then, nearer still, "Suppose that, being charmed as you seem to be with the beauty of those trees under whose shade we rest, you should long for nothing so much as to *taste some delicious fruit of theirs*." And following this "sordidly luxurious" and "absurd" fancy, he returns to "the fairest human face," the example that initiated Philocles' worries: "Can you not then, on this occasion, said he [Theocles], call to mind some other forms *of a fair kind* among us, where the *admiration of beauty* is apt to *lead to as irregular a consequence?*" (127, emphasis added). Philocles admits that he sees "where this would end" and is "apprehensive you would force me at last to think of certain powerful forms in human kind which draw after them a set of eager desires, wishes, and hopes; no way suitable, I must confess, to your rational and refined contemplation of beauty."

Thus Shaftesbury excludes the needs and desires of the body from the virtue *or* the beauty of disinterestedness. He does, however, in the central argument of *The Moralists,* have Theocles and Philocles talk about a "friend," generalized and rendered disinterested into "friendship." There is no moment at which the "friend" is designated as female ("fair face" is not connected to a gender). The example of the disinterested or interested pleasure in *The Moralists* is friendship: as we might expect, Theocles sees friendship as extending to all mankind, while Philocles (like E. M. Forster) cannot see beyond a particular friend whom he prefers to his country and mankind. As they walk together, Philocles tells Theocles

> I feared I should never make a good friend or lover after his way. As for a plain natural love of one single person in either sex, I could compass it, I thought, well enough; but this complex, universal sort was beyond my reach. I could love the individual, but not the species. This was too mysterious, too metaphysical an object for me. In short, I could love nothing of which I had not some sensible, material image. (2:38–39)

Theocles responds with the case of epistolary correspondence (one remove from conversation): Philocles loved someone in a "long correspondence which preceded [his] late personal acquaintance"—he began to love Palemon in correspondence, and was therefore "forced to form a kind of material object, and had always such a certain image of him ready drawn in my mind whenever I thought of him." In the same way he must now attempt to "raise any such image or spectre as may represent this odd being you would have me love." Theocles' second example is the Romans (again, of course, males) about whom Philocles read in his history books.

Plato's Beautiful *(to kalon)* in the *Symposium* and *Phaedrus* was a kind of perfection that is related to love *(eros),* but the Platonic discourse was "ascetic rather than aesthetic, stressing preparation for immortality by philosophic discipline":[3] the lover ascends from bodily to ideal beauty to "wisdom, goodness, and the like," by which lover becomes philosopher. In Shaftesbury's version of Platonism, the lover is purified into the civic humanist, governor, and arbiter of taste. The Platonic *ascesis* becomes the disinterestedness of the landholder and, returning to the Platonic origin, the lover of boys *(orthos paiderastein),* who, it is supposed, is more disinterestedly focused on *to kalon* than the heterosexual lover.

If Shaftesbury's aesthetics was in fact a formalizing of his grandfather's politics, it might also be relevant to consider it as a formalizing of his own homoerotics. His fear of "effeminacy," a fear of women reflecting his own sexual ambivalence, leaves little question that when he married it was for duty rather than pleasure. (He had hoped that his younger brother Maurice would produce the Shaftesbury heir.) His preference for the mental over the physical in *The Moralists* is figured in a mental "birth" metaphor in which the conception is autochthonous—or rather, requires not a man and a woman in the sexual act of conception but a man and a midwife (specified as another man) to serve, by way of conversation, at the birth (2:134–35).

Among other things, Hogarth's work, from his *Harlot* to his *Analysis of Beauty,* serves as a comment on Shaftesbury's motive for rejecting the Judeo-Christian tradition of religion, which wholly condemned sodomy, and replacing it with the classical tradition, in which the naturalness and acceptability of pederasty were taken for granted. A sculpture of the Emperor Hadrian's minion Antinous, whose image Hadrian set up throughout the empire as an object of worship, appears off to the side of *Analysis* 1 (fig. 23), accompanied by a disinterested Shaftesburian aesthetician admiring male beauty, offering an alternative to the heterosexual pair of Venus and Apollo at the center. But, as the Mandevillian observer would have noted, beneath the aesthetic disinterestedness the civic humanist dancing master is more likely propositioning Antinous.

The Beautiful Woman

Shaftesbury dismissed the Old Testament deity as well as Jupiter, the one cruel and capricious, the other too sexually oriented (always seducing and raping women), and substituted a Platonic figure of fraternal love and order. Politically, he defined his polite philosopher against the cavalier rake of the Restoration court, a figure of disorderly pleasure whose object was a woman. (Philocles describes his correspondence with his friend Palemon as a "monument of . . . Conversation, so opposite to the reigning genius of Gallantry and Pleasure.") The civic humanist was politically a response to the Jacobite threat of a strong monarch, his rakish libertine courtiers, and their seduction of beautiful women. One recalls how Charles II mistakes, at the end of Marvell's "Last Instructions to a Painter," Britannia for one of his whores. Against this sensuality Shaftesbury projects a fraternity of aristocrats, men of civic responsibility in politics, men of taste in art and literature. Stoic masculinity corrected both the past excesses of the Restoration court and the current ones of the Pretender's court in France.[4]

As it appeared to Mandeville, Shaftesbury had politicized disinterestedness; his hidden agenda was that Whig lords—rather than, as prior to 1688, a monarch—should rule England, politically and in matters of taste. Mandeville's strategy in the 1724 edition of *The Fable of the Bees* was to expose the desire, economic and sexual, under the supposed disinterestedness of Shaftesbury's civic humanist. Following Mandeville, Hogarth begins in *A Harlot's Progress* to reveal beneath the supposed disinterestedness and benevolence of the Shaftesburian man of taste (the connoisseur and collector) a subtext of ownership, control, and desire; and, in *A Rake's Progress*, beneath the idealized classical images, their use by Whig politicians for purposes of status and power. Hogarth's response can be interpreted either as saying that aesthetic experience *can* be interested—for instance, the aesthetic experience of common people who do not possess enough to distance objects—and/or as saying that there is no such thing, even (or especially) among the elite, as disinterestedness. When a civic humanist gentleman regards a Roman sculpture, he sees a possession that proves his status or an icon that says he is himself a Roman senator or emperor—or even, as in the *Antinous,* an object of desire.

However, Hogarth also substitutes for Shaftesbury's ideal classical sculptures and his male "friend/friendship" the figures of particular living (identifiable) harlots, drummeresses, actresses, and the like. Mandeville had focused on the absent female in his critique of Shaftesbury's art theory. In his discourse on painting (first dialogue in *Fable of the Bees,* pt. 2) he uses the woman Fulvia to speak for reason and common sense against the idealism of Horatio and to supplement the ironic Cleomenes (Mandeville's spokesman). As Mandeville knew, Shaftesbury would have regarded Fulvia as another figure of effeminate Pleasure.[5] Hogarth, coming at the issue from the art academy, focuses on Shaftesbury's doctrine that "the best artists are said to have been indefatigable in studying the best statues: as esteeming them a better rule than the perfectest human bodies could afford" (noticeably ungendered bodies). This Hogarth rewrites in the key sentence of his *Analysis of Beauty:* "Who but a bigot, even to the antiques, will say that he has not seen faces and necks, hands and arms in *living women,* that even the grecian Venus doth but coarsely imitate?" (emphasis added).[6] The practical source of this aesthetic may have been the controversy centered as early as the 1730s in the St. Martin's Lane Academy on the question of whether to copy the cast (a copy) of a canonical sculpture, or a living nude woman. Included were jokes linking disinterestedness to the former and interestedness to the latter.

But there was a deist source as well. In his version of nature, Toland had replaced Christianity with a more heterogeneous Nature—specifically, he replaced Jesus on the cross with the "Great Mother" Nature, who reappears as Diana Multimammia, the source of her fecundity being unveiled, in Hogarth's *Boys Peeping at Nature.*[7] This print, the subscription ticket for *A Harlot's Progress,* presents the *Harlot* as a new art form, whose epigraph is Virgil's "Antiquam exquirite matrem" (Seek out your ancient mother) but then demystifies (or historicizes) the *mater* in plate 1 as the bawd "Mother" Needham vis-à-vis the young woman who becomes a harlot.

M[ary?] Hackabout is in fact revealed to be probably Roman Catholic. The holy medal (abhorred by Protestants) she has on her wall in plate 3 (fig. 8) must indicate that she is Roman Catholic, or at least an idolater (Macheath and Sacheverell are her "idols") and that any religion tends toward such idolatry. It could also be cited to support the idea that the Harlot is a Jacobite, which Paul Monod educes from her white (Stuart) rose in plate 1 as well as the portrait of Sacheverell,[8] supported also by her probably Scottish origin (the York Wagon in which she has traveled to London originated in Scotland). Monod sees her as a Jacobite innocent destroyed by the new money men of the rising commercial class.

With the external threat of Jacobitism fading and with the scandal of the South Sea Bubble of 1720, the Shaftesburian civic humanists found a substitute within society, in corruption and cover-up, in the upstart steward or stock-jobber, embodied in the center of power by Sir

Robert Walpole. But the *femme fatale* returned for Addison in female figures of Credit; for Swift in Flimnap's wife, the empress of Lilliput, the Brobdingnagian maids of honor (vs. the child Glumdalclitch), and the loathsome Yahoos who try to rape Gulliver; and for Pope in the Goddess Dulness. Dulness is a Hanoverian mother figure (the royal title had descended through the female line).[9] Hogarth's motherly Diana of the Ephesians is, among other things, a positive alternative to Pope's symbol of idiot fecundity, Mother Dulness, as well as to Mother Needham.[10]

Thus one locus for the translation of religion into aesthetics was Hogarth's "modern moral subject," and its metaphorical unveiling of the "Great Mother" Nature—which meant showing the truth (the historical truth, in a deist sense) beneath the New Testament miracles, in the significant form of a woman. And this woman becomes the center of anti-Shaftesbury statements about art in Hogarth's works from the 1730s onward, beginning with his parody of the Choice of Hercules in the *Harlot*. Insofar as his analysis is by way of Mandeville, he reveals beneath the disinterested civic humanist mask of male public service the subtext of desire for a woman's body: beneath the canonical sculptures of Venus, Apollo, and Hercules a disruptive romantic tri-angle (*Analysis*, plate 1 [fig. 23]).

In *The Sleeping Congregation* of 1736 (fig. 13), we have seen, *Dieu* is replaced by the monarch and a family coat of arms; but in this church, where God is absent (whether as the result of society's usurpa-tion or his own transcendence), worship itself has been displaced to the one open eye—of a clergyman—which is turned away from the text of the Scriptures to the breasts of a young woman; worship has become a sensual response to a beautiful object. While this is a satiric comment on the clergyman (another Hercules, who has chosen Pleasure over Virtue)—and the woman is in fact dreaming of matrimony—for the spectator, the viewer of the print, this recalls the breasts of Mother Nature in *Boys Peeping at Nature* and adumbrates the Hogarthian model of aesthetics. Even the lion who supports the royal motto dis-plays a prominent erection, which is *his* response to the pretty young woman; and he is presumably intended to be our surrogate, demon-strating the connection between eroticism and aesthetics.[11]

Another example of unveiling followed two years later in the safer context of classical myth and the theater. In *Strolling Actresses Dressing in a Barn* (1738; fig. 14) Diana, the goddess of chastity, is revealed as a real, disheveled woman (another Pleasure figure from the Choice of Hercules), an actress performing the role of Diana; but this also suggests how the demystification of classical-Christian myths in Hogarth's "modern moral subject" is only a way station toward a *re*mystification in an allegory of beauty. Like the woman in *The Sleeping Congregation,* the Diana manqueé is spied on from above by a human Actaeon (through holes in the roof of the barn), and worship is again replaced by admiration and desire; the scene is backstage, and we, like the rustic Actaeon, are voyeurs in the situation of aesthetics.

Pope wrote of Belinda in *The Rape of the Lock* (1714),

On her white Breast a sparkling *Cross* she wore,
Which *Jews* might kiss, and Infidels adore.
(canto 1, ll. 7–8)

When Belinda's cross is turned into an art object, Shaftesburian aesthetics is born; when the sparkling object draws attention to her bosom, Hogarthian aesthetics follows. Pope leaves the question open as to whether the object of adoration is the form of the crucifix or of Belinda's breast: a question that may have inspired Hogarth's *Sleeping Congregation.* Toland's replacement of Jesus on the cross with the "Great Mother" is materialized in the 1750s by Hogarth's painting of the freethinking Sir Francis Dashwood, founder of the Hell-Fire Club at Medmenham Abbey: Christ is replaced on the cross, as the object of Sir Francis's devotions, by a nude female (fig. 16).[12] Here, in its libertine form, is one end result of Shaftesbury's civic humanist connoisseurship: The Dilettanti Society, a drinking club consisting of Dashwood and other Men of Taste, became in the 1750s the Medmenham Monks, who allegedly conducted black masses and imported prostitutes to assist in their mock sacraments.

But Hogarth offers, though he was patronized by some of the Monks, another possibility. The fallen but faithful Sarah Young, the Rake's cast-off mistress (in *A Rake's Progress*), is formally interchangeable with the Jesus of Hogarth's St. Bartholomew's Hospital mural, *The Pool of Bethesda,* a contemporary work (see figs. 17, 18). The parallel is exact: As the fallen Sarah succors the faithless Rakewell, Jesus performs a miracle of charity on the Sabbath, for which the Levites chastize him, and, in the pendant, the Good Samaritan offers a human version of charity by interposing where the priests and holy men had (like the deity) absented themselves. In *Christianity Not Mysterious* Toland had associated Jesus with a creed of "Simplicity" and claimed that he shunned "pompous Worship and secret Mysteries," preaching "the purest Morals."[13] This creed, Toland argued, was later corrupted by priestcraft, and it was a deist's duty to show the common man the way back to the immediate and eternal laws of morality, preached by Jesus before the intervention of priests. Accordingly, the Parable of the Good Samaritan was given a deist reading by both Hogarth and Fielding (in the St. Bartholomew's paintings and, five years later, in *Joseph Andrews*), as much about the priests and the Letter of the Law as about the Samaritan and the Spirit.[14]

The christological aspect of the woman continues in "modern moral subjects" with the poet's wife in *The Distressed Poet* (fig. 19) and the milkmaid in *The Enraged Musician* (fig. 20). Charity is the common element, but in *The Pool of Bethesda* (fig. 18) Charity is juxtaposed, as a kind of moral choice, with sexual love, the figure of Christ with the beautiful Titianesque nude suffering presumably from a venereal disease (her way into the curative waters of the pool having been bought by her wealthy lover). It is significantly the Titianesque nude—the Harlot again—who reappears as Venus, the symbol of Beauty, in *The Analysis of Beauty,* and later on Sir Francis Dashwood's crucifix (fig. 16). She designates the shadowy area where Hogarth the voice of the "common man" and the corrector of Shaftesbury's civic humanism meets Hogarth the client of libertine aristocrats, followers of Shaftesbury.[15]

In the *Analysis* (figs. 21–22) Beauty is figured as a serpentine line, a pure form (Joseph Burke referred to the *Analysis* as the first purely formalist art treatise), but Hogarth locates the largest concentration of such lines in the human body, above all in the female body (preferred to the male), and illustrates this Line of Beauty in the figure of Venus (fig. 23).[16] Venus, goddess of love, is the terminus of Hogarth's aesthetics, the ultimate attraction of the male gaze which keeps "the eye and the mind in constant play" with "imaginary pursuits." Indeed, the male gaze focuses ultimately on the woman's hair, a recollection of Belinda's fatal seductive lock, the symbol of her sexuality.

In the chapter "On Intricacy," Hogarth's argument moves ineluctably from serpentine lines to "pursuit," to "love of pursuit," and to "wanton" pursuit; from a commonplace domestic item, the smokejack, to men and women dancing and to female hair as the source of sexual attraction. It is significant that besides the woman, Hogarth takes as examples smokejacks, candlesticks, stays, and chair legs, the most democratic of possessions.[17] A few years later, in *Enthusiasm Delineated* (figs. 22c, 22d, 36), he includes two symbols of the Trinity, which he treats in the same way: God the Father holds out a common trivet, and a triangle with Paraclete and Tetragrammaton sits atop a pleasure thermometer that rises from "Love-Heat" to "Lust-Hot" to "EXTACY" to "Madness" and "Revelation." Of the two types of examples, one represents the reduction of the religious image to a utilitarian object; the other, to an object of physical desire. The first is a typical case of Protestant iconoclasm, the Trinity reconstituted as a device for holding hot dishes; the second reflects the attacks of Swift and other satirists on enthusiastic sects by showing that the basis for their mystical experiences is no more than sexual desire. In relation to Shaftesbury's theory, these represent the exposure of interest in supposedly disinterested objects; and of beauty in what Shaftesbury would regard as rude mechanical utility or gross heterosexual desire.

Hogarth's pursuit is primarily of desire, which he focuses on the woman's serpentine lock of hair: "the flowing curl; and the many waving and contrasted turns of naturally intermingling locks ravish the eye with the pleasure of the pursuit" (45). He recovers the subject in the chapter "On Quantity," where the lock is singled out when displayed asymmetrically, "falling thus across the temples, and by that means breaking the regularity of the oval" of the face. The lock (with its associations of both Eve and Belinda) serves Hogarth as the contingency that distinguishes the real from Shaftesbury's ideal, the living woman from a sculptured simulacrum. He later remarks that "what has been hitherto thought so unaccountably *excellent* in its general appearance, hath been owing to what hath seem'd a *blemish* in a part of it" (101).

The consequence of this "blemish," Hogarth explains, is "an affect too alluring to be strictly decent, as is very well known to the loose and lowest class of women," by which, of course, he means harlots (51–52). The aesthetic object as well as its observer is "common" (in both Toland's and the demotic sense). Speaking of the laws of Beauty, Hogarth notes that "not only ladies of fashion, but . . . women of every rank, who are said to dress prettily, have known their force" (51). This is followed by an account of dress and undress, the basis of "curiosity" and "play" in the tantalizing revelation (curiosity must be "not too soon gratified") of the body (53).

The whole passage is a nexus for significant echoes and anticipations, which we shall later examine in detail: Fielding's naked Virtue and the flaw (in both character and the work of art) that authenticates its beauty; Cleland's associations of beauty, allure, and prostitution; and William Gilpin's example of the hair, which, ruffled, makes a beautiful female face "picturesque." Indeed, Hogarth himself sums up the erotic elements with the conclusion that the effect "is extremely picturesque" (46).

Two years after publishing the *Analysis* Hogarth was commissioned to paint his one New Testament painting for a church, the *Resurrection* triptych for the altar of St. Mary Redcliffe, Bristol (1755–56). The central miracle, the *Resurrection,* had been dealt with by Woolston, first as the Ascension or Transfiguration (in the first *Discourse*) and climactically in the *Sixth Discourse* as the Resurrection itself: his focus, of course, was on the deception of the priests. From Woolston's notorious demystification followed further demystifications by Peter Annet, Thomas Morgan, and Thomas Chubb. When Hogarth painted his altarpiece of the Resurrection he emphasized the sealing and breaking of the tomb in the side panels, and, in the central panel, he focused on Mary Magdalen in the foreground, thrusting the Ascension itself into the far distance, virtually illustrating Woolston's argument.[18] Although the church was dedicated to Mary the Mother, the subject is Mary Magdalen, a redaction of his first serial paintings, the *Harlot's Progress,* and of the Venus of his *Analysis.* From this vantage, looking back at the *Harlot* we see an obvious Mary Magdalen figure, placed in the story of Mary the Mother of Christ—the paradigmatic female figure who combined virgin and whore.

The Gospels tell of at least three Marys, the most significant of whom are found in Luke and John. Luke makes her a fallen woman whom Jesus befriends, thus outraging Simon the Pharisee, in whose house the encounter takes place: she washes Jesus' naked feet with her repentant tears and dries them with her hair. Her chief attribute, as Hogarth would have been well aware from the graphic tradition, was her flowing hair.[19] She was conflated, by such painters as Titian, with Venus, her palpable bodiliness transformed by repentance and God's love into spiritual essence. Hogarth's portrayal of her in his *Ascension* panel invites us to focus on the aspect presented in the Gospel according to John. This is the Magdalen (as Hogarth shows her in one of the wings) who goes alone to weep at the empty tomb and, still alone, is the first to see the risen Christ, and at his behest carries the news of the Resurrection to the disciples (as he shows her doing in the *Ascension*). Within the maze of serpentine lines, and in the context of the subscription ticket for the *Analysis (Columbus Breaking the Egg)*, which situates Columbus-Hogarth in the position of Christ in a *Last Supper*, we are also invited to connect the Good News she brings to the disciples with the Good News of Hogarth's theory of the serpentine Line of Beauty. In this interpretation Hogarth designates her, as the first prophet of the new "religion," as the symbol of his aesthetics.

The Doctrine of the Trinity: Romantic Triangles

Hogarth likes to include in his prints a triangle conflating Trinity, Masonic symbol, and geometrical figure (as in *Sleeping Congregation* or, twenty years later, *Enthusiasm Delineated*). He uses the triangle on the title page of the *Analysis* (fig. 21) to contain the serpentine—literally snake-headed—Line of Beauty; labeled "VARIETY," the combination suggests a visualization of "composed variety." It also suggests, as I have noted above, a substitution of the Line of Beauty for the Name of God in the traditional symbol of the Trinity. In the text he writes that "There is no object composed of straight lines, that has so much variety, with so few parts, as the pyramid" (39). But he also connects it, clearly, with a demystification of the Doctrine of the Trinity, and this with the romantic triangle of sexual desire.

According to the Athanasian Creed, there is "one God in Trinity and the Trinity in unity, neither confusing the persons nor dividing the substance" *(neque confundentes personas, neque substantiam separantes)*. This was the orthodox position, that the Son, while consubstantial with the Father, was subordinated to him in both nature and order. In Thomas Gordon's satire, churchmen argue that "This is trinity in unity; three in one, and one in three; not three, but one; nor one, but three," in cadences that show how easily doctrine could be absorbed into nursery rhymes.[20] The Athanasian, Socinian, Arian, Unitarian, Tritheist, and Sabellian positions, depending on questions of unity, dominance of the Father, and independence of the Son, offered situations fraught with possibilities for fictionalizing and parodic play.

A point of origin for the controversy was William Sherlock's *A Vindication of the Doctrine of the Holy and Ever Blessed Trinity* (1690), where we read of the Socinian heresy: "The fundamental mystery of the Christian religion is the stupendous love of God in giving his own Son . . . for the redemption of mankind. If Socinianism be true, God did not give any son he had before, but made an excellent man, whom he was pleased to call his own begotten son."[21] Thus Christ was a man, miraculously born of the Virgin Mary, but was not God. One corollary of the jettisoning of dogma was that judgment in the afterlife would depend only on conduct. Sherlock quotes a Socinian: "a good life is of absolute necessity to salvation, but a right belief in those points that have always been controverted . . . is in no degree necessary."[22] More broadly, Clarke's statement of the essential doctrine, "the plain and practical Doctrine of Scripture" which has been "puzzled . . . with endless speculative Disputes," emphasizes the oppressive power of the Father modulated by the mercy of the Son and the mediation of the Holy Spirit: "The *Supremacy* of *God the Father* over all, and our *Reconciliation and Subjection* to him as such our *Supreme Governour;* the *Redemption* purchased by *the Son;* and the *Sanctification* worked in us by the *Holy Spirit;* are the Three great Articles of our Creed" (xxvii).

It is easy to see what political readings could be made of the doctrine and of its various versions. For Fielding, there is Joseph Andrews, who is not (in different senses) either Adams's or Wilson's ostensible son but only "an excellent man, whom he [Wilson] was pleased to *call* [at length, at the end of the novel] his only begotten son." There is Tom Jones, the bastard and foundling, the flawed heir, combining with Jacobite-Hanoverian politics to deny the divinity of the Son or his coexistence with the Father. In short, in Luke Milbourne's words, "denying the Divinity of our Saviour, a heresy detestable to every sober and intelligent Christian," was the same as denying the direct line of the Stuarts.[23] Again, in *Tristram Shandy* there are shadowy triads galore—Walter (or is it Yorick?), Tristram, and Mrs. Shandy; Walter, Toby, and the Widow Wadman; Yorick, Tristram, and Toby.

In plate 1 of the *Analysis* (fig. 23) the pyramid of the title page reappears as the two tripods that frame the *Laocoön* and the statue of Julius Caesar being stabbed by another Roman (presumably Brutus), who is in turn being stabbed by a third (Apollo). The first tripod, elaborating on the serpentine Line of the title page (and of the frontispiece), connects the serpentine entanglement of Laocoön and his two sons with the "romantic triangle" of Hercules, Venus, and Apollo—and perhaps implies another in the dancing master and Antinous, as Antinous looks away from his male (Shaftesburian) admirer toward Venus. The sexual triangle is then reflected in the political, involving Caesar, Brutus, and Caesar's avenger (Apollo does double duty as lover in the sexual triangle and avenger in the political [as Hackabout did in the two gestalts of *Harlot* 1]).

In the text of the *Analysis,* in the chapter "Of Proportion" (96–106), Hogarth starts with "two extremes" and proceeds to the grotesque image of Atlas "throwing off by degrees, certain portions of bone and muscle" and Mercury "augmenting" his figure and "growing towards an Atlas"; indeed the two "may be imagined to grow more and more alike, till at a certain point of time, they meet in just similitude." The last inevitably invokes the "divine Similitude" of the Son in the third book of *Paradise Lost* when the Atonement and the Trinity are worked out. Hogarth immediately follows (after a semicolon) with the secular equivalent of "an exact medium between the two extremes," but, as he continues to elaborate, the Beauty of proportion emerges as the aesthetic version of the theological doctrine. The next example is the rainbow, where

two opposite colours . . . form a third between them, by thus imparting to each other their peculiar qualities . . . and blend by interchangeable degrees, and, as above [with the Ajax and Mercury], *temper* rather than destroy each other's vigour, till they meet in one firm compound; whence, at a certain point, the sight of what they were originally, is quite lost. (98)

This three-in-one rendition of the mystery of the Trinity, in Hogarth's example, involves the colors yellow and blue merging in a green "which colour nature hath chose for the vestment of the earth, and with the beauty of which the eye is never tired"—a plain conflation of the deist Nature with aesthetics.

In the next paragraph the rainbow is replaced by a painter's palette, and so implicitly (as in the subscription ticket–frontispiece) the deity is replaced by the artist, who confounds nature and art (the object has been to show "how such characters are composed when we [the spectators] see them either in art or nature").

The argument is framed by the insistence on perfecting such "matters by common observation" and "appealing to the reader's eye, and common observation, as before" (96, 102), and by the dismissal of "the blind veneration that generally is paid to antiquity" and the dispersal of religious mystery by the human understanding: such principles "not having been since sufficiently understood, no wonder such effects should have appear'd *mysterious,* and have drawn mankind into a sort of *religious esteem,* and even *bigotry,* to the works of antiquity" (105, emphasis added).

The mysterious, much-debated relationship of Father, Son, and Holy Spirit in the Doctrine of the Trinity was already parodied by Hogarth as a romantic triangle in works of the 1730s, for example in his painting of Prospero, Miranda, and Ferdinand in *A Scene from "The Tempest"* (Collection, Lord St. Oswald). The theological dimension is most obvious in his painting *Satan, Sin, and Death* (fig. 25), illustrating Milton's satanic parody of the Trinity in *Paradise Lost.* But Hogarth gives it the form (which no artist before him had used to illustrate the scene) of a daughter mediating between her father and her lover. Hogarth had begun to play with secularized or demystified versions of the Trinity as early as the conversation piece based on Gay's *Beggar's Opera* (1728–29; fig. 26), which indeed served as the model for *Satan, Sin, and Death:* Macheath choosing between his two wives Polly and Lucy (as Hercules chooses between Virtue and Pleasure); Polly mediating between Macheath and Mr. Peachum, her lover and her father; and then, in the *Harlot's Progress,* M. Hackabout, a female Hercules, choosing between a Virtue and Vice who have exchanged roles and attributes; Hackabout and Colonel Charteris being mediated (introduced) by

Mother Needham; Hackabout as a female figure (like Polly) of mediation who is placed by chance and the demands of society (in other words, "priestcraft") in a false, male situation of choice and thereby destroyed.

In the *Rake's Progress* Hogarth returns Hercules to the male gender but accompanies this figure, now named Tom Rakewell, by a female, Sarah Young, who loves him and attempts to mediate between him and the brutal world of bailiffs and the warders of prisons and madhouses. In plate 4 (fig. 17) her charitable act is commented on by a lamplighter's accidentally dripping oil on Rakewell's head, "anointing" him with a demystification of heavenly grace. And Sarah's pose, we have noticed, is formally echoed by that of Jesus, healing the lame man, in *The Pool of Bethesda*. In effect, Hogarth has conflated Sarah (as he implicitly conflated Mary by the end of the *Harlot*) with Jesus himself, feminizing—and this means, in Hogarth's terms, aestheticizing—the Christ (and in terms of the Trinity, the deity). Replacing Jesus with a beautiful woman confirms the appropriateness, in the *Analysis,* of replacing the Tetragrammaton with the Line of Beauty, which finds its incarnation (Hogarth suggests) in the beautiful woman. This also goes some way to explain the effect of the juxtaposition of the Harlot, the feminized Christ, with the grotesque figures of a *Flagellation.* The contrast between the beautiful face of Christ and the faces of his tormentors was precisely the point of Dürer and Massys. For contemporaries, one of the most gripping features of Hogarth's series, beginning with the nucleus of plate 3, was the joining of beautiful femininity and these contrary elements including imprisonment, torture, and death.

In the same way as Sarah succors Rakewell, the Poet's wife, a couple of years later, must deal with the milkmaid who demands payment of the Poet for her milk (1737; fig. 19). But here, outside the strong narrative line of the "progresses," the figure appears in a more static triangle consisting of poet, wife, and society, and the subject is now art rather than moral choice. The triangle is also (especially in the painting, where the wife's dress is blue, the traditional color of the Virgin's) located in a scene that invokes a Nativity—or replaces it, in the sense that Hogarth replaces the deity.[24] The natural offspring is juxtaposed with the artistic—the Poet's poem "On Riches" contrasted with his baby (crying, presumably for the milk that cannot be paid for by a poem on riches) and the cat who is nursing her kittens. Both the Poet and the Musician (in *The Enraged Musician* of 1741 [fig. 20]) are taking their inspiration from "scriptural" texts—the first from Edward Bysshe's *Art of English Poetry*, the second from a musical score.

The milkmaid in *The Enraged Musician,* however, more clearly than the Poet's wife, is a sort of natural muse whose song mediates between the bars of written notation and the indiscriminate noises of the plebeians on the street and *should* inspire the Musician.[25] In this print, four years before the Line of Beauty made its official appearance on Hogarth's palette in the self-portrait of himself and his pug (National Gallery, London), it is inscribed on the Musician's violin. But the violin is beside him, unused, an indication that he is responding as a connoisseur, criticizing the sounds in the street, rather than as an artist. The Lines of Beauty in nature are found in the figure and dress of the singing milkmaid, who mediates between the extremes of connoisseurship and the demotic.[26]

To summarize, Hogarth's response to Shaftesbury's disinterestedness is with interestedness—first (following Mandeville) an interest exposed as the reality under apparent disinterest, and then a living woman in whom a man is interested and whom he pursues and with whom he engages in some sort of erotic play: a paradigm intended to replace Shaftesbury's arid, abstract version of aesthetics. But Hogarth's response to the Christian interestedness in rewards and punishments is the truly disinterested figure of Sarah Young and, concurrently, of Jesus, both examples of love and charity as corrective to the priest's reliance on promises and threats. This figure, associated with breasts, milk, and motherhood, is the mediator (or muse) at the center of the cohesive triangles that produce a *concordia discors* out of opposites.

Here we should distinguish between kinds of romantic triangle: They share the generational element of old man (father, husband), young woman, young man; but one is a cohesive group in which a woman mediates between extremes, and the other a cuckold triangle in which a woman tempts, flirts, deceives, and surprises (a convention of theatrical comedy going back to *commedia dell'arte*). These two female figures and their accompanying men make up the "mystery" of Beauty that is intended to replace the mystery of the Trinity. The enabling image was the scene Hogarth painted from *The Beggar's Opera* (fig. 26), with two overlapping gestalts similar to the ones he used in *Harlot* 1: In one gestalt, which in Gay's text echoes a Choice of Hercules, Macheath is trying to choose between Polly and Lucy, his two "wives"; this shifts (as in Gay's text) into a second in which Polly tries to mediate between her lover Macheath and her angry father, Mr. Peachum. This may have been the origin of Hogarth's replacement in *Harlot* 1 of Hercules-Macheath by a female as well as plebeian equivalent.

This woman is of the lower orders, an actress, drummeress, or whore—the "Venus" of the wealthy keeper in *The Pool of Bethesda*. As she ascends the social scale she becomes both more beautiful (has more Lines of Beauty) and less "virtuous." From being her husband's helper, she becomes his cuckolder. In the *Analysis* plates Hogarth associates the cuckolded husband, the mere collector and possessor of a beautiful object, with Shaftesbury's connoisseur. The woman's deviance from virtue seems to increase with her husband's status. The Harlot cuckolds her keeper because this is the way a "lady" behaves, and in *Marriage A-la-mode* the merchant's daughter who becomes a countess cuckolds her husband. In plate 1 of the *Analysis* Venus cuckolds Vulcan-Hercules, and in plate 2 a beautiful woman of the country gentry cuckolds her older husband, while, opposite this group, a couple apparently of the nobility, consisting of Lines of Beauty, is associated with the Woman of Samaria (Annibale Carracci's beautiful serpentine figure of an adulteress)—all being responded to, in the margin, by a plebeian Sancho Panza in "the comical posture of astonishment" (fig. 24). Sancho, whom Hogarth elsewhere associates with himself, reminds us that the Poet/Musician was a Quixotic artist, as opposed to plebeian figures of common sense who comment on his Quixotism.

Hogarth is out to demonstrate the discrepancy between the Shaftesburian and Hutchesonian equation of beauty and virtue (and status). This sense of virtue is the *conventional* one: socially it is fidelity within marriage, and theologically the maintenance of the trinitarian three-in-one. From the beginning, in his "modern moral subjects," this has been a secondary transgression, subordinated to the abandonment or exploitation of the lower orders by the priestly governing class. Compared to this evil, cuckolding or committing adultery is a peccadillo, and, perhaps for that reason, appropriate for examples of aesthetic response. For one thing, cuckoldry comes with the credentials of a long tradition of comedy, and as Hogarth's chapter "Of Quantity" shows, the cuckold triangle is the prime example of comic incongruity, the comic consequence of the "pleasure of pursuit." Neither "Trinity" is in fact cohesive: in one the male figure is divisive, in the other the female. Even cuckoldry is an acceptable form of the Trinity, in art if not in life, because it defies the conventional equation of beauty and virtue *and* because it is the best illustration Hogarth can find of the way aesthetics in fact operates. From a respectable "moral" position (marriage, the unity of husband and wife) variety is created by the pursuit of pleasure-desire-wantonness. This produces the aesthetic situation of the utmost variety within apparent unity. And, as a revision of Shaftesbury's simple equation of beauty and virtue, deformity and vice, Hogarth implies that Beauty is to comedy as the Ugly is to satire.

What Hogarth called "modern moral subjects" began as "progresses" (the progress of a harlot and of a rake) based of course on an irony: not progress but decline, "crime" followed by rigorous punishment. Even in the "progresses," however, Hogarth held the spectator's attention on each scene, plucking objects for an instant out of the teleological pull and permitting the savoring of pure spectacle. The "progresses" were followed by a series of single plates on the subject of poets, musicians, actresses, and performers. Teleology was here replaced by contrast and (complicating the contrasts, questioning the polarities) Hogarth's other aesthetic principle, variety. The effect is less admonition or satire than comic contemplation, and the impartial weighing of competing interests with (via variety and the woman) an eye to the affirmative whole. The reading structures of *The Distressed Poet* (fig. 19) demonstrate the transition. In the painting (the reverse of the engraving), reading left to right, the eye follows the "progress" from the poet's (in)action to the consequences in his clothes, beleaguered wife, and unpaid milk bill. But in the engraving, Hogarth's end product, the figure of the milkmaid (representing the outside, the real world) is contrasted to the poet in his cubicle (his dream world), and mediated by the poet's wife, thus simulating the parodic Trinity.[27]

In these works leading to the *Analysis* and beyond, Hogarth produces his own version of Shaftesbury's "divine example" as an alternative both to the fictions of equal rewards and punishments and to the real world of reversed rewards and punishments, which he had dramatized so forcefully in his "progresses." He does this again by parody, by replacing the teleology of the New Testament narrative with the theological doctrine of the Trinity and the schema of a father, rebellious son, and pretty paraclete. Out of these emerge the formalist principles of contrast, variety, serpentine lines, even pursuit (within the individual plates), and so of aesthetics as a theme. I am suggesting that from this static relationship of people and qualities—one that denies the teleological direction but is full of inner contrasts and serpentine movements for the eye to pursue—derives the aestheticizing direction of Hogarth's later work.

Play and Rhetoric

Hogarth puts Shaftesburian disinterestedness in question in fundamental ways. Against Shaftesbury's disinterested contemplation he poses desire for a pretty woman (as against the ideal sculptured figure, a living creature), and the practical utility of commonplace domestic objects. But if disinterestedness defines the aesthetic experience, Hogarth's interestedness raises a question: Is he proposing an alternative aesthetics, one that is anti-idealist, antiacademic, and anti–civic humanist, or is it an antiaesthetics?

From Hogarth's point of view, in the *Analysis* at least, it is a true, *because* an anti-Shaftesburian, aesthetics. Although of course he never uses the word "aesthetic," he recovers its original sense ("AESTHETICAE"), first used by Baumgarten in his *Meditationes Philosophicae* of 1735 and further developed in his *Aesthetica* of 1750. Derived from the Greek *aisthetikos,* it means simply "perception" and has nothing per se to do with art or beauty; Baumgarten applies the word to poetics and discourse. In the *Meditationes* he writes: "Therefore, *things known* are to be known by the superior faculty as the object of logic; *things perceived* [are to be known by the inferior faculty, as the object] of the science of perception, or *aesthetic.*"[28] His attempt to raise the lower faculty of perception to the level of thought in poetry (which Addison had accomplished with the intermediate word "imagination") parallels in interesting ways Hogarth's in the visual arts. The parallel could explain the enthusiastic response Hogarth's *Analysis* received in Germany.[29]

Faced with the highly abstract world of Shaftesbury's Beautiful,

Hogarth associates his own works (and his theory as well) with Nature (or bodily life) rather than art, sensations rather than ideas, things rather than thoughts, concrete images rather than conceptualizations, the material rather than the immaterial, and practice rather than theory. The basic dichotomy expressed is at the heart of the *Analysis,* in the juxtaposition of the theory in the text and the practice (as well as application) in the illustrations.

Interestedness and physical desire, however, stop short of gratification; they do not spill over into the sexual act, precisely because the "pleasure" is in the pursuit and not the fulfillment. In a key passage Hogarth writes that "Pursuing is the business of our lives"—"This love of pursuit, merely as pursuit, is implanted in our natures, and design'd, no doubt, for necessary, and useful purposes." To this he adds, as if in explanation, "It is a pleasing labour of the mind to solve the most difficult problems; allegories and riddles, trifling as they are, afford the mind amusement" (41–42). The crucial words are "pursuit, merely as pursuit," "necessary, and useful purposes"; "solve the most difficult problems," "trifling," and "afford . . . amusement." But Locke's "Pursuit of Happiness" and Mandeville's "eager Pursuit after Pleasure" are refined by Hogarth to "pleasure of pursuit" (or "love of pursuit" or of "the chase")—an important distinction, which shifts the emphasis onto the pursuit itself. Yet pursuit is not an end in itself but is "design'd . . . for necessary, and useful purposes." These, however, are designated as the solution of puzzles, allegories, and riddles—which are called trifles and amusements, that is to say, play and games. Pursuit does not, in short, pass beyond the solution of a puzzle, the winning of a game. The chief object, to judge by the metaphors of sexual pursuit and the chase, is a woman or a fox; but when the pursuit passes beyond seduction or capture to possessing or killing, it is no longer within the range of the Beautiful.[30]

Hogarth's aesthetics began, after all, as deist hermeneutics, and the *Analysis* is an extension of Toland's method of interpretation. Hogarth starts with demystification, the end of which is understanding, and he carries this directly into his aesthetics, essentially an unprejudiced, detached understanding. To see or know things properly, as opposed to under the aegis of authority and its various forms of priestcraft, was also essentially Hogarth's definition of morality (i.e., he casti-gates the Harlot's folly but leads the viewer to understand how it came about, where the responsibility really lies); and he merely reformulates this in the *Analysis* as Beauty. He explodes the myth of Shaftesburian (and Hutchesonian) disinterestedness by advocating interestedness (the pursuit of a woman or fox); but only in order to distinguish between interestedness and action, knowledge and possession. Shaftes-bury's disinterestedness (as Mandeville saw) in fact conceals power (political, economic governance) and possession (collecting, forcing ideological programs on painters, taking over—as Burlington did—the Board of Works and imposing his Palladian style on British architec-ture). It is therefore a factitious and fraudulent disinterestedness, while Hogarth's "true" disinterestedness stops short with solutions to puzzles. Between the mere amusement of a game and the killing or possessing lies what Hogarth shows us, here and in his whole body of work, is "analysis" (as his title suggests) or knowledge without power, without possession.

But if he posits the desire of a woman, he balances it against the utility of a smokejack. His term "Fitness" refers to utility as well as decorum; he notes that parts "adapted thus to the uses they are design'd for" comprise "one sort of beauty" (32–33). And returning to the sub-ject in his chapter "Of Proportion," he goes beyond the idea of "orna-ment," something applied "merely to entertain the eye," to the "per-forming of *motion, purchase, stedfastness,* and other matters of use to living beings"—which amount to "one part of beauty to the mind tho' not always so to the eye" (84). He presumably includes rhetoric in this account.

Certainly to the knowledge of the solution of puzzles Hogarth adds judgment. The presence of a funerary memorial to a judge in plate 1 (labeled Obit. 1753) suggests that with the *Analysis* a new, truer judgment is revealed. Understanding in Toland's hermeneutics was followed by judgment, and interpretation by evaluation, which implies some sort of an action. Beauty is "analysed," and *this* object, stance, form, or line is judged more "beautiful" than *that.* And judgment, it is implied, is supplemented by one sort of action which accords with it: enjoying a certain object, drawing a certain figure, perhaps purchasing it—an option the practical Hogarth cannot but have had in mind.[31] And this sense of judgment carries over into the "modern moral subjects" of the illustrative plates.

Hogarth's juxtaposition of text and illustrative plates invites the reader to ask whether there is such a thing as *rhetorical play*—whether play and rhetoric may function together in the *Analysis*. Hogarthian aesthetics, or religion (or morality) turned into play, may be an even more politically subversive agent than the denial of the equation of beauty and virtue. Hogarth is utilizing an "aesthetics" in order to criticize other systems such as religion and conventional (ruling-class, Shaftesburian) morality. The question that follows is whether these acts were intended as satire, or as transgressions for their own sake (as in the desecration of the church porch or the sacrilege of the Medmenham Monks), and therefore as "aesthetic." To produce a parodic Trinity, a satanic serpent that replaces the Name of God, and associate it with sexual temptation and the Fall: These are unquestionably transgressive acts. W.J.T. Mitchell has asked of the reference to Satan: "Does the Satanic character of the serpentine line suggest that beauty is simply independent of moral status? Or does it suggest that beauty is actively *subversive* of morality, order, and rationality, and that the 'curiosity' aroused by beauty is the same that lured Eve into her wanton, lustful fall?"[32] The fact that Hogarth raises these questions is probably more important than the answer.

The questions themselves are, in the context of the *Analysis,* aesthetic. In this context the illustrative plates expose matters of style rather than morality; even their questioning of Shaftesbury's assumptions distances those assumptions *as aesthetic* from their moral consequences, distinguishing the *Analysis* plates from the "modern moral subjects" that preceded the aesthetic theory—perhaps even from the artist satires (*Distressed Poet, Enraged Musician*), which may initially have been read in the context of the moral "progresses" that preceded them rather than the aesthetic theory that followed.

Variety, intricacy, contrast, all of Hogarth's aesthetic terms are clearly intended to describe, justify, and theorize in retrospect the method of the "modern moral subjects" (the "pleasure of pursuit" was the experience of "reading" them); but thereby these terms in effect aestheticize the morality of the earlier works. In the "progresses" Hogarth had at least expressed indignation, though less directly at the immediate perpetrator than at a more distant culprit, largely institutional and often absent (whether God, a clergyman, or a governor of the poor). In the retrospect of the *Analysis* we see that the object of the "progresses" was knowledge and judgment without power—without a call to action, which would have made them dangerous in the sense of prosecutable (Hogarth was no Woolston). Aesthetics dramatizes Hogarth's constant distancing of his works from—to begin with—the religious dimension of the Christian "progress" (such as of a pilgrim), but also from moral injunction. The fact that no one (unless a John Trusler) can say, without radical reductionism, that the *Harlot* shows crime punished and urges young women to avoid the life of prostitution, indicates the common ground between Hogarth's morality and his aesthetics.

Hogarth himself, for all his particularism, did not in the *Analysis* escape the trap of Shaftesburian abstraction. His object was to find the principle of beauty in all of those sensuous concrete particulars which discredit the abstract—to reveal, we might say, the structure of the concrete. (The subject of his concrete particulars and how to deal with them is wrestled with by all of his commentators, from Rouquet to Trusler, Ireland, and Lichtenberg: see below, chap. 10.) In this way Hogarth the practical artist betrayed the theorist's need to find a reason behind his practice. In the *Analysis* the tension (even contradiction) between his concrete particulars (including both the smokejack and the living woman) and the absolute principle of the one-and-only "precise" serpentine Line of Beauty had two effects: His critics (supporters of the proposal for a state academy) found the discrepancy risible; we may find the principle a way for Hogarth to distance those particulars, control them, and make them safer and more palatable. By finding Beauty in the concrete particulars of the "progresses" and thus abstracting them, he attempted to valorize and justify that world (as the Columbus reference of his subscription ticket implies) of sensations, bodies, and material objects and privilege it against the conventions of reason and the other forms of the immaterial. But he also retrospectively aestheticized it and perhaps indicated the sense in which it had been even at the time aestheticized.

THREE

Addison's Aesthetics of the Novel

The Beautiful and the Novel / New / Uncommon

Shaftesbury's aesthetics was based on the old dichotomy of the Beautiful and the Ugly or deformed: there is the Beautiful and all the rest is deformed. Although Shaftesbury designated the beautiful object (as a friend, friendship, and ever larger systems of society) and its qualities (balance and harmony, unity in variety), he was concerned primarily with the response and responder rather than the object itself. He attempted to define the refined sort of pleasure that can appreciate the beautiful object, primarily the disinterestedness that distinguishes the appreciation of a beautiful from a merely useful or desirable object. Shaftesbury's nonbeautiful, in terms of artifacts, reiterated the academic view (still echoed by Addison in *Spectator* No. 83) that the Italians painted the Beautiful—that is, history paintings—while the Netherlandish painters, mere craftsmen ("mechanics"), tended to paint the Ugly.[1] By the latter was meant dungheaps, boors, and assorted low-life subjects, including most aspects of landscape and still-life.

Martin Price has seen the Sublime, like the Picturesque, as "a revolt against the tyranny of beauty."[2] I take this to be Price's shorthand for the view that initially there was only the Beautiful, set off by ugliness and deformity, and that post-Shaftesbury aestheticians attempted to carve out, whether from the Beautiful or the Ugly, areas of the Sublime and then the Picturesque. In the eleven-essay series "The Pleasures of the Imagination" (*Spectator* Nos. 412 ff., 1712), Addison opened a space for the stigmatized or marginalized areas of enjoyment in Shaftesbury's system. From the Beautiful and/or Ugly he extracted the Great and what he called the Novel, New, or Uncommon—the latter being the area that naturally interested him most. His spectatorship itself was, after all, not something that could be categorized as "beautiful" in the Shaftesburian sense.

This was also the area that interested Hogarth most. Addison's identification of the "Pleasures of the Imagination" with the sense of sight—one of the lower faculties—would have attracted Hogarth the graphic artist at the outset.[3] The objects represented in his story-telling prints were essentially those described in the *Spectator*. When he came to write his own aesthetics he utilized both the Beautiful and the Novel. His *Analysis of Beauty* is indebted to Addison's triad, but his sense of the word is neither a passive feminine Beautiful nor a masculine aggressive Great. The aesthetic object (small, smooth, curved) corresponds to Addison's Beautiful, but the experience of the Beautiful derives from the middle term, the Novel, with the name appropriately congruent with that of the emergent literary form. Hogarth combines the serpentine lines of the beautiful object with the epistemology of the Novel (also, in its own way, serpentine). The qualities Addison associates with the Novel are "surprise," "the pursuit of knowledge," "curiosity," and "variety." "It is this," he writes, "that recommends Variety, where the Mind is every Instant called off to something new, and the Attention not suffered to dwell too long, and waste it self on any particular Object" (No. 412, 3:541). It "gratifies" the soul's "Curiosity." He remarks that the Novel can absorb aspects of both the Beautiful and the Great: "It . . . improves what is great or beautiful, and makes it afford the Mind a double Entertainment." The Great is only an expansive version of the Novel. Although a kind of object (vast deserts, huge mountains, and oceans), for Addison greatness is not "the Bulk of any single Object, but the Largeness of a whole View": "Our Imagination loves to be filled with an Object, or to grasp at any thing that is too big for its Capacity" (3:540).[4] The awe of greatness is essentially the curiosity of the Novel *un*satisfied.

The experience of greatness, of being "flung into a pleasing Astonishment at such unbounded Views," leads into Addison's paeon to liberty ("The Mind of Man naturally hates everything that looks like a Restraint upon it. . . ."); but the passage looks both back to the Great and forward in the following paragraph to the "*new* or *uncommon*," which is defined by filling "the soul with an agreeable Surprise." The Novel "*gratifies* its Curiosity, and gives it an Idea of which it was not before possest": while sharing the opening up of vistas, it resolves the unresolvable experience of the Great.

In the terms of Whig politics, Addison can be said to have created in his "Pleasures" an epistemology based on liberty, as a reaction to Jacobite and Roman Catholic tyranny (with their associations of imperial Rome, France, and greatness). And while the epistemology of liberty, openness, and discovery includes the Great, it clearly subordinates it to the Novel or Uncommon.[5]

The Beautiful itself is little more than cosmetic: beauty "gives a finishing to any thing that is great or Uncommon," for example by the addition of color, a secondary quality (3:542–44). Defined in relation to the Deformed, it is implicitly a kind of form, a closure, which counters the openness of liberty. In political iconography the Beautiful has Stuart associations—the female nation, the debauched Britannia, of Restoration imagery but also, more benignly, the gender of the last of the Stuart monarchs, Mary and Anne. The counterexperience Addison defines and aestheticizes is the middle term associated with the fraternal Spectator Club and the homosocial ethos of civic humanism.

The beautiful female, for Shaftesbury, threatened the crucial disinterestedness that he posited as what distinguishes a civic humanist and a man of taste from the vulgar: as a property owner, he is above considerations of ambition, possession, consumption, and desire, indeed of gender, and therefore capable of a "rational and refined contemplation" of beauty. Mr. Spectator's "beholding all Nature with an unprejudic'd Eye; and having nothing to do with Mens Passions or Interests," is certainly another form of disinterestedness (No. 4, 1:19). The more accommodating Addison, however, modulates the austere virtue of civic humanism into politeness, and extends the amenities across a broader spectrum of society, noting that the "man of a Polite Imagination" feels "a greater Satisfaction in the Prospect of Fields and Meadows, than another does in the Possession"—precisely because it is *not* his own property and he sees it in the perspective of commerce and paper money rather than inheritance, upkeep, and tenantry. To enjoy the "Pleasures of the Imagination," as he says in the first "Pleasure" essay, "is but opening the Eye, and the Scene enters" (No. 411, 3:537–38), another precedent for Hogarth's refrain, "see with our own eyes," not with the occluded eyes of "gentlemen."[6]

Addison again modifies Shaftesbury's sense of disinterestedness when he argues that the Beautiful focuses on procreation—each species "is most affected with the Beauties of its own kind":

> [God] has made every thing that is *beautiful in our own Species* pleasant, that all Creatures might be tempted to multiply their Kind, and fill the World, with Inhabitants. . . . unless all Animals were allured by the Beauty of their own Species, Generation would be at an end, and the Earth unpeopled. (3:542–43, 546)

Though a modification, this is not a rejection of Shaftesbury's more Platonic end of wisdom applied to governing, good taste, and political disinterestedness. While addressing himself ostentatiously to the issue of including the feminine, "the female World" (Nos. 4, 10), within his audience, Mr. Spectator reduces the female as a figure to the unfortunate Yaricko and the recalcitrant Widow who rejects the advances of Sir Roger de Coverley. (It should be recalled that Yaricko is Steele's creation and is adduced as a counterexample to the Matron of Ephesus, the prototypical lecherous widow.) Thus we come upon Mr. Spectator's observation of a beautiful young woman in Covent Garden Piazza, "newly come upon the Town," who is seduced by a bawd (No. 266, the author is Steele): "as exact Features as I had ever seen, the most agreeable Shape, the finest Neck and Bosom, in a Word, the whole Person of a Woman exquisitely beautiful." But "falling into cruel Hands," she is "left in the first Month from her Dishonour, and exposed to pass through the Hands and Discipline of one of those Hags of Hell whom we call Bawds" (3:534–35). Mr. Spectator's description, which could have served as the first idea for the *Harlot's Progress,* and his refusal to involve himself on the girl's behalf, join spectatorship to voyeurism and the object of male desire.

Addison's charmed circle, "the Fraternity of Spectators," is a male group with decidedly unsexual interests (No. 10, 1:45–46). Mr. Specta-

tor, "born to a small Hereditary Estate," is the civic humanist gentleman; Captain Sentry, like Sterne's Captain Shandy, is a man of "in-
vincible Modesty"; and Will Honeycomb, though familiar with "the
Gallantries and Pleasures of the Age" and an honest man "where
Women are not concerned," yet is described as a tatler rather than a
lover seriously engaged with any woman. Sir Roger, insofar as he pursued the Widow, is associated with the old Restoration story of Hudibras and his widow and with the revisionist relationship of Mirabel and
the Widow Wishfort. But his significant relationships are with the
male servant who saved his life and the fraternity of spectators, who
show no interest in women.[7]

Addison and Steele are central sources of the counterdiscursive
Novel, but they also retain a polite version of the fraternal aspect of
Shaftesbury's civic humanism: they transmit the Shaftesburian aesthetic of contempt for the "interested" reproductivity of heterosexuality and the corollary investment both in the desexualized idealization of woman and, more tacitly, in the homoerotic valuation of strictly
"masculine" desire—and in this respect Hogarth parts company with
them when he centers his version of the Novel on the pleasures of the
pursuit of the beautiful and living woman.[8]

One of Addison's favorite metaphors is of life-as-a-chase. In the
paper that opens the series commemorating Mr. Spectator's visit to Sir
Roger's country house, he notes that

> Odd and uncommon Characters are the game that I look for, and most
> delight in; for which Reason I was as much pleased with the Novelty of
> the Person that talked to me [Will Wimble], as he could be for his Life
> with the springing of a Pheasant, and therefore listened to him with
> more than ordinary Attention. (No. 108, 1:448)

The metaphor of the chase would seem to be best materialized in the
country, as William Gilpin and the theorists of the Picturesque later
realized. But at the end of the visit to Sir Roger, Mr. Spectator acknowledges—using the words *start, hunt, pleasure, variety, odd Creatures, puzzle, chace*—how much more appropriate the metaphor is to life in London (No. 131, 2:19). And a bit later he reminds us that "curiosity" is his
"prevailing passion" (No. 156, 2:111). In short, Addison associates the
metaphor of the chase as one form of "pursuit" most clearly with Mr.

Spectator himself. The same words associated with the Novel are applied to him: "odd," "insatiable Thirst after Knowledge," and "Curiosity" (No. 1, 1:2).

In No. 412 what was first associated with Mr. Spectator comes to be defined in terms of the "Pleasures of the Imagination" as the distinguishing category of aesthetic experience between the Beautiful and the Great—a new, uncharted category. Indeed, he announces the "Pleasures" series itself as "entirely new" (No. 409, 3:531)—an adjective both Hogarth and Fielding echo when writing of their innovative genres. To judge by the title of his journal, the Novel or Uncommon may have been the category that inspired his excursion into aesthetics. Of his three terms, the Novel was the most literary, the most *Spectator*-like. It should not surprise us that Hogarth's almost readable prints develop the mode of the Novel—or rather, find their artistic rationale in the term—and that in his *Analysis* he presents his exposition of aesthetic theory twice, once in the text and once in the concrete examples of the spectatorial plates.[9]

Hogarth's crucial modification is to change Addison's pleasure of the "chase" or the "Pursuit after Knowledge" to the "pleasure [or love] of pursuit" itself, which reverses Mandeville's "pursuit of pleasure" and recalls Locke's metaphor of the mind's "searches after truth [which] are a sort of hawking and hunting, wherein the very pursuit makes a great part of the pleasure." But in No. 116 Addison also follows Locke's version of the metaphor, urging the hunter to stop the chase short of killing the fox and to enjoy the "diversion" for its own sake (1:478, quoted below, 161).[10]

There is then an epistemological stratagem, which Hogarth, locating it in the aesthetic area of the Novel, focuses on a beautiful object, a woman. Or, by focusing on a woman he automatically locates it in the aesthetic (as *Fanny Hill* and *Amelia* will do—and *Sentimental Journey* in a different way will do—and *Tristram Shandy* will perversely *not* do). To curiosity, problem solving, and the pursuit of truth he adds pleasure and wantonness. The spectator's searching and pursuing mind is excited or inspired by the undulating shape of the beautiful woman. Responding to Shaftesbury's idealized sculpture of the human body, Hogarth's definition of Beauty focuses on sexual curiosity, voyeurism, and pursuit (which imply seduction) of the human female body. He thus joins the Beautiful in name and in a central female presence with the libertarian epistemology of the Novel in a way that is not directly opposed to Addison's formulation but is quite different in spirit.

He also discards Addison's triad, returning to Shaftesbury's (and Hutcheson's) dichotomy of Beautiful and Ugly.[11] Nevertheless, in the illustrative plates he retains Addison's Trinity, or his own parodic form of it, with the female mediator between opposing males.[12] *Spectator* No. 419 ended with a sample of "Imaginary Beings" of the Strange, which concludes with Satan, Sin, and Death (discussed earlier in his Milton essays). A favorite of Addison's, the Miltonic parody of the Trinity indicated that the Great has to be the Father, the Beautiful the Holy Spirit, and the Novel/Uncommon—Addison's favorite—the Son. But, typically, the mysterious and uncharted area in the middle, the Novel, is male. Hogarth retains the middle ground of the Novel while gendering it female and naming it (after Sin) the Beautiful.

We must be careful not to blur the distinctions, first, between natural and represented objects, and second, between epistemology and ontology, that is, between novel response and novel object. After privileging the primary Pleasures of the Imagination over the secondary (nature over art), Addison shifts his attention in the later essays to justifying the secondary (representations, in paintings, statues, and particular descriptions). Hogarth seems to be taking note of Addison's shift, for while he privileges nature over art, he nevertheless does so in a work of art, to which he draws attention in his programmatic subscription tickets and newspaper advertisements. We have traced his dichotomy between Shaftesbury's sculpture of Venus and a living woman, but we must add to this his own representation of a living woman (whether she is representative or particular). The fact is that he produces fables of aesthetics rather than (properly speaking) aesthetic objects, establishing by this means a rationale for his joining in the *Analysis* the epistemology of the Novel with the beautiful object by way of the serpentine lines (of perception, of the body) they share. In this sense the *Analysis* (as its illustrative plates suggest) is merely a continuation of his "modern moral subjects."

The Novel then is less an object than a discursive mode, which exists by incorporating the Beautiful, or sometimes the Great, or sometimes both the Beautiful and the Great. The novel object itself is anything that elicits curiosity and surprise, and this calls for an epistemology based (like its comic version, the ridiculous, to which Hogarth also devotes space in the *Analysis*) on contrast and incongruity. In works of the 1730s such as *Southwark Fair* and *Strolling Actresses Dressing in a Barn*, *The Distressed Poet* and *The Enraged Musician*, but to a lesser degree in all his works, Hogarth juxtaposes the novel response of a subject with a beautiful object, the Addisonian spectator with a woman.

Ultimately the Novel is necessary to keep the Beautiful from being (in Addison's terms) merely cosmetic and to question the possibility of a disinterested contemplation of the Beautiful itself, either in the sexual or the politico-moral sense: a program that must inevitably emerge from the amalgamation of Addison's Beautiful and Novel. Mere Beauty, following Shaftesbury, assumes in an ideal world an equivalence to virtue as to some kind of harmony; and every harmonious work implies an allegory of political well-being, while a disharmonious work—per se a novelistic work—implies, as Hogarth if not Addison realized, an allegory of social pathology.

Spectatorship and Providential Design

If one of Addison's favorite metaphors for life is the chase, another is the stage. If it is possible to see us as hunters pursuing, or at least playing with, a prey (which Sir Roger at any rate catches and kills), it is more accurate to see us as an audience watching an actor assuming different roles.

The disinterested "Fraternity of Spectators who live in the World without having any thing to do in it" is defined as "every one that considers the World as a Theatre, and desires to form a right Judgment of those who are the Actors on it" (No. 10, 1:45–46). In the essays that lead up to the essays on the "Pleasures of the Imagination," the favored subject is "spectatoring," the favorite metaphor life-as-theater.[13] They remind us that the social dimension of spectatoring (and so of the Novel) is, in the long run, the most significant one.[14] Whereas Addison wrote as a pious Anglican, he drew uncritically on the sensationalist psychology of Hobbes as well as on Locke and projected in his own polite form a very provisional sense of words/things and custom/reality, including politeness itself.

The opening *Spectators* go from an account of a "spectator" to references to gestures without words, and to theaters, operas, entertainments, tragedies, and comedies (Nos. 10, 12, 40, 371). The playhouse, for example, is "the Seat of Wit" (No. 65). In No. 86 the idea of experience gained only through the senses—and first the sense of sight—leads to an emphasis on seeing, gesturing, and acting on a stage.

The most influential rendition of the metaphor, however, is religious. In No. 219 it is related to the operation of divine providence on the distribution of rewards and punishments. According to one metaphor, from Scripture, men are "Strangers and Sojourners upon Earth, and Life is a Pilgrimage," but according to the other, Epictetus's metaphor, the world is "a Theatre, where everyone has a Part allotted to him" and is judged by how well he plays his part (2:353).[15] The pilgrimage stresses teleology: whether the Christian pilgrimage or the epic journey, whether the travels of Adam or Odysseus or Aeneas, it must have a destination and follow the road or cut across fields. (Parson Adams, in the main journey of *Joseph Andrews*, has a habit of splashing across rivers although a bridge lies just ahead.) The aspects of providence Addison stresses in the theatrical metaphor are its apparent arbitrariness, inscrutability, and incalculable distance from our everyday concerns—as well, of course, as its aspect of disinterested spectatorship which relates back to Shaftesbury's critique of rewards and punishments, but in the context of Epictetus turns disinterestedness into indifference.

This metaphor, he says, is "wonderfully proper to incline us to be satisfied with the Post in which Providence has placed us" (Epictetus himself, he reminds us, was a slave), for there may well be a discrepancy between the fate of the dramatis personae and the fate of the actors who played them:

> The great Duty which lies upon a Man is to act his Part in Perfection. We may, indeed, say that our Part does not suit us, and that we could act another better. But this (says the Philosopher) is not our Business. All that we are concerned in is to excell in the Part which is given us. If it be an improper one the Fault is not in us, but in him who has cast our several Parts, and is the great Disposer of the Drama. (2:353)

Here in the present the pattern is seen as in a glass darkly; in heaven we will be able to look down, so to speak, and appreciate the pattern, which he describes as "an Entertainment" or "a Scene so large and various" offering "so delightful a Prospect" (No. 237, 2:420): terms that will contribute to the conception of narrative employed by both Hogarth, the graphic artist, and Fielding, the ex-playwright.

However, the example Addison gives is a grim one: Moses on Pisgah is shown by God a scene on a roadway, a spring where a soldier on his journey stops to drink and forgets his purse. When he has departed a child comes up, sees the purse he has dropped, and takes it; and then an old man arrives ("weary with Age and travelling") and rests under the tree. The soldier returns to seek his purse, assumes the old man has taken it, and kills him. This scene causes Moses to fall on his face "with Horror and Amazement" (2:353), but God explains that what he has seen is divine justice, for some years ago the old man had murdered the child's father. Thus Addison is far from denying a providential pattern, but he distances it far beyond man's reach, portraying life as a journey interrupted by a scene in which three travelers come together in various roles, from the past as well as the present. To these people life is a journey; but to Moses, the human consciousness who observes them, it is a scene, and moreover, one that can only be interpreted by the playwright himself.

For Addison, the theatrical scene seems necessary to replace the determinedly teleological pilgrimage with a series of provisional structures, roles, and scenes, which are more appropriate to man's life in society (and are related to the role of religion in the writings of the deists). The pilgrimage does not disappear, indeed it structures Hogarth's *Harlot* and Fielding's *Joseph Andrews* and *Tom Jones* (not to mention *A Journey from This World to the Next*); but it is now divided into "scenes" and (as we have seen) in Hogarth's work leading to the *Analysis* it is fragmented into independent or (as in *Before* and *After*) merely contrasting scenes. Hogarth best caught the idea in graphic images of playacting, but Fielding elaborately developed the metaphor in both plays and novels, and Goldsmith utilized it in his one novel: we are actors assigned roles by a playwright or stage manager—not a deity but the ruling, policing order of his surrogates on earth, who take little interest in the appropriateness of role to actor. Clergymen promise at some distant time a reward for the way we play the role assigned to us— and this promise keeps us comforted and operational.

The educational aspect of the theater is emphasized throughout. The reference is to the playhouse as the model of the world: we learn both our moral duty and our social manners through emulation, and we will be judged in both cases by the perfection of our performance. In the essays on wit Addison writes that "The Seat of Wit, when one speaks as a Man of the Town and the World, is the Playhouse. . . . The application of Wit in the Theatre has a strong Effect upon the Manners of our Gentlemen" (No. 65, 1:278). If Addison sees the theater as a means of social education, it follows that manners and politeness are a function of acting, and proper sociability depends on a true correspondence between inherent virtue and social manner. People act out the manners they see in the playhouse, and therefore manners involve emulation and become a function of acting (of role-playing). Manners are "theatrical" both in the sense of originating in the theater and of being parts played in the world-as-stage.

It also follows that if people learn how to act by seeing actors, it is incumbent on the playwright to present in his plays true wit. To affect the manners of those above you and to appear "greater than you are" is a species of false wit. The problem of false wit is that the exterior does not correspond to the interior. Properly polite writing must unite interior virtue with exterior manner and teach that manners should embellish, not belie, virtue. Thus the satiric playwright's proper subject will be affectation, and the effective basis of the Novel will be theatrical.[16]

Aside from the discussion of theatrical imitation in the *Spectator,* Addison's collaborator Steele had introduced the general theme in *Tatler* No. 63, which, while dismissing satire as an irresponsible literary mode, admits that ridicule can serve "to bring Pretenders and Imposters in Society to a true Light," if the central characters are exemplary.[17] For example, in *Tatler* No. 27, while sympathizing with the figure of the rake (many of whose qualities he shared) Steele turns his satire onto the rake's "Mimicks and Imitators": "How ought Men of Sense to be careful of their Actions, if it were meerly from the Indignation of seeing themselves ill drawn by such little Pretenders? Not to say, he that leads, is guilty of all the Actions of his Followers: And a Rake has Imitators whom you would never expect should prove so" (1:207). He goes on to attack "second-hand Vice" and "the Fatality (under which most Men labour) of desiring to be what they are not," which "makes 'em go out of a Method in which they might be receiv'd with Applause, and would certainly excel, into one, wherein they will all their Life have the Air of Strangers to what they aim at." Hogarth adopts Steele's particular sense of "rake" in *Tatler* No. 27 for his *Rake's Progress*, which depicts the miserly merchant's son who, attempting to raise his status (become "polite"), foolishly emulates the rake. But imitation applies also, and for the *Rake's Progress* in particular, to aesthetics: to the Shaftesburian (or Richardsonian) Man of Taste who merely "mimicks" the Shaftesburian fashion for old master paintings or Palladian houses.

Steele puts the dramatic theory he presents in the *Tatler* into practice in his comedy *The Conscious Lovers* (1722). The secondary characters are "mimicks and imitators": on the bourgeois level Mrs. Sealand tries to act like a lady, and among the servants Tom and Phillis try to talk like gentlefolk. Gay employs the comedy of imitation in *The Beggar's Opera* (1728), but he moves the emulators to center stage (though they remain essentially servant types like Tom and Phillis). And Gay's phenomenally popular play served as a primary model for the early works of both Hogarth and Fielding. Fielding, in his *Champion* essay on Hogarth of 10 June 1740, gives Hogarth's "progresses" a dramatic reading, and in his preface to *Joseph Andrews* he describes the essence of the ridiculous as affectation, essentially a matter of assuming inappropriate roles, which complicates even the central characters of Joseph and Adams, though it is most blatantly evident in Lady Booby, Slipslop, and the minor characters.

Prior to Fielding's breakthrough in *Joseph Andrews,* the diary and the autobiography were the normative models for what we might call novelistic fiction (as opposed to, though by no means leaving behind prominent memories of, romance). In the 1730s Hogarth, in his "modern moral subjects" or "progresses," introduces the model of the theatrical performance, with the self-reflexive metaphor of life-as-theater and scenes that (unlike the quick succession in a play) are frozen in time, open to unlimited unpacking by their "spectators." In the later 1730s, in his single-sheet artist satires, he turns from "progresses" to single scenes, approximating Addison's own movement in the *Spectator* from morality to aesthetics. In the same years, out of the practice of both Gay and Hogarth, Fielding develops a self-consciously theatrical play, which takes the form of a *rehearsal* of a play, whose scenes are unpacked by the commentaries of the author, actors, critics, and others in attendance. Despite his claim in the preface to *Joseph Andrews,* his new fictional mode is based on (that is, justified by) Aristotelian principles of the drama; the model is Hogarth's version of Addison's Novel or Uncommon.

Theatricality for Hogarth, then, is suspect as affectation (playing an inappropriate role) but normative, or at least descriptive, as a symbol of the provisionality of social forms. It also serves as the model for his own art: "my Picture was my Stage and men and women my actors who were by Mean[s] of certain actions and express[ions] to exhibit a dumb shew," he wrote in his "Autobiographical Notes" in the early 1760s (*Analysis,* 209).

He brings his final chapter of the *Analysis,* "Of Action," to a close with the incommensurability of life and a "stage action," of primary and secondary imaginations: "It is known that common deportment, such as may pass for elegant and proper off the stage, would no more be thought sufficient upon it than the dialogue of common polite conversation, would be accurate or spirited enough for the language of a play" (160–61). On the last page he reaffirms three of the basic points of the *Analysis:* that actresses are more beautiful than actors, that "mischief . . . attends copied actions," in this case "on the stage" ("confin'd to certain sets and numbers, which being repeated, and growing stale to the audience, become at last subject to mimicry and ridicule"), and that the "comedian, whose business it is to imitate the actions belonging to particular characters in nature," is preeminent over tragedians and others; it is presumably with the comedian that Hogarth identifies himself.

He distinguishes comedian (performer), theorist of the principle of Beauty, and author. The particular "actions" that assist and enforce the "authors *[sic]* meaning" "must be left entirely to the judgment of the performer," while the theorist of action and gesture merely shows "how the limbs may be made to have an equal readiness to move in all such directions as may be required" (161). Nevertheless, "for whatever he [the comedian] copies from the life, by these principles [i.e., of the serpentine line, variety, intricacy, etc.] may be strengthened, altered, and adjusted as his judgment shall direct, and the part the author has given him shall require" (162). This "author," which conflates the

Author and the author, above and below in the metaphor of life-as-stage, returns Hogarth the theorist to Hogarth the "author" (as he called himself) of his "modern moral subjects."

Novel / News

The word "novel" appears in Steele's *Spectator* No. 254 as part of the pair "Romance and Novels," that is, the novel was a genre defined by its opposition to romance, from which it was distinguished by its sense of the "new." ("Novel" was in fact a synonym for "news.") The Italian *novella* had dealt with contemporary events, as opposed to the distant past of epic or romance.[18] Fielding, for example, makes Wisemore respond in *Love in Several Masques* (1728) to a surprising revelation ("news"): "What novel's this?" (4.4). But when he refers to the literary form "the novel" he invokes the erotic narratives of Eliza Heywood (Mrs. Novel). The action of the puppet-play of *The Author's Farce* (1730) is the marriage of Mrs. Novel with Signor Opera, followed by her seduction of the Presbyterian parson Murdertext—an Addisonian allegory of the degenerate "novel" that conceals its erotic intent under moralizing (on which Fielding focused his attention a decade later in Richardson's *Pamela*): This is the "novel" Fielding sets out to replace, partly by the Mandevillian strategy of revealing its erotic intent.[19]

Addison's sense of the word makes it a variant of "uncommon." But a philosophical sense had been confirmed by Locke in the sections of his *Essay* on "Wrong Assent, or Error," where he opposed novel not to romance but to "a received hypothesis":

> Would it not be an insufferable thing for a learned professor, and that which his scarlet would blush at, to have his authority of forty years standing, wrought out of hard rock, Greek and Latin, with no small expense of time and candle, and confirmed by general tradition and a reverent beard, in an instant *overturned by an upstart novelist*? (emphasis added)

The context was religious belief, and the unfortunate fact Locke noted was that "men will disbelieve their own eyes, renounce the evidence of their senses, and give their own experience the lie, rather than admit of anything disagreeing with these sacred tenets."[20] Interestingly, recalling the unveiling of Nature in Hogarth's *Boys Peeping*, the figure Locke uses is of the "novelist" who must "disrobe himself at once of all his old opinions, and pretences to knowledge and learning" and "turn himself out stark naked, in quest afresh of new notions."[21]

Locke remained prudently within the bounds of orthodoxy, but Toland picked up his sense of "novelist" in *Christianity Not Mysterious* and applied it to himself (Locke apparently read the manuscript, which he answered in *The Reasonableness of Christianity*). In his apologia, *Vindicius Liberius* (1702), Toland put it this way:

> And indeed He trifles extremely with the World, who is not convinc'd, that, at least, he makes Things clearer than they were; if He explodes no vulgar Errors, detects no dangerous Fallacies, nor adds any stronger Light or Proof to what was generally receiv'd before. Those and such like are the real or pretended Motives of all Authors, of *Divines* as well as others; and they actually advance new *Notions, Expositions,* and *Hypotheses* in their Books every Day.[22]

This sense of "novel" may have been in Hogarth's mind when he was drawn to Addison's intermediate term between the Beautiful and the Great; it coincides with the assumption that clearly underwrites his own mature work, from the *Harlot's Progress* on. Addison's Novel, however, suggested discovery in the exploratory or scientific sense. A specific example of the "new or uncommon" was the Iroquois sachems who visited London in 1710 (*Spectator* No. 50). Hogarth, with his deist strain, suggests discovery as exposing the truth under false authority or opinions.

For Toland this exposure of truth also included, as he explains in *Christianity Not Mysterious,* a certain obscurity that (in Stephen H. Daniel's words) "provoked new insights in others" and was "the obscurity necessary to novelty" even when "unintended by an author."[23] This provocative obscurity relates, of course, to Toland's dichotomy of "exoteric and esoteric" meanings. But, as the works of Swift and his followers show, irony, the master trope of the period, supports the sense of "Novel" as revealing a truth or reality beneath appearances (beneath the official or priestly interpretation)—the hidden real beneath misleading appearances.

The deist phenomenon introduces us to one version of the conjunction, out of which the new forms of "novelistic" fiction arise, between the older world of traditional wisdom and the new realm of empiricism, of information embodied in the journalistic press, the world of the "novel" or "news." Semidocumentary genres have the effect of generating a "liberty" of their own from prevailing aesthetic standards and conventions. Located outside traditional canons, they furnish "new," unusual, even startling insights into spiritual life. There was also a more general sense of antiauthoritarian and anticanonical "news" which was enunciated by Daniel Defoe at about the same time. Defoe contrasts the journals and their reader, the "True-Bred Merchant" who attends to his business of the moment, with the learned who read classical texts. The journal reader is an "Improver of . . . Learning" because he can understand "Languages without Books . . . [and] Geography without Maps." With his broader, more liberal education, he is "a Universal Scholar . . . qualified for all sorts of Employment in the State, by a general Knowledge of Things and Men."[24] Addison, we recall, opens the "Pleasures" with the remark that to enjoy them is but to open the eye: no learning, no Latin or Greek, is required for aesthetic pleasures—*or*, Toland and the deists would add, for reading the New Testament.

Let us now compare the two senses of "the Novel," as novel/news and as discovery of the new. Hogarth's *Harlot's Progress* materialized the news of the *Daily Courant* or *Daily Advertiser* concerning Needham, Charteris, Ann Bond, Kate Hackabout, Sir John Gonson, and the rest. The *Harlot* was virtually of a piece with the London newspapers of 1730–32, right up to its publication (with the deaths of Needham and Charteris).[25] The second sense of Novel was summed up in Woolston's demystifying of the miracles of Christ and Hogarth's rewriting of the "romance" or "ancient" story, whether of the Shaftesburian Choice of Hercules or the New Testament Visitation, revealing its novel/news or (with reference to the unveiling of Nature in the subscription ticket) novel "Truth." Hogarth continued this mode not only in his prints but also in his most ambitious paintings. In the altarpiece commissioned for the church of St. Mary Redcliffe (1755–56), as we have seen, he "novelized" the Resurrection in the side panels into a satire on priestcraft and in the central panel, focusing on Mary Magdalen, into a reprise of his *Harlot's Progress*. And in *Paul before Felix*, a painting for the Benchers of Lincoln's Inn (1747–48), he treated the story in Acts by focusing on the reversal of accused and accuser (the guilty judge is condemned by the innocent accused), and in particular on the sexual transgression of the Roman judge Felix, his liaison with the Jewess Drusilla, suggested by Hogarth's placement of St. Paul's hand with a bit of false perspective to indicate the cause of the transgression, her sex.

A similar "novelization" was at work—and I am sure with Hogarth in mind—in Laurence Sterne's sermon "Felix's Behaviour towards Paul Examined," which is remarkably like Hogarth's painting, down to its emphasis on the sexual nature of Felix's crime. The date of Sterne's sermon is uncertain, but it was first published in 1766 and may have been inspired by Hogarth's painting, which was in place by 1751, or by the print, published in 1752.[26] But a plain example is the sermon Sterne preached for the opening of Lord Hertford's embassy in Paris in his newly furnished residence (the Hôtel de Brancas). He chose the story of Hezekiah's pride in showing his palace to the messengers from Babylon (2 Kings 20:13–17, AV):

> And Hezekiah hearkened unto them, and shewed them all the house of his precious things, the silver, and the gold, and the spices, and the precious ointment, and all the house of his armour, and all that was found in his treasures: there was nothing in his house, nor in all his dominion, that Hezekiah shewed them not.
>
> Then came Isaiah the prophet unto king Hezekiah, and said unto him, . . .
>
> . . . What have they seen in thine house? And Hezekiah answered, All the things that are in mine house have they seen: there is nothing among my treasures that I have not shewed them.
>
> And Isaiah said unto Hezekiah, Hear the word of the Lord.
>
> Behold, the days come, that all that is in thine house, and that which thy fathers have laid up in store unto this day, shall be carried into Babylon: nothing shall be left, saith the Lord.

Aside from the ironies involved in choosing this particular text, Sterne's version (according to his account to William Combe) included insertions:

And Hezekiah said unto the Prophet, I have shewn them my vessels of gold, and my vessels of silver, and my wives and my concubines, and my boxes of ointment, and whatever I have in my house, have I shewn unto them: and the Prophet said unto Hezekiah, thou has done very foolishly.[27]

In the printed sermon he used the genuine text, focusing on 20:15. But David Hume, among those present at the performance, saw what he was up to and at the dinner following teased him about the miracle of the sun's shadow in the story of Hezekiah.[28]

Arthur Cash, Sterne's biographer, regards these sermons as a reflection of the unconsidered pranks ("the brisk gale of his spirits") of Sterne's Parson Yorick, one "utterly unpractised in the world."[29] In fact, they bear interesting parallels to Hogarth's treatment of holy texts, drawing on both Woolston's critical deism and Addison's Novel, which may more precisely define Yorick's "spirits."

This sense of "novel" does not exclude the sense Ian Watt has eloquently written of as the elevation of the momentary.[30] But Watt's sense of "new" cuts a much broader swath than the Hogarthian Novel/ Beautiful, including most dramatically the prose narratives of Defoe and Richardson, which were consciously written within orthodox theological traditions. The Hogarthian mode is a secular, philosophical, and heterodox one, relying more on Toland's sense of novelty as discovery, though utilizing the more general sense of the momentary as well.

An example can be found in the journalistic accounts that followed upon the great storm of November 1703, including Defoe's *The Storm*. They all characteristically transmit (in their own words) "a distinct and true Account of that unheard of fatal Accident," an "Exact Relation," a "Faithful Account"; but one which "will stand as a Monument of the Anger of Heaven, justly pour'd down upon this Kingdom to all posterity."[31] The traditional meaning assigned to the particular novel facts of the storm corresponds to the same relationship in the novels of Defoe and Richardson. This orthodox interpretation is just what Hogarth, Fielding, and Sterne avoid in their works: when they indicate such a topos or commonplace they put it in question. Fielding's revision of Richardson's *Pamela* in *Shamela* and *Joseph Andrews* is, like Sterne's surprising revision of 2 Kings, a "novelizing" procedure in the Addisonian and Hogarthian sense. Thus we could say that Fielding "Novelized" the "novel." In the *Analysis* itself Hogarth begins by reversing Francis Hutcheson's thesis in his Shaftesburian treatise *An Inquiry into the Original of Our Ideas of Beauty and Virtue* (1725). Hutcheson's definition of beauty was the spectator's pleasure of recognizing the "Uniformity amidst Variety," as in a duodecagon or a mathematical theorem. But Hogarth changes recognizing to discovering—that is, he emphasizes the active process as part of the aesthetic experience—and reverses variety-in-unity to unity-in-variety: thus making aesthetic pleasure the discovery of variety in uniformity ("infinite Variety," the more variety, the more Beauty [35]); and producing a form of the New and Uncommon based on surprise. The central principle is variety ("All the senses delight in, and equally are averse to sameness" [35]); which contains not only Addison's Novel but the general aim of news in the journals as well as "novelty" in the deist sense.[32]

The Strange: Credulity and Curiosity

As Addison gravitates in the later essays of the "Pleasures of the Imagination" toward the secondary Pleasures, he moves also toward what he refers to as the Strange. The Strange began as another synonym for the Novel/New/Uncommon in No. 412 (3:544) and returned in No. 417, where Addison divides *Paradise Lost* into its beautiful, novel, and great components. The Novel-Strange is associated with "the Creation of the World, the several Metamorphoses of the fallen Angels, and the surprising Adventures their Leader meets with in Search after Paradise" (3:565). (Ovid is the classical example cited.)

Following the categorizing of Beautiful, Great, and Novel-Strange in No. 417, Addison then proceeds from the description in No. 418 of a dunghill or "what is Little, Common or Deformed," which is improved by representation, to the "kind of Writing, wherein the Poet quite loses sight of Nature" in No. 419. The subject now is fairies, witches, demons, and ghosts, which produce a "pleasing kind of Horrour" and "those secret Terrours and Apprehensions to which the Mind of Man is naturally subject"; but the effect is related not, as one might expect, to the Great but to the Novel. The reason is that these are representations, examples of the secondary imagination, and the effect is to "amuse [one's] Imagination with the *Strangeness and Novelty* of the Persons who are represented in them" (emphasis added). What Addison describes causes us to "be delighted and surprised when we are led, as it were, into a new Creation"—a reference back to "the Creation of the World" in *Paradise Lost* and a phrase Fielding will apply in its Shaftesburian sense of secondary creation to *Tom Jones.*

The Novel as Strange only accommodates a theme that had been operative as early as Nos. 7 and 13, if not No. 3, which introduced the first of Addison's many dream vision allegories in the *Spectator* (others had appeared earlier in the *Tatler*). Old English ballads such as "Chevy Chase" and "The Children in the Wood" are analyzed in No. 77 and a number of subsequent papers. Addison defines the Strange as an area further removed than the Novel from the Beautiful and Great. In particular he directs our attention from Novel/New as modern, local, and indigenous, to remote times and regions, and from adult literature to superstitions and fantasies. And the distance seems to be in terms of transgression, raising the stakes of the more normative positions first taken by the Novel.

Most important, Addison locates superstition not in "the Ancients" (classical writers) but in "the Darkness and Superstition of later Ages, when pious Frauds were made use of to amuse Mankind, and frighten them into a Sense of their Duty," and in "apprehensions of Witchcraft, Prodigies, Charms and Enchantments"—for which read, miracles or divine interpositions: "many are prepossest with such false Opinions, as dispose them to believe these particular Delusions; at least, we have all heard so many pleasing Relations in favour of them, that we do not care for seeing through the Falshood, and willingly give our selves up to so agreeable an Imposture" (3:571–72, emphasis added). This is a mild, Addisonian version of Woolston's critical deism, safely addressed to papist and rural superstitions. But we no longer look upon these fictions with "reverence and horrour" but now in the 1700s our response is "enlightened by Learning and Philosophy." And that juxtaposition or perspective—that secondariness—describes the aesthetics of the Strange.

The "enlightenment" Addison includes in the enjoyment of superstition is a form of disinterestedness, and so a sort of curiosity
distinct from credulity. Superstition becomes an aesthetic object when
belief is replaced by curiosity. Thus credulity is an exaggerated, self-
consciously delusive form of belief—one that asks to be related to the
pragmatism of the deists for whom the question of religion rests not so
much on whether or not it is true as on (its social function) whether it
can give virtuous people the sense of happiness they experience when
they consider how God will reward them for their virtue.

But if curiosity is the principle of the Novel/Uncommon, it is
significant that Addison extends it to the Strange with its acceptance,
though bracketed by inverted commas, of credulity. Swift's "Digression
on Madness" in his *Tale of a Tub* had notoriously played with the
extremes of curiosity and credulity, discrediting both. Addison then,
perhaps reacting against Swift, makes curiosity *and* credulity the dual
basis for his aesthetics of the Novel. He regards the Strange as another,
an extreme object of curiosity, surprise, and discovery, parallel with the
Novel/Uncommon and with "news" such as the arrival of Iroquois
sachems in London. This places the spectator's response somewhere
between credulity and curiosity, between delusion and the exposure of
delusion.

"Imagination" is the term Addison uses to bridge the gap (un-
bridgeable to Swift at least) between the curiosity of the Novel and the
credulity of the Strange. Imagination mediates between (to use Baumgarten's terms) the higher and lower faculties, thought and sensual
perception. But, as his acknowledged derivation of it from Locke's primary and secondary qualities suggests, Addison's imagination (which
he equates with the fancy) falls, with colors and other secondary qualities, on the side of credulity, the aesthetician's substitute for belief.[33]

In the *Spectator* the fictional locus of the Strange is Mr. Spectator's trip to the country to visit Sir Roger—and here the Addisonian
woman finally makes her appearance as the Widow who spurns Sir
Roger's advances and is associated with witches, gypsies, and pain of
various sorts. Then in *Spectator* No. 523 Addison houses the aesthetics
of the Strange in the genre of the pastoral. Denigrating the Pope-Virgil
pastorals with "Classical Legends" added only to give them "a more
poetical Turn," he praises the pastorals of Ambrose Philips:

One would have thought it impossible for this Kind of Poetry to have subsisted without Fawns and Satyrs, Wood-Nymphs and Water-Nymphs, with all the Tribe of Rural Deities. But we see he [Philips] has given a new Life, and a more natural Beauty to this way of Writing, by Substituting in the Place of these antiquated Fables, the superstitious Mythology which prevails among the Shepherds of our own Country. (4:362–63)

Thus to the classical (decorative) mythology of "Fawns and Satyrs" Addison opposes the "superstitious Mythology" of rural areas of "our own Country," and he says that this material provides "a new Life," which he associates with "a more natural Beauty." The pastoral serves as his vehicle for modernizing and translating classical elements into a native English form, based on his principles of beauty and nature. What is called for are the reliques (or ruins) of papist myth, which, among other things, recoup the Christian religion by aestheticizing it as pre-Reformation or Old English faerie.

The transformation of Novel into Strange is carried further by Addison's disciple Thomas Tickell in the direction of the representation of a naïve credulity. As we follow the Strange from the *Spectator* into Tickell's *Guardian* essays on pastoral of a year later (April 1713), we see why the pastoral swain is given "something of Religion, and even Superstition" as a "part of his Character":

For we find that those who have lived easie Lives in the Country, and contemplate the Works of Nature, live in *the greatest Awe of their Author.* Nor doth this *Humour* prevail less *now* than *of old:* Our Peasants as sincerely believe the *Tales of Goblins and Fairies,* as the Heathens those of Fauns, Nymphs and Satyrs. (emphasis added)[34]

Tickell adds to "the greatest Awe of their Author" (i.e., God) the qualification that the shepherd's belief is a "Humour," and this includes the element of happy "delusion" (No. 22, 106–7).

The issue at stake is whether "truth" or something else is the end of pastoral. That end is in fact happiness: The poet will "amuse himself by writing Pastorals" and the reader "gives himself up to the pleasing Delusion" of the poet's half-truths and concealments; and this "is because all mankind loves Ease." What follows is a nucleus of Hogarth's vocabulary based on "pursuit" and "pleasure": "We seek Happiness, in which Ease is the principal Ingredient, and the End proposed in our most restless Pursuits is Tranquility. We are therefore soothed and delighted with the Representation of it, and fancy we partake of the Pleasure." In these terms—which recall the function of the *Spectator's* theatrical metaphor to "incline us to be satisfied with the Post in which Providence has placed us" (2:353)—the poet

> must give us *what is agreeable* in that Scene; and *hide what is wretched.* It is indeed commonly affirmed, that Truth well painted will certainly please the Imagination; but it is sometimes *convenient* not to discover the *whole Truth;* but *that part only which is delightful.* We must sometimes show only half an Image to the Fancy: which if we display in a lively manner, the Mind is *so dexterously deluded,* that it doth not readily perceive that the other half is *concealed.* (106, emphasis added)

Thus in pastorals the poet will portray the "Tranquility" and "Simplicity" of the life but "hide the Meanness of it" and "cover its Misery." The poet can include "such trifling Evils" as "the Loss of a favourite Lamb, or a faithless Mistress" or the "stealing of a Kid or a Sheep-hook."

In one sense Hogarth followed the Addison-Tickell-Philips line as he found himself in his last years returning to the "superstitious Mythology" of rural areas in *Credulity, Superstition, and Fanaticism* (1762; fig. 37) and other prints ridiculing superstition, and he increasingly calls for an art deriving from "our own Country." The latter program ended in the Signpainters' Exhibition of 1762, which included actual signboards from taverns and shops; the exhibition was mounted by Hogarth and his friend Bonnell Thornton both to satirize the pretensions of the Society of Artists' Exhibition and to offer an alternative based not on Continental models but on native English ones. But of course this is only a hypothetical, a satiric, alternative, not one that is in any way demonstrated by Hogarth's own practice. The signboards were enlivened by satiric touches. In a typical pair, of a Queen's Head and a Saracen's Head, the "artist" modifies the eyes so that they appear to be leering lasciviously at each other.[35]

While Hogarth was as critical of the Popean (Virgilian) pastoral as was Addison,[36] his practice was closer to Gay's in his supposedly Popean defense, the double-edged *Shepherd's Week* (1714), than to Philips's pastorals. In his "Fifth Pastoral" Philips writes of his shepherd,

He builds her Tomb beneath a laurel Shade:
Then adds a Verse, and sets with Flow'rs the Ground,
And makes a Fence of winding Osiers round:
A Verse and Tomb is all I now can give,
And here thy Name at least, he said, shall live.

(ll. 112–16)[37]

In his parody of Philips, "Friday; or, the Dirge," Gay writes:

With wicker Rods we fenc'd her Tomb around,
To ward from Man and Beast the hallow'd Ground,
Lest her new Grave the Parson's Cattle raze,
For both his Horse and Cow the church-yard graze.

(ll. 145–48)[38]

While Philips's "Fence of Winding Osiers" is merely decorative, Gay's fence of "wicker Rods" protects the grave from the depredations of the "Parson's Cattle." The indigenous "realism" of *The Shepherd's Week* is not an end in itself but operates in the service of satire, whether aimed at the poetaster Philips or at exploitative clergymen. Realism consists of watering thirsty herds as opposed to making love songs (Popean, we must add); the swelling of cows' udders and the awakening of cowherds by sunrise as opposed to a "sleepless lover" or a "swain dying for love." The effect is a lower, more demotic version of Pope's own "Sleepless Lovers just at twelve awake" in *The Rape of the Lock,* where "sleepless" designates the pastoral convention.

But in terms of the *Guardian* essays on pastoral, and the *Spectator* on the Strange, Gay is exposing the happy "delusion" of Philips's swain. More precisely, a year later in his rehearsal play *The What D'Ye Call It,* he reveals beneath the "delusion" (presented as playacting) that tries to pass off the "trifling Evils" of the "stealing of a Kid or a Sheep-hook," or loving a maid who loves another swain, the real "miseries" of injustice: farm boys illegally impressed and, thereafter, hanged for desertion; young women seduced, made pregnant, and abandoned by the squire's son, and, thereafter in prison, whipped until they miscarry.[39] These are the "miseries" Addison felt should be "concealed." The pastoral (or, in *The What D'Ye Call It,* the tragic) form only emphasizes the "pleasing Delusion" the reader of the Addisonian form "gives himself up to" ("because all Mankind loves Ease").

The effect is also analogous, Hogarth would have seen, to the deist historicizing of New Testament miracles. While he learned from Gay, most particularly from his dramatic works, and shows most emphatically the "miseries" under "pleasing Delusion," he picks up the association of "religion" and "theology," which Addison aestheticized into superstition ("Fairies, Goblins and Witches"). To these he applies the deist approach that substitutes New Testament subjects for classical. (Fielding, in his imitations of Gay, will return to the classical context.) In the same way that Gay's mode is based on mock forms, Hogarth's Novel, stopping short of the Strange, requires the vestiges of both classical and Christian "superstitions," not as picturesque ruins but as sets of contemporary manners that deform their possessors (as do the artworks on the walls of his progresses).

Thus Hogarth stays within the Novel, which involves the "discovery [of] the whole Truth"; whereas Addison goes on in the Strange to acknowledge the virtue (itself Shaftesburian, and utilized at times of pragmatic need by Fielding) of the partial truth, "that part only which is delightful," or rather useful, which becomes a part of the novel mode when it modulates into the Strange. Hogarth reacts against this aspect of Addison's doctrine; needless to say, the Addisonian aesthetic and world view fail to contain him.

How different writers can use the Strange, with its dark (Roman Catholic) past, is shown in the emergent novels of Fielding, Sterne, and Goldsmith. The rustic "humour" of religion, which includes superstition, and makes great "use of Proverbial Sayings," is what Goldsmith will employ positively in the *Vicar of Wakefield.* He associates the Strange and its accompanying elements with pastoral, and the effect is precisely the disinterestedness of aesthetics. This sort of writing also, as Addison noted, "[brings] up into our Memory the Stories we have heard in our Child-hood" (3:571) and will produce, as well as the novels mentioned, children's books such as *The History of Little Goody Two-Shoes.*

Finally, Hogarth's utilization of both text and illustrations (of both discursive prose and vivid images) in his *Analysis* draws attention to a feature that distinguishes Addison's aesthetics from others such as Shaftesbury's or Burke's, or later, Kant's. They occasionally exemplify their theory (by illustrating it with examples, sometimes richer and more revealing than the discursive part), but Addison extends theory into practice—into the fictions and assumptions of the *Spectator* itself—specifically the fiction of a group of London gentlemen, one of whom (Mr. Spectator) travels to the country to visit another of them, Sir Roger, the servant who saved Sir Roger's life, the recalcitrant Widow, her confidante, the gypsies, suspicious country folk, possible witches, and a fortune teller. (This is not to deny that practice may have engendered theory as well as the opposite: in the *Spectator* the fictions tend to come first.) Addison alone, before Hogarth and Fielding, blurs in interesting ways the line between the theory and practice of aesthetics (which means, of course, also between aesthetics and morality). Most spectacularly, Fielding, in *Tom Jones,* theorizes and at the same time embodies his theory in a fiction.

Addison does this, however, with only one of his aesthetic categories, the Novel/Strange. He strolls around London as a curious spectator, surprised by the variety of what he sees. He even travels to the country, replacing the Novel with the Strange. Then, in Nos. 412 and following, he places this spectatorial experience in aesthetic categories—that is, privileged categories that are outside the discourse of religion and morality. We might say that he does the same with the traditional explanation of comedy as moral satire by discrediting ridicule; or (closer to aesthetics) by carving out a new area, the purely comic (laughing *with* rather than *at* somebody), based on sheer incongruity, isolating ridicule as a Tory eccentricity; and thus rendering ridicule also aesthetic, and incidentally another aspect of the Novel.

He does not stroll out, and find and respond to mountains and oceans or to gently rolling hills or beautiful women. And of course, in any case, with his description he turns the primary into the secondary imagination. The *Spectator* itself embodies the secondary imagination. When Addison renders greatness—in his allegories or his dream visions—he is producing a response not to nature but only to a fiction that reflects the Great. This fiction is at a second remove, a tertiary imagination. And it relates less to the Great than to the "faerie way" of the Strange—and so remains another aspect of the Novel.

Addison is subordinating the Beautiful to the Novel, with that aspect of the Novel he calls the Strange a way to accommodate the

Great: As he says in the "Pleasures," it "improves what is great or beautiful, and makes it afford the Mind a double Entertainment" (3:541–42). In this sense he creates and theorizes a various and heteroglossic form that will produce in practice one of the original literary forms of eighteenth-century England (both visually and verbally, in both Hogarth and Fielding)—a form that can similarly accommodate, though subordinate, the Beautiful and the Great.

Addison in fact produces a monolithic aesthetics in the *Spectator;* but paradoxically (or not paradoxically) he uses the aestheticizing of moral categories as he does the aestheticizing (or rendering disinterested) of satire in order to re-moralize with a more convincing and powerful rhetoric. His final end is persuasion, political and ideological. While he carves out a space from Shaftesbury's Beautiful to accommodate—and justify, advertise, and theorize—this spectatorial and Whiggish area, he folds it back into moral suasion. The strategy is to make rhetoric or satire appear to be disinterested, that is, aesthetics or pure comedy—while in fact producing a more convincing, deceptive, and affective (as well as effective) mode of persuasion. Hogarth, we have seen, does much the same, starting with the morality and then placing his moral discourse within the aesthetic in order to reach a higher effectiveness of rhetoric.

Addisonian disinterestedness is based not on property ownership but (a truer disinterestedness) on *not* owning land, and thus being free from the various interests of tenancy, cultivation, inheritance, and all the accompanying worries. Mr. Spectator himself, never participating, only reporting, is the prototype of a new kind of disinterestedness (Sir Andrew Freeport is its mercantile spokesman). But also, in the same sense in which Addison's aesthetics turns back into rhetoric, he suggests a new, more effective form of participation (or persuasion) based on journalism—the Novel or novelty or news—and on the spectator's writing and printing his observations rather than participating. Thus the spectator (as Addison notes in No. 5) is silent, takes in experience with his eyes and ears, and writes it all down and prints it, and on sheets that anticipate in one sense the graphic sheets of Hogarth and in another the prose pages of Fielding. (The Novel is, in its point of origin in the *Spectator* as well as in its later manifestations, essentially prose; poetry tends to be used as the medium of the Sublime.)

This literary or political disinterestedness, in short, like its economic equivalent, is based not on land but on paper. As is well known, the year 1695 saw not only the lapse of the Licensing Act and so of censorship, with the consequent deluge of paper condemned by writers like Swift and Pope; but also the founding of the Bank of England and the rise of paper credit. Addison's deistic version of Anglicanism reminds us that "faith" in paper, as in its economic transactions, is also part of Mr. Spectator's Novel: responsive experience must be written down and printed. These issues arose in the *Tatler,* and its point of origin in Swift's Bickerstaff papers. Swift had responded to Partridge's almanacs (*true,* as physical, print, and sincere; *false* as prediction), which were really written by Partridge, with Isaac Bickerstaff's almanac, which was in fact written by Swift (a fabrication, but *true* in the sense of ideal). "Bickerstaff" had predicted Partridge's death, and this was confirmed by a fabricated commentator, also impersonated by Swift, on a false death that was, however, in terms of an ideal world, *true.* The *Tatler* then, written by "Bickerstaff," printed "bills of mortality" of men who, though in fact alive, were ideally and morally dead. The question—which was in fact a secular version of the central question of religious faith—is in whom to put your "faith," whether Partridge or Bickerstaff, or (in another case, *The Narrative of Dr. Robert Norris* of 1713) John Dennis or Dr. Norris (actually Pope). The answer is based on the reality of paper and print, the new authority that was substantiated in the crucial economic dimension by the authority of paper money—that is, by the mercantile "faith" in "credit." The difference between Novel and news is essentially the difference between Bickerstaff and Partridge: One, writing fiction disguised as fact, exposes the hidden truth of the other, which though "true" (it is indeed written by Partridge and is an almanac) is shown to be, in a profounder sense, fiction disguised as fact.[40] And thus Mr. Spectator's "credit" and Sir Andrew's, one literary and one economic, are parallel, as Addison makes abundantly clear.

FOUR

The Conversation Piece

Politeness and Subversion

Novel and News in Hogarth's Conversations

The painterly form used by Hogarth initially (following his work as a satiric engraver) to articulate his antiacademic discourse and to bridge the news and the Novel was the conversation piece—a small group portrait containing recognizable likenesses of contemporaries shown in their own parlor or saloon, defined by their interrelations and surroundings.

Civic humanist theory called for history painting, the artist's highest aspiration; and English history painting in the eighteenth century, such as it was, was predicated on the discourse of civic humanism. But the diminished bourgeois world of the 1720s produced the conversation piece. According to David Solkin's narrative in his *Painting for Money,* the conversation piece emerged as an accommodation to the new, more realistic discourse of "politeness."[1] This discourse called for (determined) a kind of painting defined by refinement and politeness.[2] Thus it is possible to distinguish the commercial discourse of politeness of Addison and Steele from the anachronistic heroics of the Shaftesburian civic humanist discourse; to distinguish history painting, a desideratum of civic humanist discourse, from the modest conversation piece, a more plausible product of the discourse of politeness. From Hogarth onward, then, the painters are civic humanists who in various ways are obliged by social imperatives and their own abilities to modulate this demanding discourse into a more malleable one of politeness, sociability, and sentiment.[3] But given his own monistic "discourse," Solkin, as a follower of Barrell, has to emphasize the social discourse at the expense of the painterly, and its hegemony at the expense of reactions to it. Indeed, he must deny that there are other discourses than the one that modulates from civic into civil humanist.

My story is a different one: Given a particular twist by Hogarth and ostentatiously joined by a band sinister to history painting, the conversation piece led directly to *A Harlot's Progress*, the "modern moral subject" or (in Fielding's terms) "comic history-painting." As a reaction to civic humanism, academic doctrine, and a bankrupt history painting, it engendered the determining painterly forms of a new tradition. From the conversation piece, plus the theory that Hogarth put forth in the *Analysis*, followed the personal variations of Zoffany, Wright, Stubbs, Rowlandson, and Gainsborough.[4] Coexisting with this tradition were the paintings of Joseph Highmore, Francis Hayman, and the other painters whose work used to be called (in stylistic terminology) rococo—called by Solkin with more accuracy polite, a term, however, with which he would like to tar Hogarth as well as Hayman.

It is plausible that, at the outset, to meet the pressures of the market and particularly the criticism of luxury central to civic humanist discourse, Hogarth developed in the conversation piece—which was already extant in the work of Philippe Mercier and others—a successful way of presenting people in the context of their luxuries without noticeably compromising their virtue. But Solkin's kind of history requires a theoretical source for Hogarth's polite practice, and this he locates in Hutcheson's revisionist Shaftesburian defense of private luxury in his *Inquiry into the Original of Our Ideas of Beauty and Virtue* (1725).[5] What this means in an early conversation, *The Wollaston Family* (1730; fig. 27), is that Hogarth has specifically devised a kind of picture in which he can present a great many people at a party in an opulent setting, based on the Hutchesonian assumption that riches are fine when they are put to good use, as in the creation of a familial or friendly society.

We can agree with Hogarth's contemporary George Vertue as well as with Solkin that Hogarth in his early conversations found a way to express and elicit "an universal agreeableness"—in " 'evidences' of amiability" and "active fellowship."[6] To this accommodation to the discourse of politeness he owed his remarkable success in the conversation line. We can also agree that Hogarth's *Wollaston Family* shows how Wollaston's wealth "enables his gracious hospitality." We can even accept Solkin's interpretation of the impudent dog in the foreground who mocks his master and musses the carpet as a small "joke," which "may have provided a source of positive reassurance to a culture that had still entirely to resolve its deeply conflicting feelings about the morality (or lack thereof) of luxurious behaviour." Quoting my observation that the dog "is parodying the host, his master," he adds that

> a motif originally devised to conjure up the realm of bestial passions has been transformed into a sign of something central to the civilising process: of the 'natural' impulse to imitation, which has prompted all of the Wollastons to pattern their own behaviour after a common model, as prescribed by the accepted norms of genteel etiquette.[7]

In short, Hogarth has found a way to "refine" the iconography of his earlier engraved satires (1721–28) in a "polite" portrait group. But Solkin stops there, failing to note that two years later in *A Harlot's Progress* (and again in *A Rake's Progress*) "imitation" turns sour and becomes the subject of Hogarth's "modern moral subjects." By this time he tends to paint conversation pieces in which the possessions (the "luxuries" despised by civic humanists) define, possess, and corrupt their owners.

Of course, the *Wollaston Family* is generically a conversation, and the "modern moral subjects" are (among other things) satires. Solkin treats Hogarth's parody "conversation," a scene of drunken stupefaction ironically entitled *A Midnight Modern Conversation* (1733; fig. 28), as another Hutchesonian defense of the good order of the "social realm," by which he means another scene "in which the getting and spending of wealth could be endowed with the character of virtue" (79). We are asked to take this brilliant satire as rather an apology for luxury-in-moderation. It would be easier to read it as a pointed examination of the close relationship between a conversation piece and scenes of drunken boors (a case of Shaftesbury's ugly and deformed). In the context of the *Harlot,* published the year before, it would be easier to read it as a demystification of a Last Supper than as an illustration of Hutcheson's "social realm."[8]

Between Hogarth's first conversations of 1728–30 and his "modern moral subjects" and mature conversations there appeared a more nuanced, a more satiric text on the uses of riches than Hutcheson's. This was Pope's *Epistle to Burlington* (1731), a work that Hogarth is certain to have read. Solkin does not mention this text, which might be used to distinguish phases of Hogarth's conversation-painting, presumably because it is a "literary" text, not a discursive text by a Shaftesbury follower. As the conversations progress into the 1730s the "jokes" increase (in the *Cholmondeley, Jones, Strode,* and *Hervey* groups), and Solkin honestly notes this fact but without asking where it leads.[9]

In the conversation pieces it is more plausible to say that the discourse of art came first, and that this was not only a supplement to but a reaction against the discourse of civic humanism. For example, Hogarth closely followed the essays on painting Steele contributed to the *Spectator.* In Nos. 142 and 172 Steele contrasted "Satyrs, Furies, and Monsters" and "charming Portraitures, filled with Images of innate Truth, generous Zeal, courageous Faith, and Tender Humanity" (which would include conversation pieces), as well as Raphael's Cartoons of the Lives of the Apostles (No. 172, 2:179; also No. 226, 2:378–81). Hogarth accepted Steele's advice not only by constructing a particular kind of conversation piece but by imitating, borrowing from, and/or parodying the Raphael Cartoons—indeed, using them as a model for the transition from conversation to "progress" and "modern moral subject." As great works of classical composition they served as models for history painting; as "Scripture Stories" (Steele's words) of Jesus and his plebeian followers they supported the portrayal of contemporary English men and women, especially of the lower orders.

Hogarth's immediate model for his conversation piece was the French *fête champêtre* or *galante* of Watteau. With neither identifiable portraits nor settings, this was not, of course, specifically a conversation piece, although it was adapted to that purpose, with the addition of portraits, by Watteau's followers. This new genre, however, was known to Hogarth directly (Watteau had been in England and his paintings were to be seen there), and its program was clear: It was a reaction against pompous official art—a reaction that was both artistic and economic. (Shaftesbury had instructed John Closterman to paint his "conversation" of himself and his brother on the scale of a heroic Van Dyck portrait. Watteau, in *Gersaint's Shopsign*, showed a grand portrait of Louis XIV being packed away.) Watteau's paintings, ostentatiously modest in scale, introduced sculpted Venuses and obscene dogs as a way of playing off high art against low, art against nature, and he focused always on love and dalliance, not on domestic (let alone official) groups. Hogarth's "families" retain something of Watteau's sense of dalliance and much of his play of nature against art. Hogarth's furnishings and paintings have a genealogy that would suggest "art" rather than (or as well as) luxury; and the intrusive dog is less a "joke" than an example of nature testing the forms of art and, by implication, the social graces of the family. All of this produced a cross-current to the polite stasis of the conversations by Mercier, Charles Phillips, and Gawen Hamilton.

Solkin argues that the polite tradition laid down a pattern for unified families and the "good society," that the unruly children embody such themes as nurture and/or civilizing—and that Hogarth illustrates these concepts. Of course, in his conversation pieces Hogarth gave the edge to unity, but as he moved from conversations to "modern moral subjects" he increasingly emphasized the variety to be discovered in apparent unity (which eventually became the thesis of the *Analysis*). The children tend to be examples less of the process of civilizing than of presocial forms of nature, in some ways an extension of the dog. After all, when he began to paint conversations, Hogarth was known primarily for his talent at catching likenesses and for the wit and satire of his engravings. While painting portraits called for a reining-in of these talents, it also attracted sitters who appreciated some liveliness in their portrait groups.

This is not to forget the occasional Dutch or Flemish contribution by such a painter as Pieter Angelis. For Hogarth's graphic model Solkin cites the Dutch "genre painters" (that is, painters of bourgeois or low-life scenes), who used sculptures and dogs for moral purposes, primarily admonitory. He draws our attention to Joseph van Aken's English versions of the Dutch conversation genre. But in the context of

English society in the mid-1720s (which included the literary works of Pope, Swift, and Gay), van Aken's classical sculptures would have been read as mock-heroic comments on the scene. A Bacchus standing above a tea service, which Solkin reads as admonitory ("Better drink tea, not strong spirits"), would more likely—depending of course on whose house it hung in, but certainly if seen by Hogarth—have suggested that the tea drinkers were to Bacchus and his grapes as Belinda and her friends in *The Rape of the Lock* were to Achilles and his wrath.

Totally omitted from Solkin's polite formulation is the literary controversy over pastoral, the realist experiments of Ambrose Philips and the mock-pastorals of Gay. The argument concerned the primacy of art or nature, classical or indigenous culture (see chap. 3, above). The unquestionable starting point and inspiration for Hogarth's conversations was Gay's "Newgate Pastoral" *The Beggar's Opera,* the subject of his first mature conversation (painted several times between 1728 and 1729). It was *The Beggar's Opera* that, as if dramatizing the *Spectator's* program, served as Hogarth's model for a conversation in which a dramatic action (a "scene") of some sort is appreciated or responded to by different spectators: a prototypically aesthetic situation (fig. 26). This model carried over not only into other conversation pieces such as *A Scene from "The Indian Emperor"* (1732), which shows the Conduitt family and friends watching their children perform Dryden's play (again, as in the *Beggar's Opera* paintings, a prison scene), but also into the first plate of *A Harlot's Progress,* where the little drama of Mother Needham's seduction of Hackabout is responded to in different ways by Charteris and the clergyman, Trusty Jack Gourlay and the clergyman's horse. Actors are played off against an audience. It was also *The Beggar's Opera,* as a conversation piece, that served as the compositional model not only for *Harlot* 1 but for *Satan, Sin, and Death, A Scene from "The Tempest,"* and other experiments in sublime history painting.[10]

A Revised History of the English School

These generic considerations complicate a history of the "English School" of painting which depends exclusively upon a social discourse of one sort. And the particular configuration of contexts suggests opposition rather than accommodation. Solkin's narrative is based on the assumption that art tends to enforce rather than subvert order, and he takes the position that even the art of Hogarth serves to contain if not reinforce the norms of politeness; that Hogarth's resistance is only apparent, and was in fact encouraged by the dominant order for its own ends.

There is, of course, always a modicum of truth in this untestable assertion; as there is also in the assumption that any artist at this time, including Hogarth, *could not* think outside the terms of the hegemonic discourse. To the extent that such a phenomenon is incontestable, Hogarth spoke not a counterdiscourse but a modified civic humanist discourse, one that constrained his attempts at innovation and led him to pay silent homage to the principles he vocally opposed.

However, the fact remains that in his prints if not his earliest paintings, Hogarth emerged from a nexus of opposition to the Walpole ministry and even (in works such as Pope's *Epistle to Augustus* and Fielding's *Welsh Opera*) to the monarch himself. It would be imprecise to say that Hogarth—or Swift (author of the hardly polite *Polite Conversation*), Pope, Gay, Fielding, and Smollett—expressed a discourse of politeness except insofar as they handled transgressive materials with an exaggerated politeness that questioned the efficacy of politeness (say, as in Pope's case, Horatian politeness in the face of Walpolian England).[11] These artists merely toyed with the concept of politeness, playing it off as style against content or, for example, Lady Booby's and Slipslop's false refinement against their Mandevillian desires. In the *Harlot* this was Hackabout's ladylike politeness in being served tea after stealing a watch from her customer, and wearing a rich gown while beating hemp in Bridewell.

In the first half of the century the most accomplished artists (by all accounts) were in one degree or another satirists, or at least began as practitioners of satire, the major literary genre. For them it was satire that replaced epic with mock-epic, or history painting with mock-history. Civic humanism seemed to them overcome by corruption, and politeness and refinement were, when employed in satire, either masks or illusions. These were simply not the significant terms for artists who were primarily writing a discourse of justice and mercy, character and conduct, moral right and wrong.

There were plenty of treatises that spoke of politeness, from the most blatant hack writing up to the high level of Addison and Steele. But even the *Spectator* not only formulated politeness but submitted it to critical analysis. Addison laid down the principles and Steele questioned their abuses, most notably in the form of affectation: the non-gentleman rising through "politeness" to be a false gentleman.[12] But it is difficult to think of any major artist of the period who actually undertook as his primary mission the "task of legitimising the elegant pleasures enabled by commercial wealth," "of cleansing luxury of its long-standing associations with human vice and folly," and of removing "polite enjoyment as far as possible from any stink of sensual vulgarity."[13] Samuel Richardson, of course, really strove for refinement, which, as the result proved, led him to write against the grain of his genius. Refinement was a strong, though highly ironized, element in Sterne's novels. Even Reynolds was quite capable of the "impoliteness," the Hogarthian "transgression," of a bawdy *Link Boy* or a *Nelly Obrien* who parodies a Raphael Madonna holding a lapdog instead of the Christ Child.

This is not to suggest that because satire was the major genre of the period it was also canonical. Those artists whose consummate works were satires, but who wrote much else as well, have to be recognized (as satirists) as counterinsurgent to the canonical respectability of the polite and refined genres—as they were, in varying degree, to the prevailing organization of social and political life (Swift an Anglican dean in Ireland, Pope a Roman Catholic in England, Hogarth a silver engraver's apprentice attempting to become a painter, and Fielding an Etonian classical scholar living by hack writing). The genres they developed, from satire itself to the novel, were fighting what counted as taste, literature, and painting in the Age of Walpole. But of course satire was aspiring to the canon by challenging it, for example by critiquing the epic, as opposed to refining it (as Pope also did in his translations of the *Iliad* and *Odyssey*).

By contrast, Hogarth's close friend Francis Hayman, as well as Joseph Highmore and lesser lights, painted politely. Possibly only Hogarth was actively campaigning against what he regarded as the ideals of Renaissance academicism. In the 1730s and 1740s he led the St. Martin's Lane artists in his "Britophil" campaign—which pitted native painters against connoisseurs who imported "old masters." Many apparently sided with him on this issue because their livelihoods were threatened. The argument was that British painters were capable of competing with the old masters but were ignored by Shaftesburian Men of Taste. Though it may not have appeared so to all the artists, this was essentially an anti-Shaftesbury, anti–civic humanist, antipoliteness campaign.

Every time Hogarth projected a new plan for advancing native English painting, his own energy was contained by the works of his colleagues. In the Foundling Hospital paintings, his most ambitious project for the "artists of Great Britain," his own *Moses Brought to Pharaoh's Daughter* cries out among the mute canvases of Hayman, Highmore, and James Wills. And yet, it is important to add, the disturbing expression of this painting, with its isolated and perplexed foundling child, is equally at odds with its lovely, pale Venetian colors and elegant forms. There is a sense in which Hogarth's paintings add something like Addison's cosmetic beauty to the resolute novelty of the *disegno,* the monochrome print, and thus bring the work more closely in line with that of his contemporary artists in the St. Martin's Lane Academy.[14]

In the 1750s the group split apart over "the elevated demands of historical art"—located in the idea of a state academy, the principle of copying, and the authority of Continental models. Hogarth was relatively isolated in the anti-Shaftesbury position he set forth in his *Analysis of Beauty,* which was taken by many of his old colleagues, including Hayman, as an attack on the idea of an academy. When the smoke cleared, his remaining supporters (Fielding, Thomas Morell, Bonnell Thornton, Sterne, and Garrick) were more literary than artistic.

In retrospect, I think we can see that Hogarth's motivation in writing the *Analysis* was antiacademic but also partly self-protective. If he resisted the social pressures of containment, he did at this point "aestheticize" his "modern moral subjects," his new art form. Containment implies and supports the idea of a hegemonic discourse; aestheticizing refers to the artist's own strategies for living with or coming to terms with his work (as in his various intentions in the creating of his particular version of the conversation piece). Hogarth aestheticized in order to elevate and justify the artistic quality of his works; but also in order to give a cover story of Beauty (or play) to what was, he must have realized, deeply transgressive in a religious sense. Pope had utilized Bishop Warburton to "moralize" his *Essay on Man,* which was regarded by some as deistic; Hogarth personally aestheticized his work, though with an aesthetics that was itself plainly deistic. In his last years he began to remoralize his work in the manner of Warburton, and this task was taken up after his death by John Trusler and others (see chap. 10, below).

At the time of the 1761 Exhibition of the Society of Artists Hogarth returned to the fold; his satires on connoisseurs and picture dealers covered the old ground he had shared with the artists in the 1730s, and they were very popular with the public who attended the exhibition—the "vulgar crowds" that were excluded the next year. Partly because of the principle of exclusivity, in 1762 there was a decisive break, and one consequence, the dissident Signpainters' Exhibition, was Hogarth's final statement on the subject, implying that the only hope was a national tradition.

Hayman by the 1750s was both proacademy and proimperialism, representing in huge Vauxhall paintings the triumphs of the Seven Years' War. He was now plainly in the camp opposed by and to Hogarth, and yet he was painting British soldiers in contemporary costumes, anticipating Benjamin West's more celebrated version of a "modern moral subject" in his *Death of General Wolfe* (1770), which was painted in modern dress against the advice of the P.R.A., Joshua Reynolds. But in Hayman's practice "modern" and "polite" are synonymous and containment is the political principle: Solkin points out how Hayman renders imperialism polite by applying to his main figure, the contemporary Lord Clive, Alexander the Great's gesture of clemency in LeBrun's *Alexander before the Tent of Darius.*[15] This appropriate modulation of heroism into "politeness" borrows the gesture Hogarth had already adapted to his conversation hosts—as part of his conscious modification of history into modern moral subject. Hogarth, however, reapplied the host's gesture in *The Wollaston Family* (fig. 27) and other conversation pieces to the bawd Mother Needham in *Harlot* 1 (fig. 3) and to Tom Rakewell in *Rake* 1, and even to Christ in his mural of *The Pool of Bethesda* in St. Bartholomew's Hospital (fig. 18).[16] Hayman has obviously observed all this, though by returning the

conversation piece gesture to the heroic context of which it was originally a parody he creates an emphasis opposite to Hogarth's. Nevertheless he keeps our attention on the continuity of the conversational and
the historical modes, which will finally be broken by West's Roman
crowd scenes (which contain and correct Hogarth's contemporary
crowd scenes, *The March to Finchley* and *Chairing the Member*).

Reynolds was quite right to feel himself isolated in the late 1750s
when he wrote his *Idler* essays attacking Hogarth and advocating the
high Shaftesbury, civic humanist, academic line.[17] In Solkin's narrative, "politeness" (as the diminished version of civic humanism) domi-
nates art in England until the 1770s, when finally the Royal Academy,
though hedged about with bad publicity and the envy of the excluded
artists, brings back a respect for civic humanism. It is at just this
moment that the conflict is clearest between the two traditions now
embodied in the Royal Academy and the Society of Artists (the re-
mainder of the polite painters as well as a few followers of Hogarth). It
is plain that royal patronage had tipped the balance, and that this was
the point of transition from the time (1700–68) when theory stood at
odds with practice—partly because the painters were unamenable,
some actively opposed—to the time when, in Reynolds's lectures and
the academy's school, theory totally dominated and bent to its will the
works of many English painters.

Zoffany and the Second Generation

The conversation piece in the Hogarthian mode continued in the
work of Johan Zoffany. His *Queen Charlotte and Her Two Eldest Sons*
(1764; fig. 29), a portrait group painted for the queen herself, projects a
dramatic (a "novelistic") situation far in excess of the subject (the
"news"). Do we, as Marcia Pointon has speculated of the painting,
expect the absent King George III to enter the queen's boudoir through
the open door?[18] And if so, what does the mirror reflection of the
housemaid's profile through the doorway imply, the reverse of Queen
Charlotte's reflection in her dressing table mirror? If Zoffany's painting
is about the absent monarch rather than the present and centered,
indeed regally posed, queen—and certainly the open door and empty

passage, as well as her regal pose, draw our attention to his absence—then our attention does fall, as Pointon argues, upon the Prince of Wales, the child standing directly before the empty doorway, who is dressed up as, of all people, Telemachus; and therefore upon the question, Where is Ulysses? There is no symbol of the king except his son and heir in the guise of Ulysses' son, who (in Pointon's words) not only "stood in for his missing father" but also went in search of him and (the oddest part) sought "to deliver his mother from the importunities of her suitors." (There are other traces of the missing Ulysses: the man-sized sword and scabard at far left, and the faithful dog who recognized him on his homecoming to Ithaca.)

Zoffany's conversations always ask questions of their viewers which are not called for by the more unambiguously celebratory paintings of Allan Ramsay (by then the chief royal portraitist) or Reynolds. These include What is central and what peripheral, what is figure and what ground, and at what point can the allusion (in this case to the story of Ulysses) be considered closed? This *is* Queen Charlotte's boudoir, and the overdoor painting shows Ulysses emerging from the sea to meet the scantily clad Nausicaa and her maidens. Nausicaa was the lady with whom Ulysses did not philander, as opposed to Circe and Calypso, with whom he did.

How much of the Ulysses story is to be applied? How much did Charlotte apply? How much did Zoffany, who at least expected the question to be asked? How much of the scene was given, and how much was Zoffany's invention? Were there in fact both a Telemachus costume worn by the Prince of Wales and an overdoor of Ulysses and Nausicaa? Pointon documents the existence of the former. Oliver Millar, in his catalogue of the Royal Collection, notes that the overdoor painting "is no longer in the royal collection," which could mean that it was Zoffany's invention. Given the fact of the Telemachus costume, the overdoor painting, which Millar thinks could be either of Ulysses or Aeneas, must be of Ulysses.[19]

The painting was made before it could have been known that George III was the only Hanoverian monarch who did remain faithful to his wife.[20] But it was the time when the Wilkites and Pittites were spreading stories about his unnatural dependence upon Lord Bute and

Bute's alleged, equally unnatural liaison with the king's mother (the real Penelope). In these years the controversy between the factions of artists, struggling over the founding of the Royal Academy, carried the political coloring of Wilkite "Liberty" versus a tyrannous monarch, and Zoffany was a leading figure in the opposing Society of Artists. Only in November 1769 did he resign as director of the Society of Artists, and in December he was nominated a member of the Royal Academy by his patron George III.

Speculation aside, we know two things: After Hogarth's works of the 1730s through the 1750s one could not look at a painting such as Zoffany's, which invites these questions, and not ask them. And Zoffany, as it seems from his being an evident imitator of Hogarth, and from a wide range of his paintings and what we know of his personal life, was quite capable of introducing the sort of "joke" Hogarth employed when he painted for the lawyers and judges of Lincoln's Inn a sublime history, showing the prisoner Paul accusing his judge Felix (and his prosecutor Tertullus). If it did not embarrass his patrons it was because, as Swift remarked, "satire is a sort of glass wherein beholders do generally discover everybody's face but their own."[21]

Although the reference in *Queen Charlotte* is classical, Zoffany did play wittily with Christian references, painting a *Last Supper* in which he portrayed members of his family and other contemporaries and, above all, including in *The Tribuna of the Uffizi* a mass of references to the Virgin Birth (1772–28; Royal Collection).[22] Zoffany's references are more personal than Hogarth's (Judas is given the face of an enemy; the Madonnas refer to his own "virgin bride" and the Child to his child). To judge by *The Tribuna* and by his self-portraits, Zoffany's wit was dark and sexually oriented. It should be obvious how Hogarth's Harlot, his anti-Venus, also carries into *The Tribuna*, which centers the Venus de' Medici as well as Titian's *Venus of Urbino*. Zoffany takes the Venus from plate 1 of Hogarth's *Analysis* and expands the narrative to extreme lengths with a crowd of artifacts interspersed with spectators and collectors, toward the ultimate (or the reductio ad absurdum) in the conversation developed by Watteau and Hogarth. A "joke" involving the figure of the homosexual Thomas Patch, for example, also goes back to plate 1—in this case to the figure of the dancing master admiring (and propositioning) the sculpture of Antinous. Though Patch grasps the frame of Titian's *Venus* with one hand, he points with the other to the equally nude *Wrestlers*, one of whose buttocks Zoffany originally adorned with a "patch." Zoffany's work represents the extreme case of what is strange and typical of one English painter of the next generation continuing to respond to Hogarth's iconographical innovations. *The Tribuna* can be interpreted as a final summation of the whole anti-Shaftesbury tradition. *Queen Charlotte and Her Two Eldest Sons,* centered on the queen herself, is unquestionably moving in the direction of *The Tribuna,* a painting that Charlotte evidently did not appreciate. We do know that we are in the presence of a characteristic Zoffany painting, and that the conversation piece remains his conduit for the counteracademic tradition.

Zoffany's conversation piece with the absent king and present queen and her eldest son dressed as Telemachus (the son of the absent Ulysses–George III) can be said to have continued the demystification of the heroic world of Van Dyck portraits begun in the 1720s and 1730s by Hogarth.

Thus Philip Reinagle's *Mrs. Congreve with Her Children* (1782; fig. 30) implicitly asks, Why are Captain Congreve and his son only present in a painting (also by Reinagle) that hangs on the wall? Simply answered, the subject is the female center of the household, Mrs. Congreve, two girls, a baby boy. The men are marginalized because this is a woman's domain (identified as Mrs. Congreve's drawing room), in which they are not welcome, or welcome only as portraits. They are presumably elsewhere—on maneuvers, as in the portrait, or with other men transacting male business. Such representations of the absent in paintings were a convention,[23] but the "joke" and "play," mild as they are, recall the Hogarth conversation.

When Pointon says she sees in the conversation piece the "construction of genealogical narratives," she means a synchronic relationship that binds the futures of the participants to the father. The patriarchal power she believes is best understood by regarding the conversation as analogous to the father's will ("a visualization of the last will and testament"), the legal document in which the protagonist is absent but imposes his "will" upon the succeeding generation. It is true that in both will and conversation "the past, present and future [are] subsumed into a single act of communication that will hold sway over a particular social grouping forever" (161), but only insofar as both are narratives of power that name some, omit others, and arrange them hierarchically. That in a conversation piece "social distinction and familial coherence could be secured and perpetuated" seems a weaker but more reasonable formulation. Pointon sees a "narrative of succession [of property or title]," whereas there are many kinds of narrative implied by conversation pieces. Of course, the narrative potential in an ostensibly synchronic form was the essence of Hogarth's conversations which projected his "progresses," each scene of which implies a before and after embodied in a pregnant present. In chapter 8 of *Emblem and Expression* I explained the conversation piece as an arrangement of spatial grids that define the relationships between family members, their genealogy, hierarchy, and property. The first plate of *Marriage A-la-mode* (1745) was the ultimate conversation piece in that it combined genealogical and anti- or countergenealogical narratives, crossed by the father Lord Squander's narrative of collecting and possessing, of both dead art and living descendants. In Pointon's terms it would be the ultimate manifestation or materialization of the absent but persistent paternal will. But here the father is present, and it is in fact the mother—that Hogarthian desideratum, the woman—who is noticeably absent.

Absence serves as an aspect of the conversation's narrative potential, though one that needs to be addressed from a perspective other than Pointon's feminist one. In the earlier period at least, the father is usually present in conversations, unless there is some pressing reason for his absence (death, military service, or the like). Pointon in fact draws our attention to a later phase of the genre in which, as in so much else, the woman has become the center of the composition. But now, as in Reinagle's painting, the absence of her mate offers a sentimental reading that focuses on the female figure and leads us to sympathize with her. It might suggest that while Hogarth's female figure is a revision of Shaftesbury's Hercules, initiating a counter-Shaftesbury tradition, she also represents an alignment with Addisonian politeness and evokes a deeper reading of Shaftesbury's own meaning. The latter would involve a sympathy that reveals Hogarth, like others of his generation, shifting his emphasis from satire to sentiment, from male to female virtues and travails, on the way to *The Lady's Last Stake* and *Sigismunda* of 1759.

If we look again at the Reinagle and Zoffany conversations we see paintings about the pathos of a wife and mother separated from husband and father in a scene that can be interpreted as in some degree an image of mourning.[24] The woman who begins as a satiric mediator has been moved into sentimental situations of distress. The male protagonist/reader witnesses the female (mediation, distress, mourning) and sympathizes. These works show Hogarth developing a new persuasive mode, transforming the satiric one of the earlier works. In the context of the charity movement of the 1730s and 1740s, the sentimental reader responds with financial or other practical assistance, associating himself with Christ vis-à-vis the sick in the mural of St. Bartholomew's Hospital or with Pharaoh's daughter vis-à-vis the infant Moses in the Foundling Hospital painting. He (the reader-viewer remains resolutely male) participates in both the suffering of Moses or the sick and the pleasure of the charitable relievers of their pain, while focused on a beautiful woman.

Hogarth and his followers keep the woman in a tension with the ironic echoes of classical texts and civic humanism and their impolite antitheses. Only in *The Lady's Last Stake* and *Sigismunda* does Hogarth align himself with Richardson and anticipate the novelists who focus on scenes that show suffering and elicit sympathy. But both of these women are transgressive, latter-day Venuses. Nevertheless, the concept of the sentimental as a kind of containment may have had some influence on him through *Clarissa* and the Richardson circle. Lady Bradshaigh, for example, was asking Richardson in 1749 for his opinion on "the meaning of the word *sentimental,* so much in vogue among the polite, both in town and country."[25] Of course (as we shall see in chap. 10), the proponents of the sentimental tradition, which privileged the visual spectacle, condemning the inadequacy of words to communicate such emotions, adopted Hogarth and made him their own.

There were also traces of the Hogarthian aesthetics among the "academic" painters. In the 1760s even so unlikely an acolyte as Benjamin West drew attention to Hogarth's position by pursuing the anti-Shaftesburian line of the *Analysis* in his history painting *Venus and*

Cupid.[26] In 1764, the year of Hogarth's death, he painted both this Venus (which strikes Solkin as "startlingly lascivious") and another version of the Choice of Hercules.[27]

West's paintings of the late 1760s leading up to *Agrippina Landing at Brundisium with the Ashes of Germanicus* (1768) are centered on a woman: in Solkin's words, "a beautiful agent who mollifies the hard brutality of a dominant male" or a "type of softening female" (186). But of course these words also apply to Hogarth's paintings of literary subjects from the late 1730s on, for example his *Scene from Shakespeare's "Tempest"* or *Satan, Sin, and Death,* as well as his "modern moral subjects" from *Southwark Fair* to *The Distressed Poet* and *The Enraged Musician.* The "Luxury and Libertinism in Colouring" (George Turnbull's words) of West's paintings, which Walpole called "very tawdry" and "abominably gaudy," could also have been applied to Hogarth's *Satan, Sin, and Death,* a history painting centered on a woman.[28] In his *Philosophical Enquiry* Burke invoked and revised this painting by omitting the woman and recovering a more conventional Shaftesburian view of aesthetics.[29] Solkin mentions such possible explanations as West's desire to attract a female audience, or to practice "the domestication of heroism" (which is, after all, one way to describe the aim of *A Harlot's Progress*), but it is more likely that West was at least in part following an antiacademic example.[30]

Of course West is not Hogarth, and we must distinguish his female-centered history, based on mourning and sentimental empathy, from Hogarth's more satiric and centrifugal one. In the *Analysis* Hogarth advocated the greatest amount of variety within unity. West returns to the Shaftesburian and academic ratio, which emphasizes unity. Everyone and everything in *Agrippina* harmonizes with and focuses on Agrippina and her urn, as in *The Death of General Wolfe* (1770; National Gallery of Canada, Ottawa) all is focused on the pathetic figure of the dying general, who combines elements both of the feminine and of Christ. This painting is important as, among other things, a synthesis: its modern dress draws upon Hogarth's antithetical conversations while invoking civic humanism in its subject; its allusion to a Van Dyck *Lamentation* draws upon but corrects Hogarth's mock-Lamentation in the eighth plate of *A Rake's Progress;* and its centripetal effect, focused on the dying Wolfe, corrects Hogarth's principle of the most variety within unity, illustrated in the *Analysis of Beauty*.

If there is a refraction of Hogarth's centralized woman even in West's history paintings, it should be no surprise to find a direct echo in Joseph Wright of Derby's *Academy by Lamplight* (1768–69; fig. 31), just as the Royal Academy was opening. The drawing class responding to the sculpture of a Venus (in fact, *Nymph on a Shell*) invokes Hogarth's *Boys Peeping at Nature* (fig. 2), which set the course from Isis-Diana-Harlot to the Venus of the *Analysis*. The Shaftesbury sculpture and Hogarth's contrary vision of the eroticized Venus are central to Wright's antiacademicism.

In his *Experiment on a Bird in the Air Pump* (1768; fig. 32) Wright replaces the Holy Spirit as dove with a bird in a scientific device, lit by a candle that replaces the divine light of seventeenth-century candlelit paintings. Characteristically, he supplements this manmade replacement with the light of nature in the moon, glimpsed through the window. A similar example is Wright's replacement of a Nativity scene with a contemporary blacksmith's shop, of the miraculous Christ Child with a glowing ingot, in *The Blacksmith's Forge* (1771; Yale Center for British Art). Long before, in his *Woman Reading a Letter* (Dresden), Vermeer had flooded a pregnant woman and her letter with light from a window, making the scene seem a seventeenth-century equivalent of an Annunciation. In the same way, Wright's paintings modernize without satiric comment, attempting to elevate and mystify the everyday; but Wright's version of history painting derives from Hogarth's conversation pieces and from the "modern moral subject" of the *Harlot*, which succeeded them: that is, from the materialization or secularization or aestheticization of mysteries (or of canonical sculptures or "old master" paintings of them). Wright also supplements the materialization with, in *Academy by Lamplight*, one artist who has fallen in love with the sculpture and, in *Air Pump*, a young couple whose love makes them impervious to the mystery of the life-and-death experience of the bird.

Wright has, of course, modulated from the size, scale, and compositions of the early Hogarth paintings to those of the 1750s *(The Lady's Last Stake, Sigismunda, The Bench)*, where more attention is given to the expressions.[31] This modification was also theorized in the *Analysis* when Hogarth contrasted the sort of picture or scene (his "modern moral subjects") in which "lights and shades . . . are scattered about in little spots, [and] the eye is constantly disturbed, and the mind is uneasy, especially if you are eager to understand every object in the composition," with a scene of "large, strong, and smart opposi-tions," which "always gives great repose to the eye" (123–24). In the following decades Wright simplifies and classicizes his compositions, focusing on the single large figure of the woman whose lover is leaving, has left, or is dead.

The more conservative West, however, after experimenting with *Venus and Cupid,* in 1769 succumbed to peer pressure and settled into painting Regulus, "an exemplary civic protagonist" who "instantiates the virtues of a superior class of men" for the Royal Academy. By 1771 he was referring to his history painting as Herculean, and his *Death of General Wolfe* is, in Solkin's words, "an attempt to mediate between academic doctrine and popular taste" (272). The whole of the Hogarth and the St. Martin's Lane tradition is now covered by the term "popu-lar." And once West has arrived, Wright's *Gladiator* and *Academy by Lamplight* can be dismissed by Solkin as "the most memorable symbols of the consensual visual culture characteristic of the period just prior to the founding of the Academy" (270). These words echo the critics who, by the 1770s, were calling Wright "deficient in taste. He seems to delight in ugliness and confusion."[32] In the 1760s the sort of small, English, unassuming, accurate representations painted by Hayman and Edward Penny, as well as the intellectually demanding sort of Wright conversation-histories, were all crudely lumped under the ru-bric of Hogarth's "exhibition of familiar life," as one critic called it. In Solkin's terms, these were equally the "new forms of historical art—by Hayman, Penny, Wright, and others—which had achieved so much popular success since the beginning of the 1760s" (270). That is the voice of the Shaftesbury tradition commenting on the works of Ho-garth. It would appear that only now do paintings at last try to live up to the civic humanist ideal—West, followed by Mortimer, Barry, Fuseli, Haydon, and so on.

In short, historically there was a time lag between the theories of Shaftesbury and the reflection of them, however compromised, in painting. There was the theory (the text) and then there was the practice of the painters; and the outstanding painters of the 1760s and 1770s (with the possible exception of Richard Wilson) simply do not fit the theory; not even Reynolds, who is one of the theorists. Of course, "outstanding painters" means merely those who stood out from the run-of-the-mill. In one sense, all that distinguishes them is in fact their deviance from the theory. But in any case their paintings—Zoffany's *Tribuna,* Wright's *Experiment on a Bird in the Air Pump,* Gainsborough's witty portraits, and Stubbs's horse-centered conversations (even West's *Death of General Wolfe*)—all take what is most distinctive about them from Hogarth's skeptical Mandevillian ethos rather than from the Shaftesburian academic one. At its best the academic discourse forced them (as it also forced Hogarth) to elevate the commonplace, to enlarge the size of the canvas, and to give an edge to unity over variety.

In 1843 William Hazlitt summed up the opposing tradition of English art when he wrote (saying that he would prefer a Cartoon by Raphael to a Dutch Family by Teniers but that he would equally prefer a Dutch Family picture to a Cartoon when both were by Teniers): "I should prefer truth and nature in the simplest dress to affection [*sic,* for affectation] and inanity in the most pompous disguise."[33] Hazlitt saw that the significant opposition was between the Greek past and the indigenous English, Hogarthian present (with the Christian church out of the picture).

Contra all the theorists of the Shaftesbury tradition, Hazlitt employs Hogarth as his protagonist. The opposition of Greek and modern English, summed up in Hogarth's comment on the difference between the most perfect antique Venus and a living woman, highlights the difference between Shaftesbury's civic humanism and a sharp contemporary eye (in Hazlitt's Wordsworthian terms, keeping one's eye steadily fixed on the object). Hazlitt was perspicacious enough to recognize that if the eighteenth century in England was important it was as a period in which theory fell far behind practice; in which the term "high art" or "canonical art" (with all of its civic humanist associations) was put seriously into question. It was a period noted chiefly for the emergence of new genres in both literature and graphic art based on materials hitherto considered inappropriate for the serious poet or painter.

Hazlitt is the villain of Barrell's narrative. His error, in Barrell's view, was to substitute for the discourse of civic humanism the more "modern" discourse of an avant garde, of an isolated artist; for the discourse of politeness (and Solkin's term "eccentricity") the discourse of genius. The difference between Reynolds and Hazlitt is that Reynolds wrote for a small ruling elite, while Hazlitt supported the ideals of the French Revolution. That Barrell championed the unlikely tradition of Shaftesbury, Reynolds, and Company may have been because, however reactionary, they regarded art as the effect of "the possible operation of historical factors" rather than, as Hazlitt claims in the 1820s, "a transaction between nature and individual genius," which is "a private transaction."[34] Thus Barrell's sympathy for the banal and pompous effusions of Barry and Fuseli, who attribute the decline of art to corruption, degeneration of society, and the privatization of art in a capitalist society. (Fuseli, of course, was an artist of the private inner closet, where heroic action melts into erotic fantasy.)

The countertradition was popularized and narrativized by Allan Cunningham in his *Lives of the Most Eminent British Painters* (1829–33), which was a part of that large body of relatively journalistic (as opposed to "philosophical") material that from the 1730s onward propagated an opposing tradition of narratives. In the narrative created by Reynolds, English art progressed in imitation of Continental art (but in practice essentially collecting) to the peak of Charles I's reign, followed by the iconoclasm of his Puritan opponents, and—except for the momentary flowering of Wren and Thornhill's St. Paul's—recovery did not come until Reynolds joined the English once again to the Continent and founded an academy on the French model. In Cunningham's story it is the Reformation that begins the process of liberating English art from foreign influence and domination (Roman Catholicism; Holbein, Rubens, Van Dyck), making way for a Protestant and therefore English artist, Hogarth. This was Hogarth's own narrative, leading up to his Signpainters' Exhibition, but more than Cunningham he developed and demonstrated, in his engraved works, the principles of Protestant iconoclasm itself. Cunningham picked up the Hogarth narrative, at its most pointed in the academy dispute of the 1750s, when Hogarth opposed the primary principle of Reynolds and his followers who argued for "the continuity of English with continental art." Cunningham's words on Hogarth could have been Hogarth's own:

> That his works are unlike those of other men, is his merit, not his fault. He belonged to no school of art; he was the product of no academy; no man living or dead had any share in forming his mind, or in rendering his hand skilful. He was the spontaneous offspring of the graphic spirit of his country, as native to the heart of England as independence is, and he may be fairly called, in his own way, the first-born of her spirit.[35]

This is, of course, another myth, as prejudiced as the Reynolds–Royal Academy one. But it is salutary to see Hogarth returned to the history of the period from which theorists from Reynolds to Barrell have removed him.

FIVE

The "Great Creation"

Fielding

Ethical Deism: "Divine Example" or Rewards/Punishments

By its hostile critics, "deism" has usually been taken to mean ethical deism, one consequence of the view that God created the world and, having set it going, abandoned it. In Fielding's own words in *The Champion,* without an immanent God "then Mankind might be left to pursue their Desires, their Appetites, their Lusts, in a full Swing and without Control."[1] Owen Apshinken in *The Welsh [Grub-Street] Opera* (1731) is an ethical deist. His argument for seduction is that "Nature never prompts us to a real crime. It is the imposition of a priest, not nature's voice, which bars us from a pleasure allowed to every beast but man."[2] But in Fielding's works the disapproval more often falls on the priest, who masks nature with his doctrine.[3]

The association of Fielding with ethical deism is based on his supposed identification in *Joseph Andrews* with Mr. Wilson and his freethinking club.[4] The "young Men of great Abilities" in the club are Shaftesburian deists who profess a commitment to "the infallible Guide of Human Reason" and "the utmost Purity of Morals," denying "any Inducement to Virtue besides her intrinsic Beauty and Excellence." In practice, however, benevolence does not hold passion in check; innate virtue is overbalanced by an equally innate but more powerful "unruly Passion," and one member of the club runs off with another's wife.

Richardson and his followers, hardly well-wishers, transmitted Fielding to the nineteenth century as a debauched skeptic whose novels were low, immoral, and possibly blasphemous. But since James Work's corrective essay "Henry Fielding, Christian Censor" (1949), and Martin Battestin's book-length *Moral Basis of Fielding's Art* (1959), Fielding has been generally accepted as a latitudinarian Anglican. Although in Fielding's day "latitudinarian" meant to many no more than a safe deist,[5] Battestin has increasingly emphasized his orthodoxy, and in an essay by Aubrey Williams he could be mistaken for an Anglican divine.[6] In his biography of Fielding (1989) Battestin judges deism narrowly and censoriously from the orthodox Anglican perspective. He mentions Benjamin Franklin's ethical deist tract *A Dissertation on Liberty and Necessity, Pleasure and Pain* (1725), "which, to his credit, he later repented of and tried to destroy"; and after referring to Franklin's failure to repay a debt to his (and Fielding's) deist friend James Ralph, Battestin comments grumpily, "Such is the cement binding the friendships of deists." When he quotes (another friend) Thomas Cooke's deist sentiment "We should divest ourselves of all Prejudices . . . we should disjoin the monstrous Associations of Ideas of the tru *[sic]* God from the Idea of such a god as the Schools teach us to worship," Battestin refers with heavy irony to "this noble enterprise" of Cook ("an utter enemy to Christian doctrine").[7]

To see deism as simply a version of "God is dead and so everything is permitted," which Fielding repudiated and Ralph and Cooke played down in their writings, is to miss the real impact of deist thought on Fielding. Although critical deism was intertwined with ethical, it was the former that primarily affected Fielding and became instrumental in the "new Province of Writing" he founded, which he referred to as his own "great Creation."

The crucial friendship may have been not with Cooke or Ralph but with Hogarth, who manifested his deism in his art. Fielding and Hogarth knew each other at least as early as 1731, when Hogarth executed a frontispiece for *The Tragedy of Tragedies*.[8] Their relationship was personally as well as professionally close. Although their association was most public in the interchange of 1742–43, when they defined their senses of "comic history painting [epic in prose]" and "character" in the preface to *Joseph Andrews* and the subscription ticket for *Marriage A-la-mode,* they continued to exchange ideas, virtually leapfrogging from one new concept and one new work to the next. For Hogarth, deism was a contemporary form of Protestant iconoclasm, one that focused not only on the deity but also, primarily, on the clergy that exploited the notions of revealed religion and an immanent deity for its own ends. For Fielding, however, deism was a more complex and ambiguous phenomenon, including both critical and ethical aspects.

Demystification of the sort practiced in *A Harlot's Progress* appears in Fielding's stage farces of the 1730s. The question, however, is where among the overdetermined sources for these plays does Woolston's critique of Christ's miracles fit? Besides the dialogues of Lucian, the primary and most admired of his models, Fielding also drew upon Scriblerian satire, in particular *The Dunciad,* which represented Grub Street authors imitating Virgilian heroes, and even upon the Grub Street puppet shows and pantomimes that amused rather than satirized by "contrasting" (to use Fielding's own term) heroic, mythological, and high-literary actions with banal everyday doings.[9] But Lucian, who held up all religions and philosophies, including that of the early Christians, to a standard of reason and common sense, would have evoked the sort of impious skepticism associated with deism. He was particularly unpopular with the Anglican clergy. The Rev. Edward Young commented that "Some Satirical Wits, and Humorists, like their Father *Lucian,* laugh at every thing indiscriminately."[10]

Fielding's use of Lucian extended from the theatrical adaptations in *Tumble-Down Dick* (1736) and *Eurydice* (1737) to direct imitations such as "A Dialogue between Alexander and Diogenes," "An Interlude between Jupiter, Juno, Apollo, and Mercury," and *A Journey from this World to the Next,* gathered in his *Miscellanies* (1743). His persona of the 1730s derives from the Lucianic protagonist (a Menippus, Cyniscus, Damis, or Diogenes, or Lucian himself) who asked questions that probed appearance, idealization, myth, and custom. This questioner began on earth with pseudo-oracles and prophets, charlatans, and sophistical philosophers, then traveled up to Olympus or down to Hades. He questioned the gods themselves and threw them into confusion, revealing their shoddy pretensions to omniscience. They proved to be only humans who think most persistently about sacrifices, the sign of man's loyalty to them; but they have long since shirked their part of the agreement, and so there is no causal relationship between prayers or deeds and rewards or punishments. Consequently, sacrifices have fallen off and man's duty to the gods is in abeyance.

The resemblance to deist rhetoric, and in particular to Shaftesbury's attack on a religion of rewards and punishments and Woolston's demystification of beliefs, would have been obvious to Fielding. Both Lucian and Woolston brought commonsense (that is, contemporary domestic) reality to bear upon false prophets: for Lucian most notably in the story of Peregrine, for Woolston in the story of Jesus.[11] But the most significant fact is that, unlike his friend the always bolder Hogarth (perhaps due to the ambiguity inherent in the visual medium), Fielding travesties only the safe classical myths of Lucian, and not Old or New Testament stories.[12] Nevertheless, he goes beyond mere travesty (in the manner of Scarron's *Virgile travestie* and its imitators) to analysis. His rehearsal plays, like Woolston's *Discourses,* are really about the bad critics and exegetes, often associated with clergymen; their structure—in both staging and book publication—surrounds a text or action with comically discrepant interpretations.

The plays obsessively exploit the self-reflexive theatrical metaphor, that favorite explanatory model for providential design. Because of its pragmatic and provisional nature this was a metaphor appropriated by the deists. Cooke, for example, opens his argument by introducing the metaphor: "I shall look on the whole World as the Scene of Action on which a continual tragic-comedy is represented."[13] When, as in *The Author's Farce* (1730), Fielding gives his characters a happy ending, and distributes rewards and punishments, it is plainly the work of the playwright, who is demonstrating the discrepancy between his world and the real world. In the last, strongly political plays of 1736–37, a prime minister (Walpole), surrogate for an ineffectual king, writes a political farce, manipulates his actors, and deceives his audience; and Fielding, the author of the play, associates himself with the minister as another surrogate farceur. He explores the discrepancy between what is shown and what is hidden behind the scenes, between actor and role, but also between the playwright's "providence" and the actual performance, marred by "chance" (another crucial Fielding term). The bailiff who intercepts the actor before he can get to the theater, or even the audience that, for extraneous reasons, hisses the play, projects a world without benefit of an immanent providence.

If Toland and Woolston were Hogarth's models, Fielding's model was the more genteel and polite Shaftesbury—not only his subtle pragmatism but his equation of beauty and virtue, the principle of internal balance and harmony, shared by the work of art and the virtuous individual. Especially significant is the fact (one that Battestin keeps to himself) that James Harris, Fielding's closest friend, from his Salisbury days onward, was closely associated with Shaftesbury and not only in all probability acted as a conduit of Shaftesburian thought to Fielding but also was himself in his writings a classical deist in the Shaftesbury mold. His mother, née Lady Elizabeth Ashley, was the younger sister of the third earl, especially close to Shaftesbury's younger brother Maurice, and dedicatee of his translation of Xenophon's *Cyropoedia,* with its strongly deist preface (1728). Harris, though he would have called himself, with Shaftesbury, a "theist," was correctly regarded during his lifetime as a "disciple" and "guardian and interpreter of Shaftesbury's reputation and moral philosophy."[14]

Shaftesbury's shadow falls over Fielding's "attack" on deism in a series of *Champion* essays of 1739–1740. These *Champions* express a more "official" view than the plays, for whose irreverence they may serve as an apology (the plays were attacked in the press as scurrilous, obscene, and impious). Fielding criticizes deism in its three aspects: the deletion of an immanent God (or, as he puts it, the desire to "believe the deity a lazy, unactive being" who will not intervene on our behalf);[15] the subsequent opening up of a libertine ethics; and the denigration of the clergy (the climactic and most extended argument, clearly the most important for Fielding). But while ostensibly condemning deism, Fielding utilizes the deist strategy of shifting attention from the question of revealed religion to the observable facts of human virtue and happiness in a social situation. The validity of religion is based less on whether it is true or false than on whether it fulfills a social function. Though ostensibly statements of orthodoxy, these essays are Lucianic, or rather (in Collins' sense of "ridicule") deist, in their rhetoric.

The argument of the opening essay, against the deist assumption that God does not interfere in human events, is couched in the subjunctive, as if hypothetical: "even *supposing* these Allegations were true, and Religion as false as they would have it imagined"; and "Was there no future state, it would be surely the interest of every virtuous Man to wish there was one." Instead of a theological argument, Fielding offers a pragmatic one:

> What a rapturous Consideration must it be to the Heart of Man to think the Goodness of the Great God of Nature concerned in his Happiness? How must it elevate him in his own opinion? How transported must he be with himself? What extatic Pleasure must he feel in his Mind. . . . If this be a dream, it is such a one as infinitely exceeds all the paultry Enjoyments this Life can afford. It is such a Delusion as he who undeceived you might be well said *Occidere & non servare,* to destroy, not preserve. How cruel woud it be in a Physician to wake his Patient from Dreams of purling Streams, and shady Groves, to a State of Pain and misery? How much more cruel then is this pretended Physician of the Mind [the deist], who destroys in you those delightful Hopes, which, however vain, would afford such a Spring of Pleasure during the whole Course of your Life. (1:208–9)

To begin with, the passage unmistakably recalls Swift, for example his account, in "The Digression on Madness," of "Happiness" "convey'd in the Vehicle of Delusion" ("How shrunk is every Thing, as it appears in the Glass of Nature?"), which is the "sublime and refined Point of Felicity, called, *the Possession of being well deceived;* The Serene Peaceful State of being a Fool among Knaves."[16] However, Fielding modulates Swift's savage irony with Addison's more sedate story, in *Spectator* No. 413, of the romantic knight errant wandering in a world of primary qualities:

> our Souls are at present delightfully lost and bewildered in a pleasing Delusion, and we walk about like the Enchanted Hero of a Romance, who sees beautiful Castles, Woods and Meadows; and at the same time hears the warbling of Birds, and the purling of Streams [all of these, secondary qualities]; but upon the finishing of some secret Spell, the fantastic Scene breaks up, and the disconsolate Knight finds himself on a barren Heath, or in a solitary Desert. (3:546–47)

Addison's "purling of streams" and Fielding's "Dreams of purling Streams, and shady Groves" recall that "purling streams" and "shady groves," as a conventional image for romantic dreams of love, appeared, for example, in Eliza Heywood's dedication to *The Fatal Secret; or, the Lucky Disappointment: A Novel* (1724).

But Addison's knight errant in his "Pleasures of the Imagination" further recalls his discussion of the reasonableness of belief in his justification of the Christian religion in No. 465:

> A Man is quickly convinced of the Truth of Religion, who finds it is not against his Interest that it should be true. The Pleasure he receives at present, and the Happiness which he promises himself from it hereafter, will both dispose him very powerfully to give Credit to it, according to the ordinary Observation that *we are easie to believe what we wish.* (4:143)

In the phrases "against his Interest" and the "Pleasure" and "Happiness" promised from the faith "hereafter," not to mention the final complacent clause, Addison offers essentially the same argument as Fielding.

Fielding's argument recalls his own dialogue between Queens Ignorance and Common Sense in *Pasquin* (1736), in which the former (whose adviser, the chief villain of the piece, is the cleric Firebrand) argues that "thinking makes men wretched; / And happiness is still the lot of fools":

> While the poor goose in happiness and ease,
> Fearless grows fat within his narrow coop,
> And thinks the hand that feeds it is its friend.

This is Fielding in his satiric mode, anticipating the stripping away of sentimental illusion a few years later in his critique of Richardson's *Pamela.*

But Fielding's invocation of "happiness," and in particular the vocabulary of *rapture, ecstasy,* and *transportation,* probably owes more to Shaftesbury than to either Swift or Addison.[17] In his *Inquiry concerning Virtue and Merit* Shaftesbury denied Hobbes's view that virtuous behavior does not produce happiness, arguing that only the virtuous individual can experience true happiness, which consists in the ability to share the joy of benevolent acts. In the sequel he sums up a benevolent god and his providential design: "For 'tis impossible that such a divine order should be contemplated without ecstasy and rapture, since in the common subjects of science and the liberal arts, whatever is according to just harmony and proportion is so transporting to those who have any knowlege or practice in the kind."[18] We have seen that Shaftesbury's basic argument is that belief in a deity is of two kinds. Fielding's views of religion from the 1730s to his death in 1754 essentially follow a course from the beautiful order of the "divine example" (the world is a work of art) to a pragmatic and provisional order based on fear and hope of rewards and punishments, to a grim necessity, beliefs essential to hold together a collapsing society.

Fielding could have been thinking of Shaftesbury when he declared repeatedly in *Tom Jones* that this work of art (like his hero Tom) may appear to some observers flawed but is nevertheless a "great Creation." Shaftesbury writes of the "moral artist who can thus imitate the creator, and is thus knowing in the inward form and structure of his fellow-creature" (1:136). He describes a world that seems to religious bigots as well as to atheists fallen and flawed but that to him seems a perfect harmonious "system" made up of other systems, parts subordinated to a unified whole. Some men "find fault, and imagine a thousand inconsistencies and defects in this wider constitution," but others ("you, my friend, are master of a nobler mind") "are conscious of better order within, and can see workmanship and exactness in yourself and other innumerable parts of the creation" (2:62).

Theocles (whose sermon on order this is in *The Moralists*) wonders that "there should be in Nature the idea of an order and perfection which Nature herself wants!" He admits that "Old Father Chaos (as the poets call him)" is ever threatening to extend "his realms of darkness. He presses hard upon our frontier, and one day, belike, shall by a furious inroad recover his lost right, conquer his rebel state, and reunite us to primitive discord and confusion" (71). This leads to the implication that the philosopher-artist's substitute cosmos is called for precisely because the actual world, in the imaging of priestcraft, is marred with "a thousand inconsistencies and defects." Thus Theocles, in his ascending scale of forms, asserts "That the beautiful, the fair, the comely, were never in the matter, but in the art and design; never in body itself, but in the form or forming power"—that is, of the artist, whether originally God or in historical time man.

There is a delicate irony in Shaftesbury's writing, which says that if religion in its Anglican forms proves conducive to happiness, he is willing to tolerate the orthodoxy necessary to preserve virtue and order, especially among the lower orders, whose members need good examples. This is an aristocratic irony Fielding would have found elucidated in Shaftesbury's writings on enthusiasm and ridicule, better known as deist irony (see chap. 1, above). Fielding's words in the *Champion* come very close to echoing Shaftesbury's " 'Tis real Humanity and Kindness to hide strong Truths from tender eyes," by which he means both the ecclesiastical authorities and the lower orders. In *Tom Jones* he cites Shaftesbury's objection to "telling too much Truth," a reference to "defensive Raillery," which Shaftesbury explained as "when the Spirit of Curiosity wou'd force a Discovery of more Truth than can conveniently be told. For we can never do more Injury to Truth, than by discovering too much of it, on some occasions."[19]

Fielding the artist, in his "comic epic in prose," gives art the primary didactic importance it carried for Shaftesbury. Representing art as a unique power for influencing those who have not yet reached a state of virtuous equilibrium, this more than any other formulation sums up Fielding's sense of his audience, his persuasive function, and his "new Province of Writing." It proclaims that the representation of a perfectly well-ordered world will produce similar order in the minds of men; that, although a fiction, the representation of the world as a beautiful and harmonious construction is on the one hand the greatest work of art and on the other the most powerful agency for improving morals.[20] It is, of course, a formulation intended primarily for an elite, whom Fielding will designate in *Tom Jones* as his "sagacious Readers" (as opposed to those who require the hope and fear of rewards and punishments).

Most important, he follows Shaftesbury in not presuming to assert (with Anglican clergymen) that this providential order corresponds to reality. I am distinguishing between the providential assumptions of the clergy, attributed to Fielding by Battestin and Williams, and the deists' view that providential design, however essential to our happiness and social stability, is a human fiction. This is not so much to claim that Fielding is necessarily himself a deist as to say that he accepts the consequences of deism; he recognizes the providential order as having been rendered by the deists no longer valid except as a fiction—as "dreams of purling Streams, and shady Groves" (in the *Champion*) or "poetic justice" and a happy ending (in *Joseph Andrews* and *Tom Jones*).

Considering the two forms of providential design, as his *Champion* essays make clear, Fielding the man—as opposed to the artist— keeps returning to the specifically Christian doctrine of rewards and punishments in the afterlife. In *The Champion* he brings the belief to bear where he felt it most keenly, in the case of the vengeful creditor who should "remember that as surely as he forgives not his Neighbour his Trespasses, so surely will his Father in Heaven deny to forgive him his."[21] But in particular, in the next few years, he needed to believe in a happy reunion with loved ones. This is strikingly evident in his proposal for dealing with the "Affliction for Loss of Friends" in his *Miscellanies* of 1743: After dismissing the "remedies" of philosophy, and focusing on his own bereavement and his wife Charlotte's existential response ("comforting herself with reflecting, that *her Child could never know what it was to feel such a Loss as she then lamented*"), he concludes, in the same language he used to defend religion against the deists, that

> Religion goes much farther, and gives us a most *delightful* Assurance, that our Friend is not barely no Loser, but a Gainer by his Dissolution. . . . Lastly; It gives a Hope, the sweetest, most endearing, and *ravishing,* which can enter into a Mind capable of, and inflamed with, Friendship. The Hope of again meeting the beloved Person, of renewing and cementing the dear Union in *Bliss* everlasting. This is a *Rapture* which leaves the warmest Imagination at a Distance. (emphasis added)

Among many other examples, we can recall Fielding's joyous meeting with his deceased daughter in *Journey from this World to the Next* and Allworthy's *consolatio* for the death of his wife in *Tom Jones*.[22] Perhaps because of the long series of bereavements he suffered (children, wife, sisters), this "hope" seems to have been Fielding's own entrée to the Christian religion. He uses this "proper matter of faith" in his personal essays but not, until the 1750s, as a guiding principle in his fiction.

Critical Deism: Priestcraft and Textual Authority

The climactic and most extended part of the *Champion* attack on deism, clearly the most important for Fielding, takes up the denigration of the clergy. A greedy, power-hungry clergy that interprets Scriptures in order to control congregations was the basic myth accepted by a fairly wide spectrum, with latitudinarians and atheists at the extremes. Fielding makes a backhanded defense, one that devotes most of its time to outlining the reasons for the contempt in which the clergy's individual members, as distinct from the "order," are held.[23] His censures are of the privileges bestowed on clerics by the civil law, and their honors, revenues, and immunities from the law—in sum (using a favorite term in his writings of the 1730s), their "greatness."[24] A preponderance of space is given to the lurid stories of Guinandus de Briland and other clergymen who murdered and raped and used the law to escape punishment. The third and the fourth essays, which are separated by an essay on vanity, define the "clergyman" simply as a good shepherd who is "entrusted with the Care of our Souls, over which he is to watch as a Shepherd for his Sheep. . . . [and] to live in daily Communication with his Flock, and chiefly with those who want him most, (as the Poor and Distressed) nay, and after his Blessed Master's Example, to eat with *Publicans* and *Sinners.*" When Fielding asks, "Can such a Man as this be the Object of Contempt?" he is anticipating Parson Adams (in particular at the hands of the roasting squire in book 3): "Perhaps indeed Boys and Beaus, and Madmen, and Rakes, and Fools, and Villains, may laugh at this sacred Person; may shake those ridiculous Heads at him." The final essay then concludes with another vivid description of what the good clergyman is *not,* rendered in great and savage detail.[25]

Clergymen are twice distinguished from deists and atheists, and Fielding, the public spokesman and (by this time) respectable barrister, wants to dissociate himself from the name of "deist." But he makes it quite clear that his sense of "the clergy" is not unlike the bugbear of the deists: the authoritarian interpreter of the law, Scripture, and doctrine. It is significant that in his plays and in *Shamela* he names as his examples of the clergy's "rotten members" Parsons Murdertext, Tickletext, and Puzzletext, names that emphasize the authority of the clergy over texts, and so focus attention on the interpretation of Scripture. Whenever the reference is political, the queen or minister is accompanied by a bad clergyman, as Queen Ignorance is by Firebrand in *Pasquin* and Robin the Butler is by Puzzletext the chaplain in *The Welsh [Grub-street] Opera.*

Joseph Andrews (1742), though it originated as literary parody, is also an attempt to resolve the religious tensions raised in the *Champion* essays. The issue of Richardson's *Pamela* (1740), greeted as it was by clerical praise, is closely linked to the clerical authority of texts, and Fielding brings in a bad Parson Tickletext to recommend and a good Parson Oliver to demystify the text. But Pamela's claims to represent "Virtue Rewarded" also focus attention on the problem of ethics. Richardson's "virtue" was founded on principle, which meant Christian orthodoxy; Fielding sets out to advocate an alternative based on something other than revealed religion.

The locus for the distrust of textual authority in *Shamela* and *Joseph Andrews* is, of course, Pamela's own text, the letters by which the servant girl controls her betters and raises her social status.[26] Like the accounts of New Testament miracles, they are in themselves nonsense, but tested against history and human psychology, they reveal Mandevillian desire.

Although Fielding plainly disagrees with Mandeville's view of human nature as unredeemedly selfish, and refers to him as "Mand-evil" (though this is some years later, when Fielding is unmistakably speaking for orthodoxy), these disavowals divert attention from a fundamental indebtedness to Mandeville in the "new" mode of discourse Fielding initiates in *Joseph Andrews* and *Tom Jones*.[27] Though the content differs, the method Mandeville employed in his critique of Shaftesbury is similar to the method used in Fielding's critique of Richardson. Mandeville's subject, in this sense, was the discrepancy between moral language and reality, and his strategy was to investigate words such as "virtue" (or "honor" or "reason") by testing them against empirical evidence, the "daily Experience" of human behavior. He played off the abstractions of Shaftesbury, as Fielding does those of Richardson's *Pamela,* against specific examples, in the process undermining the meaning of stock moral and ecclesiastical terminology. Fielding follows him in suggesting the artificial nature of "virtue," as an imposition of the clergy, and specifically as self-denial and repression of the senses. "Virtue," as Mandeville said (in his own version of Shaftesbury's fictionality of religion), is the work of "Lawgivers and other wise Men, that have laboured for the Establishment of Society"; not "the pure Effect of Religion" but "the Contrivance of Politicians," "the skilful Management of wary Politicians," a "contrivance" necessary for both social order and personal happiness.[28]

In *Joseph Andrews*, for the first time, Fielding travesties the Bible—the Old Testament stories of Joseph and Potiphar's wife and Abraham's sacrifice of Isaac. In 1740, in the third volume of his deist tract *The Moral Philosopher*, Thomas Morgan had treated Joseph and Abraham much as Woolston had Jesus; and similarly, Fielding corrects the implausibilities of the biblical stories, revealing the historical Joseph and Abraham under the biblical paragons.[29] Beginning with his first chapter he is writing about "examples," good and bad, the former based on love, the latter on principle masking antisocial passions. Joseph rejects Lady Booby (Potiphar's wife), ostensibly because he acts according to the examples of the Old Testament, Pamela's letters, and Parson Adams's sermons (Joseph as model of chastity), but in reality because he is in love with a buxom young maid, Fanny Goodwill.

At the same time, however, Fielding privileges a *New* Testament text, the parable of the Good Samaritan, which informs as a positive model the central sections of Joseph's trip back from London to Booby Hall. Thus a coachload of "respectable" folk leave the wounded Joseph to die; one poor postilion gives him his coat; in the Tow-wouses' inn, the single exception is the "love" of Betty the chambermaid.[30] The lawyers, innkeepers, physicians, clergymen, and other respectable people who act from selfish motives are employed as analogues to the pious-speaking Pamela, but we do not forget that in the Good Samaritan parable they were Pharisees and Levites. The parable, employed recently by Hogarth (in his 1737 painting in St. Bartholomew's Hospital),[31] is being read in the Woolstonian way as in fact about the priests and the letter (as opposed to the spirit) of the Law. It amounts to a citation of the morality of Jesus, which the deists praised and contrasted with the "religion" created by the church fathers and subsequent clergymen for their own interest.

Chapters 13 and 17 of book 1 focus on Parson Barnabas, whose name suggests what he *should* be, first to Joseph and then to Parson Adams (a "son of consolation," a companion of St. Paul's in Acts 4:36). In chapter 13, while Barnabas invokes doctrine, Joseph invokes a theology of love focused on his beloved Fanny. Thinking he is dying, Joseph says that his only sin is "the Regret of parting with a young Woman, whom he loved as tenderly as he did his Heartstrings," and Barnabas assures him "that any Repining at the Divine Will, was one of the greatest Sins he could commit; that he ought to forget all carnal Affections, and think of better things."³² Barnabas, who has treated the wounded Joseph with anything but Samaritan charity, tells him he must "divest himself of all human passion, and fix his Heart above," which he can only do "by Grace," that is, "By Prayer and Faith." Pamelian virtue, grace, clergy, and the church are being contrasted to a Christian ethic founded on charity and sexual love (the Pharisees accused Jesus of mingling with publicans and harlots [Luke 21:32]).

In chapter 17 Barnabas is brought together with Parson Adams; the subject is sermons, and Adams's religion is defined in terms of the preaching of George Whitefield: "such Heterodox Stuff," as Barnabas says, "levelled at the clergy. He would reduce us to the example of the Primitive Ages forsooth! and would insinuate to the People, that a Clergyman ought to be always preaching and praying." Barnabas associates the Methodist Whitefield with "the Principles of *Toland, Woolston,* and all the Freethinkers," but Adams says that in fact he agrees with Whitefield insofar as his aim is to strip the church, or the clergy, of its political authority and to return to a primitive Christianity: "I am myself as great an Enemy to the Luxury and Splendour of the Clergy as he [Whitefield] can be. I do not, more than he, by the flourishing Estate of the Church, understand the Palaces, Equipages, Dress, Furniture, rich Dainties, and vast Fortunes of her Ministers" (1.17, p. 82). However, he does object to Whitefield's doctrine of faith over works and the concomitant "Nonsense and Enthusiasm"—that is, the irrational belief in the direct intervention by God in man's affairs, and in the existence of ghosts and other superstitions, which were the object of the deist attack on the church.

Adams's criticism of the principle of faith over works leads him to assert the deist commonplace "that a virtuous and good *Turk,* or Heathen, are more acceptable in the sight of their Creator, than a vicious and wicked Christian, tho' his Faith was as perfectly Orthodox as St. *Paul's* himself."[33] When Barnabas and the bookseller cry him down, he responds by citing the authority of Benjamin Hoadly's *A Plain Account of the Nature and End of the Sacrament of the Lord's-Supper* (1735), "a Book written (if I may venture on the Expression) with the Pen of an Angel"—a work that has survived the enmity and attacks of the clergy (one of which was to be found in Shamela's library). Barnabas responds by calling Adams a Woolstonian deist, a Hobbesian materialist, a Muslim, and the Devil himself.

Just as Adams asks Barnabas whether he has ever actually read Hoadly's book, there is a great uproar: Mrs. Tow-wouse, who has discovered Mr. Tow-wouse in flagrante delicto with Betty, is calling her a bitch. Betty, of course, is the one person in the Tow-wouse household who has shown kindness to the poor, battered Joseph.[34] She objects not to the statement that she was in bed with Mr. Tow-wouse, a matter of empirical fact, but to being called a bitch—which, given her history of charity, and the facts of Mr. Tow-wouse's seduction of her, is a matter of dispute. That Betty's natural act can be mislabeled by the angry Mrs. Tow-wouse suggests that the religion of Adams and Hoadly is similarly misconstrued by the orthodox Barnabas.

In the episode of Mr. Wilson's freethinking club, Fielding shows that the deists, however cogent their critique of Christianity, failed to formulate a convincing positive alternative, a version of "natural religion" grounded in the unaided human reason. But if Shaftesbury is wrong, and "natural religion" does not work, the same applies to the externally imposed order of the clergy, which serves only as a hypocritical cloak for such as Barnabas and the egregious Parson Trulliber, who judges a clergyman's worth solely by the quality of his clothes.

By contrast with both, Parson Adams so little resembles a clergyman that he is seldom recognized until he brings his learning into play. Beneath his tattered and discolored cassock he is a lusty man, the progenitor of six children, and able to outrun a coach. He exemplifies the good nature described in the *Champion* (27 March 1740), which combined "perfect simplicity" with strong fists and a crabstick (his equivalent of Hercules Vinegar's club) used to chastise obvious knavery, especially as it threatens those he loves. The crabstick is the physical manifestation of the religion that is required to substantiate good nature.

Adams's natural good nature, however, is at odds with his sermons, his superstitions, and—as seems clear—his whole religious order. He is inordinately vain of his teaching abilities and his sermons (especially the one on vanity). He preaches the word of the Bible, significantly the Old Testament, while he acts according to the New. The model of Abraham (his namesake, and the sacrifice of his son Isaac) causes Adams to defend the father's sacrifice of his son, but when he hears that his own son has drowned he reacts with frantic love and grief. The sacrifice of Isaac was the paradigmatic example of Old Testament Law, which Hogarth had affixed to the Harlot's wall; it summed up the patriarchal family, filial obedience, and arbitrary justice, as opposed to the individual and somewhat subversive love and mercy preached by Jesus.

However, except for the influence he has had on Joseph and Fanny, Adams's example ("Piety, Meekness, Humility, Charity, Patience, and all the other Christian Virtues") has no effect on the Pamelas and Cibbers, Trullibers and Barnabases, roasting squires, dishonest justices, and greedy landlords he encounters. "Bless us!" he exclaims, "how Good-Nature is used in this World!" If Lucian was the literary model behind the farces, then Cervantes informs *Joseph Andrews* ("Written in Imitation of the Manner of Cervantes"), and that means that we are invited to read Adams as a lone Quixote fighting a losing battle with windmills—with Joseph serving as his down-to-earth Sancho Panza. The parallel is unavoidable: Quixote's knight errantry, imbibed from his reading of chivalric romances, is Adams's Christianity, imbibed from his reading of the Scriptures and (must we add?) equally a noble delusion.

Indeed, if Adams is seldom recognized as a priest, Joseph himself, though no priest at all, comes closest to embodying the beautiful harmony of virtue and passion posited by Shaftesbury and lacking in the freethinking club and even in Adams.[35] This despite the fact that he is anything but "disinterested" in his feelings for Fanny. He begins by mediating his actions through the "religious" authority of Pamela's letters and the sermons of Adams (though obviously Fielding values one more than the other), and he requires Adams to insist that he and

Fanny declare the banns before they consummate their passion. All in all, Joseph illustrates the ability of what Fielding defined in the *Champion* as the good-natured man, assisted by the "divine example" offered by an Adams, to learn to control his passions and at crucial moments to instruct even the good clergyman.

Fielding retains the figure and ethic of the New Testament Jesus, embodying them in a few good characters (the postilion, Joseph, and Adams). As to the "divine example," he reproduces, in the figures of the Pamelas and Cibbers of society (and their imitators), Shaftesbury's picture of priestcraft imposing and obstructing. This is a vision not unlike that expressed in Hogarth's *Harlot* (though Joseph is more innocent and Christlike, less affected, than Hackabout), but Fielding supplements the *Harlot*'s godless, priest-ridden world with Shaftesbury's world of order in which beauty, virtue, and order do overcome these elements of chance. Joseph, no matter how harmonious a balance of affections he builds within himself, requires a Fielding—not a God who rewards with equal providence—to get him through it; thus reminding the reader that, as Joseph Andrews is his own "simile" (3.6, p. 241), so *Joseph Andrews* is itself the "divine example" available to us in this world.

Bishop Hoadly and the Sacrament of the Lord's Supper

Woolston, besides being the referent of deism in Hogarth's *Harlot's Progress,* was, of course, as poor and out-at-heel, as simple and downtrodden, and as misunderstood as Adams. The more successful, latitudinarian Bishop Hoadly was the ecclesiastical authority most often cited by both Hogarth and Fielding, but he too was regarded by many as little better than a deist.[36] Whitefield, distinctive among many other critics only for his Calvinist perspective, saw the doctrine of the latitudinarians as "only Deism refined."[37] Hoadly's position on the Bangorian controversy (a position supported by Toland, who saw a chance to cover himself with the cloak of ecclesiastical respectability) coincided in important respects with the deist position: "that God's favor depended on sincerity rather than creed, that Christ's supernatural laws were not subject to interpretation by any ecclesiastical body and that, consequently, the church had neither doctrinal nor disciplinary authority."[38]

Adams's description of Hoadly's *Plain Account* of the Lord's Supper was in the following terms: "for what could tend more to the noble Purposes of Religion, than frequent cheerful Meetings among the Members of a Society, in which they should in the Presence of one another, and in the Service of the supreme Being, make Promises of being good, friendly and benevolent to each other?" (1.17, p. 83). What we find when we turn to the *Plain Account* is a redefinition of the Eucharist as just such a society as Adams describes. Like Hoadly's treatise, Adams's description is in effect a homely, demystified version, not unlike Woolston's, of the miracles of Christ, except without the satire. Hoadly, in turn, makes a case for religion which is remarkably like Fielding's in his *Champion* essays on deism. He wants to protect his parishioners from

> all those uneasy impressions of *Superstition*, which They had a right to be freed from, [and thus] I made it my care to state and explain the Commands peculiar to *Christianity*, from the first Declarations of *Christ* himself, and his *Apostles*, in such a Manner, as that They might appear to Honest Minds to have as little Tendency to create Distress and Uneasiness, as They were designed, in their first Simplicity, to have. (iv)

He has eliminated superstition and reduced Christianity to "the first Declarations of *Christ* himself, and his *Apostles*," and his hope is that these doctrines may "appear" to free "Honest Minds" from "Distress and Uneasiness": in short, once again, the realist position of keeping our minds at ease and happy.

Hoadly focuses on the sacrament of the Lord's Supper, "which had been rendered very Uneasy to Them [his parishioners] by the *Notions* They had, by some means or other, embraced about it." He is interested in "removing any *Error*, or *Superstition*, from this part of *Christianity*," which means "to shew the *Religion* of *Christ* to the World, as He left it: and . . . to remove from it whatever hinders it from being seen as it really is in itself" (viii). This means that he demystifies the Lord's Supper in a conventional Calvinist way, reducing it from an altar to a dining table and from the immediate divine presence in the bread and wine to a commemoration of Christ's sacrifice for men.

Underlying this demystification is Hoadly's belief in the least amount of priestcraft and dogma, and thus in the efficacy of works rather than rituals and ceremonies: follow the command "*love our* Lord Jesus Christ *in sincerity,*" extend this to our fellows, and little more is needed (vii). With such "orthodox" authority, Fielding can focus morally on love (though epistemologically he focuses on the difficulty of ascertaining the love).

While the "mystery" that seemed most interesting and problematic to Hogarth was the Trinity, for Fielding (as for Hoadly) it was the Eucharist and the question of the immediate divine Presence. If Hogarth plainly denied the possibility of an immanent deity in both art and life, Fielding focuses on the question itself, and its implications, as his central interest. Why he does so is evident in his concern, from his plays onward, with the relationship between divine and authorial providence in a world dominated by contingencies and epistemological confusions. At this point I want to suggest how he combines the notions of the Presence and Christ's love, as does Hoadly, in the Lord's Supper.

The form the Supper takes for Hoadly can be seen in his reliance on St. Paul's *Second Epistle to the Corinthians,* in which Paul attacks the Corinthians for their handling of the Lord's Supper (chaps. 10 and 11). Hoadly makes the distinction "between the *eating* and *drinking* in memory of their *Master;* and their eating and drinking indecently at a Common Meal." He argues that

> the ill Behavior of the *Corinthians* was occasioned by their joining the *Lord's Supper* to a *Meal,* or preceding *Entertainment,* of quite another Sort; in which they both ate and drank to please their Appetites, in such a manner as to distinguish Themselves from their poor and needy Brethren; and to render Themselves unfit to partake afterwards of the *Lord's Supper* in a *worthy* manner. (x–xii, 72, 69)

Hoadly's "Corinthian Sinners," those who "place the least hope in their partaking of the *Lord's Supper,* whilst they continue in the practice of their Sins" and are "guilty of *eating and drinking Unworthily*" (84, 85), serve as a gloss on Tom's dinner with Jenny Waters (*Tom*

Jones 9.5). Fielding is distinguishing between love and lust, the proper Supper and the improper, as focused on his central question of whether Tom can love Sophia and yet betray her with Molly, Jenny, and Lady Bellaston. The sequence begins with Tom's fascination with Jenny's bare breasts, a parody of the iconography of Charity, which sets in motion the lust that is at first satisfied with the food placed before him but, when that is used up, finds satisfaction in Molly herself, another "choice morsel." The dinner at Upton distinguishes between the mere satisfaction of hunger by eating and drinking, which as long as they last keep Tom from Jenny's arms, and the true love Tom has for Sophia. Blifil, for example, sees Sophia as no more than a succulent piece of roast beef.[39]

As Fielding's novels are constructed around scenes in inns, they focus on meals, both good and bad. In *Joseph Andrews* the "cheerful Meeting" (as Adams calls it) with the Wilsons is followed by the meal, the secularized Eucharist, held by Adams, Fanny, and Joseph—the good priest and his two parishioners—in a beautiful meadow with overtones of Eden: they are eating food sent with them by Mrs. Wilson, and they give thanks for the Wilsons' charity and also for the succor of the peddler who earlier paid Adams's inn bill (3.7). And this good meal is followed by its Corinthian perversion in the meal imposed upon them by the roasting squire, and is eventually fulfilled in the meal of reunion with Adams's family, where they are all shown "enjoying perfect Happiness over a homely Meal" in Adams's home (3.1, p. 218).

Tom Jones opens its first chapter with a "bill of fare," which introduces the metaphor of eating, with the author as chef and the readers as the diners at a grand feast that is the work itself, *Tom Jones.* The bill of fare appeared earlier in *The Grub-Street Opera*, where Owen Apshinken's lust was associated with French delicacies and Mrs. Apshinken's meanness with reduced menus, while Susan the good English cook vigorously sang, "O! the Roast Beef of Old England." The strongly patriotic strain takes the form of celebrating tobacco and roast beef in contrast to the French taste. The dual senses coalesce of gourmet-gourmand (Blifil versus Tom), of French foppery and stinginess against the largesse-generosity of old England and the superabundant Tom, and the good and bad Lord's Suppers. But also evident, in the case of the Apshinkens as well as in the first chapter of *Tom Jones*, is the source of the meal, which in the first case is Mr. and Mrs. Apshinken, allegorically the king and queen of England; and in the second is Fielding, the author of *Tom Jones*.

Fielding pointedly distinguishes the author as one who keeps a public ordinary, with paying guests, from the landed gentleman who "gives a private or eleemosynary Treat," which his guests must take or leave. The former offers a bill of fare, after reading which his guests "may either stay and regale with what is provided for them, or may depart to some other Ordinary better accommodated to their Taste." The civic humanist gentleman is opposed to the inn-keeper, the take-it-or-leave-it deity to the author of a whole world ("Human Nature") of the imagination. Within limits, Fielding believes in the power of the author; as he grew older he increasingly came to believe in the social and personal need for the belief in an immanent deity and the rewards and punishments of an afterlife.

The Lord's Supper brings together the two questions of Christianity that are of most interest to Fielding (as they were to Shaftesbury). If one central concern is the ontology and authority of the author in a world that is or is not governed by an immanent God with "special providence," the other is the question of love, its motives and morality, and its relationship to the Shaftesburian issue of interestedness and disinterestedness.

Tom Jones is, as Fielding suggests, his *Essay on Man*, even (in its diction and scorning of rhymed couplets) his *Paradise Lost*.[40] It is his "Creation," precisely the sort of "system" on which Shaftesbury bases his philosophy of harmony and order. And with a figure named Allworthy who owns Paradise Hall and has a nephew named Blifil (rhymes with Devil), he makes it clear that he is writing about both creation and demystification. A Christian reading of *Tom Jones* hinges upon the line from *Paradise Lost* "The world lay all before him" (7.2, p. 331), heralding Tom's expulsion from Paradise Hall by Mr. Allworthy. Blifil invents the lie of disrespect for Allworthy which leads this figure of flawed deity, influenced (his authority replaced) by his delegated representatives Thwackum and Square, to expel Tom. Thus far it is a Hogarthian *deus absconditus* story, a faint anticipation of Blake's revolutionary retellings of the same story in the 1790s, centered on a Urizen figure.

The overt demystification, however, is carried out by invocation of the Abbé Banier's euhemerism, a safe version of Woolston's critical deism.[41] Banier of course never mentions the Scriptures, but it was obvious (as the French philosophes realized) that, as in the earlier model of Lucian, the euhemerist interpretation of the Greek gods applies equally well to the life and miracles of Jesus. Banier's euhemerist analysis of myths is the basic methodology Fielding brings to bear on the Jacobite myths in the contemporary *Jacobite's Journal* of 1748 (Nos. 6 and 12), and this is the methodology's focus in *Tom Jones* as well, with its central events of the Jacobite rebellion of '45 and Roman Catholic mystification. But besides being safer, Banier carries a more complex and far-reaching sort of analysis than critical deism. Fielding's real subjects in *Tom Jones* are the demonizing and deifying of historical human acts, both Tom's and the author's, the most hyperbolic version of which is the Pretender's myth of Jacobitism.

More than *Joseph Andrews,* Fielding's masterpiece is about the fictions people create in order to live in the world, variations on the larger fiction of Fielding's novel itself. There are the provisional social structures of roles, names, words ("love," "honor"), emphasized in the essay "A Comparison of the World and the Stage," which opens book 7; and there are the classical myths and Arab stories, the Christian religion and "providence," but especially the rewards and punishments of the afterlife. These comprise a spectrum that reaches from the travestied order of Blifil and Bridget Allworthy to the no less fictional order of virtue and beauty of Tom and of Fielding's novel itself, which are repeatedly equated.

Tom Jones is literally a Shaftesburian "system," a Palladian structure with perfectly balanced elements, and yet Tom grows up in Paradise Hall, which is a "*Gothick* Stile of Building" (1.4, p. 42), and Fielding acknowledges that he is constructing an imperfect world—a good pattern, he tells us in the dedication and often thereafter, which may contain some incidental flaws. This is presented as a replication of the actual world: Tom is preferred to a Pamelian paragon (thus a hypocrite) like Blifil, as the work *Tom Jones* is preferred to more idealized and idealistic works of art. The "foundling" Tom is related to the "foundling" art form that Fielding is launching as a corrective to the more idealizing one that Richardson is writing at the same time in *Clarissa*.[42] Thus Fielding radically narrows Shaftesbury's distinction between the contingent world and the beautiful world of art. Presumably this is a realistic step beyond Shaftesbury toward both the real, "mixed" character *and* the "mixed" fictional model of the world. Balance and harmony of the Shaftesburian sort remains, but in the generic mode of comedy, where lower types are expected.

At the same time, Fielding renders comic the fantasy of omniscience in his Shaftesburian narrator: "Reader," he announces early in book 1, "I think proper, before we proceed any farther together, to acquaint thee, that I intend to digress, throughout this whole History, as often as I see Occasion, for which I am a better Judge than any pitiful Critic whatever" (1.2, p. 37). He provides and withholds information, often in a seemingly willful way, and he repeatedly tells us that his world corresponds to the real, as it does to his hero, in being flawed. This "mixed" quality includes a radical doubt as to his own, or anyone's, ability to sort out, let alone judge, actions such as Tom's. The historical analogue to the action (centered on the chaotic '45), however, suggests that perhaps it is not so much a flawed world as one governed as the political world is governed—not by a tyrant, an absolute monarch, but by an analogue of England's balanced government of monarch, Lords, and Commons: by author, actors, and audience.[43]

Fielding, in *Tom Jones,* posits three worlds: the actual world of change, accident, and disorder—evil rewarded, good punished; the ideal, comic, simulated world of *Tom Jones,* with its Palladian structure and good rewarded, evil punished; and the false, parodic order of Blifil's "system," which is illusory as against the good nature, the love and charity, of Tom. The last is the "Doctrine" or the "system" of Fielding's novel itself.

Virtue and Interested Love

In the second *Champion* essay attacking deism (24 January 1739/40), Fielding begins with Shaftesbury's figure of Virtue, projected by Theocles in *The Moralists* (Theocles' version of the ekphrasis of Prodicus or Cebes), leading a Roman triumph over "monsters of savage passions . . . ambition, lust, uproar, misrule, with all the fiends which rage in human breasts . . . securely chained" (2:44). But to this the skeptical Philocles opposes "an authentic picture of another kind," in which Virtue is the captive and "by a proud conqueror triumphed over, degraded, spoiled of all her honours, and defaced, so as to retain hardly one single feature of real beauty" (2:45). While Philocles' picture is characterized by his more pious companions as libertine and atheist, Theocles recognizes that the "proud conqueror" is not the atheist but "religion itself"—those who, pretending to expose "the falsehood of human virtue, think to extol religion," but instead "strike at moral virtue as a kind of step-dame, or rival to religion." These are the clerics who "would value virtue but for hereafter"—the advocates of rewards and punishments in the afterlife. Virtue, in short, even Theocles admits, is better without religion of *this* sort.

Fielding goes beyond Shaftesbury, however. As if recalling Hogarth's *Harlot* i, he summons up the classical paradigm of Shaftesbury's (indeed, by now Hogarth's) Choice of Hercules, but he rejects not only the harlot Pleasure but also Virtue, the latter seen as "disagreeable," "rigid," with "intolerable Penances," "Thirst and Hunger, Whips and Chains" (1:212). To get at true Virtue he must strip both women. He begins with the mistranslation of Plato which he will use again in the dedication to *Tom Jones:* "That could Mankind behold Virtue naked, they would all be in Love with her."[44] Under the "tawdry, painted Harlot," Pleasure will prove to be "within, all foul and impure," and under Virtue's clerical-puritanical demeanor she will prove not "of that morose and rigid Nature" but alluring. "Virtue forbids not the satisfying our Appetites," he writes, "Virtue forbids us only to glut and destroy them. The temperate Man tastes and relishes Pleasure in a Degree infinitely superior to that of the voluptuous" (1:213–14). Fielding keeps Virtue within Shaftesbury's ascending scale of aesthetics to ethics, body to mind, and his two women prepare us for the figures of lust and love, Molly and Sophia, in *Tom Jones.*

Nevertheless, orthodox Christian virtue as a humanized, sexually desirable young female is a surprisingly provocative metaphor for a warning against deist libertinism. The metaphor involves not only dressing and undressing Virtue but her "embraces," and the "pursuit" and "possession" of her. As *Tom Jones* shows, while Fielding retains the

Shaftesburian scale, he awards Tom his sensual "pleasure allowed to every beast but man" with other women; he distinguishes Tom's lust for Molly (and Jenny Waters and Lady Bellaston) from his love for Sophia, which however clearly includes the other.

Shaftesbury's central term "disinterestedness" is focused, in the religious context, on the distinction between a disinterested love of God and an interested one based on "belief in a future reward and punishment": he concludes that "to serve God by compulsion, or for interest merely, is service and mercenary" (2:55). Fielding's own moral program, however, is devoted to justifying the "interestedness" of virtue: Tom's benevolence is based on neither the religious principles of Thwackum nor the Shaftesburian "natural Beauty of Virtue" advocated by Square. It is based on a "love" of the *other* which, though extended to a general sympathy, is posited on physical desire. This "love" is qualitatively different addressed to Molly, Jenny, and Lady Bellaston, but only because with them it remains at the level of physical hunger (one of Shaftesbury's terms for interestedness), whereas "love" leads Tom to give up Sophia when he knows that it will be harmful to her if he does not.

In short, Fielding refutes Shaftesbury's assumption that virtue and interest are opposed principles by presenting an elaborate proof that virtue has to do with interested relationships between people. These relationships are distinguished not by Shaftesbury's ascending scale of body and mind but by appetite: in Bernard Harrison's words, "a desire for some goal which can be fully specified without at all mentioning the conscious states of other people" ("a desire to use somebody's body, without the slightest concern for any mental state of the person concerned"); as opposed to human needs, or "desires for goals which cannot be specified without mentioning the conscious states of other people." Human needs lead us "into connexion with each other, and out of that solitary egoistic self-absorption" of mere appetite.[45] Human needs include both an internal sense of empathy and an external sense of duty to the loved one.

One significant detail in Tom's story, in terms of the Miltonic model, is the asymmetry of the Fall and the Expulsion. Book 9, the book of Tom's Fall at Upton, is the central book, rather than book 6, the Expulsion itself; and this is because in *Tom Jones* the Expulsion does not follow from, is not a consequence of, the Fall. The ostensible reason is the amour propre of Allworthy, compromised by lies motivated by the hatred (or jealousy) of Blifil and his henchmen Thwackum and Square. Tom is expelled for one reason (Allworthy's), but what matters to Allworthy and later to Sophia (respect for their names) does not matter to Fielding. He focuses on Tom's betrayal of his love for Sophia—and explains and justifies it, at the moment by a materialist hydraulic metaphor (if a passion cannot find release at its proper outlet, it will find another),[46] but in retrospect by the duty that is part and parcel of love (and not of the letter of the law).

Allworthy, the God substitute, is very close to Shaftesbury's version of the Christian deity. Tom (according to the lies of Blifil) does not worship him sufficiently, and so Allworthy, representing a religion of rewards and punishments, casts Tom out. It is this religion, embodied in Allworthy's self-regarding definition of the "Fall," which Fielding replaces by the religion of love/charity, transgressed in Tom's "Fall" with Molly and embodied in his love of Sophia.

At the center, in books 7 to 9, leading up to the Fall, Fielding supplements the Christian paradigm with the classical Choice of Hercules between Pleasure and Wisdom (as Hogarth had in *Harlot* 1). Tom makes the wrong choice in a sexual situation. But this is only to remind us that he deserved the Expulsion of book 5 because he had betrayed Sophia (Virtue-Wisdom) with Molly (another whorish Pleasure). This is a Puritan-Richardsonian reading, which is discredited when Sophia and Tom both agree to ignore it; but it is also one which, as the asymmetry of Expulsion and Fall suggests, Fielding himself takes seriously. And contra both readings (Christian-Richardsonian or classical), Fielding proposes his moral philosophical reading (his "Great Doctrine"), which attributes the sexual transgression to Tom's good-natured motive for giving up Sophia (and taking Molly and Jenny): the love of Sophia, which prevents him from ruining her life.

This motive is only one of several, however, for Tom's Fall is explained by multiple motives, which on the one hand sound exculpatory and on the other suggest the doubtfulness of which explanation to choose, so evident in the basic grammatical structure of *Tom Jones:* "Whether this or that . . . I cannot say, but. . . ." And the guilty reading of the act has to be contrasted with Sophia's own position on Tom's transgression, which claims that it was his indelicacy as to her name and reputation. The comedy of Sophia's reliance on "name" (perhaps to parallel Allworthy's, perhaps to screen her true jealousy) looks ahead to book 12, chapter 8, where it finds its parallel in the word "providence," another mere "name."

In *Tom Jones,* Fielding is morally opposed both to Mandeville, who sees humans as all appetite, and to Shaftesbury, who sees them as all human needs but of a single sort, based on the model of the disinterested country gentleman in a coffee house or in Mr. Spectator's club. Fielding's human needs are based unashamedly on heterosexual desire. Even Tom's "friendship" for Black George, it is strongly hinted, is based at least partly on his sexual attraction to George's daughter Molly. Tom's refusal to betray George can be taken as parallel to his later sense of duty to Molly when he thinks he is the father of her child and offers to give her "a Sum of Money."

Fielding's position, though drawing upon memories of his late wife Charlotte, derives from the Mandevillian exposure of interest beneath Shaftesbury's disinterestedness. Fielding marginalizes the economic aspects of interest which are Mandeville's focus, leaving primarily sexual desire—but not entirely, since it is precisely Sophia's economic dependence on her father which weighs heavily with Tom in his decision to leave off his courtship. By narrowing egoism to the primary role of sexual desire, Fielding can return with a more realistic psychology to Shaftesbury's distinction between lust for an individual body and general benevolence. He can contrast the pleasure Tom gets from Sophia, as an end in itself (Sophia is only a means to that end), with Sophia herself, whose happiness and well-being give Tom pleasure. And this is different not only from the position of Shaftesbury but also from that of Hogarth, for whom it is the pursuit that gives the pleasure.

What Fielding has produced out of the Shaftesburian principles of order and harmony, mind over body, and disinterested pleasure is an alternative ethics of pleasure centered on the body of a real woman—an aesthetics, in short, which, while probably drawing upon Hogarth's *Strolling Actresses,* differs in significant ways from his *Analysis of Beauty* of four years later. Tom takes no "pleasure" or "love" in the "pursuit" or "chase" of Sophia for its own sake—though, true to the Hogarthian model, Fielding's sagacious reader is encouraged to enjoy the pleasure of satisfying his curiosity as the author lays out his story.[47]

The Retrieval of Rewards/Punishments

The alternative ethics of deism and of Anglicanism explored in *Joseph Andrews* reappear in *Tom Jones* as equally bad alternatives, those Allworthy-surrogates, Thwackum and Square; but again a compromise is worked out. Only Square the deist (a lusty man who shares Molly with Tom) is capable of reformation. He is converted on his deathbed to religion, specifically to belief in an afterlife. Battestin points to the influence on Fielding of Lord Lyttelton's *Observations on the Conversion and Apostleship of St. Paul,* published at about the time Fielding was writing the concluding books of *Tom Jones.* Possibly Square's conversion is an analogue to Tom's success at controlling his potentially anarchic impulses; but, knowing he is dying, Square needs consolation, that belief in an afterlife which was the feature of Christian belief that most concerned Fielding. It is Square the deist who is converted and confesses the truth he knows about Tom, while Thwackum the clergyman remains to the end cold-hearted, self-righteous, self-seeking, and hypocritical. This says, as Fielding reiterated after the *Champion* essays, that deist morality of the Shaftesbury sort can be corrected—as both control and consolation—by a pragmatic belief in Christian examples and eschatology; the Christian clergy, although there is an occasional Parson Adams, is unredeemable. Parson Supple, the best the clergy can show in *Tom Jones,* is summed up in his name (he cannot control the violent impulses of Squire Western) and his marriage to Jenny Waters.

Like St. Paul, Square was a persecutor and is now converted. But he is vouchsafed no Pauline vision, no divine intervention (nor is the recovering of his sight a miracle), only the same pragmatic belief advocated by Fielding at the end of his essay on bereavement. This is a matter of some importance because Lyttelton's aim in his book is no less than to prove, on the strength of this Pauline text, that Paul's conversion and its aftermath "did all really happen, and therefore the Christian religion is a divine revelation."[48] I do not mean to suggest that Fielding is subverting his friend Lyttelton's pious tract. But *Tom Jones* is written in a generic form that, as defined by Fielding, cannot advocate both divine presence and belief in the divine: the one, as the deists taught him, is not historical; the other is necessary for human survival.

By book 7, however, with the news of the Pretender's invasion (which coincides with Tom's departure from Paradise Hall, his descent into the fallen world of history), Fielding no longer permits himself to be equivocal in his respect for the clergy and the belief in Protestant Christianity. The Anglican cloth and patriotism are at this time and place in history necessarily equated.[49] This event changes his attitude toward religion, albeit still in a pragmatic way. After *Tom Jones,* as Westminster magistrate and official spokesman for the government, he speaks for orthodoxy without irony or ambivalence. If earlier, his reliance on rewards and punishments in the afterlife had seemed to satisfy a personal need, in his later years it satisfied a social one. In the 1750s he simply materialized doctrine in *Examples of the Interposition of Providence in the Detection and Punishment of Murder* (1752), although in an advertisement he explains that "No Family ought to be without this Book, and it is most particularly calculated for the Use of those Schools, in which Children are taught to read."[50]

In *Joseph Andrews* the author's system of order does not include rewards and punishments, or at least not punishments; in *Tom Jones,* however, the order is far more emphatic, elucidated in every formal element of the work, but the denouement balances the rewards of Tom and Sophia and the "good" characters with the punishments of Square and Thwackum, Black George and Blifil. Where earlier Fielding was obsessed with the belief in a happy afterlife of reunion and reward, now he begins to shift his emphasis toward punishments (though softened by Tom's mercy).

Fielding's last novel, *Amelia* (1751), advocates the Christian religion, pious education, and the necessity of belief, on the one hand; and a strong and honest judiciary and police force, on the other. A final mention of rewards and punishments comes from Dr. Harrison, the grim successor to Parson Adams: he believes that religion is useful specifically because it "applies immediately to the strongest of these Passions, Hope and Fear, chusing rather to rely on its Rewards and Punishments, than on that native Beauty of Virtue" advocated by the deists and Shaftesbury.[51]

Looking back from the 1750s, Fielding ironically defined "Religion" in the "modern Glossary" of his *Covent-Garden Journal* (1752) as "A Word of no Meaning; but which serves as a Bugbear to frighten Children with" (No. 4). No. 6, an imitation of Swift's "Dedication to Prince Posterity," takes up the uses to which forgotten books are put: Too great a dissemination (e.g., through the utilization by pastry cooks) of deist tracts is dangerous because they were meant for "the Use and Inspection of the few" but "are by no means proper Food for the Mouths of Babes and Sucklings."[52]

As often is the case, however, Fielding's irony includes a hard Mandevillian truth: not only are the old deist tracts impious and now unread, used by trunk-liners and pastry cooks, but there was, in those days (when Fielding was young), a distinction between the thinking few, who were entitled to play around with these skeptical, freethinking ideas, and the public as a whole, who required the guidance and protection of religion. The *Covent-Garden Journal* draws our attention back to the way Fielding felt before he bore responsibility for public order and saw society as dangerously degenerate, and back to the pragmatic function he assigned religion in public life as well as (in the matter of grieving) in his own private life. And the reference to children (which recalls Locke on their simplicity) exposes, at least to the "few" (those he referred to as his "sagacious readers" in *Tom Jones*), his realistic appraisal of the public, as his portrait of Booth exposes his realistic appraisal of himself in middle age.

In the *Enquiry into the Late Increase in Robbers* and the other legal tracts of 1751, and in the *Covent-Garden Journal,* he shows that to keep order in a disintegrating society religion is as essential as the law; in *A Charge to the Grand Jury* he draws attention to the statutes against irreligious writings; and in *Amelia* he includes as his own surrogate a deist, Billy Booth, who believes in a world governed by chance and at the end is converted to Christianity. Square's conversion was in the face of death; Booth's is less interested or pragmatic but also much less probable.

While not ruling out the possibility of a "conversion" like Booth's (perhaps down to the specifics of reading Isaac Barrow), I see deism and orthodoxy as coexisting for Fielding on different levels of belief; but, for both personal and professional reasons, orthodoxy gained the final ascendancy. Even then, one can imagine the aging Fielding still joking while the official voice proclaimed whatever was necessary to maintain order in London.

For Shaftesbury a religion of rewards/punishments could be useful, though it does not make a person virtuous. He could argue for the efficacy of this religion without believing in it. Fielding seems to have agreed, as when, putting his beliefs into action, he adjusts his words to different audiences, whether men of sense or children. But at other times he seems to have found it useful to act as though he believed—or to actually believe.

Postscript: Reading Richardson

In all fairness, Richardson's position deserves to be clarified in relation to the Novel/novel. As well as serving Fielding with an "orthodox" text to demystify and parody, he also shared in his own way Fielding's strategy of treating secular texts (and his own text) as parodic of Scripture, for example in *Pamela* identifying Mr. B. variously with Lucifer and Christ. Mr. B., however, sees himself as the devil and sees Pamela as an angel; and Pamela sees him "as cunning as Lucifer," "an implement . . . in the Hands of *Lucifer*," one who "does the devil's work" (45, 61, 65, 181, 112). The question raised by *Pamela* is how much of the heroine's subjectivity is intended by Richardson as "scriptural" truth, corresponding to the certainty of "Virtue Rewarded" on the title page.

Let us take as an example the sacrament of Pamela's marriage. Mr. B. suggests to Parson Williams, as the text for his wedding sermon, Luke 15:7 ("*There is more Joy in Heaven over one Sinner that repenteth, than over Ninety-nine just Persons that need not Repentence*"), applied of course to himself; Parson Williams suggests Luke 2:29–30, applied to *him*self ("*Now lettest thou thy servant depart in Peace; for my Eyes have seen thy Salvation*"), but Pamela applies "servant" to *her*self (she has seen Mr. B.'s "Salvation"). Mr. B. demurs, reminding her that she is not going to "depart in Peace" but marry him. To which Pamela replies that the *proper* text is Luke 1:46–52, the Magnificat, which celebrates "the low Estate of his [Mr. B.'s] Handmaiden" and how he "exalted one of low Degree." Pamela's self-portrait returns us to *Harlot* 1, but unlike

Hackabout, Pamela *is* exalted—not by the deity but by Mr. B. Though she ostensibly requires no Hogarth, the artist who replaces the deity, to exalt her, the fact is that Richardson, in his innovative novel *Pamela,* is doing just this, and (to judge by his copious comments on his novel, preceding and following the text), he obviously knew it. The scene in question recovers not only the scriptural significance of the Magnificat but also the aesthetic dimension in which the artist serves as a surrogate deity.

The scene also draws our attention to a common theme, even to common assumptions, about the exalting of low subject matter. The subtext in the *Harlot* and in *Pamela* is the same: the oppressive social structure crushes an innocent plebeian girl or, in the "editor's" (Richardson's) words, "Riches and Power conspire against Innocence and a low Estate" (90).[53] Richardson and Fielding share the repudiation of ethical orthodoxy; both use the novel to teach not theological but moral truths. Richardson's social heterodoxy—his anti-elitism and social progressivism—also parallel Fielding's insofar as he engages in the skeptical critique of such aristocratic ethical absolutes as "honor" and "virtue," in the "mixing" of such character elements as low social standing and elevated virtue. These are important features of any posture critical of a strictly civic virtue, and they are shared by Richardson and Fielding as well as Hogarth.

The opposite of Woolston's strategy, however, Richardson's comes from the Puritan tradition of spiritualizing nature—scripturalizing ordinary everyday events, as in Bunyan's *Grace Abounding* or (in the novel) Crusoe's spiritualizing of every event on his island. The point is that Richardson deals with the spiritual and existential levels of experience in a very different way from the deist. Although he would say that he legitimates real life by portraying it in relation to religious texts, there is a sense in which he legitimates religious texts by portraying them through real life: and that is the sense attacked by Fielding.

Like *Robinson Crusoe* (1719), *Pamela* is a spiritual autobiography in which the author plainly means the reader to accept the reality of God and of conversion and rehabilitation, the truth of his providential pilgrimage. And yet, as Defoe reveals by the conflicting accounts he prints of Crusoe's arrival on the island (in retrospect, he thanked God for his delivery; in his diary he ran about distracted and cursed his fate),

the whole story of the conversion is a fictionalizing of events by the old
and pious Crusoe who writes this "spiritual autobiography." The overlapping of narrative structures and discourses produced an effect that
was beyond the author's conscious intention.

What was called for was a deist reading of *Robinson Crusoe*. And
not long after its publication, in *The Life and Strange Surprising Adventures of Mr. D— De F—, of London, Hosier* (1719), the deist Charles
Gildon accused Defoe of the "coining of Providences," of recovering
Crusoe's inconsistencies by placing them in a pattern of divine providence which makes them seem intelligible but blasphemes by claiming
God's power to "mint" signs in the world merely to suit Crusoe's
desires. Every time Crusoe invokes providence as guiding his actions he
is merely giving his own desires a veneer of divine sanction. Gildon
accuses "Defoe" himself of claiming a special relationship with providence, an ability to detect "secret Hints" by which God communicates
his wishes personally to him.[54]

As Gildon's critique of *Crusoe* suggests, Richardson's process of
spiritualizing is the opposite of Hogarth's demystifying in the *Harlot,*
but, like Defoe's retrospective rewriting of events, Richardson's conflation of the immediate evidence of Pamela's diary, the retrospect of
"Virtue Rewarded," and his own editorial commentary opens the door
for Fielding's Gildonesque response in *Shamela,* which, based not on
the "witnessing" of spiritual autobiography but of a theatrical representation, distinguishes between the words of Richardson/Pamela's spiritual interpretation and Shamela's true Mandevillian actions—the spiritual and the (deist) historical reading, the first with and the second
without providence. "I resolved to go away, and trust all to Providence,
and nothing to myself," Pamela writes. But as her story of fishing and
catching a carp tells us, there are two ways to read an allegory. Pamela
reads the carp as "the unhappy *Pamela*" and herself, the fisherwoman,
as "my naughty Master"; but even the most sympathetic reader might
reverse the roles (84–85). Fielding is the typical post-deist reader of the
Novel/novel, which provokes curiosity, discovery, uncovering, and the
bracketing of credulity.

The theatrical metaphor, however, is never far from Richardson's
thoughts. The text Parson Williams actually chooses to preach is Proverbs 11:24–25 on "the right Use of Riches" (" *The liberal Soul shall be*

made fat: and he that watereth, shall be watered also himself"), which strongly implies the desirability of contributions to Williams's church— the underlying economic motive Mandeville would, and Fielding did, discern beneath the scriptural citations. Williams's text serves as a dramatic capstone to the series of self-serving (in fact comically self-serving) texts for the wedding ceremony suggested by Williams, Mr. B., Pamela, and her father, which are presented as a small comic drama.

Earlier, Pamela, deciding to prefer the life of a scullery maid to that of Mr. B.'s lover, sets out to determine what it would be like scouring pans. To this end she recalls the bishop who "was to be burnt for his Religion" and tried "how he could bear it, by putting his Fingers into the lighted Candle." Pamela accordingly applies her fingers to a pewter plate and reports that "[I] blister'd my Hand in two Places" (77–78). From Richardson-Pamela's point of view, this is the same as Bunyan's constantly fitting himself into the role of Christ while fearing he may have slipped into the role of Judas, Peter, or Esau. From the equally theatrical perspective of Hogarth-Fielding it is the historicizing of religious myth.

Preparing for the wedding ceremony, Pamela insists that the ceremony be performed not in Mr. B.'s chamber (his bedroom), as he characteristically wishes, but in the chapel, a place long abandoned and now used only to store lumber (262–63). But when she visits the iconoclasted chapel with Mr. B., Parson Williams, and her father, her response is a mixture of the aesthetic ("pretty . . . pretty . . . prettily") and religious ("the Solemnity . . . such blessed Prospects"): she admires the art and then, as she says, "[I] poured out my Soul to God." Pamela is mixing aesthetic and religious responses—and the question is whether to read the scene as the complexity of response recorded in a diary or as the comic incongruity of a scene in a Fielding comedy. In the latter case, Pamela's role as potential mistress of the house coexists with that of the pious *religieuse.*

Pamela is also, notoriously, a work about spectatorship. In the *Spectator* itself spectatorship was active in its pursuing of a quarry but without agency, as in the episode of the inn yard when the disinterested Mr. Spectator watched the Hackabout and Needham figures meet without lifting a finger to protect the girl. Hogarth, of course, requires that we act as well as see, at least in a moral sense. But in his aesthetic treatise he comes to depend more than we might expect on the model of *Pamela*. In Richardson's novel voyeurism has become a central concern of the villainous Mr. B., whose end is seduction or even rape. The act itself is judged bad, but, as Fielding among others noticed, the reader is placed in the same interested position as Mr. B. vis-à-vis Pamela. In the *Analysis* Hogarth takes a position not unlike Mr. B.'s clearly interested one, but he validates it in terms of an aesthetics, not a morality. We might say that he theorizes the general situation of *Pamela* including its happy ending, which renders it religious for Richardson but aesthetic for Hogarth. However, as we shall see in the next chapter, Cleland's *Fanny Hill* (1748–49), which spelled out these aspects of *Pamela* for him, intervened.

Three volumes of *Tom Jones* (books 1–9) were in print by September 1748; in October five volumes of *Clarissa* were in print, and on 15 October Fielding wrote his letter of praise to Richardson, which Richardson had copied and sent to his friends, presumably as self-vindication. Traces of the book *Clarissa* begin to be felt in the later volumes of *Tom Jones*. In book 15, letters begin to play an important role in the plot, showing the way letters should be used—embedded in the narrative, as part of "a nice train of little Circumstances" (916), rather than uncontested witnessing; and pointed and witty rather than prolix and repetitious.[55] The contrasts between Sophia and Clarissa also intensify in the last volumes.[56]

The most interesting response, however, came in Richardson's postscript to the final volume, which Fielding cannot have seen before he finished the relevant parts of *Tom Jones* and before he wrote his letter to Richardson. Richardson says that his intention in *Clarissa* was to produce not a "History" but a "Dramatic Narrative"; he means that the letters are to be read as speeches in a play, and that his genre (not a Puritan diary, spiritual autobiography, or saint's life—although of course it is all of these) is tragedy. Tragedy, of course, is implicitly contrasted with comedy, Fielding's genre. And the further distinction he insists upon is between happy and tragic endings; in terms of "poetic justice," immanent providence, in the one, and in the other the assumption that "good and evil happen alike unto ALL MEN on this side the grave: And as the principal design of Tragedy is to *raise commiseration and terror* in the minds of the audience, we shall defeat this great end, if we always make Virtue and Innocence happy and successful." His intention is to produce not the easy relief of a happy ending and poetic justice, but the catharsis produced by the pity and terror of tragedy (he cites Aristotle). But his tragic catharsis in life presupposes the "happiness" of a belief in rewards and punishments in the afterlife.

What is interesting is the emphasis, which Richardson and Fielding share, on the reward of virtue only in the afterlife. They clearly do not disagree on this point, but they arrive at a solution by different routes: Richardson by the belief of all his characters, himself, and presumably his audience in the afterlife to which, in their different ways, Clarissa and Lovelace are destined *following* the tragedy of this world; and Fielding, himself less certain, and addressing himself to a more sophisticated audience that would not accept such a fiction with such certainty, by substituting a harmonious, beautiful fiction of his own, however artificial.

In his revision of the postscript (third edition, 1750), Richardson is even more plainly thinking about *Tom Jones*. His irony is heavy-handed: "Others, and some gentlemen, declared against Tragedies in general, and in favour of Comedies, almost in the words of Lovelace, who was supported in his taste by all the women at Mrs. Sinclair's, and by Sinclair herself" (8:278). The sentence also connects with the story he liked to tell that Fielding, on the basis of his reading of volumes 1 through 5, had begged him to preserve Clarissa and give her a happy ending. The happy ending envisioned is to reform Lovelace and marry him to Clarissa, which sounds very like the conclusion of Tom and Sophia's romance:

> To have a Lovelace for a series of years glory in his wickedness, and think that he had nothing to do, but as an act of grace and favour to hold out his hand to receive that of the best of women, whenever he pleased, and to have it thought, that Marriage would be a sufficient amends for all his enormities to others, as well as to her; he [the author] could not bear that. (8:278)

The author, Richardson writes, "had a great end in view," for "He has lived to see Scepticism and Infidelity openly avowed, . . . The great doctrines of the Gospel brought into question, . . . And taste even to wantonness for out-door pleasure and luxury, to the general exclusion of domestic as well as public virtue, industriously promoted among all ranks and degrees of people" (8:279). That too obviously is aimed at the author of *Tom Jones.*

However, if Richardson follows Aristotle's definition of pity and terror caused by our seeing the catastrophe of great or good men, he is describing an aesthetics of tragedy. If he looks for the distribution of rewards and punishments, he is describing morality (or an "English tragedy"). Addison made this distinction in *Spectator* No. 40, where he prefers Aristotle's sense of tragedy to that of the moderns, which follows the rule of "an equal distribution of rewards and punishments, and an impartial execution of poetical justice": "Terror and Commiseration leave a pleasing Anguish in the Mind; and fix the Audience in such a serious Composure of Thought, as is much more lasting and delightful than any little transient Starts of Joy and Satisfaction" (i.e., from the just "distribution of Rewards and Punishments" [1:169]). There is no reference to pity and terror in Addison's account of the Great in the "Pleasures" essays, but No. 40 suggests that this is a possible interpretation of Aristotle's theory. Richardson would have it both ways in *Clarissa:* focusing on the aesthetic, he puts off the moral to the afterlife. Fielding is simply writing not tragedy but comedy—and the aesthetics of comedy (as set forth in the preface to *Joseph Andrews* and later in Hogarth's *Analysis*) involves laughter caused by incongruous juxtapositions.

The staunch Richardsonian reading of *Tom Jones* by Frank Kermode focused on the incest chapter (17.2), not the genuinely problematic chapters in books 5, 6, and 9–10. Kermode saw Fielding fudging the one real test of Tom's sexual license—the ultimate taboo of incest. But incest for Fielding is the ultimate topos of *mock* tragedy, accompanied by a momentary return to the diction of *Tom Thumb,* so egregiously theatrical precisely because it caps the illusory sequence of events set in motion by the tragedy of *Hamlet* (interpreted in Fielding's time as about the duty of sons to fathers), with citation of the Aristotelian example, the tragedy of Oedipus.[57] It is even possible that Fielding, having read or heard about Richardson's postscript, with its invocation of Aristotle and pity and terror, at that point decided to throw in the reference to a mock-Oedipus.

In fact, in *Clarissa* Richardson portrays evil as victorious and good as disabled, and enjoys the catharsis of it. But this involves the assumption that his audience must *know* that there will be rewards and punishments in the hereafter for these characters. Furthermore, in Richardson's "tragedy," while the good character is imprisoned and raped, by the end, though she dies, she is accepted by everyone as a saint (good is rewarded); and the bad character has been shamed, shunned, and executed (evil punished). Although equally grim (and hardly, in the Fielding-Shaftesbury sense comic), the Hogarthian progress stops at the first stage. Hardly a villain, though certainly not a paragon like Clarissa, the Harlot is legally and extra-legally punished, while the clearly guiltier characters who exploit her are rewarded or at least continue on their evil ways unscathed. The doctrine of equal rewards and punishments is tested and found wanting, both in this life and in the next. There is no pity or terror, only condemnation and admonition, with no hint of anything to follow—in that sense, morality denies the religious response and opens a door to the aesthetic.

SIX

Aesthetics and Erotics

Cleland, Fielding, and Sterne

Desire, Pleasure, Pursuit, and Penetration: Cleland's *Fanny Hill*

The transitional work between Hogarth's graphic satires and his *Analysis of Beauty* was *Memoirs of a Woman of Pleasure; or, Fanny Hill* (1748–49), which showed how the morality of *A Harlot's Progress* could be aestheticized.[1] John Cleland (another deist or freethinker) constructs a plot focused on a woman and demonstrates her (and her readers') growing awareness of erotic experience. His plot is a rewriting of *A Harlot's Progress* in that it represents the "scandalous stages of my life," as Fanny refers to her story, not as an ironic "progress" ending in punishment, disease, and death but as a progress from which (she says) "I emerged at length, to the enjoyment of every blessing in the power of love, health, and fortune to bestow, whilst yet in the flower of youth, and not too late to employ the leisure afforded me by great ease and affluence."[2]

Cleland (in this respect following Fielding's parodies of Richardson's *Pamela,* to the extent of having Fanny invoke the Shamelian "Vartue") fills in the "stages" of his heroine's successful progress with sensory pleasures rather than disasters or self-denials. He refers to his scenes as "pictures," and indeed voyeurism is central to his novel—not in the closed, prurient sense of *Pamela,* but as one aspect of his exploration of the senses in a young woman who explores her own senses in the first person singular in fashionable London and ends with a fortune and a husband she loves. Fanny's successful "progress" is toward both fullness of erotic knowledge and wealth, marriage, and conjugal happiness.

Erotic writings before Cleland had been primarily an excuse for anticlericalism.[3] In this sense, Hogarth's *Harlot* was itself a form of eroticism (and literally *pornography* in its Greek sense: "writing about prostitutes"). His anticlericalism was essential to the genre, as was the undercurrent of libertine sacrilege. The latter may cast a more sinister light on Hogarth's act of defecating on a church porch following the publication of the *Harlot*. This was a libertine desecration (in theory at least extending to the altar and pulpit) that goes beyond the deist principles of Toland, let alone Shaftesbury.[4] The parody Trinity, and the association of Beauty with the Temptation and Fall and with sexuality on the title page of Hogarth's *Analysis,* point to his painting of Sir Francis worshiping the nude woman on the crucifix. Countertraditions of the sort Hogarth introduces are on a spectrum of transgression which may deliberately lead beyond polite limits. The libertine mode, however, as in the Society of Dilettanti and the Medmenham Monks, addressed upper-class gentlemen—essentially Shaftesbury's civic humanists—while Hogarth (the Freemason) addressed, originally at least, and in theory if not always in practice, a wider social spectrum of the sort envisaged by Toland.

The most notorious scene in *Fanny Hill* was the sodomy committed by two young gentlemen, a scene emphasized by its climactic position in the narrative. The rationale for sodomy among libertines was that the history of Greece and Rome showed that it was a characteristic of republics, strengthening the bonds between men, and that attachment to women was associated with weakness and despotism.[5] Cleland includes the scene while labeling it from the nonlibertine perspective (it is through Fanny's horrified but fascinated eyes that we observe the act) a perversion, as Hogarth did also in the encounter of Antinous and the dancing master in *Analysis* 1. Fanny does, however, provide both perspectives: while she provides a focus on the vagina, her own eyes are always alert to the male sexual organ.

Of her friend Polly's vagina, she writes that its "lips vermillioning inwards, expressed a small rubied line in sweet miniature, such as *not*

Guido's touch or colouring could ever attain to the *life* or delicacy of."
But the same is true, from Fanny's perspective, of men: of her beloved
Charles's body, she comments that it is "surely infinitely superior to
those nudities furnished by the painters, statuaries, or any art, which
are *purchased at immense prices.*" Compared to Charles's real body,
Fanny denigrates both antique art and its monetary value; and she adds
that "the sight of them *in actual life* is scarce sovereignly tasted by *any
but the few* whom nature has *endowed with a fire of imagination,*" once
again distinguishing living bodies from "all the *imitations of art,* or *the
reach of wealth to pay their price*" (68, 82, emphasis added).

Cleland follows the anti-Shaftesbury line in having Fanny judge
the work of art to be inferior in beauty to the human body and,
officially at least, focusing on the female. Drawing on Hogarth's disheveled Diana in *Strolling Actresses* (fig. 14), he has Fanny describe
herself lying on a couch, "*in an undress* which was with all the *art of
negligence flowing loose,* and in a most *tempting disorder: no stays, no
hoop*—no encumberance whatever" (108). In short, Cleland's variations
on the Harlot give her a positive valuation and raise her life, her sensuality, her art of seduction (which is her "art of negligence"), into an
aesthetics. It is an aesthetics based on seduction, in which morality and
beauty (a simple unity for Shaftesbury and Hutcheson) are at odds.

The book begins with an invocation of Naked Truth, a glance
back to Hogarth's image of Nature unveiled in *Boys Peeping at Nature,*
which introduced the *Harlot* (and to Fielding's "naked Truth" in the
Dedication to *Tom Jones*); and this of course anticipates the many
strippings of Fanny and other women to the state of nature, but always
specifically preliminary to sexual intercourse.[6]

Cleland takes his reader from aesthetic disinterestedness not only
over into sexual desire but into the pleasure of the act itself. One could
argue that Fanny retains a certain detachment from the act (which is
always first carried out by others) by the distancing of her observation,
contemplation, and commentary, as she retells it to her correspondent
some years later. An aesthetic distance is held in an unstable and, in
many cases, clearly comic tension with the immediacy of the act, as the
euphemism of the style is with the frankness of the content. But there
is no denying that Cleland means to redefine aesthetics and elevate

erotics into an aesthetics—or reveal aesthetics to be an erotics—by focusing on a woman, making her a prostitute, and putting in question the whole concept of disinterestedness.

His focus is first on the aestheticizing and then on the penetration of Fanny's vagina, and a disproportionate emphasis is given to the breaking of her hymen. Fanny's initiation into orgasm is by voyeurism and foreplay, by herself and with her female colleagues. But this is only preparatory to the central event of volume 1, which is her deflowering by Charles, her first and ultimate lover (and destined husband). The description is extended and elaborate, the act is difficult, and the long account is centered on the mixture of pleasure and pain, or more specifically pleasure preceded by (initiated or authorized by) pain. The questions posed to a reader are about the relationship between beauty, pain, and sublimity, between art and love—questions closer to the formulations of Burke in his *Philosophical Enquiry* of 1757 than to those of Shaftesbury or Addison.[7]

Volume 2 then takes Fanny to the bordello of Mrs. Cole, whose first assignment for her new recruit is to pass for a virgin, thereby returning to the penetration of her maidenhead, an *initial* penetration. But first Fanny is presented with three more deflowerings, recalled as narratives by the more experienced prostitutes Emily, Louisa, and Harriet, and these memories are repeated in the present with men at the brothel, followed by Fanny's own intercourse with a young client who judges her still able to pass for a virgin. The voyeurs, who contribute to the questioning of disinterest in the scene of Fanny's own intercourse, are Mrs. Cole, the other girls, and of course the reader.

Finally, Fanny participates in her long-awaited "deflowering" by Mr. Norbert, a man associated with degenerate sexual practices. The episodes that follow are of sexual perversions, from Mr. Barville's desire for flagellation to an old gentleman's harmless eccentricities, to a masquerader's attempt to sodomize Emily, who is misleadingly dressed as a shepherd ("losing a *maidenhead* she had never dreamt of" [192]), and finally to Fanny's own appalled observation of a homosexual tryst— "two young gentlemen" in "so criminal a scene" (193). After this, before the dispersal of the bordello crew, the affair with the elderly merchant of Cadiz who makes her affluent and independent by leaving her his fortune, and the reunion with Charles, there is only the episode of the well-hung idiot, Dick, whose unnatural state gives pleasure that also produces a sort of anxiety in Fanny and her friends.

The obsessive repetition of the single act of initial penetration, as necessary preparation for independent acts of love, is remarkable. Of course, Richardson's *Pamela* and *Clarissa,* though they leave the act itself a blank, were obsessively concerned with defloration, and introduced as well the situation of the woman persecuted by an immoral male.[8] But Cleland, by focusing first on the defloration by the beloved Charles, renders the experience aesthetic: he presents the primal penetration, followed by earned repetitions and then artful imitations, and these by perverted simulations or displacements of the natural act. The experience of first penetration or breakthrough is presented as the only legitimate or natural one, at least until the return of Charles. The value of maidenheads ("that darling treasure, that hidden mine, so eagerly sought after by the men, and which they never dig for but they destroy") lies in their uniqueness, designating the crucial distinction between a "maid" and a "woman." (Charles becomes "infinitely endear'd" to Fanny by his "complete triumph over a maidenhead" [79].)

In the interim, as a whore Fanny herself is forced to combine the qualities of property and "art" (in the artificial deflowering) decried in her initial description of Charles and reiterated throughout her life of prostitution. These remain essentially unsatisfactory substitutes for the absent Charles, on a descending scale from him to those for whom she has to serve as first a possession or artifice and then an assistant to sexual perversions.

To judge by the early contrasts of sculptures and the bodies of living men and women, the suggestion is that the pseudo-virgin and pseudo-deflowering offer a false artful repetition of the natural act Fanny carried out with Charles. Cleland figures art as a "secondary," a theatrical substitute for nature (in the sense that Fanny is assuming the "role" of a virgin). His freethinking aesthetics of the "pleasure of pursuit" outlines the possibility of an aesthetics of the body which Hogarth then elaborates three years later in his *Analysis of Beauty.* The two illustrative plates reveal under every formal configuration the subtext of desire. This is the notion that an active participation in and experience of the variety of the formal and affective attributes of sensuous objects is necessary to a full understanding of their beauty; and these features are worked out in the paradigm of a woman, a man (whether husband or father) who possesses her favors (in Shaftesbury's sense of property), and her true love.

In the *Analysis,* however, Hogarth never claims that desire and pursuit spill over into the sexual act, precisely because the "pleasure" is in the pursuit, not the fulfillment. There is, of course, a sense in which Cleland illustrates the open nature of desire, which corresponds to the endless movement of the eye around a Hogarth print or along the lines of beauty and grace. Although there are many orgasms, and Cleland brings Fanny full circle to a happy closure with her "husband" Charles, the impetus of the novel could be construed as toward an endless string of erotic episodes—desire prolonged indefinitely, analogous to the continuous "joy of pursuit."[9] The movement only comes to an end with marriage, perhaps because at that point the *dulce* of play is definitively closed by the emphatic *utile* of procreation. For Cleland suggests that the aesthetic experience must be extended to the pleasure of intercourse so long as it is play and does not have the end of procreation. Once into marriage, Fanny's narrative must end. The great threshold is of deflowering, not of child-making. The hymen is the liminal area where disinterest and interest meet.[10]

Penetration for Fanny also means a focus on the male organ rather than the female; and this suggests that Cleland uses her to project an aesthetics of the male body (although obviously, since the male reader sees Fanny as well, supplemented by the female). Insofar as Fanny is the perceiver, the first person singular, and the judge, she becomes the subject and the man the object of Cleland's aesthetics; and the beautiful *male* body is treated from the novel perspective of the *female*'s perception, quite reversing Hogarth's categories as they had appeared incipient in his works of the 1730s–40s (and possibly leading him to correct Cleland's emphasis in the *Analysis*).

This is also, like the body of Hogarth's aesthetics, a body that is democratic, to be judged only by itself. While Fanny's rich keepers, Mr. H— and the merchant of Cadiz, exemplify moral issues in their treatment of her (and her of them), in terms of their beauty they are clearly subordinated in Fanny's eyes to Mr. H—'s servant Will and the déclassé Charles. Mr. H— is the brother of an earl and, though understanding and benevolent, discharges Fanny as a master does a servant when he catches her with Will. The other keeper, a respectable merchant, is essentially a friend who gives her dignity and a settlement, treating her socially as an equal and bequeathing her the disinterestedness she will need to marry Charles. On the other hand, Will, a Charles manqué (or substitute), is a servant, and Charles himself is economically and socially a failure. Both, however, have beautiful bodies. In this sense even Dick, the idiot who has only an admirable sexual organ, is regarded like Will and Charles as an aesthetic object.

The criteria Cleland validates (parallel to Toland's and Hogarth's) are both social and economic, and so Fanny represents not only the Beauty of a kind of extreme interestedness and novelty but also, in economic terms, a sort of Shaftesburian *dis*interestedness. Both interestedness and disinterestedness are grounded in her case in social equality. Sexuality, as Hogarth had realized, makes all men equal, and so permits one to judge in terms of beauty rather than either status or wealth, those Shaftesburian bases for disinterestedness.

Amelia's Nose: The Aesthetics of Flawed (Mixed) Character

In the *Champion* essay, Fielding's female figure of Virtue was a real, desirable woman who, under robes decorated with whips and chains, has the charms of Vice without her aspect of the "tawdry, painted Harlot." She is precisely what Hogarth had offered in *Southwark Fair,* just a year after the *Harlot's Progress,* and in *The Distressed Poet, The Sleeping Congregation,* and *Strolling Actresses* of the years following. The first and last show actresses (tantamount to harlots in contemporary sentiment), and *Strolling Actresses* echoes Fielding's own classical travesties.[11] The strolling actress is naked in the sense that, playing the role of Diana (as Chastity), she is losing her dress—and so recalls the unveiling of Diana of the Ephesians (Diana as Nature) in the subscription ticket for the *Harlot.*

From the *Champion* Fielding carries this figure into the dedication to *Tom Jones,* where he makes two provocative statements: Following his declaration that there will be "nothing prejudicial to the Cause of Religion and Virtue," he connects "Example" and "a Kind of Picture, in which Virtue becomes as it were an Object of Sight, and strikes us with an Idea of that Loveliness, which *Plato* asserts there is in her naked Charms"—this immediately after having said he will show nothing "which can offend even the chastest Eye." And he asks two indulgences of the reader: "First, That he will not expect to find Perfection in this Work; and Secondly, That he will excuse some Parts of it, if they fall short of that little Merit which I hope may appear in others" (7–8).

In the introduction to book 4 he introduces Sophia (who is in fact later stripped, but only in the imagination of the lecherous puppetmaster) to his "Male Readers," whom he advises "that however amiable soever the Picture of our Heroine will appear, as it is really a Copy from Nature, many of our fair Country-women will be found worthy to satisfy any Passion, and to answer any Idea of Female Perfection, which our Pencil will be able to raise" (4.1, p. 154). Sophia, representing the "Beauty" of "Nature," is linked to "our fair Country-women." In a passage that immediately precedes this one, Fielding locates Sophia at the end of a spectrum that runs from the Venus de' Medici (the sculpture of a goddess, the Shaftesburian ideal of physical perfection) to the Hampton Court Beauties (portraits, however idealized, of real ladies) and to the real woman Charlotte Cradock Fielding (whom, Fielding tells us, she actually resembles most). This, the real physical female body with its "naked charms," is of course antithetical to the position of both Shaftesbury and Addison and anticipates Hogarth's central formulation in the *Analysis* about the "living woman" who is more beautiful than the most perfect sculpture of a "Grecian Venus" (the Venus de' Medici in plate 1).

Three years later, in *Amelia*, Mrs. James's unsympathetic critique of Amelia's appearance goes all the way back to Addison's triad of Beautiful, Great, and Novel. Mrs. James (who has just been called by her husband "tall," "a tall awkward Monster") responds that Amelia is neither tall nor short but in a middle area between the "pretty" and the "fine" (Addison's Beautiful and Great):

> "There is such a Thing as a Kind of insipid Medium—a Kind of something that is neither one Thing or another. I know not how to express it more clearly; but when I say such a one is a pretty Woman, a pretty Thing, a pretty Creature, you know very well I mean a little Woman; and when I say such a one is a very fine Woman, a very fine Person of a

Woman, to be sure I must mean a tall Woman. Now a woman that is between both, is certainly neither the one nor the other." (11.1, pp. 454–55)

Mrs. James's formulation is intended to be negative, but Fielding's response is not. Amelia's "beauty" falls into the area of the Novel, which Hogarth was redefining at this time in his *Analysis* as the Beautiful.

Amelia, with her scarred nose, is both a specific memory of Charlotte Cradock (whose nose was in reality damaged) and a more schematic extension of the "mixed" or flawed nature of the moral norm in Tom and in *Tom Jones,* connected by way of the "flawed" work of art with the aesthetic object. The distinction would seem to be between the "paragon" of female perfection in a sculptured Venus and the real "Country-woman," now with a scarred nose.

A year later, in his *Analysis,* Hogarth stresses not only the "living woman" but the flaw or contingency—the lock of hair that breaks the perfect oval—which comes from the "mixed character" and work of art described by Fielding in *Tom Jones,* but also from the physical flaw that enhances beauty in Cleland's *Fanny Hill.*[12] Fanny describes her own face as "a roundish oval, except where a pit in my chin had far from a disagreeable effect" (52), and mentions other "flaws" such as a smallpox scar and (most significantly in the present context) the stretch of her vagina following her deflowering (159, 160).

Sophia's "exactly regular" nose is succeeded by Amelia's, "beat all to pieces," which makes Amelia a type of the flawed more in the manner of Fielding's hero Tom and his novel *Tom Jones* than in that of Sophia. "Exactly regular" does not, however, idealize Sophia; she is a mixture of what Reynolds would call "ideal" and "characteristic" beauty—perfect symmetry of limbs but "middle-sized," with a low forehead, and so on. But the aggression and violence of Amelia's nose being "beat all to pieces" requires more than passing notice—as Fielding's critics showed.

In the second edition of *Amelia,* Fielding corrected his embarrassing omission in the first, inserting the successful surgery on Amelia's nose and the argument that the scar actually increased her beauty. The aesthetic dimension—the idea of imperfection (going back to "mixed character")—is added to Mrs. James's account of Amelia's middling status between the Great and the Beautiful. Colonel James, defending

Amelia's appearance, has already described Booth's own nose as "a Nose like the Proboscis of an Elephant," asking, "He handsome?" (11.1, p. 454). The reference is clearly Fielding's to his own nose—which, in the absence of a reference to Amelia's, makes one wonder if unconsciously there was not an aesthetic dimension to Amelia's disfigurement from the outset which linked it for him with his own and led him to overemphasize it—as I shall also suggest, it is linked to the same need Cleland expressed in his fixation on the painful deflowering of Fanny.

We can assume that Fielding made his corrections to Amelia's nose soon after publication of the first edition and the first hostile reviews, but it supposes discourse, perhaps give and take, with Hogarth. What he adds (which will not see print until the first collected edition of his works in 1762, but which has to be read in the context of Hogarth's *Analysis of Beauty* of 1753) is Mrs. James's remark that—in addition to Amelia's neck being "too protuberant for the genteel Size," and "her Eyebrows . . . too large"—"her Nose, as well proportioned as it is, hath a visible Scar on one Side" (1:454). And earlier he adds the remark, which is significantly the author's and not Booth's: "I know not whether the little Scar on her Nose did not rather add to than diminish her Beauty" (4.7, p. 184). This will be precisely Hogarth's argument, concerning the contingencies without which Beauty cannot exist, and the argument is also relevant to Samuel Foote's noseless sculpture on the frontispiece of his farce *Taste* (a satiric dig at Amelia): Hogarth's central claim is for an aesthetics of nature as opposed to art, in which the most perfect antique Venus is nothing compared to a living woman.

It is significant that Fielding makes Amelia's nose into a rationale for the Beautiful—a basis for redefining the Beautiful as he had already redefined his protagonist as "mixed" rather than a paragon in *Tom Jones*. So if *Amelia* is, in the context of the other works of 1751–52, didactic, it is also, given the presence of the specifically beautiful and cathected Amelia, aesthetic. The aesthetic begins as the personal, the private, although Amelia's beauty is also obviously related to the public beauty of Virtue which Fielding equates with his public theme. The two strands are so mingled that we need to distinguish and explicate them.

Beauty before Amelia—before her appearance—is embedded in Newgate, characterized by appearance disguising an unbeautiful (immoral) reality; it is associated with sexual attraction, seduction, betrayal, jealousy, revenge, and "murder." Though this is closer to Hogarth's sense of "Beauty," Fielding intends it, presumably, as a false beauty, corrected with the memories of Amelia, anticipating her actual arrival. Initially these seem to be throwbacks to *Joseph Andrews,* satiric structures exposing the reality under appearances or disguises. But with the recounting of his courtship of Amelia, Booth seems to be contextualizing her in a series that includes not only the "very pretty Girl" whose looks do not correspond to her morality but also the two pretty but pathetic young women who lead up to Miss Matthews, whose beauty conceals a murderess. These are examples of beauty versus or minus goodness, or plus seduction. For Miss Matthews's and Booth's narratives (the latter concerning Amelia herself) do serve to seduce Booth—and under the protestations of conjugal love reveal misdirected, adulterous desire of the sort Hogarth associates with Beauty in the two *Analysis* plates. First, we learn the truth about Dido-Pleasure (vs. Aeneas-Duty); about the naïve Shaftesburian assumption of the correspondence between beauty and virtue; and about Booth's own naïve assumption of the "intrinsic beauty" associated with the "conventional image of femininity," in the Swiftean sense of delusion (in his "Dressing Room" poems).[13] Then we go on to the analysis of Amelia.

From this point Amelia is the object of the "pleasure of pursuit" or of "the chase," a metaphor significantly echoed in the masquerade scene by Miss Matthews (disguised as a shepherdess) and applied to Colonel James: "You are a true Sportsman, . . . for your only Pleasure, I believe, lies in the Pursuit." She translates this to mean: "He gets every handsome Woman he can" (10.2, p. 412). Later Captain Trent is described as the Noble Lord's pointer or setter, on the "Scent of Amelia," a hunter for whom Amelia is the "Game" (11.3, p. 471). At the extreme of this argument, the rankness of the guilt adds zest to the sin (10.2, p. 415), and even Booth's pleasure "lies in the Pursuit" of Amelia.

In book 5, chapter 9, Fielding revives Addison's categories by equating beauty with liking, great qualities with admiration, and good qualities with esteem, but love only with love (226); and in the next chapter, which opens book 6, Amelia's beauty, anticipating the epigraph on the title page of the *Analysis,* is evoked in a series of quotations from *Paradise Lost* in which Adam describes Eve's beauty, but as she appears not to Booth but to Colonel James, the Satan of the story, arousing his passion. The passage is about the power of beauty over men, once again linking beauty and love (230–33).

The retention of Amelia as object, Booth as subject, opens up the issue not only of Amelia's nose but of Booth's peculiarly sadistic treatment of her. In the early books, where he tells the story of Amelia to Miss Matthews, both express misogynist assumptions toward her, with Booth seeming to follow Miss Matthews's lead (indeed, she is instructing him). One suspects that once again (as in Tom, Molly, and Sophia) Fielding is thinking of Booth-Aeneas in terms of the classical choice between two women, one representing seductive Pleasure and the other Virtue. The latter is the Amelia who, misunderstood and egregiously badgered by Booth himself—who instructs her in his theory of the passions—has finally to instruct him. While he condescends to Amelia's womanly inability to philosophize, she expresses her fears for his "atheism" and urges on him (indeed represents) the Christian religion. But Booth first falls in love with Amelia and then, much later, accepts her virtuous instruction (even so, by way of Isaac Barrow, another man). Hogarth's aesthetics stops short of—or ignores—this distinction; or rather, Hogarth sees and explores only the negative, the Miss Matthews or the aspect of pure Pleasure. Nevertheless, though it is Colonel James who most fully embodies the Mandevillian, Booth himself in his own way mistreats and tests Amelia, treating her as if she were a patient Griselda whose patience masks interest.

There is a remarkable sequence of actions in book 2, chapter 2, in which Booth turns his attention to Miss Osborn, telling Amelia he loves another woman, which causes her intense suffering. His behavior is rationalized as on the model of Tom Jones's to Sophia: he loves her so much that he feels he must give her up rather than ruin her (later we hear the old refrain: "the dreadful Idea of having entailed Beggary on my *Amelia* and her Posterity" [9.4, p. 368]). But this explanation is both obscurely put and incommensurate with the strangeness of his stratagem (as compared with Tom's straightforward one). It seems rather a testing of Amelia, taking its place in the larger plot in a series of tests of her virtue—threats that are also tests—by the Noble Lord, Colonel James, but also by Booth himself in his errors and stupidities and cover-ups for the originating act of adultery with Miss Matthews.

Booth's treatment of Amelia can be seen in a number of contexts: the problematic case of Tom; the testing of a paragon (following his reading of *Clarissa,* Fielding's first positive experiment with a Richardsonian heroine); the testing of Shaftesbury's equation of beauty and virtue against Hogarth's skepticism; and the scarring of a nose as the flaw that proves both beauty and virtue. The strange delineation of and emphasis on the pain Booth gives Amelia just prior to the pleasure of marriage and, implicitly, the initiation into sex, may even be seen as a displacement of the deflowering, so crucial for Fanny Hill. The pain that Amelia and Fanny suffer, each at the hands of the man she loves, can be interpreted, among other ways, as a sort of initiation rite that includes distancing the object, along with testing her and causing her to be flawed. (The piquant affect of the Harlot was in part due to the contrast of beauty with imprisonment, flagellation, disease, and death.)

Booth's treatment of Amelia has also to be related to the Noble Lord's behavior to his own women. Mrs. Atkinson says: " 'Good Heavens! what are these Men! What is this Appetite, which must have Novelty and Resistance for its Provocatives; and which is delighted with us no longer than while we may be considered in the Light of Enemies' " (303)—words that could apply to Booth's behavior in book 2, chapter 2, to his abrupt departure to his beloved sister without saying a word to Amelia, and, in some degree, to his behavior throughout. His obtuseness and fecklessness almost—as if he wanted to—permit Amelia's dishonoring. The louche plot of Fielding's play *The Modern Husband* (1732) is not only projected in the Trent plot but is implicit in Booth's acts, which allow readers to enjoy the same antithetical games he plays with Amelia in courtship and permits to be played by the would-be seducers in London. Fielding, Booth, the reader—all on some level find aesthetic experience in the erotic possibilities that go from seeing Amelia with her scarred nose or dressed in rags, to seeing her apparently transgressing at the masquerade (in fact it is Mrs. Atkinson).

All of this evokes Fielding's principle of contrast: not only Booth's quick turns vis-à-vis Amelia but the abrupt contrasts, turns, and surprises of character and plot. These are associated most frequently with that puzzling character Dr. Harrison, who one minute is for and the next against the Booths, having Booth arrested or freeing him; but also with Mrs. Harris, who agrees to Booth's marriage proposal and, while he is away with his dying sister, accepts another suitor—and (apparently) turns on Amelia, repudiating her and cutting her out of her will. These contrasts include the social cuts and snubs of Colonel and Mrs. James, as well as the quick turnabouts of Miss Matthews. They are only partly explained by "changes of fortune," "Surprising Accidents."[14] In *Tom Jones* Fielding put it this way:

> This Vein is no other than that of Contrast, which runs through all the Works of the Creation, and may probably have a large Share in constituting in us the Idea of all *Beauty,* as well natural as artificial: For what *demonstrates the Beauty* and Excellence of any thing *but its Reverse?* Thus the Beauty of Day, and that of Summer, is set off by the Horrors of Night and Winter. And, I believe, if it was possible for a Man to have seen only the two former, he would have a very imperfect Idea of their *Beauty.* (5.1, p. 212; emphasis added)

There was an aesthetic moment based on contrast in *Tom Jones* (9.2): Tom, Partridge, and the Man of the Hill enjoy the prospect from Mazard Hill, which is "most noble" (Addison's Great) but indescribable—inaccessible in this sense to the reader. For Tom, however, the affect is clearly of the Beautiful: he associates the view with Sophia, love, loss, and distance. The experience is similar to an earlier shared view of the moon, which for Tom elicited thoughts of Sophia-love, for Partridge thoughts of dinner.

But at this moment they hear the "most violent Skreams of a Woman," which draw attention to the attempted murder of Jenny Waters. The aesthetic experience has changed, and the responses are different but equally defining. Tom acts to prevent the catastrophe and save the woman. We hear nothing of Partridge's response, but from past experience we infer cowardice. The Old Man, misanthropic and disinterested—the Shaftesburian qualification for enjoying the aesthetic experience—though he has a firearm, sits apart and meditates on the scene. As to the readers, though we have the proper detachment, we probably regard the scene as a moral exemplum, one that the Old Man has rendered aesthetic but to himself only. It is not so to Tom or to Jenny or to Northerton. In short, an aesthetic prospect (which has to be defined as beauty equals love) is broken, interrupted by a terrible sound and act; and Tom's response is moral, virtuous, benevolent, outreaching, an extension of his love of Sophia.

The aesthetic affect of Fielding's chapter, however, is based on the principle of contrast. However Fielding would classify this affect, Addison would have placed it in the area of the Novel. Fielding, like Hogarth, conflates it with the Beautiful, producing another aesthetic fable. If the criteria for the Beautiful are applied, for example, to Jenny Waters, we would conclude that Tom finds her beautiful (sexually attractive, as distinct from the feeling he had for the memory of Sophia) because she has beautiful breasts; or perhaps because she is flawed, homely above the neck but (by contrast) attractive below. When Jenny turns to Tom it is actively to seduce him, a simple anticipation of Miss Matthews's seduction of Billy Booth in *Amelia;* and it is schematized (as in Sophia vs. Molly) to recall Shaftesbury's paradigm of Hercules' choice between Virtue and Pleasure, which has just been materialized for us in the Old Man's story of his unfortunate choices between different forms of virtue and pleasure.

This form of aesthetic experience—the one associated with Jenny Waters, as later with Miss Matthews—is distinguished from the aesthetic experience of Sophia, as lust and appetite are distinguished from love. But in one respect it overlaps with the experience of Sophia, and later with that of Amelia, and that is in the association of beauty with nakedness, threat, rape, and—above all, in the case of Amelia, in this respect a divergence from Sophia—a physical flaw: that is, with violent contrasts both external and internal.

In *Tom Jones* contrast included all the foils set off against Sophia and Tom, but in *Amelia* it is focused only on Amelia and is much more prominent—as in so much of this novel, eccentrically so. It suggests not that something can only be defined by its opposite or negative but that there is a beauty in sheer contrast. In the broadest, most public terms, Amelia's virtue—her lovableness, "so amiable and great a Light"—is set off or defined by Booth's "own Unworthiness" (498).[15]

Amelia is a central symbol of beauty, moral and aesthetic, but she is always seen by men—whether with the Hogarthian "pleasure of the pursuit" of Colonel James or with the protective and loving but unfaithful possessiveness of her husband, Booth. As long as the symbol of Beauty is a woman, the female spectator cannot be curious, desiring, and pursuing. In his play *The Wedding Day* (produced in 1743), Fielding had Mrs. Plotwell remark, "For a Woman to pursue, is for the Hare to follow the Hounds; a Chase opposite to the Order of Nature."[16] The exception was a Mary Hamilton, in Fielding's *Female Husband* (1746), who is a lesbian and so, to Fielding, a perversion of nature. She must disguise herself and try to pass as a man in order to enjoy the experience of her aesthetic (or cathected) object.[17]

Richardson, of course, did raise the question of whether he is addressing a female subject in the same sense that Fielding addresses a male. He also posed the distinction between the subjectivity of a female reader and that of the female object (of the lust of a male subject) within the novel. Pamela is clearly as much a subject as Tom Jones is, and although she writes to her mother and father, she projects a reader of her own gender.

Sophia Western is, within the plot of *Tom Jones*, as much a subject as Tom; his regarding her as such (rather than as a mere object of pleasure) is the moral center of Fielding's novel. In this sense Amelia, thematically at least, represents the case of a subject who, regarded throughout by the men as an object, eventually comes to be accepted (we are told, rather than shown) as another subject by her husband— as she has been throughout by Serjeant Atkinson and her children. In his plays Fielding had written roles for strong actresses, women who played strong, virtuous females, but with a sexual subtext (double entendres, ambiguous gestures), which corresponded to the actresses who played virtuous heroines but were known (or at least supposed) to have immoral private lives (a view of actresses carried over into Hogarth's Diana in *Strolling Actresses*). Thus, in the dedication to *Tom Jones*, female Virtue combined desire (located as the "Beauty of Virtue") with "true Interest." But while she appeared off to the side of Tom as Sophia against the extreme Pleasure of Molly and Jenny (and the "Virtue" of the Man of the Hill's retirement into misanthropy), in *Amelia* Virtue is centered and embodied in a heroine.

For structurally, Amelia is not in the Sophia position but in the Tom position—misread and misrepresented in one way or another by all the characters (except Atkinson and her children, who idolize her).

The characters, good and bad, including both Booth and Dr. Harrison, see her through "misogynist assumptions," and (as Angela J. Smallwood notes) "The reader's concern about the unfair treatment of the heroine in *Amelia* is thus much more widely diffused than in *Tom Jones,* and more comprehensive than the concern of any of the characters who surround her."[18] But if she is in the Tom position as center of interest, and we remain seeing her as we saw Tom from the outside, she nevertheless remains peripheral to the central moral action, which is Booth's—a man's, in what is clearly still, in Shaftesbury's sense, a man's world in which Amelia remains a symbol or, as we have seen, both a moral and an aesthetic object. She is a love object (for all the men), a muse for the author, a wife for Booth, a mediator between Booth and the world (the role Hogarth had given his women in the later 1730s and 1740s), and above all a Charlotte Cradock redivivus. In her, Fielding associates (like Shaftesbury more than Hogarth) beauty, morality, and love.

If the question in *Tom Jones,* and at the outset in *Amelia,* is how Booth can love Amelia and sleep with another woman, by shifting attention from Booth to Amelia—placing, as I have said, Amelia in the Tom Jones position—Fielding sets a new problem: how to get at Amelia, how to represent her virtue, her beauty, how to win her—how to represent her virtue after marriage, how to relate her beauty and virtue (questions that apply to both Booth and the author of the novel). And the answer seems to be: through contraries, deviously, through flaws, and ultimately (in the largest sense) through her flawed, erring husband, as well as her would-be seducers, and all of those who fail to understand her virtue-beauty.

Sentimental Love: Sterne's *Sentimental Journey*

Cleland, according to James Boswell's report, thought "Sterne's bawdy *was* too plain." "I reproved him," Cleland told Boswell, "saying, 'It gives no sensations.' Said he: 'You have furnished me with a vindication. It can do no harm.' 'But,' I *said,* 'if you had a pupil who wrote C— on a wall, would not you flogg him?'"[19] Cleland is presumably referring to *Tristram Shandy,* book 2, chapter 6: "My sister, mayhap, quoth my uncle *Toby*, does not choose to let a man so near her ****." He blurs the distinction between the word (and, indeed, its euphemism, as in his own case) and the act—between *writing* cunt "on a wall," and representing its penetration. Sterne plays with the word but maintains a distance, never letting "a man so near her ****."

The aesthetics of the Novel continues to dominate *Tristram Shandy* (1759–67) and *A Sentimental Journey through France and Italy* (1768), which consistently reveal, under abstracted thought, sensations ranging from sympathy to sexual desire. These narratives, particularly the second, materialize a sequence of pursuit, flight, and dawdling that is obsessively centered on a woman's body. In *A Sentimental Journey*, Parson Yorick is the man of taste seeking (pursuing) an aesthetic experience based on constant movement and variety, but always with a sexual subtext that not only replicates Hogarth's advice in the *Analysis* but now introduces the terms of travel which William Gilpin will call Picturesque (see chapter 9, below).[20]

However, Sterne seems to be reclaiming aesthetics from both Hogarth and Cleland by recovering, or at least redefining, disinterestedness. Yorick makes *sentimental* love into an artful substitute for both aspects of Mandevillian interest, sexual and economic. He feels no inclination to give alms to the Franciscan monk (whom he associates with popery and French imprisonments and confiscations) until he sees him with a woman, Mme de L***, at which point his veins distend in a parody of tumescence as his purse strings loosen, and he presses her hand throughout most of volume 1. But while every scene is about sexual desire and its pleasures, the scene always stops just short of the act.

Yorick's approach to intimacy with Mme de L*** is held in check in volume 1 by the memory of his "sentimental love" for Eliza, who is bodily in India and whose portrait only is in his hand (the hand with which he holds the hand of Mme de L***). Later, "conscience" causes him to follow the chapter called "The Temptation" (on temptation by the Fille de Chambre) with one called "The Conquest." Volume 1 gets only as far as Mme de Rambouillet's urethra, ending with her "Rien que pisser," as Yorick urges her to "p——ss on" and invokes the decorum of worshiping (as a source of his poetic inspiration) at the "fountain" of this "chaste Castalia" (recalling Tristram's ability with his "lover"

Jenny only to "pisser"). And volume 2 ends literally with a fille de chambre's "End" being "caught hold of" through a curtain: a closure that is left open.

It is instructive to note that Ralph Griffiths, reviewing *Sentimental Journey* in the *Monthly Review,* commented on the Fille de Chambre episode, which is a mass of double entendres but not physically consummated: "Is it *possible* that a man of *gross ideas* could ever *write* in a strain so pure, so refined from the dross of sensuality!" The exception was the final chapter, with its "ludicrous *hiatus*" at the end.[21]

It is as if Sterne is responding to Cleland's emphasis on breaking the hymen with the risqué but acceptable substitute of breaching a curtain, a harmless parody of sexual penetration, which for Yorick at least offers the possibility of going beyond virginity without physical intimacy—without losing his disinterestedness, which in the clerical context means without disgracing himself.

Sterne returns to the borderline situation, the threshold of sexual intercourse itself, and will not go over it. Only once, near the end of volume 1, in a sequence of sections that proceed from the visual translatability of the old officer's French in the theater to the explicit language of Mme de Rambouillet ("rien que pisser"), does Yorick leave the word *connection* intact with both its senses, communication and sexual intercourse. He reports another of these translation/connection encounters going to a concert in Milan, this time with the Marquisina di F**:

> —so I instantly stepp'd in [to her coach], and she carried me home with her—And what became of the concert, St. Cecilia, who, I suppose, was at it, knows more than I.
>
> I will only add, that the connection which arose out of that translation, gave me more pleasure than any one I had the honour to make in Italy. (173)

A Sentimental Journey sets out to define and explore the limits of "sentimental love," and I suspect that the encounter with the Marquisina di F** is only intended to try the limits, which remain intact. Yorick penetrates purses and plackets instead of vaginas. The requirements are not sexual intercourse but sympathy and courtship, first embodied practically in Sterne's *Journal to Eliza* (1767) and then dramatically and theoretically in *A Sentimental Journey.*

In the *Journal to Eliza* (addressed to Eliza Draper), Sterne goes back to Shaftesbury's example of disinterestedness in epistolary correspondence by which, Philocles says, he was "forced to form a kind of material object, and had always such a certain image of him [of Palemon] ready drawn in my mind whenever I thought of him" (*Characteristics* 2:39). The limits are on the one side formal (marriage) and on the other sensuous (sexual intercourse with a lover outside marriage). But sentimental love is also defined in terms of other forms of limitation and excess: the limits of reason and sense, one checking the other, reason distancing the senses; or, closer to the deflowering of Fanny, the limits of pain and pleasure. Pain in Yorick's case is the disgracing of his cloth or his sense of Shandean "politeness." Yorick is a clergyman, and he makes this very clear by carrying his clerical attire with him to France: he will appear as a clergyman in the various dubious *affaires de coeur* in which he engages. The clerical attire both prevents him from going too far and adds a poignancy to every encounter. Thus pain obviously outweighs, though it may also contribute to, the pleasure.

Both Sterne and Yorick are clergymen. Also relevant are the reputation of the author of *Tristram Shandy* (it was disgraceful for a cleric to write such a book) and the casual physical encounters in which he had previously indulged—an extreme of libertinage which Sterne's readers would have associated with his friends John Hall-Stevenson and John Wilkes. Sterne joined Wilkes at one party in Paris with (in Wilkes's words) "two lively, young, handsome actresses," a pair of whores.[22] "Sentimental love" was played out at more sedate parties in conversations characterized by Sterne's addressing Shandean double entendres to women (as opposed to the acceptable practice of clergymen speaking obscenities to other men). His "friend" Garrick described him as a "*lewd companion,* even wilder in society than in his writings, usually driving away all the women through his obscenities." We can only guess at these, but in a letter to "Mrs. F" he writes with typical double entendre that he will run into "Satyre & sarcasm—scoffing & flouting—rallying & reparteeing of it,—thrusting & parrying in one dark corner or another."[23]

The other distancing factors in the case of the *Journal to Eliza* were Eliza Draper's relative youth and frail constitution, her marriage to a brute she did not love, her residence in far-off India, and Sterne's own estrangement from his wife. "I'm half in love with You," he writes. "—I ought to be *wholly so*—for I never valued . . . or thought more of one of Y^r Sex than of You" (298). The public show of affection—especially when she is herself absent—is permitted because there is nothing physical, and thus, in terms of the cloth, shameful. But primarily the affair is conducted in writing—and writing that is a mixture of the real and the fictional, a real diary passed off as fictional, real and fictional names mingled ("Draper" for Draper, but "Yorick" for Sterne) in a document that is both intensely personal and was read aloud by Sterne to friends at parties. He showed Eliza's picture and letters to friends, referred to her by name in *Sentimental Journey,* and even wrote to her husband: "I fell in Love with y^r Wife, but tis a Love You would honour me for—for tis so like that I bear, my own daughter" (349). Indeed, when his daughter Lydia returned following the abandoning of the *Journal to Eliza,* she replaced Eliza in the same relationship of sentimental love.[24] The writing itself is a mingling of erotic and infantile, as well as of conventional love imagery and comic innuendo, fantasizing and truth-telling (for example, on Easter Sunday concerning the severe pain in his testicles [138, 141–42]).

Showing Eliza's picture and talking about her with a lady at a party, Sterne reports himself to Eliza as saying,

> O my dear Lady, cried I, did you but know the Original—but what is she to you, Tristram—nothing; but that I am in Love with her—et caetera—said she—no I have given over dashes—replied I—

The syntax and punctuation are ambiguous, but Sterne seems to mean us to read "[her] et caetera" as spoken by the lady, filling in the pause as Sterne's Tristram would have with an obscene pun; with Sterne himself now replying penitently: "—no I have given over dashes" (183).

Sentimental love, as Sterne practiced it and analyzed it in *A Sentimental Journey* ("sentimental" implies that he did both), is precisely equivalent to an aesthetics that is a revision or refinement of, in their different ways, both Cleland's and Hogarth's. Sterne, in effect, argues that the erotic has to maintain a certain distance between subject and object; if the sexual "pursuit" and innuendo crossed over into sexual contact it would no longer be aesthetic; it would be once again life—in this case, in the sense of indecorum, a married clergyman having sexual relations with women, married and unmarried.

It is possible, looking back, to argue that Hogarth's woman was also something other than just a woman; she was an actress in the role of Diana, or a sculpted Venus with a living woman trying to get out (catching the eye of the Apollo Belvedere). There is, however, a more significant contrast between Sterne's man, and Hogarth's woman slipping out of her Diana costume, or the woman emerging from the Venus imposed on her by convention (by art, by stage managers). He is, after all, as Yorick or an Englishman (the church and nation get the blame), like the poor starling who cannot get out of his cage—his own repressions, the prison of his body—and join Bevoriskius in putting down his writing long enough to count the number of copulations carried on by the sparrows on his window sill (228–29).[25]

In *Sentimental Journey* Sterne and Parson Yorick are practicing "sentimental love" to avoid giving sway to their sexual urges. In *Tristram Shandy* Uncle Toby, the sketch for a sentimental lover, is shocked to discover the Widow Wadman's sexuality. But neither he, who ends "in a resolution, nevermore to think of the sex,—or of aught which belonged to it," nor Walter, who (once he has become a husband) detests love and women, is to be imitated. Yorick may be Sterne's response to the failure of Toby and Tristram, both of whom are prevented by their wounds from sexual intercourse. Being a sentimental lover, Yorick can keep love aesthetic, at the crucial moment stepping back to maintain his Shaftesburian balance.

So far, the structure has seemed to be that of the Freudian joke, with the tendentiousness of the jest (the Hogarthian pursuit) aimed as a kind of sexual attack on the woman. As we saw in the case of Amelia, this objectivization is apparently the only way the woman gets into the aesthetic experience. We can define the objecthood of Yorick's woman by placing her in Eve Sedgwick's argument that the monk and M. Dessin mediate Yorick's desire for Mme de L***; that it is the monk and not the woman who is the focus of Yorick's attention, as part of a Shaftesburian, homosocial community.[26] My argument would suggest that, in fact, seeing the woman with the monk is what causes Yorick to give the monk alms in order to make himself look good in the eyes of the woman. But if she is the object in the aesthetic (or distanced erotic) experience, she is not necessarily the subject addressed.

If Yorick's obscene puns are (in the Freudian sense) aimed at the woman, then a female reader is implied, as in the social situation described by Garrick and others in which Sterne addressed sexual innuendos to women at parties in order to shock them. In the *Journal to Eliza* Eliza is literally the reader, but there are also the men and women to whom Sterne read passages, and there is even Eliza's husband, whom (to judge by Sterne's letter to him) he is including in the address. This would explain "sentimental love" as love in which the aggression—the sexual act—is verbal rather than physical, another version of Toby's reconstructed fortifications vis-à-vis the actual battles, and intended for the pleasure (including edification) of a third party. Tristram/Sterne reveals sexual innuendo under every reference but, at the same time, retreats from every female (perhaps obscene puns are a form of retreat in the Shandean world rather than, as Freud argued, a form of seduction).

At the least, the aesthetic object still consists, as it did for Hogarth and Fielding, of more than the living woman. In Hogarth's scenario there was the beautiful woman and the pursuit of her in a larger "novelistic" situation involving her husband, an artist's representations of her, and a young man who carries the Shaftesburian aesthetic (or possessive) contemplation over into pursuit. This triad was essentially repeated in Cleland's Fanny, Charles, and the paying customers of the brothel. In Sterne's scenario, however, the lover is sentimental and the husband indifferent, and total attention is focused on the representation of the woman. Words are substituted for actions, as in the maps and verbal substitutes for Toby's wound in his groin. For, we might add, while the fortifications of Namur were the ostensible object of Toby's reconstruction, an aesthetic object made of commonplace domestic items such as those recommended by Hogarth (sash weights, jackboots, spouts, gutters, and pewter shaving basins), the reader soon comes, with the Widow Wadman, to see the true object as Toby's groin. And Toby's wounded groin is, of course, only a digressive analogy for the book's central subject, Tristram's wounded body.

Sir Roger, Uncle Toby, and the Two Widows

Tristram Shandy is centered on the human body and the senses' coming to terms with the body. But the body in question is the male body, not the female as in either *Amelia* or Sterne's own sequel, *A Sentimental Journey*. It is as if in *Tristram Shandy* Sterne consciously replaces the female body with a male. The woman's body, while always present, is only implicit in the *other*, in the Widow Wadman's—whereas the central concern is the Widow Wadman's in Uncle Toby's body.

In *Tristram Shandy* the female aesthetic object (of pursuit) can be formulated in either of two ways: as a de-idealization or a disappearance. If the first, the book can be read as another work in the Hogarthian anti-Shaftesbury tradition. But if the second, it represents a parodic return to Shaftesbury's civic humanist ideal. The society of Shandy Hall is resolutely male. Uncle Toby is certainly an arms-bearing civic humanist (though not of the militia, preferred by civic humanists to a standing army) but now retired and with his masculinity in question: whether as a result of his service or of his natural "modesty" is never certain. But Shandy Hall does not idealize its females; rather, it elides or marginalizes them. The blank page in volume 6, where the reader is supposed to visualize for himself the Widow Wadman, is the crux—the only place where a potentially idealized woman appears. Mrs. Shandy is herself virtually a "blank page," and Jenny, whose conversation consists largely of asterisks, serves Tristram as an equally disinterested lover.

Although the Widow Wadman's image is a blank, she is very concretely represented by her disposal of the corking pin and by the dirty thumbprint she leaves on the map of Bouchain, both aggressive love tokens. We should note that the Widow Wadman comes to *Tristram Shandy* by way of the threatening figure of Sir Roger de Coverley's Widow in the *Spectator*. Wadman reverses the situation: the disinterest of Sir Roger's Widow was focused on her suitor Sir Roger; Wadman discovers the disinterest in her male suitor Toby, at least once he has ascertained why she wants to know where he was wounded.

In terms of Addisonian aesthetics, the associations given the Widow, Sir Roger, and their courtship are of the Strange. In the papers on the visit to Sir Roger's country house, Mr. Spectator finds his attention turning toward the "country" or "faerie" subjects of ghosts (No. 110), witches (No. 117), and gypsies and fortune telling (No. 130). In this setting Mr. Spectator's role as spectator of the Novel leads the country folk to take him for a murderer, a conjurer, a "white witch," and a Jesuit—transgressive figures with the qualities of the Novel become the Strange, and very much outside the range of Shaftesburian aesthetics. Thus, when observation and observer become the observed, as was often to prove the case, the Novel becomes the Strange and Mr. Spectator becomes an object that stimulates from others (from his own spectators) a "variety of opinions" (2:20).[27]

Sir Roger's unfortunate "courtship" of the "amorous" Widow is detailed in his own words (No. 113):

> a Beautiful Creature in a Widow's Habit . . . born for Destruction of all who behold her . . . this perverse Woman is one of those unaccountable Creatures that secretly rejoice in the Admiration of Men, but indulge themselves in no further Consequences. Hence it is that she has ever had a Train of Admirers, and she removes from her Slaves in Town, to those in the Country, according to the Seasons of the Year. . . . She has certainly the finest Hand of any Woman in the World. I can assure you, Sir, were you to behold her, you would be in the same Condition; for as her Speech is Musick, her Form is Angelick; but I find I grow irregular while I am talking of her, but indeed it would be Stupidity to be unconcerned at such Perfection. (1:466)

I would emphasize the words "Angelick" and "Perfection." The Widow rejects Sir Roger, and in No. 115 Mr. Spectator reports:

> The perverse Widow, whom I have given some account of, was the Death of several Foxes, for Sir Roger has told me that in the Course of his Amours he patched the Western Door of his Stable. Whenever the Widow was cruel the Foxes were sure to pay for it. In proportion as his Passion for the Widow abated, and old Age came on, he left off Fox-hunting, but a Hare is not yet safe that Sits within ten Miles of his House. (1:473)

The chase of the Widow, equated with the chase of foxes and hares, is not unlike Hogarth's version of the metaphor, and Sir Roger's "amours" surely found their way into "my Uncle Toby's amours." In No. 116 Mr. Spectator comments on the "innocent," "lively Pleasure" of the hunt, though he is somewhat concerned "on the Account of the poor Hare, that was now quite spent, and almost within the Reach of her Enemies":

> [Sir Roger] took up the Hare in his Arms; which he soon after delivered to one of his Servants, with an Order, if she could be kept alive, to let her go in his great Orchard, where, it seems, he has several of these Prisoners of War, who live together in a very comfortable Captivity. I was highly pleas'd to see the Discipline of the Pack, and the Good-nature of the Knight, who could not find in his Heart to murther a creature that had given him so much Diversion. (1:478)

Next comes the paper on witches (No. 117), followed by another on the Widow (No. 118), and one on the evil counsel of the Widow's female confidant, and finally one in No. 130 on gypsies and the fortune teller who predicts Sir Roger's "future." Here, in its most sensitively fictional spot, Addison's Novel associates women, love, and hunting, with irrational elements, where spectatoring comes dangerously near to losing its disinterestedness but "Curiosity" is still the "prevailing passion."[28]

No. 412, we recall, completed the trajectory from the "Pleasures" of the Novel or Uncommon to the Strange, indeed from pleasure to pain. Addison focuses on Fancy (usually a female figure), and goes from there into abstruse or inappropriate allusions, analogies, or allegories.[29] The latter (a memory of the essays on false wit) he associates with the Novel or Uncommon, rather than the Great or Beautiful, and his first example is of thwarted love: "I have read a Discourse upon Love, which none but a profound Chymist could understand." While he brings the "Pleasures of the Imagination" to a climax with his analogy between the poet's power "of affecting the Imagination" and the Creator's (the poet creates "Objects which are not to be found in Being," "Additions to Nature"), he actually ends with a coda on "those contrary objects, which are apt to fill it with Distaste and Terrour; for the Imagination is as liable to Pain as Pleasure": "When the Brain is hurt by any Accident, or the Mind disordered by Dreams or Sickness, the Fancy is over-run with wild dismal Ideas, and terrified with a thousand hideous Monsters of its own framing" (3:578). This strangeness is located in the "mortifying" sight of "a Distracted Person," and Addison's example is again about love: a simile from the *Aeneid* in which the delusions of Pentheus and Orestes, caused in both cases by mothers, are used to explain the madness of Dido following Aeneas's desertion. It would seem to be relevant that Virgil, the poet, sees from the point of view of Aeneas, Pentheus, and Orestes rather than of the women whose madness produced the response. Nor, failing to complete the simile with the name Dido, does Addison distinguish from the madness of Pentheus and Orestes the absence of affect Dido's madness has on Aeneas (whose ears had been sealed by the gods and denied "the thrill of grief"). And, continuing to deny the presence of the obviously central woman, he concludes by emphasizing "the influence that one Man has over the Fancy [again, a female personification] of another." Having at this point left behind both the woman and the Novel/Uncommon/Strange, he ends by giving the Great the emphasis Burke will give it: "In short, he [the poet of the Great] can so exquisitely ravish or torture the Soul through this single Faculty [the imagination], as might suffice to make up the whole Heaven or Hell of any finite Being" (580).

In one sense Sir Roger is Addison's rewriting of Swift's Grub Street Hack and other figures of modern solipsism (e.g., the spider, the Banbury Saint) but revalued as a Tory and reinterpreted by a sympathetic Whig: a sketch for the strategy Sterne applies to Walter, Toby, and Tristram. In the background, in Addison's theory of comedy, Sir Roger is "something of an Humourist; and . . . his Virtues, as well as Imperfections, are as it were tinged by a certain Extravagance, which makes them particularly *his,* and distinguishes them from those of other Men" (No. 106, 1:440). As Addison well understood, this humor figure was Swift's normative country gentleman. But while Swift would have ridiculed the humor figure into which Addison turns him, this is precisely the eccentricity and slight madness for which Mr. Spectator, the members of his club, and Sir Roger's neighbors all love him.

In political terms, Addison is drawing on the Restoration imagery of widows. Aside from the folklore of lecherous widows, the most notable precursor was Hudibras's widow, who was courted for her "riches" and rejected the Puritan in no uncertain terms. This, the main plot of Butler's mock epic (1662 ff.), may have been in Addison's mind when he substituted a Tory country gentleman for the Presbyterian Hudibras. George Etherege's *Comical Revenge* (1664) formulated the counterplot in which the cavalier succeeds as the Puritan had failed with the widow who is surrogate for the restored nation.[30]

The other side of the coin, however, is the homosocial circle whose integrity is threatened by the Widow (as by witchcraft and the Strange). The visit to Sir Roger's house includes the picture gallery, which represents a cross-section of English history in Sir Roger's ancestors (No. 108, 1:449 ff.). (The sequence ends with a demotic portrait of Sir Roger as a revision—of the sort later carried out in Hogarth's Sign-painters' Exhibition—of the sign of a Saracen's Head [No. 122, 1:500].) The crucial picture, however, precedes the picture gallery and is of his male-bonding with the servant who saved his life (an anticipation of Corporal Trim). It shows the naked Sir Roger with his liveried servant, and it prompts his explanation that it was only at the servant's insistence (Sir Roger has rewarded him with property of his own) that he was portrayed in the livery he wore at the time when he saved his master's life (No. 107, 1:445). Addison projects a relationship of Sir Roger, his servant, and Mr. Spectator which is very much at odds with Sir Roger's supposed desire for the Widow, who is subordinated to his more substantial desire for the homosocial pursuit of foxes and hares.[31]

Sir Roger and Uncle Toby comprise a polite and gentlemanly version of Shaftesbury's aristocratic civic humanist. It seems that one thing at stake here, at a deeper level, is Shaftesbury's negative emphasis on the feminine (and this is also part of his Platonic denigration of the body, which tends to be female) and therefore the intersection of his discourse of civic humanism and one of homoeroticism (the need for "the citizen to triumph over his own [hetero]sexuality").[32] Sterne creates a comedy of disablement centered on Toby, Tristram, and Yorick, who are contrasted with the vibrant young plebeians Trim, Bridget, and Trim's brother Tom and his Portuguese widow. Indeed Tom's widow echoes Toby's (and Sir Roger's) as the popular symbol of extra-lusty womanhood and the threat she poses to the Shandean civic humanism. Like the Beguine, the widows have been forced into a conventual life from which they seek an outlet, however unsuccessfully. The source of the ethos in the *Characteristicks* and the *Spectator* is the primary evidence in favor of the interpretation of *Tristram Shandy* as a homosocial world and of *Sentimental Journey* as a series of encounters based on homosocial desire in which the men are the real focus of the attention aimed at women. If *Tristram Shandy* offers any precedent, Uncle Toby addresses Walter—and shies away from addressing the Widow Wadman directly. (She is always, like Mrs. Shandy, listening in, eavesdropping, or spying; like Sterne's female addressee, she always misinterprets the text and must be corrected.) The Shandean male-bonding—the triumph of Adam without his Eve, remaining in the safe Shandean garden—has to be contrasted with Yorick sailing out into wartime France, where, however, he remains as untouched as Toby. In these terms, the monk, M. Dessin, and the other males are complicit, used by the speaker Yorick as accomplices, and the man and his approval are the real center of attention—and in that sense, we have to distinguish between an aesthetic object (the woman) and a rhetorical subject (the man): he is the one being acted upon rhetorically, being persuaded. In this sense, Yorick/Sterne's real subject is Eugenius, Garrick, Hogarth, and the monk, even Mr. Draper; and the sentimental situation implicitly includes the male who desires (and aestheticizes) the female.

Burke's Beautiful and Sublime

In his *Philosophical Enquiry into the Origin of Our Ideas of the Sublime and Beautiful* (1757), Burke privileged the Sublime, but, as Frances Ferguson has noted, the Burkean Sublime and Beautiful both lead to the same stasis: if the Sublime *forces,* the Beautiful *flatters* us "into compliance."[33] And the Beautiful does so by feigned "imperfections" (what Hogarth referred to as the contingency of the lock of hair that breaks the perfect oval of the face). To these "imperfections" are added "weakness," by which Burke means that women "learn to lisp, to totter in their walk, to counterfeit weakness, and even sickness," because "Beauty in distress is much the most affecting beauty. Blushing has no little power; and modesty in general, which is a tacit allowance of imperfection, is itself considered as an amiable quality, and certainly heightens every other that is so" (110). This is not so much Hogarthian as a recollection of the affected politeness of a man without a limp carrying a cane—a fashion criticized by the *Spectator*—or of Belinda's "purer blushes" in *The Rape of the Lock*. The "gradual variations" of the body shape, especially the breasts, serve, according to Burke, to create a "deceitful maze, through which the unsteady eye slides giddily, without knowing where to fix, or whither it is carried" (115). These words could again be Hogarth's, applied to the same object, but for Burke they carry an almost Shaftesburian negativity. The physiological responses he describes in the male observer ("The head reclines something on one side; the eyelids are more closed than usual, and the eyes roll gently with an inclination to the object, the mouth is a little opened, and the breath drawn slowly, with now and then a low sigh; the whole body is composed, and the hands fall idly to the sides") suggest something quite different from the pursuit and achievement of pleasure described by Hogarth. Burke's result is instead "an inward sense of melting and languor" which "very much enfeebles the tone of the stomach" (149, 154). "The best remedy for all these evils" of the Beautiful, cited by Burke as a sort of cold shower, is in fact the Novel, or what Hogarth called the Beautiful: "exercise or *labour;* and labour is a surmounting of *difficulties,* an exertion of the contracting power of the muscles" (135). But this remedy returns Burke to the Sublime.

The fact is that Burke, although he posits an aesthetic subject that is not elite but universal, does partake of the Shaftesburian anti-Venus fraternity. His example of the Trojan War illustrates, in Ferguson's words (51), "beauty's disastrous consequences not only for the body but for the body politic as well":

> It may be observed, that Homer has given the Trojans, whose fate he has designed to excite our compassion, infinitely more of the amiable social virtues than he has distributed among his Greeks. With regard to the Trojans, the passion he chooses to raise is pity; pity is a passion founded on love; and these *lesser,* and if I may say, domestic virtues are certainly the most amiable. (158)

Although in this minor sense the Burkean Sublime is the heir of the founding Shaftesburian tradition of aesthetics, in a larger sense it is an innovative attempt to replace the "ethical" mode of that tradition, and in that sense it provides an alternative distinct from both Shaftesburian and Hogarthian traditions. But if Burke's Sublime provides an alternative to the Shaftesburian Beautiful, Hogarth and those sympathetic with his aims respond to what they would regard as the mystification of the Sublime with the extension of Addison's Novel into the Strange.

As to *Tristram Shandy*, the above passage could be taken as virtually an epitome, equating the Shandys and the Trojans. Sterne is accepting Burke's negative interpretation of the Beautiful, but without seeing it as a foil to the Sublime. Let me quote Ferguson's description of Burke's Beautiful: "For although the sublime inspires us with fear of our death, the beautiful leads us toward death without our awareness"; "the beautiful associates itself with a slow and almost imperceptible movement toward death" (52). Applied to Tristram's main concern, his impending death, these words suggest both the opposite of his own solution (a Hogarthian or Swiftean "vive la bagatelle") and, sadly, the drift of the Shandy family toward extinction.

In both *Tristram Shandy* and *Sentimental Journey*, for the aesthetic situation to obtain, the family, which remains the central unit of both Fielding and Smollett, has to come to an end; the social love of the Beautiful has to dissolve into something—just offstage—that is based on power and pain (and death). Aesthetic or sentimental love, like Shandean impotence, produces no offspring, unless as texts, which of course it does produce in abundance. *Sentimental Journey* is thus the discovery of sentimental (proper) communication outside the family, which is obtained only occasionally and with great difficulty within the family.[34] It is simplistic to say that the homoerotic ethos is life-denying, art-reifying, but this is essentially the message of the civic humanists from Shaftesbury (in its strongest form), to Addison (in its most accommodating), to Sterne (in its most ironic, cynical, and self-defeating). But with the beautiful object marginalized, left blank, or *estranged*, all that remains is to push the epistemology of the Novel in the direction of the Strange.

The reader of the first volumes of *Tristram Shandy* was invited to a Hogarthian pursuit, based on pleasure, curiosity, and surprise. Curiosity, or inquisitiveness, as a principle first set forth in the beginning of volume 1, leads straight to the last page of the volume, with its challenge to the reader to guess what is coming on the next page. Introduced in the early chapters (a corrective to the regularity and obstinacy of Walter Shandy and Mrs. Shandy's association of clock and sex), curiosity focuses on the overly precise dating of Tristram's conception; though he assures us his birth was a full nine months later, the gestation adds up to only eight months, which focuses the "curious" reader on the question of paternal identity and the first stage of dismantling the idea of "family."

The centerpiece is the birth, once more historicized as a mysterious Nativity of the sort Hogarth implied in the *Harlot's Progress*. There is the triangle of aged, sciatic father, aggrieved mother (by the legalism of her marriage contract), and—perhaps—Yorick himself, the lively jester and cleric whom Tristram much more closely resembles, in both body and spirit, than his "father." The theological discussion of the efficacy of Tristram's baptism hinges on such issues as whether the words *"in nomino patriae & filia & spiritum sanctos"* would still be efficacious with the wrong terminations. The opinion reached from the learned arguments is that neither mother nor father is "kin to her child": "It is held, said *Triptolemus*, the better opinion; because the father, the mother, and the child, though they be three persons, yet are they but (*una caro*) one flesh; and consequently no degree of kindred—or any method of acquiring one *in nature*" (4.29, pp. 326, 330). This is, of course, the vocabulary of the Trinitarian dispute (above, chap. 2). Walking out of the conference, Yorick concludes that "no mortal, Sir, has any concern with" Tristram's birth,

> for Mrs. *Shandy* the mother is nothing at all akin to him—and as the mother's is the surest side—Mr. *Shandy*, in course, is still less than nothing—in short, he is not as much akin to him, Sir, as I am—
> —That may well be, said my father, shaking his head. (4.30, p. 331)[35]

When the pleasure of pursuit involves Tristram himself in volume 7, it is a flight from the pursuit of Death; and only once he is out of Death's reach can he pursue the Nut Brown Maid and the ideal of *vive la bagatelle*—but this proves to be a dance *away from* the Maid's open placket, the sight of her naked flesh. Volume 7 ends with this dancing, and the pattern of his dance goes straight onto the page on which he is inscribing volume 8, the amours of Uncle Toby. The dance takes the form of the lines on the page and then the words and the rest of the Shandean paraphernalia of communication, exactly paralleling the relationship, in plate 2 of Hogarth's *Analysis,* of the country dance with diagrams representing it and with the verbal (theoretical, aesthetic, rhetorical) account of it in the text of the *Analysis*. Throughout the spatial metaphor, based on the reading of Hogarth's prints and its formulation in the *Analysis,* Sterne equates the pen, pencil (paint brush), chisel, and fiddlestick that trace the lines, making them "swell" toward a "true Beauty," with sublimations of the sexual drive (anticipating in this respect the graphic representations of Rowlandson).

Sterne's sense of writing partakes of both the play of Hogarth's *Analysis of Beauty* and the death-wish of Burke's Beautiful, but resolutely avoids the Sublime. His dedication rewrites Fielding's dedication to *Tom Jones:* Sterne says that his work is not a great work of creation, merely an "endeavour to fence against the infirmities of ill health, and other evils of life, by mirth." While Fielding invokes the order of a balanced work of art (of religion, law, and art), Sterne hopes that his work will "[add] something to this Fragment of life." Tristram attempts to *reconstruct* (show where he was wounded), which he depicts as a mirthful activity, and the hobbyhorse is his grotesque version, if not parody, of Shaftesbury's and Fielding's work of art.

The *Analysis* clearly mediates between *Tom Jones* and *Tristram Shandy,* where obliquity is now the criterion, rules are flouted, and sheer curiosity and inquisitiveness draw on the reader, who is on a wavelength with Tristram, who is trying to understand his origins and so explain them to the curious reader. This is opposed to the regularity (obstinacy) of his father, his mother's association of sex and winding the clock, and the precise dating of Tristram's conception. Curiosity and imprecision join in the search for the exact time of Tristram's conception, which begins the series of flaws, misadventures, and accidents—contingencies that mimic poor Amelia's nose in one scene and replace it with Tristram's penis in another. While Fielding, even in his dedication, draws attention to the "flaws" in his great work of creation, Sterne moves Hogarth's lock of hair that breaks a perfect oval, as well as Fielding's blemishes, from the margins to the center.

He takes off also from Burke's feigned imperfections. He did not need Amelia's nose, but if we regard noses as a nexus of intertextuality in the tradition of the Novel, we might note that beginning with Hogarth's lock of hair, Fielding materializes the notion of flaw in a crushed nose, and Sterne then proceeds from Tristram's crushed nose to Slawkenbergius's interminable nose, which is the cause of the fall of Strasbourg, and to the Shandy nose, which is the emblem at least (if not the cause) of the fall of the house of Shandy. We are seeing the flaw that distinguishes a kind of beauty from Shaftesburian sculptural perfection exaggerated and mythologized and hyperbolized. And, also characteristic of the development from Beautiful/Novel to Strange, if volume 4 begins with Slawkenbergius's nose it ends with an altogether different kind of a disaster, which places all the others in perspective: Brother Bobby's death. Tristram's pain is only implicit, but Walter's— and, above all, Toby's—is on stage.

If in *Tom Jones* the problem addressed was in the question Does Tom really love Sophia? (Does Black George really love Tom?) the problem addressed in *Tristram Shandy* was in the question Where was Toby wounded? And whereas neither writer relied on divine presence for an answer, Fielding embodied the answer in the "great Creation" of Fielding's parallel world of art, while Sterne tentatively and provisionally added fragment to fragment including words, maps, models, simulations, in vain attempts to communicate and be understood. The efficacy of the Shaftesburian substitute world is no longer present to bolster the belief in the moral sense.

Although Hogarth absolutely opposed his Beautiful and the Burkean Sublime in his final print, *Tail Piece; or, The Bathos* (1764), as beautiful serpentine lines are broken into total disjunctions by the forces of chaos and death, Sterne shows that the opposition is not absolute. For Hogarth the political surrogate of the Burkean Sublime was William Pitt, the symbol of grandiloquent oratory and expansionist politics. Sterne said that he came to London in order to associate two people with his work—Hogarth and William Pitt.[36] Hogarth supplied illustrations and Pitt accepted the dedication of the book. In the spring of 1760 Pitt was at the height of his popularity, power, and success; to Sterne (as opposed to Hogarth) he would have represented politics outside the old electoral system, a new voice, a great orator addressing the "people" and circumventing the "politicians"; and, of course, he was expanding the British empire with incredible military victories. But with his name would also have gone unavoidably some sense of the casualties of his wars, on the Continent as well as in all corners of the globe. Addressed to Pitt, Sterne's version of the Novel is an attempt to "[beguile] you of one moment's pain," and the application would have been public as well as personal, the Seven Years' War and Toby's wound as well as the "woundings" of Tristram. The War of the League of Augsburg and the War of the Spanish Succession—Uncle Toby's wars—were equivalents of the contemporary Seven Years' War. When the peace of 1763 is concluded, Toby's war also comes to an end—with volumes 5 and 6.

In the next two volumes, 7 and 8, Sterne seems to have remembered a particular Hogarth print (which Hogarth had composed as an homage to *Tom Jones*), *The March to Finchley* (1750; fig. 33). The Abbess of Andouillet's departure from her convent, with all her nuns at the windows, is described in terms of the rows of whores protruding from the geometrical grid of windows of the Finchley brothel—Sterne's way of suggesting the analogy of convent and brothel and of variety exceeding uniformity (7:12, p. 505). But he also picks up on the soldier who is painfully trying to urinate at the left edge of *Finchley* and the liquidity that unfolds to the right in wine, gin, and other intoxicants. Starting with Tristram's ability only to **** in volume 7 (528) he follows in volume 8 with the "rill of cold water dribbling through my inward parts," which can set a girl on fire, and a flow of emphatic water imagery (543):

> In swims CURIOSITY, beckoning to her damsels to follow—they dive into the centre of the current—
> FANCY sits musing upon the bank, and with her eyes following the stream, turns straws and bulrushes into masts and bosprits—And DESIRE, with vest held up to the knee in one hand, snatches at them, as they swim by her, with the other—

Hogarth used these liquids as part of a sublimation of the blood of warfare into forms of intoxication focused instead on drinking and love-making. The original "family" disintegrates underneath the sign of Adam and Eve in a fist fight (between a Cain and an Abel) and thence, moving from left to right, "dissolves" into the whores, loose women, and their brothel on the far right. But parallel with the dissolution of the family, we see warfare itself dissolving into the preferable lifestyle of drinking and love-making.

What is most noticeable in the "Amours of My Uncle Toby" is

that love follows after war is ended, though the military metaphor is retained: after the Peace of Utrecht Toby falls in love with the Widow and the military becomes an amorous "blow"; after Trim is wounded, he and the Beguine fall in love. *The March to Finchley* may have served Sterne as a model for the transformation of the family into isolated individuals, of warfare into love-making, and of clear issues of right and wrong into aesthetic contemplation.

Nevertheless, the emphasis in *Tristram Shandy* is different—not on love as a positive alternative but on love as another form of death. If love for the Shandys is a sublimation of, or reprieve from, war, it remains just as deadly. For Walter love is poison, for Toby a blister or the cut of a "gap'd knife across his finger," though this presumably refers to the second of the two kinds of love in Walter's formulation: the love of the brain and that of the liver (rational and natural). Even Trim, recalling the Beguine, reports that "Love, an' please your honour, is exactly like war, in this; that a soldier, though he has escaped three weeks compleat o' *Saturday*-night,—may nevertheless be shot through his heart on *Sunday* morning" (572).

I have tried to suggest that Sterne in various ways reflected and deflected the vogue for Burke's Sublime. He goes considerably beyond the Beautiful/Novel, reflecting Burke's death-drive of the Beautiful, changing the love of pursuit from the pursuit of a beautiful lady to the flight from death (or from the lady). The family as normative patri-archal microcosm, perhaps reforming in conjugal units, now fragments into extreme forms of disinterestedness, impotence, homosociality, and solipsistic monads. The normative Shaftesburian work of art is carried to extremes of artificiality, feigning, and fantasy.

In Sterne's case, in his most purely aesthetic work, *A Sentimental Journey,* the terms still remain Hogarthian. Once Yorick is in Paris the sexual innuendo, which had been an undercurrent, comes to the sur-face and becomes intrusive: He cannot keep his mind off the subject. In the chapter called "The Wig. Paris," the pleasure of sexual innuendo is set against the Sublime. Yorick is forced by a French barber to substi-tute a French wig for his English one. When he questions whether one buckle (lock) will hold firm, the barber says, "You may immerge it . . . into the ocean, and it will stand—"

> What a great scale is every thing upon in this city! thought I—The
> utmost stretch of an English periwig-maker's ideas could have gone no
> further than to have 'dipped it into a pail of water'—What difference!
> 'tis like time to eternity. (159)

The English mode has been set against the French as a pail of water
against the ocean. Further, Yorick's point is that in the "French sublime"

> the grandeur is *more* in the *word;* and *less* in the *thing.* No doubt the
> ocean fills the mind with vast ideas; but Paris being so far inland, it was
> not likely I should run post a hundred miles out of it, to try the
> experiment [i.e., of dipping his wig in the ocean]—the Parisian barber
> meant nothing.—
>
> The pail of water standing besides the great deep, makes certainly
> but a sorry figure in speech—but 'twill be said—it has one advantage—
> 'tis in the next room, and the truth of the buckle may be tried in it
> without more ado, in a single moment.
>
> In honest truth, and upon a more candid revision of the matter, *The
> French expression professes more than it performs.* (159)

Yorick then makes two determining gestures: he adds that he believes
he "can see the precise and distinguishing marks of national characters
more in these nonsensical *minutiae,* than in the most important matters of state." And, once out of the hands of the French barber, he
"walked forth without any determination where to go" (160). Where
his steps take him, in the next chapter ("The Pulse"), is to the grisset,
her pulse, her husband, and her gloves; in short, back into sexual pleasure, however controlled and "sentimentalized" (the whole sequence
ends with "The Conquest").

Sterne is summing up the area that is equally not French, not
foreign, and not sublime. This is defined by the small and manageable
versus the illimitable; "minutiae" like the pail "in the next room"
(what Jean André Rouquet, referring to Hogarth, called *mille petites
circonstances*)[37] versus "matters of state"; profession rather than performance (or theory vs. practice, or word vs. thing); and sauntering
after erotic pleasure rather than seeking and enjoying the sublimity of
power.

Postscript: Sterne's Critical Deism

In *Tristram Shandy* the villains are Roman Catholics (including the egregious Dr. Slop), but not far behind are the Anglican clergymen, with one Adams-like exception in the outspoken and unfortunate Yorick. The subject is the religious doctrine of Presence, in this case of Toby's and Tristram's, and accompanied by analogous sub-christological woundings. As in biblical scholarship, the demand for presence leads to the demand for documentation, and this leads on the one hand to an exaggerated importance placed on the document as document—the Bible, the marriage contract, and the excommunication, and in general the text as poor substitute for presence. But, on the other hand, these are all put in question by the Widow Wadman's "Where?"—which subordinates all other senses (including Toby's) of presence focused on historical documentation, the geographical and physiological placement of the wound, to the sheer question of whether he can give her sexual pleasure.

Is there any sign of religion in this work written by a Church of England clergyman (admittedly a Yorick sort of clergyman)? Certainly there is no trace of the doctrine of rewards and punishments. No doctrine, no biblical story, no sacrament appears without elements of parody. John Wilkes, himself reputedly author of the scandalous *Essay on Woman* (c. 1762) and a Medmenhamite Monk, observed that "Tristram [Sterne] pleads his cause well [i.e., in his sermons], tho' he does not believe one word of it."[38] Was Sterne a crypto-deist—as Wilkes's remark would suggest—or simply a libertine (one of the Yorkshire Demoniacs) in shepherd's clothing? Parson Adams has become Yorick, namesake of a jester, regarded as a Lucian disrespectful of authority among clerics named Phutatorius, Didius, and Ernulphus. Noticeable is the Fieldingesque distrust of all texts, including sacred ones. It is possible to see the Roman Catholic elements such as excommunication, but also the sacraments of baptism and christening, as mercilessly parodied. The Tristram-Walter-Yorick relationship (as I have suggested) may be another play on the Christ-Joseph-deity joke on the Son–Father–Holy Ghost centered once again on the question of Tristram's paternity.

The crux is Yorick's Sermon on Conscience, the centerpiece of the first two volumes. It is first of all a Shandean sermon, a catachresis emblematic of the novel itself. It follows from and balances Dr. Slop's appearance on the scene; it anticipates, with its references to the Spanish Inquisition, the excommunication of Obadiah's knot in volume 3 and Slop's crushing of Tristram's nose which follows. The common elements are Roman Catholicism, rigid orthodoxy, "theory," imprisonment, and torture.[39]

The sermon makes the un-Shaftesburian argument that religion and morality (for which read conscience, moral sense, and benevolence) must both be present in any situation; without one, the other cannot operate. Religion is the external, rationalized, authoritarian, and coercive pole (related to Walter's use of authority rather than love with his wife concerning her laying-in; Dr. Slops' forceps and squirt, the Inquisition and Trim's brother Tom, and so on). At the other pole is the Shaftesburian moral sense, which by itself is inefficient too, embodied in Toby, who is unable to communicate his physical experience at Namur, and Yorick, who is unable to work within conventional modes, including that of the church (his sermons get lost, he is misunderstood, and authority is used against him, ultimately with lethal effect).

The message of the sermon is that morality without religion is no better than religion without morality. But the sermon is delivered by Corporal Trim, interrupted, commented on, and contextualized in various ways by Toby, Slop, Walter, and of course Trim. "Religion" is carried off into, merging with, the Roman Catholicism of Slop and the Spanish Inquisition, whereas the other, sentimental pole comes to be represented by the Shandys and Trim, with special emphasis on Trim's brother Tom.[40]

The sermon is also contextualized, both before and after, in a strange mixture of fiction and reality, by the fact that it has been published by Sterne and fictionally misplaced by Yorick in the copy of Stevinus he borrowed from Toby, will be retrieved after its one "reading" by Trim, but then will be lost before Yorick can deliver it, and finally years later will be delivered by another member of the chapter and published by Sterne in *Sermons of Mr. Yorick.* Thus, the sermon is another text, but it is Yorick's sermon. We can conclude that Sterne's satire is on the side of the innate moral sense, but he recognizes that within the nature of things it (the sermon as an aspect of poor Yorick) cannot function without the forms of religion too. The text's rendering modifies its import and destabilizes its official (textual) message, and if that destabilization is not a demystification, and the text itself is not subjected to critical analysis, the procedure is nevertheless one that could not have been accomplished without the silent absorption of the principles of critical deism.

SEVEN

The Strange, Trivial,
and Infantile
Books for Children

The Child as Aesthetic Object or Subject

If "play" for Hogarth was not, as one would expect, disinterested, why is this? To understand, we might begin with Solkin's discussion of the containment of transgression in Vauxhall Gardens. This was a pleasure garden opened in 1732 in which, as Solkin puts it, commerce refined the passions because Jonathan Tyers (its projector) "devoted a great deal of time and energy to devising ways of keeping vulgar elements outside his establishment."[1] He cleaned up the old garden, excluding the harlots and pimps who traded there, enclosing it and charging admission to keep out "the inferior sort." What this meant in terms of morals was the elimination of " 'pretty women' of alluringly dubious character" (107); in terms of art the replacement of hurdy-gurdy players and penny prints of vulgar subjects by an orchestra playing Handel and rustic scenes painted by Hayman on a large enough scale to appear historical.

Although the original conception of employing English artists to decorate the pavilions had been Hogarth's, Francis Hayman was the primary artist employed to paint rustic scenes on the walls of the supper boxes; these were, according to Solkin, "negative examples [that] foster[ed] the sort of conduct Tyers invoked his clientele to embrace." "If Vauxhall's most important political function was to confirm the polite character of its public, it did so above all by defining that character over and against representations of the popular" (129, 135). The underlying assumption is that the audience wanted to "define" themselves or "confirm" themselves as "innocent and polite." One difference between Hogarth and Hayman is that this need to "confirm" or "embrace" politeness was precisely the pose Hogarth satirized in his Harlot and Rake.

Though rusticity was itself "transgressive," Hayman painted his rustic subjects in the ostensibly polite setting of a supper box and excluded more serious "transgressions." Woman was the central transgressive element for Shaftesbury, and sexuality and the mixing of genders and classes served this purpose at Vauxhall Gardens, but Hayman rendered these transgressive elements polite or nonexistent. In *The Play at See-Saw* (fig. 34) Solkin detects some "transgressive" sexual mixing of social levels, a gentleman in bagwig making a pass at a plebeian girl. But I see no sign of a bagwig or any sort of a wig (which might designate a gentleman) on the boy at the left. His hair is his own and untended, though held at the back by a ribbon, like that of his opposite (rival?) on the other end of the see-saw. Hayman has in fact avoided the ribald potential of a see-saw by placing the boy at the high point and the girl at the low (cf. Fragonard's use of the same situation in *The Swing*). Hogarth, however, is supposed to have had copies of his *Four Times of the Day* (1738) hanging in one of the supper boxes at Vauxhall, and these unmistakably mix high and low, heterosexuals and homosexuals, genders and races.[2] Lusty women figure in three scenes and a man in drag in the fourth. The two painters shared the same audience in the supper boxes, but Hayman contained while Hogarth retrieved the transgressive elements.

Solkin also notes the "preponderance of children" in the supper-box designs at Vauxhall. He explains the "basic reasons for this bias towards the infantile" as the identification of childhood with "a phase of life opposed to adulthood in much the same way as Vauxhall stood apart from the everyday world outside its walls—in both cases the crucial distinction being between leisure and labour, and possibly between innocence and corruption."[3] Thus childhood's "negative connotations, of frivolity and folly, of impulses that adults were meant to suppress, while simultaneously regarding them with fascination and nostalgic longing"—and these, of course, he associates with the "lower orders" and with "play" (138). "Play" he develops "as the realm of childish games or vulgar folly," which, he notes, accurately I think, "made it difficult to represent polite adult diversions in an unequivocally positive light" (147).

"Play," this transgressive word associated with children, infantilism, the vulgar, and folly, is of course the term Hogarth invokes at the center of his hedonistic aesthetics, alongside the Shaftesburian anti-Venus. The woman playing the role of a Diana or Venus is not the only aestheticized figure in *The Analysis of Beauty*. Hogarth also, drawing on the children in his earliest conversation pieces of families, substitutes for an angel "an infant's head of about two years old, with a pair of duck's-wings placed under its chin, supposed always to be flying about, and singing psalms." As he continues, "there is something so agreeable in their form, that the eye is reconciled and overlooks the absurdity, and we find them in the carving and painting of almost every church. St. Paul's is full of them" (50; referring to fig. 22 of plate 1).

To contextualize this image in the *Analysis* it is necessary to remember two earlier pictures. One, the conversation of the *Beckingham-Cox Wedding* (1729–30; Metropolitan Museum, New York), shows a pair of floating angels, somewhat dangerously releasing a cornucopia over the heads of the marrying couple; but at the same elevation, in a gallery above the altar, two urchins are looking down on the ceremony: parallel angels and living boys, perhaps alternative explanations, divine and secular. The other painting, from 1746, was *Moses Brought to Pharaoh's Daughter*, painted for the Foundling Hospital (engraved in 1752, a year before the *Analysis*). Here Hogarth utilizes the obviously transgressive aspect of the foundling child itself, representing Moses as another urchin, looking lost and uncertain between his two competing "mothers," the true mother being the less beautiful.[4]

Hogarth's opponents within the St. Martin's Lane Academy, in the 1750s when the two traditions clashed openly over the founding of an official state academy on the French model, associated his Beautiful—the physical, bodily, and pleasureful—with just those transgressive qualities of the nursery and the lower orders. In the midst of this quarrel Burke's *Philosophical Enquiry*, while respectful of Hogarth's beautiful serpentine line, treated these elements (beginning with curiosity) as a trivializing alternative to the Sublime (in which curiosity is replaced by delight). Subsequently, in Samuel Johnson's *Rasselas* (1759) these elements were infantilized into the nursery world of the Happy Valley, out of which Rasselas and his friends escape into a world of mature choices, which include Burkean Sublimes both secular and religious. In Horace Walpole's *Castle of Otranto* (1765), where the issue was class, they are isolated in the simple-minded servants who are trying to understand the sublime activity going on around them, which in fact is no more than an issue of property and inheritance, but is focused on the flight of the beautiful Isabella, pursued by the tyrant Manfred (her prospective father-in-law), who intends to rape her.

Shaftesbury, we recall, contrasted two senses of "pleasure," physical and mental; the former he associated disparagingly with children and animals: "For as highly pleased as children are with baubles, or with whatever affects their tender senses, we cannot in our hearts sincerely admire their enjoyment, or imagine them possessors of any extraordinary good."[5] From here he draws a line descending to the enjoyment of "mere animals" and the "low and sordid pleasures of human kind" (which, a page later, in a phrase that may have caught Hogarth's eye, he calls "a hoggish life").

Although they were private jottings, Shaftesbury's hysterical exclamations in his notes advocating "manliness" project the terms of the counterdiscourse to civic humanism: "Childish, womanish, bestial, brutal," he exclaims, asking himself if these are anything more than words: "But how then [is a man] not a child? How least like a woman? How far from the beast? How removed and at a distance from anything of this kind? How properly a man?" Then again, "A man, and not a woman, [who is] effeminate, soft, delicate, supine, impotent in pleasure, in anger, talk; pusillanimous, light, changeable, etc; but the contrary to this in each particular." He is, of course, describing Hercules' Pleasure, also connected by Shaftesbury, in his dedication to the *Judgment of Hercules* pamphlet, with the "effeminate . . . Taste" of the English baroque (an anticipation, Michael Levey believes, of "the feminine bias of the rococo").[6] But he goes on: "—A man, and not a beast: . . . A man, and not a child; . . . the contraries: Manhood, manliness, humanity—manly, humane, masculine."[7] The associations are most instructive, suggesting the demonizing of both woman and child in the Shaftesburian system of masculinity.

Shaftesbury's tutor Locke used childhood (along with idiocy) as an exemplification of the tabula rasa in his *Essay concerning Human Understanding*. The purpose of learning is to fill the tabula rasa, the empty slate, the dark room open to the day only through a small chink in the wall, or the empty head of the child or idiot. Three years later, in *Thoughts concerning Education* (1693), the presiding authority for the empiricism of teaching in the eighteenth century, he insists that learning to read should not seem to curtail the child's essential love of liberty. He hopes that "Learning might be made a Play and Recreation to children":

> The Natural Temper of Children disposes their Minds to wander. Novelty alone takes them; whatever that presents, they are presently eager to have a Taste of, and are as soon satiated with it. They quickly grow weary of the same thing, and so have almost their whole Delight in Change and Variety. It is a Contradiction to the Natural State of Childhood for them to fix their fleeting Thoughts.[8]

The first thing we notice is the vocabulary: "wander," "novelty," "delight in change and variety," as opposed to the weariness "of the same thing," the fixity of repetition. Therefore, Locke suggests, instruction and the teacher's main aim, "to get and keep the Attention of the Scholar," can best be carried out by offering the child pleasure and variety, taking advantage of the phenomenon (itself essentially "childish") of the association of ideas. The children's book entails materials over which the viewer's eyes wander in order to enjoy "the love of pursuit" which was celebrated both by Hogarth in the *Analysis* and by Locke in the opening section, "To the Reader," of his *Essay concerning Human Understanding*.[9] As the bookseller John Newbery was quick to see and exploit, a pleasant series of associations can "fix" the letter, word, or idea in the child's memory; and this can best be done through simple additive units, letter followed by word, image, and sentence (a moral aphorism).[10]

Isaac Kramnick, in his essay "Children's Literature and Bourgeois

Ideology," asks us to believe that "from its beginnings in the late eighteenth century, children's literature in English has been designed to serve ideological objectives." He argues that *The History of Little Goody Two-Shoes,* published by John Newbery in 1765, was a self-conscious attempt on the part of adults to inculcate "the values of the middle class" in children.[11] By ideology Kramnick means the verses Margery Two-Shoes assembles from her alphabets: for example, "Early to Bed, and early to rise; / Is the Way to be healthy, and wealthy, and wise" (76). But his austere view should be contrasted with Locke's emphasis on pleasure and variety—or, more recently, F. J. Harvey Darton's view that "Children's literature" emerged precisely when the *utile-dulce* ratio began to shift its emphasis from the aim to teach the alphabet (or inculcate thrift) to sheer play.[12] The emphasis here is on sheer play, but it is not easy to distinguish this from the intellectual form of play, like Hogarth's, which opens closed doors and is tendentiously heterodox. Locke's association of ideas could function either to fix subliminally certain ideas in the child's mind or to free the child's imagination to a kind of play (which admittedly might then fix the certain ideas in his or her mind). One of the phenomena recognized in children's books in our time is that "the scenes and figures of any picture-book can always have a double significance . . . both for what such things mean objectively, and also for what they come to signify to the child, in terms—for example—of safe or dangerous, pretty or ugly, nice or nasty, silly or sensible, funny or serious."[13] These binaries include other categories than the ones that would appear to the ideologue parent or perhaps even to Locke. For example, the supplementing of judgment with fancy (other Lockean terms) is a phenomenon applicable to every utterance in a children's alphabet book, especially when, as in the eighteenth century, the words, sentences, and visual images served as relatively disjunctive additions to the letter.

A simple alphabet, ordered from *A* to *Z,* is made a "children's book" by being augmented by illustrations and verses, moral and story. In practice this amounts to adding to the arbitrary alphabetical order requiring that *A* be followed by *B,* and that the sequence conclude with *Z,* another order that is illustrative, by placing spatially adjacent to the letter a word, and near that a corresponding verbal image, and a sequence that does not necessarily close as simply as the *A*-to-*Z* series. The result is an extension outward in imagination. At its simplest, in an alphabet book of circa 1740, *Tom Thumb's Play-Book:*

> A Apple pye
> B Bite it
> C Cut it
> D Divide it
> E Eat it. . . .

And each is accompanied with a picture.[14] Built into the instruction is a particular pleasure in the form of a "fixed," an absolute and arbitrary sequence compromised, augmented, in some sense broken or, we might say, "varied." The regimentation of memorization is accompanied by a freedom to let the fancy explore the proliferation of meaning in words and then in a visual image—and, indeed, the juxtaposition of reason and fancy, above all of unity and variety.

In Newbery's *Little Pretty Pocket Book* (1744) a letter of the alphabet is linked to a story:

> Great A, B, and C,
>   And tumble down D,
> The Cat's a blind buff,
>   And she cannot see, . . .

And these are followed by small *a, b, c,* and similar stories. "The Great E Play" is the game of shuttle-cock:

> The Shuttle-Cock struck
>   Does backward rebound;
> But, if it be miss'd,
>   It falls to the Ground.

And the game is followed by a "Moral":

> Thus chequer'd in Life,
>   As Fortune does flow;
> Her Smiles lift us high,
>   Her Frowns sink us low.

As the imagery leads the child from shuttle-cock to a maternal figure of Fortune whose smiles elevate and whose frowns depress, variety also replaces uniformity of interest, the sheer play of imagination begins to usurp the page, and genuine "children's literature" begins to emerge. When an alphabet begins "A was an Archer and shot at a frog" and ends "Z was one Zeno the Great, but he's dead," the process is well under way toward the "nonsense" of Lear and Dodgson.

One analogy might be between the child's rambling, fanciful thoughts, which produce strange combinations and associations, and, on the adult level, the poetic though regressive imagination of the dunces, ridiculed by Pope in *The Dunciad*. In Locke's view, we recall, "Inadvertency, forgetfulness, unsteadiness, and wandring of Thoughts, are the natural Faults of childhood": a picture not unlike Pope's of the dunces; but Locke had added: "and therefore where they are not observ'd to be wilful, are to be mention'd softly, and gain'd upon by time."[15] The dunces, of course, were willful, and so the just object of satire. But the analogy retains its basis in the waywardness and wandering thoughts—which is, of course, precisely what is privileged in Hogarth's theory. One might reply to Kramnick that the adults' stake in the children's book was perhaps less indoctrination of the child than a freeing of their own imagination through a recovery of childhood.

The History of Little Goody Two-Shoes

In *Spectator* No. 419, on the Strange, Addison advised treating "the Darkness and Superstition of [the Dark] Ages, when pious Frauds were made use of," not with "reverence and horrour" but with a perspective "enlightened by Learning and Philosophy" (3:572). As Fielding's *Examples of the Interposition of Providence* showed, in the mid–eighteenth century children were the model audience for such strange works. There is no better example of the doctrine of rewards and punishments as a social curb than Isaac Watt's *Divine Songs Attempted in Easy Language for the Use of Children* (1715, with many reprintings). In song 23, on lying, the child is admonished:

What heavy Guilt upon him lies!
　How cursed is his Name!
The Ravens shall pick out his Eyes,
　And Eagles eat the same.

> But those that worship God, and give
>   Their Parents Honour due,
> Here *on this Earth* they long shall live,
>   And live *hereafter too.*
>   (emphasis added)

Watt's emphasis on interested virtue is laid out in his posthumous *Discourse on the Education of Children and Youth* in *The Improvement of the Mind* (1782), where he argues that those children who follow his precepts will prosper in both this world and the next (as opposed to children whose very limbs are "wild Instruments of Madness and Mischief"). His is a world with an immanent deity "Who is for ever nigh":

> Creatures (as num'rous as they be)
>   Are subject to thy Care:
> There's not a Place where we can flee,
>   But God is present there.
>   (song 2)

In this world there is an ever-present Redeemer:

> Remember all the dying Pains
>   That my Redeemer felt,
> And let his Blood wash out my Stains,
>   And answer for my Guilt.
>
> O may I now for ever fear
>   T'indulge a sinful Thought,
> Since the Great God can see, and hear,
>   And writes down every Fault!
>   (song 9)

This is just the sort of children's book *Goody Two-Shoes* is correcting or rewriting from a perspective now "enlightened by Learning and Philosophy."[16] The only traces of an immanent God of the sort Watt supposes are added as a specifically superstitious overlay to the actions of the humans and animals. Both explanations are offered, and the child can choose between them or accept both.

As its introduction announces, *Goody Two-Shoes* is written with this double perspective, for children but for adults as well. The salient characters include a female orphan who rises to the status of both lady and Christ-like redeemer—who shows how to compensate for personal loss (of home, family, brother) by the addition of a second shoe (the completion of the eponymous pair) and how to deal with oppression and want through alphabetic constructions that make words and then proverbs—so that the spelling of "bread" or "plumb pudding" can substitute for the absent food; and who supplements every providential explanation with a social one. Children are saved from their collapsing school building by a miraculous dog, *and* the community is admonished to correct the faulty construction of its schools.

We have dealt with a deistic writing that habitually addressed two audiences, a popular and an elite. The Novel/Beautiful of Hogarth required both a "reader of greater penetration" and an "ordinary reader." *Pilgrim's Progress* also employed its figures and similitudes "for Boys and Fools; but as for thee," the adult reader, "Do thou the substance of my matter see";[17] and these types of readers are equivalent to adult and child in books for children. *Goody Two-Shoes,* a "children's book," as its introduction announces, is written for children but for adults as well: "it is intended, Sir, not for those Sort of Children, but for Children of six Feet high" (11). Here we see the intersection of deist rhetoric, Puritan rhetoric, and the rhetoric of books for children. Children's books perforce address both the child and the adult who reads the book to the child, bracketing the child's fantasy with the adult's realization of hard social facts—and vice versa. It is also both printed text and oral recitation. The children's book gives us in its purest form the jointure—the juxtaposition—of the fantasy world of children and the world of adults in which the former is providential signs and the latter human agency.

The nucleus of *Little Goody Two-Shoes* is an alphabet book, with its implications of the child's learning, cooperating, and making larger units out of smaller. However, although it employs alphabets the book is not itself an alphabet book. For like Robinson Crusoe's conversion and spiritual autobiography, the alphabet of the primer, with its verses and pictures, is absorbed in *Goody Two-Shoes* into a larger story, and its nature is changed and commented on by the literary (or merely imaginary) structure to which it is subordinated. Though a book for children, *Goody Two-Shoes* also asks to be seen in the context of the prose fiction that flourished in the first half of the eighteenth century: that is, the novels of Fielding or, more immediately, Goldsmith's *Vicar of Wakefield.*

For *Goody Two-Shoes* reads in some respects as a children's rewriting of the *Vicar*, which is ostensibly a novel for adults but is about a family characterized as "equally generous, simple, credulous, and inoffensive" who inhabit a children's world, animistic and governed by malign and benign spirits in the form of squires, justices of the peace, and landlords. The two books were coeval: the *Vicar* was written and in Francis Newbery's hands between 1762 and 1766, when it was published, and *Goody Two-Shoes* was published by John Newbery (Francis's father) in 1765.[18] It is conceivable that they were both written by Goldsmith. Both share a central fiction of a character who is a modern Job (Primrose and, though in this case in a story-within-the-story, Lovewell), and a voice that attempts to resolve the same central question: how to deal with adversity. The expulsion of Margery Two-Shoes's family from their farm is analogous to the expulsion of the Primroses, and both books dissolve an originally stable family structure into a picaresque series of comic, ironic, and sentimental episodes, increasingly exaggerated and fantastic (in the *Vicar*, "theatrical"), punctuated by inserted verses, aphorisms, proverbs, and parables. The original family of Margery Two-Shoes dissolves and is replaced by her own "family" of children and animals, and this dissolves into miraculous picaresque adventures of Margery and her animals. Both the *Vicar* and *Two-Shoes* are what came to be called novels, one for adults and the other for children, yet both define themselves by blurring the lines between the worlds of adult and child: by infantilizing adult experience.

On the title page of this children's book, beneath the title *Little Goody Two-Shoes,* the words continue:

WITH

The Means by which she acquired her Learning and Wisdom and in consequence thereof her Estate; set forth at large for the Benefit of those,

Who from a State of Rags and Care,
And having Shoes but half a Pair;
Their Fortune and their Fame would fix,
And gallop in a Coach and Six.

And below this is the self-consciously satiric (and literary) remark: "See the Original Manuscript in the *Vatican* at *Rome,* and the Cuts by *Michael Angelo.* Illustrated with the Comments of our great modern Critics."

The juxtaposition suggests that we are still in or near the mode of Swift's *Tale of a Tub,* Pope's *Dunciad,* Gay's *Trivia,* and Fielding's *Tragedy of Tragedies; or, the History of Tom Thumb,* as well as his novels. It suggests less the sort of juxtaposition in which the title *Pamela* is followed by the explanatory subtitle *Virtue Rewarded* than the mock-heroic relationship (as in *The Rape of the Lock* or *Tom Thumb*) between the small, indifferent subject of children—or more precisely the story of Two-Shoes (her "State of Rags and Care," her "acquiring" of "Learning and Wisdom," and thereupon "her Estate")—and the sublime subject of the Fall, Redemption, and Last Judgment painted by Michelangelo in the Sistine Chapel (and well known in England through engraved "cuts").

The message of the verses by themselves is totally conventional. In *A Little Pretty Pocket Book* Newbery printed, following the alphabet, a letter with a woodcut of a little boy riding in a coach and six: this little boy had "learned his Book" so well, and been so "dutiful to his Parents and obliging to his Playmates" that "every Body loved him," and eventually he rose (in the hyperbole typical of children's books) "from a mean State of Life to a Coach and Six, in which he rides to this Day." It is in the relationship between this popular wisdom and the world of Vatican manuscripts and Sistine frescoes on the subject of Man's Redemption that the author of *Goody Two-Shoes* strikes a distinctive note, or rather one that connects his book with the tradition of satiric fiction for adults—and, with the particular authority of *Gulliver's Travels,* with the shadowland between adult and child.

Following the title page, the "Introduction" opens with Adam's Fall. Two-Shoes's father, Mr. Meanwell, "a considerable Farmer in the Parish," falls and is expelled from Eden but not, significantly, through his own sin: suffering "Misfortunes which he met with in Business, and the wicked Persecutions of Sir Timothy Gripe, and an over-grown Farmer called Graspall, he was effectually ruined" and driven from his farm. This is not quite the Fall Michelangelo portrayed; it is closer to the ambiguous expulsion Fielding describes in *Tom Jones.* The implication—of title page and Introduction—that Two-Shoes is a small (a mock) redeemer, who emerges from the fall of her mother and father to save the good and punish the evil, is fulfilled in the sequel. She even carries out a Last Judgment on the Gripes and Graspalls. Thus the book is announced as *about* a child as hero, moreover with overtones of the Redeemer, but also recalling the redeemed ("Suffer the little children," "be as little children"), and conflating our usual notions of redeemer and redeemed.

The story continues in chapter 1, with the death of the Meanwells, Two-Shoes's parents, and the wanderings of the two orphans, Margery and her brother Tommy. The sequence characteristic of this book (which starts from the nucleus of an alphabet book) is introduced when brother Tommy is carried off to sea and Two-Shoes first weeps uncontrollably ("she ran all round the Village, crying for her Brother"); but then, when the shoemaker appears with her eponymous new shoes, she recovers her composure: "Nothing could have supported Little Margery under the Affliction she was in for the loss of her Brother but the Pleasure she took in her two Shoes." We should notice that, whereas her name is Margery Meanwell, it is important for her that she is thereafter called Two-Shoes for the event that establishes her personal support system. Perhaps we should say "completes," for the emphasis is on "two," and on putting them into words. She runs out and cries to everyone she meets, "Two Shoes, Mame, see two Shoes"—"and by that Means obtained the Name of Goody Two-Shoes" (20–21). The shoes, by way of her verbalizing of them, earn her a name; they serve as a possession, a compensation for loss, and an article of practical use, shoes that protect her feet from stones and permit walking (as opposed to a dress or bonnet).[19]

They are also a pair. The importance of the title, *Goody Two-Shoes* (and the verse on the title page, "having Shoes but half a Pair"), lies in its reference to the completion of a pair, the addition of one shoe to another: for the addition of the second shoe overshadows the additive employment of the alphabet by which Margery attains her "learning and Wisdom" and indeed the whole function of reading in Two-Shoes's story.

Immediately following her acquisition of the second shoe, Margery—who is being sheltered by Mr. and Mrs. Smith—is cast out again.

Graspall has ordered Mr. Smith to expel her. Mr. Smith and his wife weep copiously but nevertheless send her away—their sentimental tears anticipating Blake's interpretation of tears in his *Songs of Experience* as a selfish substitute for charity ("pity would be no more, / If we did not *make* somebody Poor")—and Mr. Smith invokes divine providence: "[He] shed Tears, and cried, Lord have Mercy on the Poor!" to which the narrator adds: "The Prayers of the Righteous fly upwards, and reach unto the Throne of Heaven, as will be seen in the Sequel" (22)—a passage that recalls some chapter headings in *The Vicar of Wakefield* (e.g., "Former Benevolence Now Repaid with Unexpected Interest") and the general juxtaposition of providential signs with human agency. This ironic sequence is followed by the next chapter title: "How Little Margery Learned to Read, and by Degrees Taught Others."

The lesson Margery learned from her first mentor, Mr. Smith, was that his goodness and wisdom were "owing to his great Learning, therefore she wanted of all Things to learn to read" (24); and this fulfills the title page's promise of showing "the Means by which she acquired her Learning and Wisdom." The whole sequence, proceeding from the need for shoes to the need to "acquire" learning, begins again with tears, then goes to the invocation of divine providence, and concludes with the practical turn to reading—first learning to read herself and then teaching others to read.

The additive sequence is therefore also Margery's way of passing on her learning to the children of the neighborhood: she gives them the alphabet in capital letters and then in lower case and then in syllables (all reproduced in the text for the young to see; first in their alphabetical order, then mixed, and then rearranged in their original correct order [fig. 35]). Next the alphabet is arranged by the students into words—and then into proverbs ("A wise Head makes a close Mouth. Don't burn your Lips with another Man's Broth"). The sequence is most suggestive: from one sort of order into total randomness, rearranged in a new, higher order; an order of convention is followed by an order of sense, "fixed" by variety, novelty, and pleasure. These alphabetic structures are then applied by Margery to human experience:

> having pulled out her Letters, she asked the little Boy next her, what he had for Dinner? Who answered, Bread. (the poor Children in many

Places live very hard) Well then, says she, set the first letter. He put up the Letter B, to which the next [student] added r, and the next e, the next a, the next d, and it stood thus, Bread. (35)

This scene is not so much a dramatized spelling lesson or what Kramnick refers to as the imposition of an ideology, a work ethic, as it is a satiric revelation of the only way to come to terms with a hard life, dinners of only bread. To see the direction of the satire we need only juxtapose the linguistic substitution for food—"Suppose the Word to be spelt was Plumb Pudding (and who can suppose a better)" (27)— with the money squandered on Lady Ducklington's funeral, which "would have been better laid out [1] in little Books for Children, and [2] in Meat, Drink, and Cloaths for the Poor" (46).

But the word "satire" must be qualified; for *Goody Two-Shoes* is more obviously a fiction that once again recapitulates the *Robinson Crusoe* or *Tom Jones* plot of the man isolated in a precarious situation who builds up a world of his own with whatever is at hand as a flawed substitute for the world he has lost; who learns how to protect himself from his intolerable plight, which learning he then passes on to his pupil Friday and the colonists of his island. Two-Shoes's schoolroom of children, and her alphabet, are her way of reconstituting her lost Eden.[20] But the vehicle of salvation is not religion but the alphabet, and the coming to terms is by the arranging of letters into talismanic words. Crusoe's experience also had to be put into words, into the words of his diary and subsequently into the words of his retrospective memoir (the book *Robinson Crusoe* itself): another lost Eden that is reconstructed specifically in terms of words.

Margery Two-Shoes is like Giles Gingerbread's father, in another of Newbery's books, who gives Giles every day a fresh gingerbread cake with the alphabet on it, "which he eat up": and so literally "lived upon learning." Or in the context of Richardson's *Pamela*, Margery can be seen as another female servant completely vulnerable and oppressed, who nevertheless goes about doing her duty but accompanies this by writing her journal; and this journal—its words—converts, teaches, serves as an example to her society, and obtains for her a rich husband.

Margery's aphorisms, it would have to be admitted, are ideologically repressive.[21] One is "The Lord have Mercy upon me, and grant that I may be always good"—to which Polly Sullen (another of those figures like Tom Suckbribe or Tom Idle whose names forever prejudice them by a fiat of their author, heavenly or literary) objects that "she did not know why she should pray for her Enemies." These words of "such a naughty, proud, perverse Girl" prompt Two-Shoes to depart in a huff, only prevented by a compromise by which some practical aphorisms are interlarded with the pious incantations (for example, "He that will thrive, / Must rise by Five") (38–39).

The form Margery develops allows for a franker, more precise social diagnosis of the plight of the poor than, for example, Fielding's in his *Enquiry into the Late Increase of Robbers,* but, on the other hand, agrees with Fielding in projecting as the only solution (or, as Kramnick would say, the one that renders the poor docile) the uttering of words, and substitution of words for substance—and here words are constructed into exorcisms that at best mingle practical advice with heavenly formulas. The power of words is presented—ironically or practically—as the only way (acceptable to the ruling class) that the poor can cope with their plight.

The power of words presupposes the primacy of literacy, but only far enough to spell out words and moral aphorisms that will content the poor. That is, the "children" learn to read only up to words that stand in for bread or plum pudding; or to aphorisms that stand in for liberty. But then there is the adult reader—or even the childish reader—who reads the whole book. For this reader the book is precisely about the fact that all one *can* do is combine harmless delusion and labor in order to survive and remain happy. We are witnessing in *Goody Two-Shoes* the absorption of the alphabet (the primer or alphabet book) into a fiction of teaching-through-play. Use is first incantatory or talismanic, but then it becomes instrumental; first a way of coping with reality, but then, in some sense that remains to be defined, a way of changing reality for the better. Part 1 ends with two episodes illustrating the consecutive phases and prepares us for part 2, as the first shoe prepared us for its mate.

After a funeral, in the middle of the night, the church bells mysteriously begin to ring. The superstitious parishioners talk of ghosts, but the rector, pooh-poohing the notion, unlocks the church door: "What Sort of a ghost do you think appeared? Why Little *Two-Shoes,* who being weary had fallen asleep in one of the Pews during the Funeral Service, and was shut in all Night." She apologizes for the trouble, saying "she should not have rung the Bells, but that she was very cold" (49–50). In short, Two-Shoes gives the appearance of a ghost, but in fact is only a tired, homeless, and cold child trapped in an empty church (one that, in the manner of the distant steeple in Hogarth's *Gin Lane,* is not very helpful to poor orphans).

While inside the church, she recalls, she had felt an icy touch on her neck and heard mysterious sounds, which she claims she never imagined were in fact only a dog (also locked in); but she had not been terrified because of (first) her absolute "Confidence" in God's "Protection," and (second) her knowledge that "there is no such Thing to be seen" as ghosts (53, 66). She has such complete confidence in God's "Protection" and in her knowledge that she descends into the vault where Lady Ducklington had just been buried and "trod on" her coffin, but "saw no ghost." The mixture of the providential and prudential, and indeed the whole world of *Two-Shoes,* is strikingly clear in her summation:

> any little Boy or Girl, [1] who is good, and loves God Almighty, and keeps his Commandments, may as safely lie in the Church, or the Church-yard, as any where else, [2] if they take Care not to get Cold; for I am sure [3] there are no Ghosts, either to hurt, or to frighten them; [4] though any one possessed of Fear might have taken Neighbour Saunderson's Dog with his cold Nose for a Ghost; and if [5] they had not been undeceived, as I was, would never have thought otherwise. (55–56)

This chapter is immediately followed by one in which Two-Shoes this time seeks shelter from a storm in a deserted barn, where four thieves also take shelter and, not seeing her, "began to talk over their Exploits, and to settle Plans for future Robberies" (58). From being the person who instructed others in verbal formulations to protect against such contingencies as storms and poverty, Two-Shoes now becomes the "ghost" who overhears others and passes on a warning to the rich families (including the Gripes) who are to be robbed. The first part thus ends with the robbers apprehended and the rich as well as the poor redeemed by Two-Shoes's teachings and her warnings, and with her reward in the appropriate form of the inheritance of a school building, which she calls the ABC College.

The title page has been fulfilled: she has acquired "her Learning and Wisdom, and in consequence thereof her Estate." But the more specific terms of God's "Protection" and the "ghost" have also been introduced, and to the term "child" has been added, however fleetingly, "dog," natural or supernatural. These, all by this time marginal materials, move to the center in part 2.

In part 2, Two-Shoes adds animals as her assistants—animals she has rescued from cruel treatment, and taught to arrange the letters of the alphabet and to assume an instructive role similar to her own.[22] But the animals, also like Two-Shoes, not only carry messages of hope from injured parents to their children but warn the children of imminent danger. The dog, the primary animal, learns the alphabet game and then serves to warn of the collapse of Two-Shoes's schoolhouse. His warning initiates a pattern that combines a providential act with an alternative social explanation (of the sort we grew accustomed to in the early chapters of part 1). It is divine providence that causes the building to collapse, but it is also the carelessness of landlords, and this carelessness should be controlled by an Act of Parliament as the providence is controlled by the intervention of the dog.

At this point Margery Two-Shoes's wise acts are misconstrued by her superstitious neighbors as witchcraft—one explanation for the strange procedures we have seen, and indeed for her employment of animal familiars. The episode carries various lessons; first, that there is no such thing as a witch (as earlier, a ghost), and second, that in fact "witch" is a *word* applied to someone old and poor, living in an ignorant community (125). If she acquires money she is no longer a "witch" but has become a "great lady." The first lesson may be thought of as the children's message, the second as the adults'. But, though Two-Shoes is of course declared no witch, there is also a sense (related to the providential function of the dog) in which her enemies are correct: she is a witch, in the same sense that she is a redeemer or a ghost. We are given the choice of calling her either, or of regarding her as only a human agency who understands the power of words. It is an error to interpret as witchcraft her use of a barometer to foretell the weather, because

"People stuff Children's Heads with Stories of Ghosts, Fairies, Witches, and such Nonsense when they are young, and so they continue Fools all their Days" (119). But a genuine fairy-tale quality is invoked by her employment of animals and alphabets and by her contiguity to a miraculous dog. This is a book that has it both ways, deflating fairy tales and producing one itself, as it offers a providential followed by a prudential explanation for actions.[23]

The ultimate case of providential reward is the way "witches" (or poor women) become "ladies" in this world. The only way, it is implied, is to earn (by her "wisdom") the love of a rich man who before long dies and leaves her his whole fortune. No fewer than two examples are given; in one case the man dies even before the wedding. This is how Two-Shoes's fortune is finally acquired, making her (after only six years of marriage) a "great lady" and a power in the community who can oversee the Last Judgment that brings back her brother Tommy from the sea (loaded with riches himself) and encompasses the ruin of Gripe and Graspall. But "Lady Margery" (as Two-Shoes is now called, having transcended the title of her book) excepts Graspall's children from the general punishment, "for they, says she, are no Ways accountable for the Actions of their Father" (135)—another satiric aside to the adult reader.

Pursuing the figure of the child, we can introduce another context for *Goody Two-Shoes*, Thomas Day's *Sandford and Merton* (published in 1783), and make a distinction between Kramnick's two examples of bourgeois ideology promulgated in children's literature. In one sense the two books are similar: both overwhelm us with their self-awareness of language, whether as alphabetic structures or as larger linguistic and literary structures—to the point of setting off this world of fiction definitively from the real world of experience and pain in which the readers are otherwise mired. The structure of *Sandford and Merton* is insistently binary, an endless series of variations on the oppositions between poor and rich, industrious and idle, skilled and unskilled, and successful and unsuccessful. Sandford is a poor boy who is educated with a rich boy. They share the same wise schoolmaster who supervises their contrary responses to each stimulus. The book projects a world that is governed by a single law: do good, work hard, achieve skills, and you will beat out your contrary. Two-Shoes, by contrast, lives in a world that is far less certain of this law, and she spends much of her time pointing out oppression and hedging her bets on the ways of controlling it rather than actively defeating it, as Sandford does. Two-Shoes herself remains until the end an outsider, liable to be charged with being a witch (and only by a kind of witchcraft finally made rich and "a lady"). She does not succeed or grow rich as a consequence of her industry: she is a teacher, a guru, perhaps in fact endowed with magical powers, and not a Harry Sandford who works productively and always wins bouts with a lazy aristocrat.

As an outsider, however, she is a descendant of the subversive child, the young *picaro* Lazarillo de Tormes, or the child who plays a peripheral part in the graphic and literary satire of the early eighteenth century (in particular Hogarth's), and culminates in Blake's rebellious children in *Songs of Experience* and his fiery Orc, the spirit of the French Revolution. The child as subverter has disappeared both into the victories of the hero Sandford and into the higher authority of the child who, though no victor, inculcates ideology in the sense of erecting defenses against the pain suffered by the powerless at the hands of the powerful. But in their different ways Two-Shoes and Sandford are fairy-tale alternative solutions for the victim who becomes a prophet of how to overcome or order a hard life.

The point of including in *Goody Two-Shoes* both the child and the animals is, I suspect, another aspect of the double-naming that goes on everywhere in the book. She is Margery Meanwell, then Two-Shoes, and finally Lady Margery; she is a "ghost" and a little girl who can warn against robberies; she is a "witch" and a woman who can teach wisdom that makes life bearable; and she is a providential redeemer whose mock-heroic status (carried on from the title page) is substantiated by her association with a providential dog. What we notice is that words denoting providence are juxtaposed with words such as "ghost" and "witch," as well as with natural or human agency, and that the intermediate terms (related perhaps to the stories of dwarves and dogs in *The Vicar of Wakefield*) are "child" and "dog."

In the early eighteenth century, for example in the graphic works of Hogarth, children and animals were interchangeable as representations of the subculture: equally subject to cruelty, and sharing the qualities of smallness, vulnerability, and helplessness, with "Suffer the little children" their motto, but with a this-worldly ability both to cause small disorders in the domains of their elders/masters and to satirically mimic them.[24]

The dog's first appearance, in the church in the first part of *Goody Two-Shoes,* was related to his older role as subverter or disturber of order, and this is in the more realistic, less parabolic half of the book. In the second half he instructs children and saves their lives, and at the very end, in the "Appendix, containing a Letter from the Printer," which connects the adult view of the Introduction with the ending, there are two more dogs. One saves his master from a bolt of lightning, for which he is treated "in his old Age with great Tenderness, and fed . . . with Milk as long as he lived"; and the other drinks alcohol and falls into a boiling pot, by which he becomes an admonitory example of temperance for the adults—and for the children who will grow into adults.

Providence and admonition, action and consequence, are related in the figure of the child as well as in that of the dog. There is a sense in which the dog qualifies and demystifies the probability of Two-Shoes, making us see that "witch" and "ghost," like the providential dog, are "children's book" sobriquets. Two-Shoes is in this sense a replacement of an adult authority figure exactly analogous to the cat in "Puss in Boots" or in the story of Dick Whittington, both retold in Newbery's *The Fairing* (1765). The traces of her odyssey, however, remain: unlike Puss and Whittington's cat, she earned her charisma, beginning as a Lockean child in a book written for Lockean children.

If it is "children and idiots" whom Locke cites to prove his point against the theory of innate ideas, it is because they do not have "naturally imprinted" on their minds the principles "most allowed title to innate," viz. "What is, is" and "It is impossible for the same Thing to be and not to be" (68). Children are creatures who do not accept the law of contradiction; for them it is possible for something to be and not to be—or for (in Pope's words) "Roses, Lillies and Daffadils [to] blow in the same Season."

> For children, idiots, savages, and illiterate people [are] of all others the least corrupted by custom, or borrowed opinions; learning and educa-tion having not cast their native thoughts into new moulds, nor by

superinducing foreign and studied doctrines, confounded those fair characters nature had written there. (77)

In *Goody Two-Shoes* we can trace a progression from one kind of childish order to another. The order Two-Shoes gives to experience, alphabetizing it and using reading as a child's defense against hardship, is followed by the dual explanations—the supernatural explanation and the prudential one, invoking, respectively, witchcraft and wisdom—that ask for a sense of both/and instead of either/or, a kind of randomness that includes the irrational and is far outside the order of Two-Shoes's alphabet—its most obvious manifestation being in the animal, especially the providential dog or cat. This strong sense of both/and is, first, in the mind of the "childish" reader of the book; and second, in the comprehensiveness of the novelist of the 1760s inherited from Fielding and Hogarth; but in terms of a Pope or a Swift it was the irrational and paradoxical area of "idiots and savages" which they incorporated into their work, producing new forms of poetry and fiction. This irrational and paradoxical area, when located in the child, became considerably less the subject of satire.

Goody Two-Shoes remains within the range of the novel of the 1740s–1760s; and Margery Two-Shoes exists in her double fashion as both pragmatic child and "witch," in the tradition not only of Pamela (both virtue and prudence) and of the postilions and peddlers who suddenly appear to save the hero in Fielding's novels, but also of the poetic figures invoked by Collins and Warton. This irrational side is repressed in the totally ordered formalist world of *Sandford and Merton*. In *Goody Two-Shoes*, children are still an intriguing but strange area of subject matter for writers—roughly another center of energy and contingency like Pope's dunces, but with the built-in poignance of victimization and the nostalgia for a freedom from "custom, or borrowed opinions" of the Lockean child in pursuit of the word. Children (and, by extension, dogs) are another of those areas outside the range of classical literary decorum which were nevertheless so poignant, and relatively unsafe, that they had to be placed, even in a children's book, within contexts of rhetoric (satire) and aesthetics (the Strange).

EIGHT

From Novel to Strange to "Sublime"

Credulity and Superstition

Accompanying the vogue for the Sublime was the turning away, beginning in the 1740s, from the model of the great poet of the period, Alexander Pope, and his overly formal (and satiric) society verse, to the poetry of passion from England's past: Spenser, Shakespeare, Milton, and the oral poetry of the folk (Ossian and the anonymous ballads collected and published in 1765 by Thomas Percy). This was also the space of folklore and country superstitions that appeared in parts of *Tom Jones,* especially connected with the '45, and about the same time was invoked by Collins in the remote "Scottish Highlands" as a proper subject for a poet.

In *Examples of the Interposition of Providence in the Detection and Punishment of Murder* (1752) Fielding sought not the hard truths of deism but, as is appropriate to children, the useful fictions of religion—not the curiosity of the Novel but the credulity of the Strange. But when Hogarth returned a few years later to Swift's version of credulity/curiosity in *Enthusiasm Delineated* (1759), eventually published in 1762 as *Credulity, Superstition, and Fanaticism: A Medley* (figs. 36, 37), he could be critiquing Fielding's *Examples,* which attributed the increase in murders to "one cause," the "general neglect (I wish I could not say contempt) of religion," and supplied many examples of "the Interposition of Providence" to expose murderers, including "many stories of apparations."[1] The Cock Lane Ghost, the subject of Hogarth's *Credulity*, could have been one of these "interpositions" before it was revealed as a hoax.

Enthusiasm Delineated and *Credulity, Superstition, and Fanaticism*, two states of a single engraving of the interior of a church, represent for Hogarth both recapitulation and watershed. In *Enthusiasm Delineated* the Name of God has been returned to its triangle, replacing the Line of Beauty and indicating England's decline back into the religious enthusiasm from which Hogarth's Line had rescued it. The "terrible" Name of God is also part of Burke's Sublime in his *Philosophical Enquiry* (63, 67–68). *Enthusiasm Delineated* shows the mysteries returning in a scene that in religious terms is Methodist and in aesthetic terms is Sublime. "To make any thing very terrible," Burke wrote, "obscurity seems in general to be necessary. . . . In reality a great clearness helps but little toward affecting the passions, as it is in some sort an enemy to all enthusiasms whatsoever" (58, 60). Hogarth sees Burke's "obscurity" (illustrated by the figure of Milton's Death) as a new version of the old Christian mysteries dealt with by Woolston. In the *Analysis* he had remarked that because the effects of antique sculptures "have appear'd mysterious," they "have drawn mankind into a sort of religious esteem, and even bigotry, to the works" (105). Now he associates "clearness" with Addison's detached and curious spectator, who appears in both versions of the print as the Muslim (the deist example of a disinterested perspective on Christianity) outside looking into the church through a window.

In *Enthusiasm Delineated* and the other prints published following the publication of Burke's *Philosophical Enquiry,* Hogarth conducts a rearguard action of his Beautiful-Novel against the threat of Burke's Sublime. The breaking of his Lines of Beauty in his last print, *Tail Piece; or, The Bathos* (1764), is a final indication of the agon he sees between his Beautiful and Burke's Sublime. As Hogarth saw it, Burke's examplar of terror, the obscure figure of Milton's Death or the tyrant Satan, has replaced the romantic agon of his own Satan and Death (mediated by Sin, the object of their attentions) with a single obsessed, self-absorbed figure. The first of Hogarth's responses to Burke was the blind gambler in *The Cockpit* (1759), surrounded by equally obsessed disciples (in the composition of another Last Supper), and the last, in the *Tail Piece*, was Father Time, the tyrant who replaces Beauty with (in Burke's words) "dark, confused, uncertain images" (62). *Enthusiasm Delineated* then is a scene crowded with such figures, each solipsistic, as if to illustrate Swift's enthusiast congregation in *The Mechanical Operation of the Spirit* that transmutes spirit into orgasm. It is significant, considering Hogarth's deist past, that the figure of this negative interpretation of the Burkean Sublime is the religious fanatic.

Solipsism and self-enclosure, like obscurity, are the opposites of Addisonian spectatorship, which looks and judges objectively. In *Credulity, Superstition, and Fanaticism: A Medley*, the published version of *Enthusiasm Delineated* three years later, Hogarth's answer to the Sublime is essentially the counterexplanation of Addison's Strange, which in effect absorbs the Sublime as superstition. From *Enthusiasm* to *Credulity* he changes his subject from religious folly (dedicated to the archbishop of Canterbury) to superstitious folly; from icons of Jesus to icons of Fanny the Cock Lane Ghost, who replaces his glory with her candle flame; from images of God the Father holding up a Trinity to a witch on a broomstick, from the Paraclete to the Tedworth Drummer, from Adam and Eve, Sts. Peter and Paul, and Moses and Aaron to the ghosts of Caesar, George Villiers, and Mrs. Veal; and from a beggar cradling an image of Jesus to the Boy of Bilson spewing nails, from a saint in ecstasy to Mary Toft the Rabbit Woman delivering her rabbits (both hoaxes that were exposed). The icons of deity and false miracles (mysteries, doctrines, dogmas) have become the superstitions of the lower orders; the religious icons based on high art representations by Continental painters (Raphael, Rembrandt, Dürer) are replaced by superstitions based on popular and local images.

The replacements, however, are carefully chosen. The replacement of God the Father with the witch is appropriate in that she mimics God's version of rewards and punishments with her more demotic one of casting spells on her enemies and their livestock. Remaining in both versions is the devil with his grill for roasting sinners in the afterlife. Fanny the ghost, who replaces the Name of God at the top of the pleasure thermometer, is, significantly, another woman (though without Venus's Lines of Beauty). In the hands and mouths of the congregation the body of Christ is replaced with the female body, the same sort of substitition Hogarth had employed in *Harlot 6*, thirty years before. However, in the *Harlot* and *The Sleeping Congregation* the woman took the place of the deity because she was a real, living woman; in *Credulity* she is merely another substitute object or representation, a contemporary version of the Christ of the Eucharist, an edible rather than aesthetic object. This edibility invokes a form of consumption that collapses the distance between subject and object and emblematizes the distinction between reader or spectator and deluded participant (in this sense Hogarth recalls Shaftesbury's definition of disinterestedness). Two weeks after he published *Credulity* Hogarth republished *The Sleeping Congregation* ("Retouched & Improved"), perhaps for purposes of comparison and to convey something of the anticlerical message he had decided not to publish in *Enthusiasm Delineated.*

As the title of the revised print shows, Hogarth is now representing credulity (the Strange) in the Swiftean mode of curiosity (the Novel). He continues to condemn these popular superstitions because the Cock Lane Ghost was accepted, in effect dogmatized, by the clergy, Anglican as well as Methodist. The preachers and congregation are *not* "enlightened by Learning and Philosophy," as Addison posited for the Strange. In both versions, by having the High Churchman's tonsured head emerge from under his wig, he expresses his opinion that High Anglicans and Papists are the same.

To the detached Muslim observer, and the viewer of the print, however, the effect is aesthetic. The representation of the objects of credulity and superstition may be more compelling than the enlightened satire directed against it. Once detached from priestcraft and lodged in Addison's "faerie" or Strange, they take on interest in their own right. They permit Hogarth to combine the news (Whitefield's preaching, the setting in his tabernacle, and the Cock Lane Ghost) with bizarre practices that recoup the emblematic structure of his earliest satires (e.g., *The Lottery* [fig. 15]). In short, in *Credulity*, he has changed the composition from the group of self-absorbed fanatics in *Enthusiasm Delineated* into a collection (a "Medley," as he subtitles *Credulity*, suggesting a mixture, a hodgepodge, or a series of songs) of folklore specimens, rather like Brueghel's *Netherlandish Proverbs* (Kaisar Friedrich Museum, Berlin).

The phantasmagoria of *Credulity* informs the other prints Hogarth published between 1760 and 1764: *The Five Orders of Periwigs* and *The Bruiser* (wigs metamorphosing into sexual organs; Hogarth's self-portrait into a bear), as well as the purely emblematic *Times, Plate 1* and *Tail Piece*. *Credulity* also lays the groundwork for the exhibition of Old English signboards, just one month later, which illustrates Addison's use of the Strange as a balance of credulity and curiosity. (Addison himself had drawn attention to signboards in *Spectator* No. 28.) In the context of the exhibition, *Credulity* itself appears to be a collection along the line of Percy's collection of Old English ballads in his *Reliques of Ancient English Poetry*. Both are based on the principle of authenticity similar to that first laid down in Hogarth's Virgilian motto "Seek out your ancient mother" (*Boys Peeping at Nature* [fig. 2]); both exhibit collections of ancient English artifacts, though somewhat "improved" by the collector. Both draw upon a simpler, more immediate response than that of Pope's "ethical poetry" or Hogarth's own "Modern Moral Subjects."

The Vicar of Wakefield

Beginning with its title page, Goldsmith's *Vicar of Wakefield* projects the *Two-Shoes* world. Its epigraph urges, "Sperate miseri, cavete foelices" (Ye miserable, take hope; ye fortunate, beware): the poor will learn to cope, and the Gripes and Graspalls will have their comeuppance. *Goody Two-Shoes* ostensibly offers hope to the poor and downtrodden in an equal providence, but it also offers practical strategies for survival: want is set against spelling, bereavement against shoes. The levels of ideology and irony, or indoctrination and satire, in *Two-Shoes* coexist as uneasily in *The Vicar of Wakefield*, in which the power of Pamela's written word has degenerated into the supposed efficacy of Dr. Primrose's sermons and "wisdom"—supposed because the relationship between word and thing is much less certain than it was in Pamela's world (and even that certainty was doubted by Fielding in *Shamela*). When Primrose preaches a sermon on divine providence there is a noticeable discrepancy between idea (or promise) and reality, between message and audience reception—a gap that is not entirely bridged by an eventual happy ending closer to the genre of the fairy tale than to that of the sermon, though hinting at an analogy between them. The providential discourse of the sermon is played off against the real world we observe in the actions of the characters, which is itself prophesied, validated, and set in perspective by the fairy-tale discourse of the inset ballads, whose words prove to be the only authoritative ones within the "novel."

However, "Sperate miseri, cavete foelices" plainly does not mean that the *good* should take hope, the *evil* beware. Goldsmith quotes Robert Burton's "Sperate miseri, cavete felices," apparently Burton's own Latin.[2] It gives a different emphasis to the Magnificat's "Deposuit potentes de sede, et exaltavit humiles," exchanging happy/unhappy and hope/beware for powerful/powerless and raise up / cast down. Goldsmith's novel is indeed about the latter, but without the real presence of God, Goldsmith makes clear, fictions that produce happiness are the only viable substitute. He shows the casting down of the powerless by the powerful, which is compensated for (as in *Goody Two-Shoes*) by proverbs, sermons, fairy tales, and theatrical scenes. In this respect, while going far beyond Fielding's rationalism, Goldsmith continues to believe in the historicity of the deists and yet knows that the "monstrous truth" (what is to be seen under the shift of Hogarth's Nature) would sap our will to live; and so he accepts religion as a noble lie, which incidentally serves to reenchant the world with fictions, similes, and vivid characters.

The *Vicar* is about happiness, not morality, and when morality is invoked it is only in the prudential and pragmatic terms of the religious belief in a reward or punishment in the afterlife. Primrose is condescending when he describes how the poor, and especially the prisoners with whom he coexists in gaol, survive their ordeals by being mirthful, but the parallel is clear enough when he tells us that the prime function of books is to help us survive, and when he follows by using his sermons for the same purpose.[3]

Goldsmith's writings leading up to the *Vicar* provide a context. In his *Enquiry into the Present State of Polite Learning in Europe* (1759), he cited the "ingenious Mr. Hogarth" for his assertion "that every one, except the connoisseur, was a judge of painting," and added, "The same may be asserted of writing. . . . And this may be the reason why so many writers at present, are apt to appeal from the tribunal of criticism to that of the people" (1:318). This will be his position in the *Vicar*. If we did not know that his essays in the *Bee* were published in the autumn of 1759 and *Tristram Shandy* did not appear in its York edition until December, we might suppose that he had read Sterne.[4] Goldsmith says in his "Introduction" to the *Bee* (6 October) that he was determined "to pursue no fixed method, so it was impossible to form any regular plan"; and that, "determined never to be tedious, in order to be logical, wherever pleasure presented, [he] was resolved to follow": "It will be improper therefore to pall the reader's curiosity by lessening his surprize, or anticipate any pleasure I am able to procure him, by saying what shall come next. Happy [would I be] could any effort of mine, but repress one criminal pleasure, or but for a moment fill up an interval of anxiety!"[5] The next sentence returns to the pragmatics of Fielding's first *Champion* essay attacking deism, contrasting "the vain prospect of life" to "prospects of innocence and ease, where every breeze breathes health, and every sound is but the echo of tranquility."

In an essay in the *Bee* on "Happiness" Goldsmith opposes "age and knowledge [which] only contribute to sour our dispositions" to the disposition "to be merry in circumstances of the highest affliction." He illustrates his thesis with a story of a slave, "maimed, deformed, and chained; obliged to toil from the appearance of day 'till night-fall, and condemned to this for life":

> yet, with all these circumstances of apparent wretchedness, he sung, would have danced, but that he wanted a leg, and appeared the merriest, happiest man of all the garrison. . . . No reading or study had contributed to disenchant the fairy land around him. Every thing furnished him with an opportunity of mirth; and though some thought him from his insensiblity a fool, he was such an ideot as philosophers should wish to imitate; for all philosophy is only forcing the trade of happiness, when nature seems to deny the means. (1:386)

A bit later Goldsmith's author remarks, "For my own part, I never pass by one of our prisons for debt, that I do not envy that felicity which is still going forward among those people who forget the cares of the world by being shut out from its ambition" (1:387). Presumably an example was the earlier story of Alcander and Septimius. After a succession of disasters leading almost to capital punishment, Alcander is miraculously reprieved, reunited with his friend Septimius, and accorded "happiness and ease," and the moral "That no circumstances are so desperate, which providence may not relieve" (1:367).

This vocabulary of happiness reappears in the *Vicar,* focused on the talk of "mirth" preserving the wretched and providence repaying their pain, especially in the prison scenes. Primrose preaches the same message, and his sermons only add the missing desideratum of reward in the hereafter. The absence of any reference to the hereafter in the essay on happiness in the *Bee* suggests how provisional and contingent for Goldsmith is the particular pill within the sugar coating of delusion. The essay on happiness offers a reprise of Addison's Strange, with the credulity that connects it to the Novel:

> Happy could so charming an illusion still continue. I find that age and knowledge only contribute to sour our dispositions. My present enjoyments may be more refined, but they are infinitely less pleasing. The pleasure the best actor gives, can no way compare to that I have received from a country wag, who imitated a quaker's sermon. The music of the finest singer is dissonance to what I felt when our old dairy-maid sung me into tears with Johnny Armstrong's Last Good Night, or the Cruelty of Barbara Allen. (1:385)[6]

As with Sterne and late Fielding (harking back to the *Champion* essays, and so back to the *Spectator* and *Guardian*), Swift's "Digression on Madness" is simply revalued, and delusion is shown to be the way for the wretched to survive, whether through religion or through some worse folly: "it is certainly a better way to oppose calamity by dissipation, than to take up the arms of reason or resolution to oppose it: By the first method we forget our miseries, by the last we only conceal them from others" (1:388). It is also significant, of course, that Goldsmith includes in this essay the conclusion that "the whole world is to them [such as the happy slave] a theatre, on which comedies only are acted" (1:386).

The most significant precursor of the *Vicar* and (whether or not Goldsmith wrote it) *Goody Two-Shoes* was *The Life of Richard Nash,* published in 1762. The point Goldsmith makes about Beau Nash's exemplary life is that such a history will "supply a vacant hour with innocent amusement, however it may fail to open the heart, or improve the understanding." Though himself inconsequential, Nash "presided over the pleasures of a polite kingdom," and his life shows "the pains he took in pursuing pleasure, and the solemnity he assumed in adjusting trifles." He is a case of "the little king of a little people" (it is constantly emphasized that he was metaphorically a monarch); and Bath, his little kingdom, is *the* city for "a continued rotation of diversions" (3:310); but "The great and the little, as they have the same senses, and the same affections, generally present the same picture to the hand of the draughtsman. . . . for nothing very great was ever yet formed from the little materials of humanity" (3:288–90). The topos of the great/ small goes back to *Gulliver's Travels* and Fielding's *Tom Thumb,* but Goldsmith has located it in a New Testament way (via the Magnificat and Christ's teachings) in the small or humble whose delusion of "sperate miseri, cavete felices" sustains them.[7]

As usual with Goldsmith, it is not easy to determine whether the author is very simple or very worldly—how much is irony and how much pragmatic truth-telling, how much is Swift and how much Mandeville.[8] Mr. Rigmarole, the author of "A Reverie at the Boar's-Head-Tavern in Eastcheap" (originally published in the *British Magazine* of 1760), takes Goldsmith's position in the *Bee,* which is also Primrose's: "I love stories, but hate reasoning"—"I am destined to hearken only to stories" (3:102, 111). But here his words are related dialectically to those of Mrs. Quickly's ghost, who reveals that stories of or from the past are different from the life of those times, dominated by superstition and priestcraft. The irony is played out in Quickly's observations: "the people of those times were not [like contemporaries] infidels, but sincere believers"; "they were too plain and simple in those happy days to hide their vices, and act the hypocrite as now" (3:106, 109). Of a woman of that vicious age she reports: "Before she was fifteen she could tell the story of Jack the Giant Killer, could name every mountain that was inhabited by fairies, knew a witch at first sight, and could repeat four Latin prayers without a prompter" (3:107). This hard life, made bearable by stories and prayers, is clearly to be distinguished from Mr. Rigmarole's stories, which bear the same comforting relation to reality in his own time.

If the reverie at the Boar's Head Tavern presents a fiction of a glorious past, the story of Asem in the *Royal Magazine* of December 1759 presents a fiction of a world without vice, and both destroy the illusion much as Swift did Gulliver's of the Struldbrugs.[9] The first depends on a fiction reminiscent of the reading of the Sermon on Conscience in *Tristram Shandy,* with religious belief in the past equated with superstition and clerical tyranny; and the second on a Mandevillian paradox of private vices / public virtues. But, it is also stressed, both Rigmarole's "stories" and Asem's "imaginary world" are useful as "reveries" to enjoy and live by, although, seen through the filter of reason, not to live *in.* The stories, however historically and reasonably untrue, can or must be used to beguile the pain.

Finally, the episode of the Cock Lane Ghost in the spring of 1762 draws together all of these strands: Goldsmith describes the "Mystery," as he calls it, Hogarth links superstition to religion in general, and Samuel Johnson investigates with his cold rational eye the superstition and declares it a fraud. Goldsmith's *The Mystery Revealed,* like the *Vicar* published for Francis Newbery, opens: "It is somewhat remarkable, that the *Reformation,* which in other countries banished *superstition,* in England seemed to encrease the *credulity* of the vulgar."[10] I have emphasized the Addisonian terms of the Strange; and Goldsmith follows them with the assertion that such superstitions are "rejected by all but the lowest class," the "vulgar," whose victims in this instance are "the poor, the ignorant, the old, or the friendless, . . . persons who were unable to resist, or who, because they knew no guilt, were incapable of making an immediate defence" (4:421). Goldsmith dissects the ghost story, concluding:

> It was the observation of Erasmus, that whenever people flock to see a miracle, they are generally sure of seeing a miracle; they bring an *heated imagination,* and an eager *curiosity* to the scene of action, give themselves up blindly to *deception,* and each is better pleased with having it to say, that he had seen something very *strange,* than that he was made the dupe of his own *credulity.* (4:437–38; emphasis added)

Goldsmith has brought together all the familiar terms, even demonstrating how "curiosity" can be used to overlap with "credulity."

In the *Vicar* Dr. Primrose is writing a story about himself, not unlike the story of Alcander, on the model of Job ("A Tale Supposed to be written by himself," we are told on the title page, above the epigraph), and his parabolic discourse is complemented by the fairy-tale discourse of his children and of Mr. Burchell, who addresses his stories to children. However, in the *Vicar* the family and its fall, which in *Two-Shoes* was seen from the child's outsider perspective, is now seen from the inside, from the perspective of the father. If a younger George—or a more resourceful Moses—had told the story, it would have been virtually a repetition of Margery's. If Margery showed how family and possessions lost could be recovered, Crusoe-like, by a child, Dr. Primrose shows what it is like to be the father whose religious discourse constantly runs up against the more accurate as well as more poetic discourse of his youngest sons, who are smaller, secular versions of himself (vs. the daughters, who are already smaller versions of their mother)—and eventually, in the most desperate circumstances, bursts forth in "Sublime" poetry.

In the first chapter he tells the old story of the Roman matron who identifies her "treasures" as not her jewels but her children—predictably with the childlike inflation of the number to thirty-two. The Roman matron is gothicized to a German count, who presents his thirty-two treasures "to his sovereign as the most valuable offering he had to bestow" (4:20). If we take the sovereign, Henry II, to correspond in this postclassical world to the republican Roman, we are also asked to envision a suitable opening to the story of a Job whose "treasure" consisted of seven sons and three daughters, seven thousand sheep, three thousand camels, and so on—of whom the Vicar is a diminutive type (as Two-Shoes is a diminutive Michelangelesque Redeemer). Then the two dei ex machina, Squire and Sir William Thornhill, are parodic versions, at a remove—a children's story version, but also a socioeconomic version in England of the 1760s—of Satan and the Lord God discussing Job. One is the Primroses' landlord, the other the landlord's own landlord or master. The Lord puts Job's "substance," "all that he hath," into Satan's hands, in effect transferring the property from its true owner, the Lord (not his servant Job), to this surrogate, with the sole proviso that Satan can do anything he wishes with the "substance" but cannot touch Job himself. This means that Job's "substance" includes his sons and daughters, seemingly confirming Dr. Primrose's own sense of his children as "treasures" and "valuable offerings."

The *Vicar* is, in a more adult (or sophisticated) sense than *Two-Shoes,* a novel about the transference—the loss and regaining—of property, including the "property" involved in marriage brokerage, but extending also to the "finery" the Vicar's wife and daughters purchase, horses he must sell, the gross of green spectacles his son must buy, and even the family portrait he commissions with current Reynoldsian iconography elevating them all into gods and heroes (another version of "finery"). Thus the Job story and the accompanying sublimity are shown to have the Mandevillian subtext of property, not unlike the story of pursuit and rape in Walpole's *Castle of Otranto.*

For the *Vicar,* which has been called a parable of providence,[11] is more properly a parable of the different kinds of making, literary and/or existential, interested and disinterested, including the prisoners' making of little useful objects and Primrose's making of a usable parable about himself. It is a novel that instructs suffering man how to survive in the hard world of experience, which involves the kind of oppression by the rich of the poor which is described in *Two-Shoes,* and so the kind of incantatory repetitions also used by Margery, including not only the useful delusions of fairy tales but also religious belief in an afterlife. But above all, far from being a parable of morality, it is in fact a novel that offers instead, as a solution to the immorality of a world of unequal providence, an aesthetic experience. However, the *Vicar* begins as a poetics. Making is introduced with the domestic chores of Mrs. Primrose, which recall the commonplace examples used by Hogarth in his *Analysis.* As the doctor never tires of repeating, she has expertise at "pickling, preserving, and cookery," at which "none could excell her" (4:18). This is expressed in the boastful words of an uxorious husband, which serve as one aspect of the constant incongruity in the novel between what is and what is said about it. Mrs. Primrose, the other central presence in the novel, is in many ways Dr. Primrose's suppressed other (his dark side, which he can comment on and blame but still uxoriously praise and encourage). Her "reputation for gooseberry wine" and her "abilities at making a goose-pye" play on the sense of simpleness (goose-egg, a zero or nothing, a score of zero in the game of appropriation of property that is being played in the novel). She is fine when she cooks and pickles, less so when she contrives to save money and "prides herself" in her contrivances, which are soon related to her "thousand schemes to entrap" Squire Thornhill into marriage with Olivia: "or, to speak more tenderly, [she] used every art to magnify the merit of her daughter," attributing to Olivia her own talent for gathering gooseberries and making gooseberry wine (4:18).

Her "contrivances," which engross Dr. Primrose, disastrously misfire when absorbed within the larger, more skillful contrivances of Squire Thornhill and Ephraim Jenkinson. Contrivance is connected with "art" (as in the unfortunate case of the family portrait), pretension, and failure, not only for the Primroses but eventually for the Squire and Jenkinson as well.

As a person involved in this kind of contriving, Primrose himself is several steps behind Margery Two-Shoes. He cannot put two and two together. He cannot connect Moses' experience selling a horse with his own. He is (as opposed to the dualism of Two-Shoes) a "monogamist," as he tells his deceiver Jenkinson, identifying himself as "that unfortunate Divine, who has so long, and it would ill become me to say successfully, fought against the deuterogamy of the age" (4:73); but he lets his wife assume the pose, in their history painting, of that notorious polygamist Venus. His problem is that he literally cannot put on the second shoe, or put together letters or words to make sense of them.

The rascally Jenkinson, by contrast, puts together nonsensical syllables and words in an incantatory way that has at least a temporary success with the Vicar (chap. 14). His speech consists of words that have nothing "to do with the business I was talking of," says Primrose; "but it was sufficient to shew me that he was a man of letters, and I now reverenced him the more." Primrose's nonsense carries him away from the business at hand into the Whistonian (monogamist) controversy; Jenkinson's nonsense, more practically and so more in the mode of Two-Shoes, acquires for him the Vicar's horse—for which end he also employs the words on paper which comprise a draught upon Farmer Flamborough "payable on sight," words that take the place of actual money, have no intrinsic worth, but do get him the horse. In a sense the *Vicar* shows how Primrose learns to utilize his own nonsense to practical ends such as coping with misery, both his own and his co-sufferers'.

Primrose, at the outset, presents his readers with the commonplace reality of the members of his family, who are (as he acknowledges, indeed boasts) "all equally generous, credulous, simple, and inoffensive"; "a family so harmless as ours," he notes later, is "too humble to excite envy, and too inoffensive to create disgust" (4:21, 76). This he implicitly contrasts with the history portrait he commissions, which is too big for the parlor wall; with the ambitious contrivances of Mrs. Primrose; and with his own vanities (her economic "management" and his "spiritual"). What the contrivance of art brings about is the joining of these incongruous, and apparently disastrously disparate, realities. This unification is possible because parallel with the bumbling contrivances of the characters is the providential pattern invoked by Dr. Primrose which takes over from them as the novel approaches its extravagant denouement.

The most effectual of what Primrose refers to as "those harmless delusions that tend to make us more happy" are the sermons he delivers to the prisoners in the final chapters. The principle is one of simple repetition (he must, as he puts it, "repeat") based on the "harmless delusion" of providential design, that is, on a heavenly reward juxtaposed with earthly pain. Like Mrs. Primrose's persistent making of gooseberry wine, the Vicar's sermon is based on two elements: a pleasant taste and repetition. In prison he breaks down the opposition of the prisoners by dogged repetition: "[I] went on, perfectly sensible that what was ridiculous in my attempt, would excite mirth only the first or second time, while what was serious would be permanent." In "less than six days" Primrose has made "some" of the prisoners "penitent, and all attentive," and this stage is followed by his setting them "to work at cutting pegs for tobacconists and shoemakers," and at selling them "so that each earned something every day" to maintain himself (4:148–49). Words have been augmented by labor to consume the tedious hours in prison and produce alleviation of discomfort. In an abbreviated form he has recapitulated Crusoe's story, being expelled (first from the eponymous Wakefield, then from his humbler home), then confined (as in the trope of Defoe's prison-island of his personal "history") and forced to reconstruct his own world, after which he builds up—by a civilizing process—a society around him, solely through his sermonizing.

The final sermon, in chapter 29, is on providence. In it, Primrose modifies the book's epigraph from "Ye wretched, take hope; ye fortunate, beware," to words that have it both ways: "to the fortunate religion holds out a continuance of bliss, to the wretched a change from pain." The sermon that follows is his version of Margery Two-Shoes's maxims about smiling in the face of disaster, and satisfying one's hunger for plum pudding by spelling the word, and fulfills the earlier thesis of "harmless delusion." Religion, he tells the prisoners (and his family and himself), "does what philosophy could never do: it shews the equal dealings of heaven to the happy and the unhappy, and levels all human enjoyments to nearly the same standard" (4:162). He sounds remarkably like Swift's Grub Street Hack, opposing philosophy to religion as dissection to painting and patching over flaws, analysis to illusion, but more like Fielding's version of the doctrine of equal providence:

> [It] has promised peculiar rewards to the unhappy; . . . To [the miserable] it is a double advantage; for it diminishes their pain here, and rewards them with heavenly bliss hereafter. . . . It gives to both rich and poor the same happiness hereafter, and equal hopes to aspire after it; but if the rich have the advantage of enjoying pleasures here, the poor have the endless satisfaction of knowing what it was once to be miserable, when crowned with endless felicity hereafter; and even though this should be called a small advantage, yet being an eternal one, it must make up by duration what the temporal happiness of the great may have exceeded by intenseness. (4:161–62)

The pleasure of the poor and downtrodden is simply richer than that of the fortunate rich because it contains the contrast of pain and pleasure. Or, closer to the message of Two-Shoes: In the afterlife there will be a time "when the luxurious great ones of the world shall no more tread us to the earth; when we shall think with pleasure of our sufferings below," and so on; the sermon ends with reference to the time "when our bliss shall be unutterable, and still, to crown all, unending" (4:163). Now this "harmless delusion" begins to be materialized in the plot: as with Two-Shoes, words generate events. In chapter 30 "Happier prospects begin to appear," and this good news is followed by strange advice: "Let us be inflexible, and fortune will at last change in our favour" (4:164).

It is also materialized, most significantly, in the metaphor of life as theater. Dr. Primrose, in his words of comfort to his son George, sees life as a journey: "Almost all men have been taught to call life a passage, and themselves the travellers. The similitude still may be improved when we observe that the good are joyful and serene, like travellers that are going towards home; the wicked but by intervals happy, like travellers that are going into exile" (4:135).[12]

The Primrose family migrates to a new parish and begins to fragment as George departs, Olivia disappears, and Dr. Primrose sets out alone on the road to find her. The climax of his providential metaphor of life as a journey is reached, ironically, when his family is completely broken up and he is confined to prison. In his sermon on providence he asks the prisoners to take comfort, "for we shall soon be at our journey's end," and "the weary traveller" will "lay down the heavy burthen laid upon" him and find his heavenly (as opposed to earthly) reward (4:163). The point is that the reward is distanced into the afterlife from this unlucky moment in the present. Earlier, when he sent George off into the world, Primrose had advised him to remember the Thirty-seventh Psalm: "never saw I the righteous man forsaken, or his seed begging their bread" (v. 25; 4:26). The context of the quotation he chose is a journey: "The steps of a man are from the Lord, and he establishes him in whose way he delights" (or, "he holds him firm and watches over his path"); "though he fall, he shall not be cast headlong, for the Lord is the stay of his hand" (vv. 23–24). Though it appears that Primrose is intended to be in some sense educated, demonstrating a progress by his statement of the doctrine of equal providence to the prisoners, the fact is that at the end of the novel a shower of earthly rewards vindicates his first interpretation (to George) of providence as justice in this world. The fact that Primrose's progress is analogous to Job's may, as Battestin has proposed, help to explain why he too was returned his lost possessions.[13] But I suspect that the answer is involved in the other metaphor that informs Primrose's progress, and of which he is seemingly unaware.

On his travels in search of Olivia he encounters George, performing in a troupe of actors, and the progress George recounts takes the
form of a journey, from the Primrose vicarage to London to Amster-
dam to Louvain to Paris, and so on, in each place assuming a different
profession: gentleman usher, writer, English teacher, Greek teacher,
tutor, rhetor, and finally actor. "I was driven for some time from one
character to another," George tells his father; and we recall that in each
case he was given the idea of what profession to adopt by a friend. It
becomes clear that Goldsmith has seen George's journey as a series of
roles adopted, and that the metaphors of life as journey and as theater
have coalesced.

Once generated, however, by the recognition scenes with Arabella Wilmot and George, and by George's performance in *The Fair
Penitent,* the theater metaphor takes over: we are hurried into the
grotesquely theatrical recognition of the lost Olivia and the revelation
of her seduction (a fair penitent), the Vicar's arrival home with her just
as his house bursts into flames, his imprisonment by the wicked seducer of his daughter, and so on; and toward the final reversals, recog-
nitions, and unmasking—a blaze of theatrical metaphor with which
the providential resolution is expressed.

Only in the denouement of a play can the lowly find hope and
the mighty beware. The fairy tales and ballad romances, even the
model of Primrose's life as Job's, are part of the system of analogies that
becomes, with the appearance of George and his troupe of actors,
specifically theatrical, with Dr. Primrose another actor. The members
of the Primrose family (like George) pick up any role offered them. At
the moment when Primrose is preaching life as a journey to an eternal
reward, he is locked in a prison that soon turns into a set for *The
Beggar's Opera,* with the Beggar himself virtually materialized to set
things right. Even Job's story, parallel at many points to the Vicar's, is
not a journey but a drama in which a puppet master takes away and
restores possessions in a most theatrical way. Sir William Thornhill,
like the Duke in *Measure for Measure,* is merely the great Puppet
Master's surrogate on earth.

The only scholar who has connected Dr. Primrose with the primrose *path* has cited *Macbeth* ("the primrose path to the everlasting bon-
fire").[14] But the germ of the Vicar and his antagonist Squire Thornhill,

as well as the novel's conjunction of metaphors, is in *Hamlet* (a play Fielding also used to inform Tom's journey at a crucial point)—in Ophelia's speech to Laertes as he departs on his journey:

> But, good my brother,
> Do not, as some ungracious pastors do,
> Show me the steep and thorny way to heaven,
> While, like a puff'd and reckless libertine,
> Himself the primrose path of dalliance treads,
> And recks not his own rede.
>
> (1.3.45–51)

Here is the pastor, the "thorny way to heaven," and the "primrose path of dalliance" in which the pastor does not heed his own counsel.[15] Here is the Vicar not only as the subject who needs to see his life as the hard journey of a Job with an inevitable reward for virtue, but also as the object whose life is actually a theater, with provisional roles and apparent rewards and punishments distributed at the denouement.

The *Vicar* sums up the various uses of the theatrical metaphor and serves as a retrospect on the period it closes. It demonstrates the two ways the metaphor was used by the contemporaries of Hogarth and Fielding. The patricians staged one form of theater for the lower orders, consisting of paternalistic gestures and costumes, and another for themselves, this one interposing masks between themselves and bodily contact with coarse realities (such as the lower orders). Both Squire Thornhill and Dr. Primrose (and his family) carry out these charades in their related ways. The Primroses imitate the Thornhills, as the hapless dwarf in the fable follows the giant into giant-battles for which he is ill equipped.

There is no question that Goldsmith in the *Vicar* is extending the Novel and Uncommon to the Strange and Fanciful, superstition and faerie; and he does this by the utilization of fables, proverbs, ballads, fairy tales, epitaphs, and (the parallelism is suggestive) sermons—all equally fictional, mirth-making, delusive, and at the same time truth-bearing and prophetic. Burchell / Sir William tells children stories and sings them ballads in the manner of Two-Shoes, accompanying his performances with physical objects he carries in his pockets, specifically "a piece of ginger-bread, or an half-penny whistle" (4:39). In chapter 30, when he reappears for the Final Judgment, he gives Bill and Dick Primrose "each a large piece of ginger-bread" (4:169)—"which," we are told, "the poor fellows [now in adversity] eat very heartily, as they had got that morning but a very scanty breakfast"—and we recall not only the Newbery story of Giles Gingerbread's father, with his fresh gingerbread cake each day, but Margery's spelling of the words "plumb pudding" and "bread." Indeed, John Newbery the bookseller of children's books, and in particular of *Goody Two-Shoes,* and father of Francis Newbery, the publisher of *The Vicar of Wakefield,* appears in the text of the *Vicar* in time to pay Primrose's bill after his illness on the road— and is, Primrose tells us, the publisher of one of his monogamist tracts (4:94).

In their contexts of consolation, the sermon and the story of Matilda are equated, and these in turn with books (4:129, 132)—all functioning to overcome misery. In this sense, simple merriment is a lesser alternative, reserved for the poor and the prisoners; in the latter case the sermon becomes an alternative (4:117, 141). However, these forms of popular literature share one significant characteristic: they are the only source of truth in the *Vicar,* though it is a truth that (like Pamela's homely analogy of herself and the carp) can be interpreted at different times in different ways. Bill's song of the mad dog (4:88–89), an exemplum of the biter-bit (taught him by the farmer whom the Primroses are using as a cat's paw to trap the squire into marriage with Olivia), first tells the truth that the Primroses are the biter-bitten (by the squire), but at the end the application shifts to the squire himself. In the context of popular or folk wisdom, the Augustan theater proves to be merely "theatrical," as in the tragedy, Nicholas Rowe's *Fair Penitent* (1703), in which George Primrose and the players are about to perform but are prevented when George recognizes his father in the audience (4:122). In the playtext, the lovely woman who stoops to folly (Callista, Richardson's model, by the way, for the "tragedy" of Clarissa) has one recourse, to die; and die she does. Her father dies in sympathy; her lover, Lothario, is stabbed by Altamont in very much the way Thornhill is attacked by George. Rowe's play suggests an alternative (a high-literary one) to the Primrose family's final happiness. Written by Rowe, *The Vicar of Wakefield* might have ended with the stabbing of Thornhill, the suicide of Olivia, the death of Primrose, and the stormy but finally stable marriage of George (Horatio) and Arabella Wilmot (Lavinia). Its narrative structure—which is replaced by that of the Book of Job—suggests an alternative perspective. Both plots center on the betrayals and catastrophes besetting a family, one depicting the family's disintegration, the other its strengthening and reintegration. Both dismiss fictions dealing with high life and the nobility. In fact, the speech George fails to deliver before the curtain is Horatio's prologue, which calls for a drama about *the people* rather than about the gentry:

> Therefore an humbler theme our author chose,
> A melancholy tale of private woes;
> No princes here lost royalty bemoan,
> But you shall meet with sorrows like your own.
>   (ll. 15–18)[16]

Goldsmith uses the convergence of the two works, one literary, with the conventions of the Augustan period, and the other with its associations of the Old Testament and the Sublime, to stress their differences: it is much the same thematic that distinguishes the reader from the Vicar, the Vicar from Thornhill, the dwarf from the giant, the elegy from the vulgar ballad, and the steep and thorny way from the primrose path.

As James Lehman has pointed out, the first part of the *Vicar* is dominated in the old fashion by Pope, Gay, and Congreve, by social satire and comedy of manners. Primrose's folly is largely because he is contained within this world, which is essentially his social-climbing family. It is his pride of family that explains, for example, his inflation of the number of the Roman matron's children and his hyperbolic charge to George to emulate his grandfather who fought with Lord Falkland (which would make Primrose well over a hundred). It is this same pride of family which defines the satiric roles of Deborah and his daughters, and indeed his son Moses. As Lehman points out, both names are parodic of Old Testament figures that Deborah and Moses emulate (the domineering, bossy wife and the female judge of *Judges;* the debating-inclined son and the lawgiver of the Pentateuch). Primrose is placed—or places himself—in "an artificially self-conscious position" based on the "concern for appearances and social status."[17]

In the second part, then, when he is forced to go on his "pilgrimage," he is cast into "the condition of genuine passion," "the natural and passionate love of his family and his fellow man," which has been adumbrated in the ballads; he now takes up the story of Job, which culminates in the sublimity of the fire and other disasters, Primrose's Joblike curse, Olivia's "death," Primrose's sermons, and the Burkean power of Squire Thornhill.

How much of this "play" is intended by Goldsmith, and how much is a function of the Novel/novel itself—its curiosity, discovery, uncovering, and bracketing of credulity? For example, an early version of the *Vicar* and its provisionality of forms was *Robinson Crusoe,* the spiritual autobiography in which Defoe presumably means for the reader to accept the providential pilgrimage as fact but, by including conflicting accounts (of Crusoe's arrival on the island) and perspectives (the immediate experience, the retelling of it by the old, pious Crusoe), he in effect demystifies the conversion story. The overlapping of narratives produces an effect that may be beyond the author's conscious intention. But a half century later, *Goody Two-Shoes* offers side-by-side the alternative supernatural and natural readings of phenomena; and in the *Vicar* Goldsmith is self-conscious enough of the theoretical issues to introduce literary discussions about them.

In the literary criticism that is bandied about in conversation, the poles (in Burchell's talk and Primrose's, and later as the players and George discuss old and current literature) seem to be Pope and Congreve, associated with wit and sententiousness, and the ballads and popular literature, which includes children's stories. The literary alternatives are presented as a comic interplay of positions and characters. But the popular invariably proves to have carried the truth of a situation or a prophecy of future events. After his son's recitation of the "Elegy on a Mad Dog," which projects the biter-bit situation in the case of both the Primroses and Squire Thornhill himself, Dr. Primrose remarks blandly (and uncomprehendingly) that "the most vulgar ballad of them all generally pleases me better than the fine modern odes, and things that petrify us in a single stanza; productions that we at once detest and praise" (4:17). These jingles are a reaction to the Popean mode ("A Lady loses her muff, her fan, or her lap-dog, and so the silly poet runs home to versify the disaster"). Primrose takes the Tickell-Philips position against the one shared by Burchell and Pope, replacing it with a mode that privileges the dog over the man (the dog, not the man, dies of the bite); and the dog is a "mad dog" rather than a lapdog. It is a parabolic tale rather than a social satire, and it includes the prophetic dimension. But then, in the strange comic dialectic that characterizes this novel, Moses replies that popular songs too are "all cast in the same mold."[18]

The central example of literary discussion focuses on the current theater—a subject that, appropriately, is materialized in the second half of the novel, where theatricality is the dominant mode. Primrose asks the players he encounters on his journey "who were the present theatrical writers in vogue"—and is told that Dryden, Otway, and Rowe are out of fashion and Jonson, Shakespeare, and Fletcher are in (surely a good thing from Goldsmith's point of view). At this point Primrose, now no longer on the side of balladry and Percy's *Reliques,* asks how "the present age can be pleased with that antiquated dialect, that obsolete humour, those over-charged characters, which abound in the works you mention?" (4:96). The player's explanation, on the face of it, undermines the argument for old comedy: people "go only to be amused, and find themselves happy when they can enjoy a pantomime, under the sanction of Jonson's or Shakespeare's name," he says—recalling for us the "harmless delusions" referred to earlier. What distinguishes this acting is "shrugs," "starts and attitudes," or presumably what he refers to as "natural" gestures, as opposed to the verbal wit of Congreve and Farquhar.[19] Modern taste is apparently based on gesture and subrational, emotional, inexplicable things that are related to the poetry of popular ballads. One opinion dialectically follows the other. But the fact remains that the wisdom, or at least the truth, of the novel (or Novel) is being carried by the popular songs—and by the strange, ritualistic level of the story—and not by the protestations and refinements of Burchell.

The Aesthetic Moment: Olivia's Song

In chapter 24 there is a scene of such black humor that it characterizes at one extreme the mode of Goldsmith's novel. The Primroses breakfast together. Olivia has been seduced and abandoned by Squire Thornhill; just recovered by her father, she is damaged goods (as Dr.

Primrose has made quite clear to her in his first response to the discovery that she is no longer a virgin yet unmarried). Their house has been burnt down and most of their property lost, including the daughters' dowries. But they sit on the same honeysuckle bank where, back in chapter 5, they first encountered Squire Thornhill pursuing an unfortunate stag. The symmetry as well as the parallel of the "chase" are plain. Dr. Primrose recalls that

> It was in this place my poor Olivia first met her seducer, and every object seemed to recall her sadness. But that melancholy, which is excited by objects of pleasure, or inspired by sounds of harmony, sooths the heart instead of corroding it. Her mother too, upon this occasion, felt a pleasing distress, and wept, and loved her daughter as before. "Do, my pretty Olivia," cried she, "let us have that little melancholy air your pappa was so fond of, [since] your sister Sophy has already obliged us. Do child, it will please your old father." She complied in a manner so exquisitely pathetic as moved me. (4:136)

Thus she sings the well-known lyric that begins "When lovely woman stoops to folly," and ends:

> The only art her guilt to cover,
> To hide her shame from every eye,
> To give repentance to her lover,
> And wring his bosom—is to die.

Among the many things to note in this scene, we may begin with the fact that "art" is required to cover her guilt—"art" both in the sense of "contrivance" (the art of her song) and in the sense of an aesthetic experience contrived from her catastrophe for the relief of her parents. The experience of the scene, which includes the message of the lyric, involves the fallen sinner, the prey of the "chase," but now in the aftermath her purgation through a fantasy of reparation or atonement. The scene, while it aesthetically pleases both father and mother, later alarms the father when, no longer distanced, the song is materialized (once again, as with the other songs and ballads, it is proved prophetic) in Olivia's death, which is momentarily accepted as true by the reader as it is by Dr. Primrose. This is another contrivance—this time a successful one—of the arch-contriver Ephraim Jenkinson, with the connivance of Mrs. Primrose.

Under the circumstances, the request to Olivia for that particular song was needlessly cruel. No character within the text raises the question of the cruelty of the request, any more than the cruelty of the later contrivance of Olivia's "death." The literary prototypes, in a scene that is charged with parody and comedy, go back to Pamela's first letter from her parents, which urged upon her the same advice—to die—in case she allowed herself to be seduced by her master; and so set up a stricture that radically limited, whatever she may say or Richardson may gloss, her subsequent actions vis-à-vis Mr. B. But more plainly than Pamela, Olivia recalls, especially in the context of the recent talk between Moses and the actors about theater and Shakespeare, the case of Hero in *Much Ado about Nothing*. Hero also feigned death to catch a lover who treated her, in terms of an alleged "fall," as barbarously as Squire Thornhill treated Olivia; and she also returned safe and sound.

In this sequence of events in the *Vicar*, however, the disturbing parodic element is the aesthetic pleasure of the mother and father, perhaps shared by the reader: The sounds of the birds and of Sophia's song, and the associations of the place in which they have chosen to breakfast, serve to obliterate for the moment Olivia's seduction and fall and their own present dismal plight. Mrs. Primrose, we are told (suggesting that the preceding sentence refers to Dr. Primrose, the speaker), "too, upon this occasion, felt a pleasing distress," which apparently causes her to weep and to love "her daughter as before"—as if this experience, with its mixture of present sounds and memories of past happiness and betrayal, has made her forgive Olivia in a way she has not managed before. The result, or rather the materialization, is her request to Olivia to sing for Dr. Primrose (who "was fond of" the "melancholy air") the song of her own fall and projected death. In one sense, her song is another popular, anti-Pope form of literature, thus prophetic, proleptic, and truth-telling. In Sterne's sense, Olivia has a story, a *sad* story, and appears to her family of spectators as Maria did to Tristram and Yorick.

Underneath this cruel mock-epitaph is Goldsmith's presentation of an "aesthetic" scene based on evident objectification of Olivia by her property-oriented parents.[20] The scene follows upon the sublime experience of the conflagration and precedes the incarceration of Primrose, Olivia's death, and her resurrection. As such it negates, or at least distances, the fiction of sublimity and the Job analogue that have come to dominate the story in the disasters that are rapidly accruing to Dr. Primrose.

The scene is followed immediately by the seducer Squire Thornhill's arrival—by his compromising proposals (to marry Olivia off and remain her lover), Primrose's angry dismissal of those proposals ("avoid my sight, thou reptile"), and Thornhill's threat of eviction and imprisonment and Primrose's theatrical speech beginning "Go, and leave me to want, infamy, disease, and sorrow." The chapter that began with Olivia's song ends with Primrose being carted off to prison in a Greuze-like scene of lamenting children around a suffering paterfamilias. As he leaves, he says, "[I] desired my son to assist his elder sister, who, from a consciousness that she was the cause of all our calamities, was *fallen,* and had lost anguish in insensibility" (4:138–39; emphasis added). The words of the song are materialized in herself, as they predict her forthcoming (fictive) death. But like earlier songs and ballads, this song turns out to be about Dr. Primrose's own disaster, which of course proves to be another's death with her resurrection in store. Olivia has to atone for Primrose's fall (into pride, avarice, and marriage-plotting), after which the deity himself (Sir William) can reappear for a Last Judgment.

At the end, after all the reversals and discoveries, Dr. Primrose tells us, "my spirits were exhausted by the alternation of pleasure and pain"; so he leaves the others "in the midst of their mirth" and retires alone. "I poured out my heart in gratitude to the giver of joy as well as sorrow, and then slept undisturbed till morning" (4:181–82). This statement, after a scene orchestrated by the "designs" and contrivances of Sir William Thornhill and Ephraim Jenkinson, sums up the aesthetic of the book as an alternation of pleasure and pain finding release in a paean to deity—a deity that has been thoroughly fictionalized within the story itself; and is a final demonstration, if one is needed, that the *Vicar* is in fact an aesthetic, not a moral, fable. As Dr. Primrose said in his sermon: the "addition" to the happiness of the poor man in a heavenly afterlife is "that he had once been wretched and now was comforted; that he had known what it was to be miserable, and now felt what it was to be happy" (4:162).

A final aspect of this aesthetics is apparent in chapter 30, where the pseudo-sublimity and pseudo-tragedy eventuate as true (or at least conventional) comedy. Sir William Thornhill, the local property owner whose misanthropy has withdrawn him from society, plays God, specifically a *deus absconditus* who is recalled by emergency to his responsibility. Thus, having seen "a good man struggling with adversity," we now see the even greater subject, "which is the good man that comes to relieve it" (4:167). Sir William comes, chastises and pardons, and passes out gingerbread to the children, in the gesture of authority and benevolence seen in children's books of the time. Then everyone sits down to dinner, and Sir William writes a prescription for Primrose's damaged arm (he is also a healer), much as Jehovah takes care of Job's boils. Now the gaoler turns into the servant who serves dinner, the lion lies down with the lamb, and (in the next chapter) judgment is passed by Sir William, the wicked Squire Thornhill is punished, and marriages are arranged.

Finally, Olivia, the aesthetic object: With prompting from Jenkinson and her mother, she has taken the advice offered by her song, pretending to die—not to wring her lover's bosom (from all reports unwringable) but to help bring her father to an awareness of his complicity in her ruin and his responsibilities to the family. She appears in the gaol cell for the finale, alive, and what is more, far from martyred: she is made proprietress of the wretched squire's remaining fortune.

The Vicar of Wakefield is a book about equal providence in the hereafter rendered immanent by an extreme form of theatricality and fictionality. Primrose, so focused upon interest, projecting a religion focused on the interest of rewards/punishments, is the exact opposite of Shaftesbury's disinterested man, and indeed the civic humanist is included doubly as the interested Squire Thornhill and the disinterested Sir William. This world, with nothing of the Palladian structure of *Tom Jones,* represents an alternative aesthetic to Fielding's as well as to Hogarth's. It sums up the effect of Addison's Strange (the so-called trivial or infantile), which I earlier formulated as the pursual of the

Novel/Uncommon beyond reasonable limits. I would now add, on the basis of the example of Goldsmith (and probably Sterne as well), that the Strange acts to carry the Novel so far that it is turned back upon itself and reabsorbed—humorously but effectively—into the *Spectator* world where it began, and where Addison himself certainly intended it to remain.

NINE

*From Novel
to Picturesque*

Gilpin and Price

William Gilpin's aesthetics of the Picturesque, formulated in the 1780s but developed as early as the 1740s, begins with Addison's Secondary Pleasures, the area of the picturable.[1] Gilpin's sense of the Picturesque as making picturable something that is beautiful or sublime goes back to Addison's Novel as that which "improves what is great or beautiful, and makes it afford the Mind a double Entertainment" or "enlivens a Prospect" (as opposed to the Beautiful, which only "finishes"). However, some of Gilpin's emphases come from Hogarth's adaptation of Addison rather than from Addison himself. Gilpin had corresponded with, if he did not meet, Hogarth (he pointed out to him the incongruity of a floating scroll in *Paul before Felix*), and after Hogarth's death he wrote *An Essay upon Prints* (1768) which included an informed discussion of his engravings.[2]

Gilpin begins the first of the *Three Essays* of 1791 with a sense of the beautiful object which corresponds to Addison's category of the Beautiful, based on "smoothness, or neatness, [and] elegance."[3] This he augments with a "picturesque representation" of Hogarth's woman, thereby producing the amalgam "picturesque [like *novel*] beauty." By this he means beauty represented, "objects chiefly pleasing in painting": on the one hand, beauty in close-up or detail (the wrinkles of a face, the "bark of a tree, . . . the rude summit, and craggy sides of a mountain") and, on the other, beauty in action or movement, for example a face or hair "agitated by passion" as a "smooth surface is ruffled," or "an elegant line" (presumably Hogarth's serpentine Line of Beauty) juxtaposed, as in the principle of contrast, with "a rough one" (6–7, 12, 17).[4]

Gilpin's focus in this first essay is on the artist, though of course he is also explaining to the observer how paintings provide an aesthetic experience. (He continues with an essay on the picturesque traveler but then returns in the third essay to the artist who sketches landscapes.) He divides the picturing (picturesquing) of nature into two aspects, the artist and the object he represents, which in practice depend on iconoclastic verbs of breaking: The artist creates ruggedness and roughness by modifying the surface of "beautiful" bodies.

In the case of Palladian architecture, the picturesque artist must be a destroyer (a role that recalls Hogarth's satires on Palladianism): "Should we wish to give it picturesque beauty, we must *use the mallet, instead of the chissel:* we must *beat down* one half of it, *deface* the other, and *throw* the mutilated members around in heaps. In short, from a *smooth* building, we must turn it into a *rough* ruin" (7, emphasis added). The same iconoclasm is called for when confronted with Capability Brown's "beautiful" serpentine gardens. Gilpin's artist is urged to

> Turn the lawn into a piece of broken ground: plant rugged oaks instead of flowering shrubs: break the edges of the walk: give it the rudeness of a road; mark it with wheel-tracks; and scatter around a few stones, and brushwood; in a word, instead of making the whole *smooth,* make it *rough;* and you make it also *picturesque.* (8)

As Gilpin's references to Capability Brown suggest, the garden was the focus of another line of aesthetic argument. In this case Brown appropriated Hogarth's Line of Beauty by itself, jettisoning the principles of intricacy and (at least in Hogarth's sense, which included the emblematic) variety—in short, taking the principle and leaving the concrete particulars from which the principle was educed. Gilpin responded (largely associating Hogarth, as Brown did, with his Line) with the case for intricacy and variety, achieved in a landscape by benign neglect. It is notable that in this essay Gilpin's Picturesque, unlike later versions by

Uvedale Price and Richard Payne Knight, supposes not gradual passive destruction by time but an energetic action by an artist.

On other occasions Gilpin did tend to sentimentalize rural poverty and, by attributing picturesque landscapes to the effects of time, accident, or fate, draw attention away from the responsibility of political agencies. In the present essay he follows Hogarth in shifting attention to agency, but specifically to the artist's. His correlation of the Beautiful with positive moral values, and the Picturesque with what is ordinarily thought of as negative (idleness and decrepitude), creates an aesthetic object. But he also asks that the Picturesque be utilized to counteract and correct the Beautiful.[5] The active verbs of breaking tend to imply the satiric aspect (or potential) of the picturesque artist, which was primary in Hogarth's intention. Indeed, picturesqueness, roughness, variety, and contrast (as of rough with smooth) were among the characteristics of the traditional satyr-satirist.

Hogarth, of course, in the *Harlot* and the *Rake,* and even in the *Analysis* (in its illustrative plates), consistently placed the responsibility for the effects wreaked on the beautiful object on outside factors—on "priestcraft," whether of clergy, magistrates, or politicians. But the Hogarthian Novel did carry oppositional force, and Gilpin follows Hogarth in privileging the local, marginal, and specifically English against the Continental "high art" tradition that homogenizes art and culture. Even in Gilpin's theory of the landscape Picturesque these oppositional assumptions remain: the scene works on behalf of the indigenous against the forces of "improvement" and is a protest against those who, ignorant or dismissive of cultural heterogeneity, seek to impose the same pattern and order everywhere.

Gilpin's essay, while not omitting landscape, focuses on human figures, and—following Hogarth—on the lock (Belinda's lock) of hair. Gilpin imagines the portraitist Reynolds disheveling the hair of his sitter about her shoulders (8). And from Reynolds's throwing his sitter's hair Gilpin moves to Virgil's "portrait of Venus," "which is highly finished in every part, [but] the artist has given her hair, / ——*dissundere ventis,*" has made it stream in the wind; as Milton represents Eve in *Paradise Lost* with "unadorned golden tresses . . . / Dishevelled, and in wanton ringlets waved" (9). This passage, echoed by Hogarth in the *Analysis,* is adjacent to the one he used on the title page as his epigraph:

So vary'd he [i.e., Satan], and of his tortuous train
Curl'd many a wanton wreath, in sight of Eve,
To lure her eye.

(bk. 9, ll. 516–18; fig. 21)

The "dishevelled" hair makes the beautiful woman picturesque; it also echoes the "wanton wreaths" of the serpent who tempts her to the Fall.

However, if Gilpin attributes the picturesqueness of Beauty to the work of the artist, he also implies the story in which the artist situates her: the contingencies surrounding the beautiful object within the representation (the history painting). His examples of Venus and Eve, Ascanius and Charon, imply stories. A beautiful body becomes picturesque (picturable) when it is "agitated by passion" or (a Virgilian metaphor for passion) caught in a wind, which produces more variety or contrast than does the merely beautiful object by itself. Gilpin takes these terms from the Hogarth-Addison middle term, Novel, and doubtless from Hogarth's practice in his "modern moral subjects":

> The lines, and surface of a beautiful human form are so infinitely varied . . . and it's limbs so fitted to receive all the beauties of grace, and contrast. . . . But altho the human form in a quiescent state, is thus beautiful; yet the more it's *smooth surface is ruffled*, if I may so speak, the more picturesque it appears. (11–12)

The example he gives is when "it is agitated by passion," and the conclusion is that "the human body will always be more picturesque in action, than at rest" (his examples of sculptures are those used by Hogarth in *Analysis* 1, the *Laocoön* and *Antinous* [12–13]). "Action," as in Hogarth's chapter "Of Action," is what Gilpin sees as the element that transforms the Beautiful into the Picturesque—specifically a theatrical action. And, as we have seen (in chap. 2, above), Hogarth sums up the erotic drift of his Beautiful with the conclusion, which Gilpin appropriates, that the effect "is extremely picturesque" (*Analysis,* 46). In one sense the Picturesque is just that aspect of the Beautiful which is useful to, or the result of, the artistic enterprise of representation.

Having made the distinction between the Beautiful in repose and in action (or in representation), he finally turns to the more familiar picturesque images of the "worn-out cart-horse, the cow, the goat, or the ass," as opposed to the beautiful "smooth-coated" horse; and now the painter (a Berghem or Salvator Rosa) has the option of choosing to represent, rather than a smooth, beautiful horse, a "lion with his rough mane; the bristly boar; and the ruffled plumage of the eagle" (14). In nature, there are certain subjects that are inherently picturesque, without the secondary interference or operations of the artist. Time makes them so in this, the passive or reactionary Picturesque. Gilpin had first introduced the subject in his *Dialogue upon the Gardens . . . at Stowe* (1748), where he distinguished between "natural and moral Beauties," or aesthetic and ethical experiences:

> Our social Affections undoubtedly find their Enjoyment the most compleat when they contemplate, a Country smiling in the midst of Plenty, where Houses are well-built, Plantations regular, and everything the most commodious and useful. But such Regularity and Exactness excites no manner of Pleasure in the Imagination, unless they are made use of to contrast something of an opposite kind.[6]

At this point Gilpin is defining the picturesque experience by its distance from ethics—its disinterestedness—as well as its "contrast" with "something of an opposite kind."

Gilpin's Picturesque is essentially a retitling of Hogarth's Beautiful/Novel, including the need for the beautiful object as a foil to the novelistic epistemology. Hogarth's beautiful object, his ontology, and his epistemology of intricacy, surprise, and curiosity, based on contrast and variety, have been suitably divided but represented within a scene in which they relate as, for example, a smooth face to the same face with its hair caught in a strong wind; and appear embodied in some sort of a story.

In the second essay, "On Picturesque Travel," the same effect is produced by the constant movement of the traveler from scene to scene, object to object: "No two rocks, or trees are exactly the same. They are varied, a second time, by *combination;* and almost as much, a third time, by different *lights, and shades,* and other aerial effects"—as well as, he adds, by being seen first as wholes and then as parts (42). In Gilpin's development of the Picturesque as a landscape category, particularity and foregrounding remain as important as they were for Hogarth; as Frances Ferguson notes of trees in Gilpin's *Remarks on*

Forrest Scenery (1791): "Trees, with names, these are trees with histories," and they are "personified by being seen in human perspective,
with foreground."[7] Oak, ash, beech, and elm trees are as individual for
Gilpin as Mother Needham, Colonel Charteris, and Jack Gourlay were
for Hogarth.

It is not surprising that Gilpin once again selects the chase to sum
up the traveler's "love of novelty" (he picks up Addison's touristic sense
of the term):

> The *pleasures* of the chace are universal. A hare started before dogs is
> enough to set a whole country in an uproar. The plough, and the spade
> [i.e., industry] are deserted. Care is left behind; and every human fac-
> ulty is *dilated* with joy.—And shall we suppose it a greater *pleasure* to the
> sportsman to pursue a trivial animal, than it is to the man of taste to
> pursue the beauties of nature? to follow *her* through all her *recesses*? to
> obtain a sudden glance, as *she* flies past him in some airy shape?

And so on, the passage continues (48). The emphasized words suggest
the equivalence of nature and "passion" as sexuality, which goes back to
the Hogarthian source and to the examples of Venus and Eve in Gilpin's first essay.

The more systematic theory of Uvedale Price, in his *Essay on the
Picturesque* (1794), starts by ostentatiously turning from pictures (representations of nature) back to nature itself. Shakespeare and Fielding,
for example, help us to see human nature—we see people better after
reading those authors; but to go from a painting to the gardens of
Capability Brown is to go from nature to art, or more specifically, from
the Picturesque (in Gilpin's sense) to the Beautiful in the limited sense
of Addison's or Burke's term, and so to a contrast similar to that embodied in Gilpin's scenario except reversed; the beautifying artist now
destroys the naturally picturesque scene. The picturesque scene in
nature is due not to the artist but to "the indiscriminate hacking of the
peasant," to neglect, carelessness, or "lucky accidents," which, however, will make a landscape thereafter "the admiration and study of a
Ruysdael or a Gainsborough," who then can copy it.[8]

Price contrasts Brown's beautiful gardens ("their exclusive attention to high polish and flowing lines"—in fact serpentine Lines of

Beauty) with the landscape before its "improvement." He bases his discussion on the two principles of nature itself, variety and intricacy:

> the first, that great and universal source of pleasure, variety, whose power is independent of beauty, but without which even beauty itself soon ceases to please; the other, intricacy, a quality which, though distinct from variety, is so connected and blended with it, that the one can hardly exist without the other. (17)

Thus "intricacy in landscape" is "that disposition of objects which, by a partial and uncertain concealment, excites and nourishes curiosity"— which he later calls "the most active principle of pleasure" (17–18, 20).

While Price, unlike Gilpin, had no direct contact with Hogarth, he adapts Hogarth's terms "variety" and "intricacy." But if he is setting out to define (and train) "a picturesque eye" he distinguishes it from a "common eye" (19), the "common observation" or "our own eyes" of the *Analysis.* He cites Hogarth's "wanton chase"—"What most delights us in the intricacy of varied ground . . . is, that it leads the eye (according to Hogarth's expression) a kind of wanton chace"—but only in order to devalue Hogarth's smooth Beautiful as against the rough Picturesque: "this [wanton chase] is what he properly calls the *beauty* of intricacy, and which distinguishes that which is produced by soft winding shapes, from that more sudden and quickly-varying kind which arises from broken and rugged forms" (198). Price wishes to associate Hogarth strictly with the serpentine Line of Beauty, which Brown used as the principle of improvement in his gardens. Nevertheless, he adheres to the epistemology of intricacy in both smooth *and* broken or rugged forms, which is Hogarth's.[9] The movement of the eye is simply augmented by the constant movement of the picturesque traveler through his estate or through the countryside. The shared assumptions are that movement is a biological necessity of "life," mental life is analogous to physical, and movement follows the need for both mental and physical movement; that mental stasis is debilitating and less pleasureful than activity; and that the highest aesthetic pleasure is not familiarity but the sense or perception of movement, therefore of novelty.

In the case of human figures, Price returns to Hogarth's and Gilpin's scenario of passion: In chapter 3 he distinguishes the Picturesque from the Beautiful and Sublime, responding specifically to Burke (that "great master" [39, also 40 ff.]) by arguing with Gilpin (and Hogarth) that the smooth features of the Beautiful become Picturesque by being "ruffled by passion" (63).[10] "The most enchanting object the eye of man can behold," Price tells us, "is the face of a beautiful woman." But for it to be picturesque once again the hair is required—"by its comparative roughness and its partial concealments, [to] accompany and relieve the softness, clearness, and smoothness of all the rest; where the hair has no natural roughness, it is often artificially curled and crisped" (92–93). And, he adds in a note which reflects the practice of Gainsborough in his portraits of women in a landscape: "In many points the hair has a striking relation to trees; they resemble each other in their intricacy, their ductility, [and] the quickness of their growth."

He characterizes the "passion excited by" Burke's Beautiful as "love and complacency; it acts by relaxing the fibres somewhat below their natural tone, and this is accompanied by an inward sense of melting and languor"; whereas picturesque curiosity "by its active agency keeps [the fibres] to their full tone, and thus, when mixed with either of the other characters, corrects the languor of beauty, or the horror of sublimity." He refers to the "coquetry of nature," which "makes beauty more amusing, more varied, more playful, but also, / 'Less winning soft, less amiably mild.'" It "excites that active curiosity which gives play to the mind, loosening those iron bonds with which [sublime] astonishment chains up its faculties" (84–86).

Roughness, the opposite of repose, causes "irritation," which is more or less stimulation, or "harassment": "the eye, instead of reposing on one broad connected whole, is stopt and harrassed by little disunited discordant parts" (123). And so "when the mind is agitated, from whatever cause, those mild and soft emotions which flow from beauty, and of which beauty is the genuine source, are scarcely perceived" (110–11). In a footnote to "irritation" Price relates this to sexual desire: "We talk of the stings of pleasure, of being goaded on by desire. The god of love (and who will deny love to be source of pleasure?) is armed with flames, with envenomed shafts, with every instrument of irritation: Of all that breathes, the various progeny, / *Strong* with delight, is *goaded* on by thee" (110 n). Earlier he has offered the example of birds who, "when inflamed with anger or with desire, the first symptoms appear in their ruffled plumage." The game cock or the peacock, "when he feels the return of spring, shews his passion in the same manner, / And every feather shivers with delight" (64).

In short, what came to be known as the Picturesque in many ways carries on the Novel, especially Hogarth's version of it as the Novel/Beautiful, applying it to natural rather than human phenomena. For example, the landscapes-with-figures of Zoffany, Stubbs, and early Gainsborough were a direct continuation of the conversation piece. The Picturesque only shifted emphasis to the distinctive landscape form of the national and local, of property with or without the presence of its owners. The furniture and works of art in the interiors became agricultural improvements and landscape gardening, enclosed fields and (by the use of ha-has) apparently unenclosed lawns. These painters, combining portraits and landscape, contained the picturesque landscape within the Novel, Uncommon, and Strange, continuing to utilize that mix of curiosity and credulity which defines it. As Hogarth did in his conversations, they always draw attention to, or problematize, the relationship between possessor and possession.[11]

Landscape was the primary vehicle of both the Beautiful and the Sublime, against which Gilpin, Price, and Payne Knight carried Hogarth's argument from history painting. They argued for an area in nature between the cosmetic and coiffeured Beautiful and the chaotic Sublime, in effect a landscape equivalent of the "modern moral subject." Price and Payne Knight regarded the Picturesque as politically as well as aesthetically a "middle term," liberty, between the extremes of tyranny (Brown's Beautiful) and license (Burke's Sublime). Brown's words, according to Price's parody, were: "You shall never wander from my walks—never exercise your own taste and judgment—never form your own compositions—neither your eyes nor your feet will be allowed to stray from the boundaries I have traced." This "species of thralldom unfit for a free country" suppresses "variety, amusement and humanity." While their attack on Brown's gardens was on Hogarth's own serpentine Line, they treated it as Hogarth had the geometrical straitjacket of Shaftesbury-Hutcheson's Beautiful, and they discredited the serpentine Line as aesthetic object by applying Hogarth's skeptical epistemology of curiosity.[12] Their distrust of the Sublime was a natural equivalent of Hogarth's fear of the anarchic political implications of

Burke, Pitt, and Whitefield. In the form of the Picturesque Hogarth's theory and practice survived in landscape, the one painterly mode that proved to be a viable vehicle for new ideas in art.[13]

Rowlandson and Gainsborough

Thomas Rowlandson based his whole practice, figural and landscape, on Hogarth's fable of the Beautiful/Novel. He knew Hogarth's work extremely well, both prints and the *Analysis*.[14] From the *Analysis* he took the play of male-female, beautiful-grotesque forms, building his formal structure on these contrasts, but he also introduced a scene of voyeuristic sex: the third party of the Hogarth parodic Trinity, a father or husband, becomes an interested (sometimes appalled, but usually excited) observer who is detached formally by shape as well as by age from the activity of a beautiful boy and girl. As aesthetic constructs—and consciously aesthetic statements—Rowlandson's drawings and prints are about response and how images of art and nature affect their viewers, and the presence of the novelistic observer—a Mr. Spectator—is required to establish the experience of the Beautiful.

Rowlandson began to work in the 1780s as Gilpin's essays on the Picturesque appeared. He turned Gilpin's smooth and rough in human terms into youth and age, and in his landscapes into the contrasting shapes of a beautiful female figure—often supplemented by a sculptured female, a Venus perhaps—and trees and foliage, rocks and ravines. The basic situation of his "Dr. Syntax" drawings parodies Gilpin: Dr. Syntax appears with a beautiful young woman and rough, shaggy beasts or trees, turning his back on the one in order to focus pedantic attention on the other.[15] The difference is that Rowlandson thinks a spectator should look at the beautiful woman (who faintly recalls the serpentine lines of Brown's gardens); Gilpin, at the picturesque scenery. In one drawing Syntax sketches cows while in turn being watched by young men and women depicted in lines of beauty and grace. Part of the joke is that his own shape is as picturesque as the cows, while the young couple is "agitated by passion."[16]

Rowlandson's literary model is Don Quixote seeking giants and encountering instead windmills and innkeepers: Syntax gets lost, is attacked by highwaymen, loses his horse, is overcharged at inns, and is attacked by a bull. The quixotic nature of Dr. Syntax's travels draws attention to the similarity between a fable of the Beautiful colliding with the Novel and the fable of an idealizing knight attacking windmills: a fable that, in Cervantes' prototype and the many imitations in French anti-romances, contributed to the "novel" of Fielding and Smollett, and also (by way of his illustrations for *Don Quixote* and the English Quixote, *Hudibras*) to the works of Hogarth. *Don Quixote* was the prototype for the erosion of credulity in the authority of the written word, whether "literary language" (Bakhtin's term), the chivalric romance, heroic tragedy, Baroque history painting of the Counter-Reformation, or Gilpin's theory of the Picturesque.

Gilpin's Picturesque is, for Rowlandson, one case for the discovery of sexual desire under the most disinterested aesthetic poses going back to Hogarth's sculptures of Venus and Antinous which turn out to be focuses of desire. Rowlandson's sexually striving male is a more active and participatory version of Addison's spectator become Gilpin's walker, who moves about the countryside merely looking for visual stimulation. Indeed, Dr. Syntax himself has become another voyeur— the aesthete to whom the picturesque viewer reduces himself; and Rowlandson not only contrasts the sexual and the picturesque figures but thereby brings out the sexual component of the picturesque scene.

For Rowlandson, as for Hogarth, disinterestedness consists of distancing from the particular to the general or universal, from the real to the ideal, from the immediate and fleshly to the antique sculpture or old master painting, and from the original to the copy. And so, for Rowlandson as for Hogarth, it ultimately centers on the fact of the Royal Academy itself, the entrance of the vulgar public to its annual exhibition of paintings by the academicians. In *The Exhibition Stare-Case* (fig. 38) he shows that even Hogarth's Line of Beauty has become academicized in the academy's staircase (as Capability Brown froze the Line in his landscape gardens). However, replacing the serpentine form of the staircase are the falling bodies, in utterly contingent poses, of the visitors to the exhibition. These poses offer opportunities for views up women's dresses and amorous embraces, which, Rowlandson proclaims here and in most of his drawings, are preferable to what they would have seen in the gallery above. At the same time, their fall, echoing Rubens's painting *The Fall of the Damned* (Alte Pinakothek, Munich), replaces the biblical paradigm of the "Fall," or at least renders it a "*fortunate* Fall."[17] As Hogarth aestheticized religion by replacing the Name of God within the triangle of the Trinity with his serpentine Line of Beauty, so Rowlandson replaces the Line itself with the sensory world of erotically interlocking bodies.

Rowlandson carries Hogarth's aesthetics to its extreme and beyond. He sums up the course we have traced from conventional classical and Christian iconography to the natural "living" human body in which human contingency (of the sort exposed by the deists underneath the New Testament "miracles") is an essential part of the effect—no longer the lock of hair that breaks the perfect oval face, or Amelia's scarred nose, but the "picturesque" shapes of the male and female sexual organs. He not only removes the fig leaf of classical sculpture, revealing the hidden "flaw," but draws in explicit detail *this* one part of the otherwise conventionalized or idealized human body. He depicts both the sexual organs *and* (in this sense illustrating *Fanny Hill*) the act of penetration. And yet it remains an aesthetic act because beautiful figures making love are being responded to by a spectator; whose response also elicits a response from the viewer of the drawing on the basis of both action *and* response within the picture.[18] This suggests that eroticism or—at its extreme, when response has turned into possession—pornography depends on such a configuration: Not just a body, or two bodies in love, but a third *watching*. Or not watching. The latter is the purely comic version of the situation, which becomes aesthetic when the spectator's attention is turned to the beautiful object without physically merging with it.[19]

Rowlandson's erotic aesthetic focuses on the distinction between detachment and voyeurism. The old man (Picturesque in the sense of permitted to go untended, spreading in all directions) is a vestige of the disinterested civic humanist, the man whose property supposedly raised him above the demands of physical desire and acquisitiveness. If sexual desire is one aspect of the demystification of disinterestedness, mere possession is the other. Thus Hogarth placed the art objects in plate 1 of the *Analysis* in a statuary yard, objects of consumption and possession; and in plate 2 the paintings on the walls were augmented by the "possession" of marriage with the old squire, subverted by the intrusion of a young lover. These two plates are the models for many of Rowlandson's most characteristic images. He shows statues juxtaposed with living and handsome young men, and beautiful wives and daughters accompanied by both aging husbands/fathers and handsome young men. Here, as in other contexts, he suggests that while the beautiful young woman is the old man's "property," the young man has the natural right to the "pleasure" of her "enjoyment."

The old man's detachment becomes a withdrawal from nature or the living woman, often an incapacity or impotence. And the old man is merely an exaggerated version of the artist (who derives from Hogarth's Poet and Musician as, in Rowlandson's terms, life-denying). The artist and the connoisseurs who presumably dictate his subject are typically seen with a painting of *Susannah and the Elders* on the easel—a paradigm of both voyeurism and the demystifying of biblical iconography (*The Connoisseurs* [fig. 42]). Like Dr. Syntax, the artist is shown *representing*—drawing, painting, and mythologizing—either her or some obviously less sensuously satisfying alternative.[20] The clergyman's cross, the physician's scalpel, the artist's quill or brush, and even the voyeur's line of sight all have their phallic significance. But, displacements as they are, they represent a negative interpretation of disinterestedness. To place the body on a cross, an operating table, a pedestal, or a canvas distances it—and this is one of Rowlandson's favorite subjects; but he always shows the aesthetic shield collapsing, or at least discredited, before the human response.

While it is evident how Hogarth and Rowlandson, reacting against academic doctrines, came at this particular definition of experience, Rowlandson has carried Hogarthian aesthetics so far as to produce a fable against aestheticizing. The gist of Hogarth's artist satires was that nature is preferable to an artist's rendering of it (primary against secondary qualities and pleasures); Rowlandson goes on to show that the spectator, whether as artist or voyeur, should be (in his explicit terms) enjoying the woman rather than aestheticizing her.

The difference lies in the fact that while Hogarth is opposed both to aesthetic distancing from the experience of life in London and to the praxis of improving it, Rowlandson concerns himself only with the first and ignores the latter. His object is the pure pleasure or play of the *Analysis* text; although he takes his compositions and contrasts from the two illustrative plates, he drops their moral subtext. He picks up and develops Hogarth's discussion of laughter in his chapter "On Quantity," and so depicts not simply a beautiful woman (which would presumably be a representation of the Beautiful) or a beautiful woman and a handsome young man "agitated by passion," but rather one or both of these played off in a variety of ways against the ugly, fat, aging, sagging, and often shaggy, animal-like creature who makes the scene, in Gilpin's and Price's terms, picturesque. He bases his groupings on the Hogarthian parody of the "Trinity." But Hogarth shifted the emphasis from the theological unity in variety of the Athanasian doctrine to the utmost variety stretched to the brink of disorder; Rowlandson goes over the brink, exceeding the limits, and (as in *Exhibition Stare-Case*) questions the principle itself. His fiction is Hogarth's of the cuckold triangle, but his endless variations on the theme leave no trace of the theological doctrine, focusing attention (as indeed Shaftesbury tried less successfully to do) on this as basis of the comic essence of the aesthetic experience.

If in the comic mode the aesthetics of the Beautiful/Novel is represented (or fabulated) by Rowlandson, in the serious mode it is exemplified by Thomas Gainsborough. We recall that, according to Uvedale Price, a landscape made picturesque by neglect, carelessness, or "lucky accidents" becomes thus "the admiration and study of a Ruysdael or a Gainsborough" (29). As a student in the St. Martin's Lane Academy, Gainsborough took as his immediate models François Gravelot and Hayman; his early works were more refined and subtle versions of Hayman's conversation pieces. But while he began as a "rococo" or "polite" student of Hayman, he clearly learned from Hogarth's works (he adapted situations from Hogarth prints in early paintings) and read the *Analysis,* imbibing the principles of the Novel/Beautiful. He employed the wit of pleasureful pursuit, contrast, and variety in his most adventurous portraits (*Sarah Siddons, Mrs. Thicknesse,* and others), and he followed the same progression as did Gilpin

from the Novel/Beautiful to the Picturesque.[21] The occasional mythologized landscape, for example *Diana and Actaeon* (1789; Royal
Collection), and the many unmythologized (or de-mythologized) versions of shepherds and their flocks descending, anticipate Price's "cav-
erns and cool retreats for the sheep . . . some lying in the niches they
have worn in the banks among the roots of trees, and to which they
have made many side-long paths; some reposing in these deep re-
cesses, their bowers / O'er canopied with luscious eglantine" (25). The
sense of Gainsborough's typical landscape is virtually formulated by
Price's recourse to dramatic metaphors such as the "large roots of trees
[which] . . . seem to fasten on the earth with their dragon claws" (30).
But the subject and the aesthetic fable go back to Hogarth's *Strolling
Actresses* (fig. 14).

At least once, however, he reveals his source in New Testament
iconography. In *The Harvest Wagon* (1767; fig. 40) he borrows the
painting's central group of figures from Rubens's *Descent from the Cross,*
a painting that Gainsborough himself had copied (fig. 41). He not only
paints the rustics in the elegant and fluent style of Rubens but evokes—
in a sense Hogarth would have understood—in these "peasants" striving upward toward a drink of wine from the "leathern Bottle, long in
Harvest try'd" (bequeathed in Gay's version in his *Shepherd's Week* by
Blouzelinda to her lover Grubbinol), a low popular version of the
figures reaching up for Christ's body and blood in the eucharistic
Descent from the Cross. The effect may have begun (if Hogarth is
Gainsborough's point of origin) as novelistic demystification but, as in
Addison's Strange, the effect is of equivalence, contemporary myth,
and credulity. Gainsborough not only suggests that these carousing
peasants are participating in some primitive fertility ritual, which is the
local "country" version of the Christian miracle, but appropriates the
subject in a design that illustrates the principle of serpentine lines
presented in the *Analysis.* As I have argued of this painting elsewhere, it
is the artist's reclamation of the scene, of the Counter-Reformation
iconography, as his own English representation.[22]

Gainsborough's landscapes "play" with natural forms to make
them expose human desire, revealing under their serpentine forms the
erotic subtexts that indicate their affiliation with Hogarth and Row-

landson. In a London scene, *The Mall* (1783; Frick Collection, New York), young women in twos and threes are emerging from a vortical landscape with plainly sexual overtones. One man is discernible among them in the shadowy background of the Mall, which was associated from the Restoration on with assignations; a pair of dogs in the foreground (staffage from a Watteau *fête champêtre*) carries the same overtones of sexual encounter. (A pair of cows have wandered in from the landscapes.) After *The Mall*, Gainsborough returns the horizontal vortex to its normal downward spiral into a dark pond in *Diana and Actaeon*. The history painting of naked nymphs and a goddess in a pond is a retrospective key to the landscapes of cows and sheep descending into a pond, as well as to the London women of *The Mall*. The male spectator on the marge is drawn by serpentine lines of attraction down into a sexualized nature, becoming indistinguishable from it.

Gainsborough is showing the transition from the Novel to a witty Picturesque, pursuing in nature the issues Hogarth and Rowlandson had pursued in society. Rowlandson produces his own comic version of the Gainsborough landscape when he shows a contemporary Adam and Eve intertwined in *S*-curves as they recoil from a large, rearing, *S*-curving serpent (fig. 39), a fleshed-out version of the upright Line of Beauty that appeared on the title page of *The Analysis of Beauty*. Nature, centered in this phallic shape and a couple "agitated by passion," reflects the human situation in trees and branches twisted into grotesquely distorted *S*'s. The serpent is the force of disruption at the same time that he gives his shape to that disruption and labels it sexual. The whole picturesque landscape, even the torrential stream, seems to be recoiling with this couple from the serpent—but in so doing becomes itself serpentine. The theological Fall, alluded to on Hogarth's title page, is here literal and naturalized in Rowlandson's comic Christian version of Gainsborough's *Diana and Actaeon* as it is in an architectural setting, within the Royal Academy itself, in *Exhibition Stare-Case* (fig. 38).

The question remains whether aesthetics in the mode I am describing—from Hogarth to Cleland to Sterne and Rowlandson—should be called an erotics, or pornography. Pornography (literally, "about prostitutes") is generally thought of as a more explicit and unvarnished erotica—hard core as opposed to soft; its primary and unconcealed aim is to excite the voyeur to self-gratification in masturbation. It is also a *representation* (say, of prostitutes), while erotics (parallel with aesthetics) indicates response. But I want to use the term "pornography" in a special sense in order to emphasize the opposition between an aesthetics of pleasure and one (to use Burke's word) of delight, a more intense but problematic experience that includes the intensity of pain. This is the contemporary definition advocated by, among others, Andrea Dworkin: Pornography is a man inflicting power and pain on a woman. Or, in the words of the MacKinnon-Dworkin Bill: "the graphic, sexually explicit *subordination of women* through pictures or words." Pornography is a product in line with the Sublime, which, as expounded by Burke in the other, far better known aesthetic treatise of the 1750s—his *Philosophical Enquiry into the Origin of Our Ideas of the Sublime and Beautiful* (1757)—is based on power and pain. I want to distinguish this pornography from what I call eroticism, man and woman in explicit sexual play based on love, sexual desire, curiosity, and seduction, that is, the Hogarthian Beautiful.

Although I am accepting Dworkin's definition of pornography, I am also delimiting it and arguing that the Rowlandsonian sex act is one of mutuality. Only the Beautiful involves the two strands I have outlined which connect aesthetics and erotics—the philosophy of the body, the senses, and pleasure; and the demystification of myths, whether religious or platonic. Sublime pornography (perhaps a tautology) involves *only* plays of power and pain carried to an extreme of mutilation and death.[23] The line usually drawn is from Burke, or the Burkean Sublime, the way of male power, leading to the fantasies of the Marquis de Sade. Sade's aesthetics merely fulfilled the fears Hogarth entertained (and represented in his final works) of the Burkean Sublime literally destroying and replacing the Beautiful.[24]

And yet no dichotomy is pure. Implicit, we have seen, in the experience of pleasure involving Sophia Western, Amelia Booth, Fanny Hill, and Olivia Primrose are clear elements of pain and power. However much displaced onto others, or left to the reader's sometimes uneasy response, these aspects of pain function, if only as contrast, to intensify the experience. They may be the result of the powerful foundational images of the Harlot and Pamela, from which it was difficult to shake loose. The strand becomes prominent in Rowlandson, taking the form of an act of subordination—which he deplores but repeatedly shows; thus the great emphasis on voyeurism. But the point at which Rowlandson shows the most striking act of subordination is when an artist reduces the live Hogarthian woman to a work of art, fixed on a canvas and preferred to the real, live model. She is being possessed, not enjoyed. Even here, however, she is only being formulated, not raped, tortured, or murdered.

TEN

The Novelizing
of Hogarth

The Hogarth Commentaries: Trusler, the Harlot, and Her Father

Lengthy commentaries on Hogarth's engraved works began to appear with John Trusler's *Hogarth Moralized* in 1768 and continued in 1791 with John Ireland's *Hogarth Illustrated* and in the 1780s and 1790s with G. C. Lichtenberg's *Ausführliche Erklärung der Hogarthischen Kupferstiche.*[1] In 1747 and 1750 brief French commentaries had appeared by Jean André Rouquet, Hogarth's personal friend, whose practical purpose was to clarify the local references in the prints for a French audience. This was also Lichtenberg's pretext, for a German audience. On the most practical level, all these commentaries were written to accompany sets of Hogarth's prints: Trusler's *Hogarth Moralized* was an attempt, with the approval and presumed supervision of the artist's widow, to make Hogarth's prints respectable and salable some decades after they were originally published (the commentary was itself accompanied by small copies).[2] By the 1760s the recovery of context had become as necessary for an English as for a foreign viewer.

Even Rouquet's commentary had served to remind a viewer that these prints, which deserved and repaid such close attention, were not ephemera. At the same time, the greater length and elevation of Trusler's discourse inevitably invoked the contemporary commentaries on English poems. The rise in the 1750s of historical-philological research that sought to recover a native literature of the distant past in all its primitive purity (Spenser, Shakespeare, and Milton), manifestly superior to contemporary forms such as the "novel," may explain why Hogarth in this same period turned away from his "modern moral subjects" to romance, allegory, and "stranger" figurations (*Sigismunda, The Cockpit, Enthusiasm Delineated, The Times, Plate 1,* and the *Tail Piece*).[3] It was to further the canonization of his prints that he himself undertook introduction, autobiography, and commentary in the last years of his life; though, as Jane Hogarth realized, commentary was better written by a scholar or a divine and preferably both.[4]

Thomas Warton's *Observations on Spenser's "Faerie Queene,"* which began as annotation and grew into commentary, had been published as a separate volume in 1754. Annotation usually consisted of enumerating the poem's associations, essentially its sources; the models for commentary, however, were biblical or classical, and commentaries were often printed parallel to the texts, paraphrasing and explaining them on analogical, anagogical, allegorical, typological, and other levels. More pertinent perhaps was Joseph Warton's *Essay on the Genius and Writings of Pope,* published in 1756, which had combined commentary with criticism and laid down the thesis that the highest poetry was of the passions, embodied in Shakespeare and Milton, not in Pope and the "ethical poets." Warton had incidentally criticized Hogarth for attempting to raise his art into the higher poetry of passion, evoking from Hogarth a response that showed how sensitive he was on the subject of genre.[5]

What distinguished Trusler was less the desire to moralize Hogarth than to raise him above the stigmatized category of satirist to at least "ethical poet" if not "poet of the passions." For Trusler this involved extricating him from his matrix of the 1720s and 1730s, the subversive opposition satire of Swift, Pope, and the *Craftsman* circle. Coming a generation later, Trusler served Hogarth as Bishop Warburton had served Pope, transmuting his witty impieties into orthodoxy. Moral admonition was one aspect of Trusler's commentary, as it was of Hogarth's prints—and it carries over into Trusler's index, with entries such as "Gaming, the folly of it" or "Hypocrisy, a characteristic of the French and Great." But as he explains his method: "While I *moralized,* I studied to *explain;* and, while I *explained,* I studied to *moralize*" (viii).

The *Rev.* John Trusler has been regarded as the "moralizer" of Hogarth, but he styled himself "Dr." both of medicine and of letters. His stated aim in the preface to *Hogarth Moralized* was "to bring some minute objects to view, which lay concealed amid a crowd of larger ones; to hold the painter forth in a moral light, and, convince the age, there is more in his design, than to ridicule and lash the follies of it." The first of these purposes Trusler shared with Lichtenberg and Ireland, and all three echoed Rouquet, who drew attention to the "thousand small details *[mille petites circonstances]* which escape most spectators."[6] This has been the basic assumption and hermeneutical mode of most subsequent Hogarth commentators.

Returning to the example with which we began in chapter 1, I take Trusler's commentary on *A Harlot's Progress* (1732; figs. 3–12). In this series, he argues, Hogarth combines the "minute objects" with the "moral light" by producing "a history full of such interesting circumstances, as must, certainly, give the *unthinking maid,* a sense of *her danger,* and, *alarm* her, lest she, also, becomes *a prey to man*" (my emphasis added throughout). "From this distressing story, let me warn my *female* readers of the lurking danger that threatens them: as there is no greater Christian virtue than *chastity,* none more pleasing to God, or, more agreeable to *man,* it is the interest of every *young lady,* to be, particularly, attentive to it" (13). Trusler warns the female reader against both the men who lay snares, and her own vanity, which is exploited by men. On pages 13 to 15 he sermonizes on the error of spending a single moment in bad male company (he likens it to entering a pesthouse) and the effect of such a lapse: the "temporal misery on your *families*" that accompanies the "eternal vengeance on *yourselves*" (15).

Such words certainly draw on the discourse of sermons, but they also recall Richardson's comment in *Pamela* (1740): "And the Whole will shew the base Arts of designing Men to gain their wicked Ends; and how much it behoves the Fair Sex to stand upon their Guard against their artful Contrivances, especially when Riches and Power conspire against Innocence and a low Estate" (90). Richardson had in fact claimed in his postscript to *Clarissa* that his novel was a more effective pulpit than the one from which clerics preached the same message.

One "minute particular" Trusler overlooks in his focus on the vulnerability of the young woman is the detail of the basket and goose addressed "For my Lofing Cosen in Tems Stret in London"—the cousin whose failure to meet her has left her no apparent alternative to the bawd who is offering her a different sort of lodging. The inference is that Hackabout's fall is facilitated by the parallel absences of her London cousin (the pun on *cozen* [i.e., to cheat] is probably intended), on the one side, and the preoccupied clergyman, who is engrossed in reading the address of the bishop of London, on the other.

This is a significant omission, because Trusler introduces his account of plate 1 with the information, which he gleaned from Rouquet's *Lettres* (he could not have inferred it from the print), that the girl is the daughter of the "country curate." (One thing to note about both Trusler and Lichtenberg is that they regard Rouquet's *Lettres,* close as they were to the source, as almost as scriptural as the prints themselves.)[7] For his French audience Rouquet had explained that:

> Priests in England are not celibate, and they take advantage of that privilege; they all marry and, since the revenue from their benefices does not support many children, their offspring and above all the girls, after the father's death and too often during his lifetime, are reduced to strange means of subsistence. This is a commonplace *[l'opinion commune]*, though perhaps only based on the lies of some fallen women who like to give themselves airs by claiming an origin and education the furthest removed from their present condition. The author, following this commonplace, has made his heroine the daughter of the priest whom he introduces in this print. They arrive together at the wagon stop.[8]

On the face of it, Rouquet's story is implausible. If the parson is the father of the girl named Hackabout (we have to imagine a *clergyman* named Hackabout), what happens to him after plate 1? What then is the function or significance of Hackabout's "Lofing Cosen in Tems Stret"? (One could as easily infer—as Lichtenberg seems to—that the "Lofing Cosen" is the bawd.)[9] There is no internal evidence in either this or any of the subsequent plates that the parson and Hackabout are related by blood.

Trusler is plainly aware of the problems involved in such an interpretation. He writes more about this one detail than about any other in the whole of Hogarth's oeuvre. He explains that the clergyman father is introduced "in order to shew us the amazing frailty of the sex; that, notwithstanding she might have been brought up, properly instructed in the paths of virtue, yet, is there such an inchantment in vice, as to allure the person on, who once gives the least ear to her persuasions" (2). He is accordingly forced to invent a story about the parson which bridges plates 1 and 2:

> One would, naturally, be led to think, that her father, from the education he must, necessarily, have had, would have seen through the deceit [by the bawd who is offering her employment], or, at least, would have been more cautious, and, counseled her otherwise; but, by his supposed consent to her acceptance of the proffered place, we are to understand, that, there are none so ignorant of the ways of life, as those, who have, wholly, applied themselves to the knowledge of books: this ignorance of men and things, led the unthinking father, pleased with this prospect of good fortune, in finding provision for his daughter, immediately, on his arrival, innocently, to consent to the ruin of his child. Thus, do we, in an unguarded moment, lay the foundation of endless misery; and, thus, commenced that series of disasters, that makes up the several parts of this story. (3)

The signs of Trusler's particular brand of moralizing are clear: the parson fails to protect the girl because he is "ignorant of the ways of life," "innocent" and "unthinking," rather than merely self-serving. He is also "pleased with this prospect of good fortune." Another detail is the paper the parson is reading, which is addressed to the "Bishop of London." Trusler essentially translates Rouquet in his explanation that the parson has come to London "in search of better fortune." But if Rouquet suggests that the daughter merely accompanied a father who was seeking his own fortune, Trusler indicates the parallel: "That this [searching for better fortune], also, was her father's view, is evident from the letter of recommendation, whose direction he is reading, addressed to some bishop in town."[10] Then, referring to the parson's "extreme necessity," he moralizes in parenthesis: "(for such is the misfortune of the clergy, that want seems attendant on their order)" (3). Trusler's stress always falls on "the misfortune of the clergy" at the hands of their backsliding flock. Hogarth's, however, always falls on the self-regarding clergyman who ignores his flock—as seen most egre-giously in the clergyman presiding in plate 6, who ignores his duty in order to grope under the skirt of the whore next to him, and summed up in the Anglican bishop in plate 2 who rewards Uzzah for saving the Ark of the Covenant with a stab in the back.[11]

Lichtenberg, who also follows Rouquet in the identification of the clergyman as father, comments in a note on what he takes to be a joke Hogarth played on Rouquet: "Since Roucquet *[sic]* knew Hogarth personally and Hogarth evidently knew that remark *[Bemerkung]*, it is very probable that the mischievous Englishman wantonly persuaded the credulous Frenchman to believe it."[12] This suggests how the "re-mark" about the clergyman as the girl's father may have originated. The witticism would have come from Hogarth: presumably the jest that many prostitutes were (in, for example, Henry Fielding's words) "the Offspring of the clergy" or that "the greatest Part of the *London* Prostitutes are the Daughters of Parsons,"[13] the reason being that daughters of the clergy were bred to a higher social situation than their expectations could justify. (And of course the joke is augmented by the fact that the choice is between the father and a "mother," Needham.)

Hogarth may have been thinking specifically of Fielding's *Rape upon Rape,* his farce based (like the *Harlot*) on the Charteris case, performed and published in 1730 as Hogarth was planning *A Harlot's Progress.* Fielding has his heroine Hilaret—whom Justice Squeezum mistakes for a whore—"humor this old villain" (as she puts it) by parodying the stereotype of a whore: When she uses the word "neuter" Squeezum responds, "Do you understand Latin, hussy?"—to which she replies: "My father was a country parson, and gave all his children a good education. He taught his daughters to write and read himself." She elaborates on the stereotype of whore, claiming she has sixteen sisters "and all in the same way of business." Squeezum concludes that literacy was what made them all become prostitutes—that is, learning to write taught them to aspire above their station. (Trusler's idea was the contrary, that "knowledge of books" left a clergyman's daughter ignorant of the world and susceptible to seduction.) As it happened, Hilaret says, a man of war harbored near their parsonage and "my poor sisters were ruined by the officers, and I fell a martyr to the chaplain."[14]

If Hogarth made this joke to Rouquet, he was only reflecting what is quite clear in the six plates of the *Harlot:* the dual themes of the clergy's self-interest and the aspiration (by the parson, the Harlot, and her Jewish keeper) to higher social status. For Hogarth (and his immediate audience) the address of the bishop of London specifically invoked Bishop Gibson, Walpole's dispenser of ecclesiastical preferment, whose *Pastoral Letter* is being used by the Harlot as a butter dish in plate 3. Although Trusler might have inferred that this is her comment on the man who failed to promote her father, in fact he remarks:

> Mr. *Hogarth,* has, here, taken an opportunity of shewing us the great degeneracy of the age, in matters of religion, by laying on the table a piece of butter, wrapt up in the title-page of a Pastoral Letter, which a great prelate, about that time, addressed to his diocese [here Trusler inserts a note identifying the prelate as "Dr. *Gibson,* Bishop of *London*"]; many copies of which, had the misfortune to be sold, as waste paper: such being the general wickedness of mankind, that every thing religious is held in disesteem. If any ludicrous or obscene publication should issue from the press, it is sure to meet with an immediate and rapid sale; every man, who is master of a shilling, is, instantly, a purchaser: but, on the contrary, an edition of any piece, tending to correct the vices or follies of the age, lies in the shop, either unnoticed, or, disregarded. (7)

Rouquet, with Hogarth at his side, had only noted with quiet irony that these pastoral letters by a distinguished prelate found their way to grocers rather than parishioners. Lichtenberg comments, closely following Rouquet: "It is said that despite the address clearly written on them, they [the *Pastoral Letters*] did not reach their destination until the grocers co-opted and undertook the delivery" (27). But for Trusler, Hogarth *must* perforce respect the clergy; and so he reads the disrespect as part of the Harlot's sin—perhaps especially after his interpretation of plate 1, in which she repudiates her father/pastor. Thus her repudiation of all clergymen. Even Lichtenberg finds it impossible to believe that Hogarth could have ridiculed the clergy. Though describing the groping clergyman of plate 6, he acknowledges that Hogarth "has made attacks on three occasions upon people in parsons' clothes" but states that he never "attacked the profession of clergyman as such" (74).

Trusler's most imaginative attempt to explain Rouquet's assertion about the paternity of Hackabout is to connect her paternity with that of Tom Rakewell in *A Rake's Progress*. While one series is aimed at the woman, the other is aimed at the man—one is the victim, the other the susceptible corruptor, but the paternity hypothesis leads Trusler to emphasize both as offspring. He must therefore distinguish between the good parson-father, whose virtuous training was not enough to save the girl when a threat arose, and the bad miser-father, "who is supposed to have hurt the principles of his son, in depriving him of the necessary use of some of that gold, he had, with the greatest covetousness, been hoarding, to no kind of purpose, in his coffers" (17).

In fact, Trusler is onto something, but his piety keeps him from seeing that with the clergyman and Harlot it is *like* father, *like* daughter. Perhaps the joke was not an end in itself but a means to an end, an analogy between the parson's relationship to Bishop Gibson and M. Hackabout's to the bawd and her clients, suggesting that the clergyman (Parson Hackabout) is another whore. In this case, one can see why Hogarth might have suggested to Rouquet that they were father and daughter.

Hogarth's coupling of old and young Rakewell is merely another materializing of a satiric topos, this time drawn from Pope's Old and Young Cotta in his *Epistle to Bathurst;* the family continues, more novelistically than satirically in *Marriage A-la-mode,* and I suspect that Trusler is reading back from this series, as he is also reading back from Richardson's exactly contemporary novel *Clarissa,* which makes the daughter's tragedy depend on her oppressive and unfeeling family. For if Trusler's first need is to find a pious explanation to cover Hogarth's impiety (or at least his contempt for the clergy), another is to fill in between the scenes, or make what is clearly drama into a narrative; and for him narrative is based on the central unit of the family, which had been established by this time in the works of Richardson, Fielding, and Goldsmith. Thus it is important for the Harlot to have a father.

Between plates 1 and 2 Trusler weaves, in addition to the story of father and daughter, a narrative in which the procuress takes the girl into her house, treats her as a friend, gradually corrupts her, and then, once she becomes "at last, hardened in infamy," sells her to the Jew (4). Colonel Charteris remains unexplained. Although Rouquet had noted that the old lecher in the doorway was a portrait from life, Trusler was apparently unaware of the pamphlets that tell how Charteris employed the bawd to hire young women just arrived (and alone) in London as maids for *his* house, where he seduced or raped them. Hogarth gives no explanation for the transitions from the bawd's housemaid to Charteris's victim to the rich Jew's mistress in plate 2. But contemporaries who recognized Charteris's portrait read him not (as Trusler does) as an alternative to the bawd, lurking in the shadows in case she is unsuccessful at attracting the girl, but rather as the bawd's employer, and as himself symbolically a surrogate for his own patron, Sir Robert Walpole (who had secured him a pardon after his capital conviction for rape). Indeed, Hogarth and his immediate audience also knew that there was actually a harlot named Kate Hackabout who was committed by Justice Gonson, and whose brother Francis was condemned when Charteris was condemned but was hanged when Charteris was pardoned.[15]

The most striking aspect of Trusler's narrativizing of the *Harlot* is the way he internalizes the moral admonition in the Harlot's conscience. In plate 4, set in prison, for example, he imagines that she is reflecting on her past life and her "tender and affectionate parents," and decides to reform. With "this pious resolution, her time of confinement expires" and she is freed, but (because at the time there was no Lock Hospital for reformed prostitutes in which she might have been rehabilitated) she can only return "to her former course" and is soon "eaten up with want and disease"—and so "she sinks into rottenness, and, falls a martyr to prostitution" (10).

Hogarth's context for his *Harlot* was the 1730s, the commodification of life and culture symbolized by the prostitute, and the particular details and political context of the Charteris rape trial. Thus Trusler replaces Hogarth's symbolic figures, his historical referents, with a psychological version of character, which internalizes moral significance and seeks psychological and narrative consistency at the expense of symbolic (or satiric) coherence.

Lichtenberg's Shandean Hogarth

Lichtenberg's Hogarth commentaries were first published between 1784 and 1786 (and were revised and republished between 1794 and 1799).[16] The conventional distinction between the commentaries of Trusler and those of Lichtenberg has been roughly the difference between the moralist and the wit. In fact, Lichtenberg's *Erklärung* derived from a similar tradition of commentary being applied to the national literature and was the first work in Germany to apply this commentary to graphic works. But more significant, I believe, was the fact that Sterne's *Tristram Shandy* had been published between 1759 and 1767,[17] and John Nichols's *Biographical Anecdotes of William Hogarth* had appeared in 1781. Accordingly, Lichtenberg begins his account of *A Harlot's Progress* with the biographical facts of Hogarth's life surrounding the *Harlot* and its publication.[18] For him Hogarth is always implicitly the protagonist of his prints, making jokes or setting the reader puzzles to solve. If Trusler filled in and elaborated Hogarth's scenes into a narrative, Lichtenberg prefers to find an anomaly such as the discrepancy between the dresses Hackabout is wearing in plates 3 and 4, noting that there would have been no time for her to change. He worries such details as a dog worries a bone, displaying the intricacies of his own thought processes, expanding Hogarth's metaphors and adding metaphors of his own. But one result is to connect, far more accurately than Trusler, with the sense of "novelty" and "play" which Hogarth formulates in the *Analysis of Beauty.*

　　With the identification of the parson as the Harlot's father Lichtenberg follows the same line as Trusler but prefers Rouquet's explanation for the York Wagon in which she has arrived—that the prettiest girls came from Yorkshire (which sounds like another remark of Hogarth's to his French friend)—rather than Trusler's explanation that Yorkshire was "far distant from the metropolis, and, as such, supposed to be least acquainted with its intrigues." While Trusler pointed out the analogy between the parson and his horse ("a sorry broken-kneed and foundered animal, who [not like our high-fed beasts] is, eagerly, catching at a mouthful of straw, in which some earthen vessels are packed; and, so full is his master of the business he is upon, as to pay no attention to the damage"), Lichtenberg interprets the "flower pots, dishes and pans and what-not" being upset by the horse as about to shatter and indicates the irony that the poor parson, dreaming about the profits derived from his advancement in the church, will in fact have to pay for the depredations of his horse (7). While Lichtenberg notices the parallel between the falling buckets and the "falling" girl, his emphasis is on the parson and his horse: "here is another use of fragile goods—tumbling down, to the detriment of the poor devil [the parson], which no bishopric will ever restore" (14). Neither Trusler nor Lichtenberg—unwilling to recognize Hogarth's anticlerical bias—notices the parallel between the horse and its rider, based on the self-interest of both.

Lichtenberg's elaboration takes off from a minute description of the parson's clothing and his nag (5–6), which is not only Shandean in tone but essentially turns the pair into Parson Yorick and *his* poor nag, described in the first volume of *Tristram Shandy*. Following a long digression on wigs (taking off from the parson's) and apostrophes to the parson and the girl ("Farewell then, unhappy pair . . ."), Lichtenberg addresses the horse:

> And you, faithful grey *[Schimmel],* in whose side I discern, just behind your rider's spur, a little spot of reality which has cost the artist but a slight pressure of his stylus, but has cost you precious blood; believe me, the discovery has made me feel for you three times more keenly. I was sorry to discover, so shortly before our parting, this sign of conjunction between you and your master. But be comforted! The similarity between the two of you is even greater than you imagine: he too all his life long has carried just such a merciless rider as you have, and it would have cost the artist more than a single stroke to depict the scars which the poor victim covers here with the clerical *Copri-miseria.* (8)

Lichtenberg is recalling, among other things, Parson Yorick's metaphorically battered head ("'tis so bruised and mis-shapen'd with the blows which ***** and *****, and some others have so unhandsomely given me in the dark, that I might say with *Sancho Pança,* that should I recover, and 'Mitres thereupon be suffer'd to rain down from heaven as thick as hail, not one of 'em would fit it' ").[19] Far from criticizing the parson, in Shandean fashion he sentimentalizes him.

Lichtenberg describes the Harlot by contrasting the stolidity of the "slow, honest, good and clumsy animal" of plate 1 with her mercuriality vis-à-vis her Jewish keeper in plate 2: "here, though seated, is she not the living image of mobility?" he asks:

> In the whole face no line and no contrasting shadow, and yet how eloquent! 'See, fellow, not so much do I care for you and your wretched

plunder; a fig for it!,' and with a snap of her finger she indicates exactly how much she thinks of the plunder. It is half a finger joint and a little sound that she brings to his notice. The right eye has something indescribably scornful. But the fellow has money and that is an important item which the left eye clearly recognizes. The feint is, I think, quite unmistakable. On her whole right wing, war is declared, while the left is at peace, or at least, some admission is made there of guilt. On the right wing the knee is raised at least a few hands above the line of modesty, and in an ugly way, so that the tip of the foot is turned inwards; and the arm stretched out so that in the Quart [a fencing term] she brings the snap of her fingers as close beneath the enemy's nose as if it were a pinch of snuff. (16–18)

We could compare this with any number of descriptions in *Tristram Shandy*, but the first that would come to mind is the one that Hogarth himself illustrated—Corporal Trim reading the Sermon on Conscience in book 2, chapter 17. The description is a page and a half long, but the central part reads:

> He stood,—for I repeat it, to take the picture of him in at one view, with his body sway'd, and somewhat bent forwards,—his right-leg firm under him, sustaining seven-eights of his whole weight,—the foot of his left-leg, the defect of which was no disadvantage to his attitude, advanced a little,—not laterally, nor forwards, but in a line betwixt them;—his knee bent, but that not violently,—but so as to fall within the limits of the line of beauty. (121–22)

Of the erotic objects on the Harlot's wall in plate 3, Trusler had said simply that they "sufficiently explain themselves, to the more knowing part of mankind, which decency will not permit me to make such of my readers acquainted with, as these pages are calculated to improve" (7; though he does blandly note the arms of the Harlot's profession in plate 6 as "three spiggots and fossets," 12). Lichtenberg takes on "the broom of education—the birch," intended presumably for a customer who wishes to be flagellated:

> We have called it terrible, but merely in accordance with linguistic custom; for these comets on the firmament of morals do just as little harm to that system as those in the sky to the system of the physical

world. Just as Newton has assumed that the latter might perhaps with their tails fan an invigorating atmosphere into the system, so it might not only be supposed but could be geometrically demonstrated that the former actually sweep a great deal of evil out of the world with theirs. (29–30)

These sentences introduce a long, convoluted digression that both reflects the Shandean prurience in all matters sexual and implicates the pious Trusler.

Lichtenberg approaches plate 4 (where Trusler internalized his moralizing in the Harlot's psychology) with an elaborate metaphor of life as a slow fermentation, as opposed to the speed with which some (the earl of Rochester, for example) degenerate; and he finally concludes: "All this is really meant for you, poor Molly. Your fermentation too is going forward very quickly. Barely twenty, and already nearing the end of the second stage, whose progress that brewery scullion in the apron beside you there will have difficulty in arresting" (41). The first person singular addresses are to the Harlot, not as a Pamela or Clarissa but as a Jenny or Widow Wadman, an Uncle Toby or Walter Shandy. The aspect of Hogarth which Lichtenberg builds upon is the wit, as the untrammeled eye moves from one detail to another within the print. He materializes the thought process that Hogarth defined in *The Analysis of Beauty* as the "pleasure of pursuit" within an "intricate" pattern, but for Lichtenberg this is mediated by the verbal equivalents invented by Sterne a few years later. Sterne's familiar address to his reader and his characters, his obsession with minute detail and gesture, showed Lichtenberg how to reproduce in writing the perception that Hogarth intended for at least one type of reader, when he retrospectively aestheticized his earlier "modern moral subjects" in the *Analysis*.

This is an epistemology of aposiopesis bordering on what we would now call indeterminacy—"play" is based on strategies close to the "pursuit" of floating signifiers. On the contrary, Hogarth's works of the 1730s still adhered to the irony of Swift, Pope, and the early Fielding, and not to the more expansive "play" advocated in the *Analysis* and *Tristram Shandy* in the 1750s. Irony, like allegory, involves two—not indeterminate—senses, as it implies two audiences.[20] Irony was an early-eighteenth-century mode, contemporary with Hogarth but lost to the pious Trusler, and complicated by Lichtenberg into what has been called romantic irony (which replaces true and false meanings with ambiguity).

The Novel and the New

As we saw in chapter 1, far from being an ideal father figure from which Hackabout has fallen away, the parson is another inadequate model offered her by society—along a spectrum that runs from the bawd and Colonel Charteris to representatives of the judiciary, the constabulary, the penal system, and the clergy.[21] This would have been quite evident to a contemporary who was familiar, for example, with Fielding's plays of 1729–32 or with the Charteris rape trial of 1730 and with Opposition politics, let alone the strategies of the critical deists.

Again, Trusler and Lichtenberg had not read (with Hogarth's original audience) the story of Mary Muffet, "a woman of great note in the hundreds of Drury, who about a fortnight ago was committed to hard labor in Tothill-fields Bridewell . . . she is now beating hemp in a gown very richly laced with silver . . . to her no small mortification."[22] Writing of plate 4 (fig. 10), Trusler believes that the warden's "wife" is stealing the Harlot's handkerchief and "casting at the same time a wishful look upon her lappets" (8). In fact, as Lichtenberg sees, the warden's wife is pointing to the Harlot's bow and lace collar, deriding the impropriety of her fancy dress.[23] But, after much witty speculation and elaboration over the question of why her dress in plate 4 is different from the one in plate 3, he supposes that either plate 4 shows a second arrest and imprisonment, or she has dressed up for her appearance before a magistrate, hoping to sway his judgment (42–43). He reads the detail on the level of narrative verisimilitude rather than—as Hogarth meant it—symbolism: the dress indicates her emulation of "politeness."[24]

Only John Ireland, among the eighteenth-century commentators, catches something of Hogarth's emphasis on the Harlot's theatrical emulation of the great. She is taken to the bawd's brothel, introduced to Charteris, "who tells her she is born to grandeur; and, by artful flattery and liberal promises, intoxicated with the dreams of imaginary greatness," seduces her.[25] But plate 3 is described as merely a *vanitas* emblem: "Here we see but this child of misfortune *fallen, fallen,*

fallen, from her high estate!' (1:10). And this leads only to the generaliza-
tion that she thus demonstrates the "important truth, that / A DEVIA-
TION FROM VIRTUE, IS A DEPARTURE FROM HAPPINESS" (1:19).
Ireland gives much attention to Hogarth's use (justified, he believes) of "minute details," "minutiae" in "little stories, which record
the domestic incidents of familiar life"—and so these prints "become a
sort of historical record of the manners of the age" (1:6). While he
connects the bottles on the Harlot's shelf with her occupational disease,
he mentions the paintings on the Jew's wall only as satire on old master
paintings (1:8, 11). His interpretation of the *Harlot's Progress* is still that
Hackabout's "*variety of wretchedness,* forms such a picture of the way in
which vice rewards her votaries, as ought to warn the young and
inexperienced from entering this path of infamy." The Harlot is the
"daughter to a poor clergyman," whose failure to protect her lies in his
inability to read physiognomy; as a "good, easy man, unsuspicious as
Fielding's parson Adams" and a Quixote (his horse a "Rozinanti"), he is
"unpractised in the wiles of a great city" (1:2, 4).
    Ireland wrote *Hogarth Illustrated* (1791) for John Boydell as a
commentary to accompany the Hogarth folios Boydell published after
buying the original copperplates from Jane Hogarth's estate. Ireland
(perhaps a reader of Johnson's *Shakespeare* of 1765) sees Hogarth as a
Shakespearean artist who "took Nature for his guide, and gained the
summit." He distinguishes his commentary from that of Trusler, who
"confines himself to *morality,*" whereas he himself deals with the *art* of
Hogarth, that is, the compositions and expressions (1:xiii). Nevertheless, his retelling also produces a wild narrative unsubstantiated by the
plates, at least as novelistic as Trusler's but now along the lines of
Fielding's *Joseph Andrews* by way of *Amelia.*
    In short, if we wish to find a more accurate interpretation of
Hogarth's *Harlot's Progress*—or at least one closer to Hogarth's own
intention and the response of his original audience—than is offered by
Trusler, Lichtenberg, or Ireland (or even by Hogarth himself twenty
years later in the *Analysis of Beauty*), we must return to the time before
he made and published these prints, and to his verbal models, sources,
and antagonists.
    Reynolds, in the third of his *Discourses*, placed Hogarth in one of
"the various departments of painting, which do not presume to make

such high pretensions" as history painting—Hogarth is one of the "painters who have applied themselves more particularly to low and vulgar characters, and who express with precision the various shades of passion, as they are exhibited by vulgar minds."[26] The third *Discourse* was delivered in 1770, just two years after Trusler's *Hogarth Moralized.* Later, in his mellower fourteenth *Discourse* (1788), Reynolds singled out Gainsborough and Hogarth as two painters of genius in their own ways, but saw Hogarth as committing the error of attempting history painting without the study and effort he had put into (Reynolds now calls it) his "new species of dramatick painting, in which probably he will never be equalled" (254). It is instructive to see Reynolds praising Hogarth and Gainsborough, who in fact, despite their different genres, participated in a counterdiscourse to the one Reynolds preached in his annual discourses.

Rouquet had distinguished Hogarth's work from history painting in much the way Reynolds did, though privileging the new mode over the old, arguably outmoded one: "The first and greatest fault I find in Mr. Hogarth's painting," he writes ironically, "is that it is totally new *[neuf]*, and it corresponds too closely to the objects it represents."[27] It has the freshness of nature, not the darkness of old master paintings. Trusler, the second commentator, writing for Jane Hogarth, makes no attempt to assimilate Hogarth to the tradition that Reynolds represented, whether we call it civic humanist or simply academic. At this point in the 1760s these categories did not seem relevant—Trusler was defending Hogarth's works against the charge of impiety or false wit. But it is significant that in the first year of the Royal Academy, that bastion of civic humanism, Trusler reveals none of the sense of counterdiscourse that was evident in Rouquet's commentary—as in Hogarth's own programmatic subscription tickets and the contemporary references of Fielding, Sterne, Thornton, and others.

One inference I draw is that by the 1760s Hogarth's works were assimilated to a category that, while it originated as a revisionary discourse of civic humanism and history painting, had come to represent so standard if not normative a genre that its defenders found no need to contest what in literary terms was an outmoded discourse that only survived in the writings of professional painters who wished to appear to be liberal artists.

In a general way I am suggesting two things: that the most accurate reading of a work by Hogarth may be found in its sources; but also that I take the above evidence to suggest that while both Trusler and Lichtenberg were assimilating Hogarth's dramatic structure to a narrativistic one—indeed, a novelistic one—Hogarth's own model was closer to the combination of genres joined in the plays of Steele, Gay, and Fielding (what Reynolds referred to accurately as "dramatick painting"). Hogarth's contemporaries had initially transferred his tableaux *back* to the stage, and Fielding noted in a *Champion* essay of 1740 that Hogarth, "one of the most useful Satyrists any Age hath produced," has created a sort of play. In short, the sense of "novel" and "novelizing" goes back to the form of the Hogarthian "progress," the implied actions in the interstices between the scenes presented, and the genealogical projections carried over from the conversation pieces (most notably in *Rake* I and each scene of *Marriage A-la-mode*).

I acknowledge the seeming inconsistency that I have argued that Hogarth's *Harlot* and *Rake* projected and contributed to the English Novel,[28] while now I argue that these same works are distorted by being novelized by their commentators of the 1760s-1780s: But both statements are true if we distinguish between what these works meant to Hogarth and to their immediate audience, which was only partly what they meant to Richardson and Fielding, and what they meant to Trusler and Lichtenberg after the mediation of the Richardson-Fielding-Sterne novels of the 1740s and 1750s. Basically Hogarth remained a "dramatic" artist, to Reynolds as well as to Fielding, and indeed to himself (to judge by his final autobiographical writings), though this may only draw our attention back to Addison's novelistic metaphor of life-as-theater.[29] And he ends the *Analysis* with a return to the stage metaphor, beginning in the chapter "Of Action" (the metaphor is introduced on 149, and runs on, mixing the dancing with commedia dell'arte performance, until the end).[30]

This conclusion does not necessarily lead us to argue that we must talk about Hogarth's prints in the discourse of dramatic theory, though it is clear that he utilized the innovatory arguments that had been set forth by George Farquhar as well those of Steele, Gay, and Fielding. But I do mean to suggest that one important dimension of Hogarth's work is lost to both Trusler and Lichtenberg because they are, by the time they write, seeing his work of the 1730s through the eyes of Richardson, Fielding, and Sterne. The latter are of value because they draw our attention to the protonovelistic elements of works that were initially conceived in dramatic terms. The fact that Rouquet wrote in 1747, not in the 1730s—indeed, after the publication of *Joseph Andrews*—is reflected in the evidence that he was already beginning (or we might say that Hogarth himself was beginning) the process of novelizing, for example in *Marriage A-la-mode*, a work much closer to the mode of Trusler and Lichtenberg. By "novelizing" we mean that he developed the potential seen by Fielding and expanded in *Joseph Andrews*, for example the opening of genealogical, filiating, biographical perspectives, as well as the replacement of emblematic with psychological implications.

Our examples, however, have also shown that there is a great divide between the way Hogarth's questioning of social forms is read in the context of the 1720s–1730s and the way it is read in the context of the second half of the century, when these social forms were relatively assimilated. Indeed, they show that the process of rendering society "polite" begun by Addison (and analyzed and critiqued by his near-contemporary Hogarth) has now been internalized and that Hogarth himself has been domesticated in this particular way (which includes but is not limited to "moralizing"). In contrasting the Trusler-Lichtenberg "readings" with what can be discerned of Hogarth's own, we have in effect distinguished between the Novel and the novel, and so between the responses of the spectators at a play and the readers of a novel—between a situation that is public, dialogical, and oppositional and one that is private, monological, and internalizing.

Shakespeare and Johnson

A symptomatic text (and another of those commentaries I mentioned at the outset) was Charlotte Lennox's *Shakespeare Illustrated* of 1753, which was significantly heralded in its subtitle "by the author of the *Female Quixote*" (a novel commended by Fielding). Lennox repeatedly cites as the sources of Shakespeare's plays "novels and histories."[31] Her use of the word "novel" is itself significant at this time because she uses it to designate narratives in prose in the context of Shakespeare's poetic and dramatic forms—and because her tendency is to elevate those at the expense of the poetry and drama. Though the "novels" she invokes were generically short romances, she interprets them as if they were the "novel" of Richardson and Fielding, stressing the "probable" unfolding of plot and delineation of character.

Lennox's sense of "novel" is based on her own work, but the quality she singles out—which in fact distinguishes "novel" from most of the pre-Shakespearean novels she cites—is "probability." She could be following Fielding's account of her *Spiritual Quixote* in his *Covent-Garden Journal* No. 24 (24 March 1752), as a work that "presents a . . . regular Story with a complete Plan." Indeed, "The Incidents, or, if you please, the Adventures, are much less extravagant and incredible in the English than in the Spanish Performance."[32] Although Fielding also stresses the deflation of "Romance" and the author's endeavors "to expose all those Vices and Follies in her Sex which are chiefly predominant in our Days," these do not fit into Lennox's image of the novel, which holds to probability of plot and characters.

In her account of *Twelfth Night* Lennox prefers Bandello's "novel" to Shakespeare's play because "the *novelist* is much more careful to preserve probability in this narration than the *poet:* The wonder is that Shakespeare could task his invention to make those incidents unnatural and absurd."[33] "Probability" for Lennox is opposed to the "unnatural and absurd," or the quixotic romance. She in effect reduces the Novel to novel/news, omitting the sense of curiosity, pursuit, and discovery, and the other elements that made up what Hogarth called the Beautiful. The Novel also included the re-allegorization carried out by Woolston after he de-allegorized the miracles of Christ by historicizing them in order to educe a satire of clerical authority, of the letter against the spirit of the law.

What Fielding referred to as satire and anti-romance corresponds for Lennox to Shakespeare's "invention . . . neither necessary nor probable," or his "contrivance," displayed at the expense of probability (1:24, 146). And these qualities are what Samuel Johnson, in the dedication of the work to Lord Orrery, found lacking in Lennox's picture of Shakespeare. Though he writes under Lennox's name, Johnson uses the occasion to criticize her sense of Shakespeare / novel, reinscribing his own sense of the novel he had expressed in *Rambler* No. 4 (1750). Not "probability" and "plot" ("the naked plot or story of his plays") but the transcendence of time and place, according to Johnson, distinguishes Shakespeare's works from novels, which Johnson in fact tends to equate with romances. It is not the improbability of characters, as Lennox would say, but the fact that Shakespeare "exhibited many characters, in many changes of situation," which distinguishes his plays: "These characters are so copiously diversified, and some of them so justly pursued, that his works may be considered a map of life, a faithful miniature of human transactions, and he that has read Shakesepeare with attention, will perhaps find little new in the crouded world" (1:x). Here Johnson automatically distinguishes the two senses of *new* or *novel:* a "map [or miniature] of life," including variety ("diversified") and pursuit ("pursued"), from merely what is "new." Of course, as his *Rambler* No. 4 shows, he also excludes the sense of "novel" that complicates and obscures, such as the "mixed" or flawed character, although it is more "probable," in favor of the moral paragon.

We have witnessed the "novelizing" of Hogarth by his literary commentators—ironic in that by this time "novel" had come to lose most of the connotations he attached to his "modern moral subject." The novel was now Charlotte Lennox's "novel," based on probability; and indeed when Johnson critiqued Lennox's view of Shakespeare he was in some ways identifying Shakespeare, as many contemporaries had, with Hogarth himself: the Shakespeare who cannot be judged in terms of standards of narrative probability and the other criteria Trusler sought to impose on Hogarth. Thus when Trusler calls his book "Hogarth Moralized" he means "Hogarth novelized" in the manner of Lennox's definition, which eliminated all the aspects of pleasure outlined in Hogarth's *Analysis of Beauty.* And we end with the definition of "Shakespearean," gathering into the argument the issue of whether the works of the national hero were in Hogarthian terms Novel, or Beautiful, or Sublime.

Johnson had developed, from his earliest years, a personal vocabulary that was basically psychological and moral. This can be followed up to the late 1750s. In his *Dictionary* (1755), defining such terms as *beauty, novelty, variety,* and *greatness* he ignores Addison's aesthetic sense of the words; for the word *beauty* he cites Addison but not one of his "Pleasures of the Imagination" essays; *sublime* for Johnson still carries the Longinian reference to rhetoric; and there is no trace of Hutcheson's, let alone Addison's or Hogarth's, senses of *variety*.

But by the end of the 1750s, with his reading of Hogarth's *Analysis of Beauty* and Burke's *Philosophical Enquiry,* and probably more the latter,[34] he evidently saw how parts of his psychological-moral discourse related to the aesthetic discourse that was becoming prominent in the 1750s. The new discourse makes its appearance in *Rasselas* (1759), where it is subsumed under the moral and placed hierarchically below the religious. For example, the aesthetic terms are applied by Johnson to Rasselas's "observations" in the same provisional way religious terms were by Fielding in his *Champion* essays:

> With observations like these the prince *amused* himself as he re-turned, uttering them with a plaintive voice, yet with a look that dis-covered him to feel *some complacence* in his own perspicacity, and to receive *some solace* of *the miseries of life* from the consciousness of the *delicacy with which he felt,* and the *eloquence with which he bewailed* them. He mingled cheerfully in the *diversions* of the evening, and all rejoiced to find that his *heart was lightened.* (emphasis added)[35]

When Rasselas complains that "I should be happy if I had *something to persue*" (16), we infer that Johnson associates happiness with aesthetic discourse, as opposed to moral or religious.

However, the aesthetic discourse, subordinated to the religious in the story of Rasselas, reappears more positively in Johnson's commentaries on the plays of Shakespeare, and where we would expect it: the Sublime is praised in *Lear* and *Othello;* the Beautiful and Novel in *Hamlet* and *Antony and Cleopatra.* But in the 1765 "Preface" Shakespeare's drama as a whole is described as "not in the rigorous and critical sense either tragedies or comedies, but compositions of a distinct kind; exhibiting the real state of sublunary nature, which partakes of good and evil, joy and sorrow, mingled with endless variety of proportion and innumerable modes of combination."[36] "Compositions of a distinct kind" recalls all the references of contemporaries to

Hogarth as supreme "in his way," and his own references to his works as "entirely new." "Variety" is now the privileged term: "all pleasure consists in variety," Johnson writes at one point, and this variety, "lessened" by adherence to the rules and Unities, is associated with the rapid "change of scenes" (7:67). In the commentary on *Antony and Cleopatra* Johnson takes the same example Hogarth cited in his *Analysis* (14–15), Cleopatra's "infinite variety," commenting that "The continual hurry of the action, the variety of incidents, and the quick succession of one personage to another, all call the mind forward without intermission from the first act to the last. But the power of delighting is derived principally from the frequent changes of the scene" (8:873). In Shakespeare he recommends the contrast of "laughter and sorrow," "serious and ludicrous characters," because the "alternation . . . approaches nearer than either to the appearance of life" (7:67).

Of course, Johnson has little good to say of "that novelty of which the common satiety of life sends us all in quest," for "the pleasures of sudden wonder are soon exhausted, and the mind can only repose on the stability of truth." But by "truth" he means "a faithful mirrour of manners and of life"—and this is based on "diligent selection out of common conversation, and common occurences." The "selection," he had remarked in the *Rambler*, is based on "essential principles" which could be violated "by a desire of novelty" (No. 156); principles which, that is, distinguish the Novel from simply the news (7:61–63). Johnson is defining the Hogarthian, or rather the Novel, mode, and at one point in the "Preface" his metaphor also makes the connection between the Novel and the Picturesque: "the composition of Shakespeare is a forest, in which oaks extend their branches, and pines tower in the air, interspersed sometimes with weeds and brambles, and sometimes giving shelter to myrtles and to roses; filling the eye with awful pomp [the Sublime], and gratifying the mind with endless diversity [the Picturesque]" (7:84).

Thus Johnson contrasts Shakespeare, "an exact surveyor of the animate world," with Milton, who fails to capture "the freshness, raciness, and energy of immediate observation."[37] Johnson's Shakespeare is one who, though his "story requires Kings, . . . thinks only on men";

who speaks not the language of poets but that of men; who "acquaints us with human sentiments or human actions . . . observation impregnated by genius"; whose plays are "always crowded with incidents," and whose "natural disposition . . . led him to comedy."[38] Hogarth and Johnson would have agreed on their general principles—what ought to be imitated, what "nature" consists of, the dangers of art, and the uselessness of polarizing art and nature.

At this point the formulation and privileging of variety may owe less to Hogarth than to what was obviously his source (and Addison's as well); in the eighteenth century the notion of variety itself derived perhaps more from Shakespeare than from any other source. One could better say that Shakespeare, variety, mixed genres and mixed characters (*pace* the *Rambler* essay on *Tom Jones*), and violation of the unities all bring together Hogarth and Johnson ideologically—and on the common ground of the drama with its "rapid succession" and variety of scenes. Hogarth, we recall, was from 1730 onward referred to by contemporaries as the Shakespeare of painters.

Yet Johnson, outside the literary context of Shakespeare's plays, consistently criticizes the aesthetic response—as in the beauty or sublimity of a scene—in favor of the humane. In practical terms this means something like human comfort and safety if not happiness itself. In his *Journey to the Western Islands of Scotland* (1775), his actual questioning of the Sublime by human and vital standards is not unlike Hogarth's. He describes Slanes Castle, precariously perched high above the sea:

> To walk around the house seemed *impracticable. From the windows* the eye wanders over the sea that separates Scotland from Norway, and *when the winds beat with violence must enjoy all the terrifick grandeur of the tempestuous ocean.* I would not *for my amusement* wish for a storm; but as storms, whether wished or not, will sometimes happen, I may say, *without violation of humanity,* that I should willingly look out upon them from Slanes Castle. (19, emphasis added)

If this is Johnson's humane critique of the Sublime, later at the Fall of Firs, broaching the Novel or Uncommon, he wishes "that our curiosity might have been gratified with less trouble and danger" (34). This is essentially a criticism by human standards of the aesthetic itself, and in that sense draws attention to the antiaesthetic dimension also evident in Hogarth's revisionist, anti-Shaftesburian aesthetic. As a discourse Johnson's "aesthetics" is qualified, devalued, and marginalized in relation to his moral-psychological discourse, let alone his religious. This is because aesthetic discourse represents for him disinterestedness as opposed to human involvement. But it follows that his antiaesthetics is therefore in close proximity to Hogarth's aesthetics, while "aesthetics" itself signifies the Shaftesburian distancing of art from life.

Illustrations

TREATISE VII.

V I Z.

A NOTION of the *Hiftorical Draught* or *Tablature*

OF THE

Judgment of *Hercules,*

According to PRODICUS, *Lib.* II. *Xen. de Mem. Soc.*

—————————————————————Potiores
HERCULIS ærumnas credat, fævofque Labores,
Et Venere, & cœnis, & plumâ SARDANAPALI.
Juv. Sat. 10.

Paulo de Matthæis Pinx: *Sim. Gribelin Sculps:*

Printed firft in the Year M.DCC.XIII.

FIG. I. Paolo de Matteis, *The Judgment of Hercules* (1713), engraving by Simon Gribelin. Reproduced by courtesy of the Trustees of the British Museum.

FIG. 2. Hogarth, *Boys Peeping at Nature* (1731), etching; subscription ticket for *A Harlot's Progress*. Reproduced by courtesy of the Trustees of the British Museum.

FIG. 3. Hogarth, *A Harlot's Progress* (1732), plate 1; etching and engraving. Reproduced by courtesy of the Trustees of the British Museum.

FIG. 4. Hogarth,
A Harlot's Progress,
plate 1
(a) detail;
(b) detail.
Reproduced by
courtesy of
the Trustees
of the
British Museum.

a

b

FIG. 5. Albrecht Dürer, *The Visitation*, woodcut. Reproduced by courtesy of the Trustees of the British Museum.

FIG. 6. Hogarth, *A Harlot's Progress,* plate 2. Reproduced by courtesy of the Trustees of the British Museum.

FIG. 7. Hogarth, *A Harlot's Progress,* plate 3. Courtesy of the Print Collection, Lewis Walpole Library, Yale University.

FIG. 8. Hogarth, *A Harlot's Progress,* plate 3 (detail). Courtesy of the Print Collection, Lewis Walpole Library, Yale University.

FIG. 9. Dürer, *The Annunciation,* woodcut. Reproduced by courtesy of the Trustees of the British Museum.

FIG. 10. Hogarth, *A Harlot's Progress,* plate 4. Reproduced by courtesy of the Trustees of the British Museum.

FIG. II. Hogarth, *A Harlot's Progress,* plate 5. Reproduced by courtesy of the Trustees of the British Museum.

FIG. 12. Hogarth, *A Harlot's Progress,* plate 6. Reproduced by courtesy of the Trustees of the British Museum.

FIG. 13. Hogarth, *The Sleeping Congregation* (1736), etching and engraving.
Reproduced by courtesy of the Trustees of the British Museum.

FIG. 14. Hogarth, *Strolling Actresses Dressing in a Barn* (1738); engraving.
Reproduced by courtesy of the Trustees of the British Museum.

FIG. 15. Hogarth, *The Lottery* (1724), etching and engraving. Reproduced by courtesy of the Trustees of the British Museum.

FIG. 16. Hogarth, *Sir Francis Dashwood at His Devotions* (1750s), painting. Collection, Lord Boyne.

FIG. 17. Hogarth, *A Rake's Progress* (1735), plate 4; engraving. Reproduced by courtesy of the Trustees of the British Museum.

FIG. 18. Hogarth, *The Pool of Bethesda* (1737), painting (detail). Reproduced by kind permission of St. Bartholomew's Hospital.

FIG. 19. Hogarth, *The Distressed Poet* (1737; republished 1741), etching and engraving. Reproduced by courtesy of the Trustees of the British Museum.

FIG. 20. Hogarth, *The Enraged Musician* (1741), etching and engraving.
Reproduced by courtesy of the Trustees of the British Museum.

THE

ANALYSIS

OF

BEAUTY.

Written with a view of fixing the fluctuating I D E A S of
T A S T E.

BY *WILLIAM HOGARTH.*

So vary'd he, and of his tortuous train
Curl'd many a wanton wreath, in fight of Eve,
To lure her eye.-------- Milton.

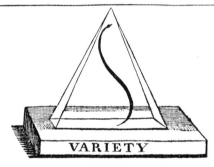

L O N D O N:

Printed by *J. R E E V E S* for the *A U T H O R*,
And Sold by him at his Houfe in L E I C E S T E R - F I E L D S.

MDCCLIII.

FIG. 21. Hogarth, *The Analysis of Beauty* (1753), title page.

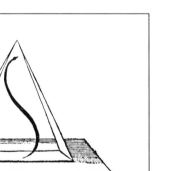

FIG. 22. *(a)* L. Cecill, title page of Thomas Heywood, *The Hierarchie of the Blessed Angells* (1635), engraving (detail, Trinity with Tetragrammaton); *(b)* Hogarth, title page, *Analysis of Beauty* (detail); *(c)* Hogarth, *Enthusiasm Delineated* (detail of fig. 36, below); *(d)* Hogarth, *Enthusiasm Delineated* (detail of fig. 36, below).

c

d

FIG. 23. Hogarth, *The Analysis of Beauty* (1753), plate 1; etching and engraving. Reproduced by courtesy of the Trustees of the British Museum.

FIG. 24. Hogarth, *The Analysis of Beauty* (1753), plate 2; etching and engraving.
Reproduced by courtesy of the Trustees of the British Museum.

FIG. 25. Hogarth, *Satan, Sin, and Death* (late 1730s), painting. Tate Gallery, London.

FIG. 26. Hogarth, *The Beggar's Opera* (1729), painting. Paul Mellon Collection, Yale Center for British Art.

FIG. 27. Hogarth, *The Wollaston Family* (1730), painting. Executors of the late H. C. Wollaston, on loan to Leicester Museums and Art Galleries.

FIG. 28. Hogarth, *A Midnight Modern Conversation* (1733), engraving.
Reproduced by courtesy of the Trustees of the British Museum.

FIG. 29. Johan Zoffany, *Queen Charlotte and Her Two Eldest Sons* (1764),
painting. The Royal Collection © Her Majesty Queen Elizabeth II.

FIG. 30. Philip Reinagle, *Mrs. Congreve with Her Children* (1782), painting.
Courtesy of the National Gallery of Ireland, Dublin.

FIG. 31. Joseph Wright of Derby, *An Academy by Lamplight* (1768–69), painting. Yale Center for British Art, Paul Mellon Collection.

FIG. 32. Wright of Derby, *An Experiment on a Bird in the Air Pump* (1768), painting. Reproduced by courtesy of the Trustees, the National Gallery, London.

FIG. 33. Hogarth, *The March to Finchley* (1750), engraving. Reproduced by courtesy of the Trustees of the British Museum.

FIG. 34. Francis Hayman, *The Play at See-Saw* (c. 1741–42), painting. Tate
Gallery, London.

Bow wow wow, ſays the Dog at the Door. Sirrah, ſays his Miſtreſs, what do you bark at Little *Two-Shoes.* Come in *Madge;* here, *Sally* wants you ſadly, ſhe has learned all her Leſſon. Then out came the little one: So *Madge!* ſays ſhe; ſo *Sally!* anſwered the other, have you learned your Leſſon? Yes, that's what I have, replied the little one in th

the Country Manner; and immedi-ately taking the Letters ſhe ſet up theſe Syllables.

ba be bi bo bu ca ce ci co cu
da de di do du fa fe fi fo fu.

and gave them their exact Sounds as ſhe compoſed them; after which ſhe ſet up the following :

ac ec ic oc uc, ad ed id od ud
af ef if of uf, ag eg ig og ug

And pronounced them likewiſe. She then ſung the Cuzz's Chorus (which may be found in the *Little Pretty Play Thing* publiſhed by Mr. NEW-BERY) and to the ſame Tune to which it is there ſet.

After this Little *Two Shoes* taught her to ſpell Words of one ſyllable,
C   and

FIG. 35. Two pages from *The History of Little Goody Two-Shoes* (1762). Reproduced by courtesy of the Trustees of the British Museum.

FIG. 36. Hogarth, *Enthusiasm Delineated* (c. 1759), etching and engraving.
Reproduced by courtesy of the Trustees of the British Museum.

FIG. 37. Hogarth, *Credulity, Superstition, and Fanaticism: A Medley* (1762), etching and engraving. Reproduced by courtesy of the Trustees of the British Museum.

FIG. 38. Thomas Rowlandson, *The Exhibition Stare-Case* (c. 1800), drawing.
Yale Center for British Art, Paul Mellon Collection.

FIG. 39. Rowlandson, *Landscape with Snake* (1790s), drawing. The Elisha
Whittelsey Collection, the Elisha Whittelsey Fund, 1959 (59.533.1667), Metropolitan
Museum of Art, New York.

FIG. 40. Thomas Gainsborough, *The Harvest Wagon* (1767), painting. The Barber Institute of Fine Arts, the University of Birmingham.

FIG. 41. Gainsborough, *Copy of Rubens' "Deposition"* (1760s), painting. Private collection, presently on loan to the Ashmolean Museum, Oxford, England.

FIG. 42. Rowlandson, *The Connoisseurs* (undated). Yale Center for British Art, Paul Mellon Collection.

Notes

Preface

1. See George Levine's introduction to *Aesthetics and Ideology,* ed. Levine (New Brunswick, N.J., 1994). I do not mean to suggest that none of the essays in the collection deals with aesthetics in the scholarly sense; I found particularly useful Oscar Kenshur's " 'The Tumour of Their Own Hearts': Relativism, Aesthetics, and the Rhetoric of Demystification," in ibid., 57–78.

2. The chief texts here are Hume's "Essay on Taste" of 1756 and Burke's response in the second edition of his *Philosophical Enquiry* of 1759. These fall outside the range of the present study.

3. For the strong and prestigious tradition of writing on the Sublime, see Samuel H. Monk, *The Sublime: A Study of Critical Theories in Eighteenth-Century England* (New York, 1935); Thomas Weiskel, *The Romantic Sublime: Studies in the Structure and Psychology of Transcendence* (Baltimore, 1976); Neil Hertz, *The End of the Line: Essays on Psychoanalysis and the Sublime* (New York, 1985); Steven Knapp, *Personification and the Sublime: Milton to Coleridge* (Cambridge, Mass., 1985); and Frances Ferguson, *Solitude and the Sublime: Romanticism and the Aesthetics of Individuation* (New York, 1992). Any list of secondary works on aesthetics should begin with W. J. Hipple Jr.'s *The Beautiful, the Sublime, and the Picturesque in Eighteenth-Century British Aesthetic Theory* (Carbondale, Ill., 1957).

4. Martin C. Battestin, *The Providence of Wit: Aspects of Form in Augustan Literature and the Arts* (New York, 1974), 1. See my review, in *Studies in Burke and His Time* 17 (1976): 234–40. To be fair to Battestin, he is using "aesthetics" in the quotation in as loose a way as is Levine in the introduction to *Aesthetics and Ideology.*

5. Michael McKeon suggests this dialectic progression in "Politics of Dis-

course and the Rise of the Aesthetic in Seventeenth-Century England," in *Politics of Discourse: The Literature and History of Seventeenth-Century England,* ed. Kevin Sharpe and Steven N. Zwicker (Los Angeles, 1987), 35–41. More recently, see McKeon, "The Origins of Interdisciplinary Studies," *ECS: Eighteenth-Century Studies* 28 (1994): 22–23.

6. Robert Sullivan, *John Toland and the Deist Controversy: A Study in Adaptations* (Cambridge, Mass., 1982), 274.

7. Bernard Mandeville, *Fable of the Bees,* ed. F. B. Kaye (Oxford, 1924), 3. In *Free Thoughts on Religion, the Church, and National Happiness,* 2d ed. (1729), in the chapter "Of Mysteries," Mandeville acknowledges that "I incur the censures of our zealous clergy, who will call this the advice of a latitudinarian, if not worse" (82)—suggesting the narrow line that separated latitudinarian (i.e., orthodox) and deist for many contemporaries.

8. See Robert Voitle, *The Third Earl of Shaftesbury* (Baton Rouge, 1984), 347.

9. E.g., *Tatler* No. 111; *Spectator* No. 459.

10. *The Spectator,* ed. Donald F. Bond, 5 vols. (Oxford, 1965), No. 465, 4:143–45. Hereafter all citations to the *Spectator* refer to Bond's edition.

11. So far as I know, I was the first to make this point, in *Hogarth,* 3 vols. (New Brunswick, N.J., 1991–93). (Hereafter this work is cited simply as *"Hogarth."*) For a brief connection between aesthetics and deism, see Robert C. Holub, "The Rise of Aesthetics in the Eighteenth Century," *Comparative Literature Studies* 15 (Sept. 1978): 275. For the general relationship of aesthetics to the decline in religious belief, see Holub, "Rise," 275–76; and McKeon, "Politics of Discourse and the Rise of the Aesthetic," 35–51. A short sketch for what developed into the present book appeared as "Aesthetics and Erotics in Eighteenth-Century English Art," in *Künstlerischer Austausch: Akten des XXVIII. Internationalen Kongresses für Kunstgeschichte, Berlin, 15–20 Juli 1992,* ed. Thomas W. Gaehtgens (Berlin, 1993), 559–67.

12. While Hipple, *Beautiful, Sublime,* has almost nothing to say about Addison's Novel (18–19), he includes an informed chapter (chap. 4) on Hogarth. Michael Kitson was correct, and virtually alone, in calling the *Analysis* "the first sustained anti-academic treatise in the history of aesthetics" ("Hogarth's 'Apology for Painters,'" *Walpole Society* 41 [1966–68]: 65).

13. For "idiosyncratic," see David Solkin, *Painting for Money: The Visual Arts and the Public Sphere in Eighteenth-Century England* (New Haven, 1993), 93; for "Cockney's Mirror," Margaret Bowen, *Hogarth: The Cockney's Mirror* (London, 1937); and for the man of the London street, Richard Dorment's review of my *Hogarth* and my replies (*New York Review of Books,* 27 May 1993, 17–20; ibid., 12 Aug. 1993, 56–57; ibid., 7 Oct. 1993, 53–54).

14. Irving Howe, "History and the Novel," *New Republic,* 3 Sept. 1990, 29.

15. Georg Lukacs, *Die Theorie des Romans,* 2d ed. (Berlin, 1963), 28–31. Michael McKeon does include a mention in *The Origins of the English Novel,*

1600–1740 (Baltimore, 1987), 81–82. He involves the deists in what he calls the "Question of Truth," in connection with which he mentions Thomas Woolston.

16. The germ of the idea can be traced to Martin Price's fine essay "The Picturesque Moment" (in *From Sensibility to Romanticism: Essays Presented to Frederick A. Pottle,* ed. Frederick W. Hilles and Harold Bloom [New York, 1965]). I began, first looking back from the context of the French Revolution, in *Representations of Revolution* (New Haven, 1983): Blake's fiery Orc elevated picturesque energy into a force with sublime effects or at least consequences, and I read something of the Blakean imagery back into Hogarth and Rowlandson. In *Breaking and Remaking: Aesthetic Practice in England, 1700–1820* (New Brunswick, 1989), I described a poetics rather than aesthetics (concerned with making rather than response) which subsumed the category of the Novel rather vaguely under the term "modern."

17. Melvyn New, " 'The Grease of God': The Form of Eighteenth-Century English Fiction," *PMLA* 91 (1976): 235–43.

18. I dealt with, besides Hogarth himself, Zoffany, Wright, Stubbs, and Gainsborough (Rowlandson was treated in a separate book): see *Emblem and Expression: Meaning in English Art of the Eighteenth Century* (London, 1975); idem, *Rowlandson: A New Interpretation* (London, 1972).

19. John Barrell, *The Political Theory of Painting from Reynolds to Hazlitt* (New Haven, 1986).

20. See J.G.A. Pocock, *The Machiavellian Moment: Florentine Republican Thought and the Atlantic Tradition* (Princeton, 1975), and his subsequent essays on civic humanism.

21. Andrew Hemingway, review of *The Political Theory of Painting,* by John Barrell *Art History* 10 (1987): 381–95; Ronald Paulson, review of *Political Theory of Painting, New Republic,* 10, 17 Aug. 1987, 39–42.

22. Stephen Copley did this, citing a counterdiscourse of writers for the periodical press (as opposed to philosophers and connoisseurs), in his illuminating essay "The Fine Arts in Eighteenth-Century Polite Culture," in *Painting and the Politics of Culture: New Essays on British Art, 1700–1850,* ed. John Barrell (Oxford, 1992), 13–38.

23. J.G.A. Pocock, "Cambridge Paradigms and Scotch Philosophers: A Study of the Relations between the Civic Humanist and the Civil Jurisprudential Interpretation of Eighteenth-Century Social Thought," in *Wealth and Virtue: The Shaping of Political Economy in the Scottish Enlightenment,* ed. Istvan Hont and Michael Ignatieff (Cambridge, 1983), 246.

24. Both Barrell and his followers have elaborated on his thesis (as in the essays he edited in *Painting and the Politics of Culture* of 1992). Happily, some of the essays in that book, while confining themselves to the "civic humanist discourse," do silently test and extend Barrell's thesis. See Ronald Paulson, review, *Times Literary Supplement,* 19 Feb. 1993, 20.

25. Cf. John Guillory, *Cultural Capital: The Problem of Literary Canon Formation* (Chicago, 1993), whose sense of tradition corresponds more closely than mine to canon (33–34).

26. Johnson's case was, however, more complex: see *Hogarth* 3:263–68; and chapter 10, below.

27. It should be noted that Hogarth only applies the words "modern moral subject" to these works in his "Autobiographical Notes," which he intended to use as an introduction to sets of his engravings, written in the 1760s (in William Hogarth, *Analysis of Beauty,* ed. Joseph Burke [Oxford, 1955], 216).

28. W.J.T. Mitchell, *Iconology: Image, Text, Ideology* (Chicago, 1986), esp. chap. 1.

29. For a better sense of the variety of input that led to Hogarth's own *Harlot* and that led to the novel, see, respectively, *Hogarth,* vol. 1, esp. chaps. 8, 9; and McKeon, *Origins of the English Novel.*

CHAPTER 1. Aesthetics and Deism

1. See below, chap. 2, p. 43; see also Howard Caygill, *The Art of Judgement* (London, 1989), 38; and Terry Eagleton, *The Ideology of the Aesthetic* (London, 1990), 13.

2. For the history of deism, see John Orr, *English Deism: Its Roots and Fruits* (Grand Rapids, Mich., 1934), and—for our purposes, the most useful source—Roland N. Stromberg, *Religious Liberalism in Eighteenth-Century England* (Oxford, 1954); but Leslie Stephen's chapters in his *History of English Thought in the Eighteenth Century* (1876; reprint, New York, 1962) remain of interest. For Shaftesbury's deism, see A. O. Aldridge, *Shaftesbury and the Deist Manifesto* (Philadelphia, 1951), which includes a list of references to Shaftesbury's deism in the eighteenth century (371 ff.).

3. Shaftesbury obsessively returns to the danger of the Christian religion's carrot-and-stick fiction of rewards and punishments in the afterlife. He first made the point in his preface to *Select Sermons of Dr.* [Benjamin] *Whichcot* (1698). His point was that the Christian view of human sinfulness is no different from Hobbes's atheistic materialist view of man; and that this was the result of priestcraft's need to emphasize rewards and punishments in the afterlife, thus replacing the love of goodness for its own sake—*dis*interested virtue (preface to *Sermons,* sigs. A5v, A6r–v, A7r). For the influence of this doctrine on Fielding, see chapter 5, below.

4. Shaftesbury, *Characteristics of Men, Manners, Opinions, Times, Etc.,* ed. John M. Robertson (New York, 1900), 1:266–67. I cite this edition for all quotations from Shaftesbury.

5. "Virtue," Mandeville wrote, is the work of "Lawgivers and other wise

Men, that have laboured for the Establishment of Society"; not "the pure Effect of Religion" but "the contrivance of Politicians . . . the skilful Management of wary Politicians," a "contrivance" necessary for both social order and personal happiness (*Fable of the Bees* 1:42, 50, 51). Benjamin Hoadly, the Anglican "latitudinarian" bishop who was close to both Hogarth and Fielding, also took this position against the idea of morality based on rewards/punishments in the afterlife. William Warburton, an orthodox Anglican bishop and an influential literary spokesman (another acquaintance of both Hogarth and Fielding), said much the same in the first volume of his *Divine Legation of Moses* (1738).

6. Hobbes's equation of beauty and virtue (in the contrast between *pulchrum* and *turpe*) was, as Oscar Kenshur notes, a way of "reinforcing his claim that goodness is merely relative by linking goodness to the merely beautiful." Whereas Hobbes "[tied] the fate of the good to that of the beautiful" (the latter dependent on shifting tastes), Shaftesbury "has each point to the intrinsic value of the other, thus allowing the perception of beauty to serve as the criterion for the recognition of the good" (Kenshur, " 'Tumour of Their Own Hearts,' " 61, 69).

7. Shaftesbury, *Notion of the Historical Draught or Tablature of the Judgment of Hercules,* first published in French in *Journal des Scavans,* Nov. 1712; translated into English in 1713 and published in the *Characteristicks* of 1714 as treatise 7; and published in *Second Characters or the Language of Forms,* ed. Benjamin Rand (Cambridge, 1914). For a discussion of the Choice of Hercules tradition, see Erwin Panofsky, *Hercules am Scheidewege und andere antike Bildstoffe in der neueren Kunst* (Leipzig, 1920); as related to Hogarth, see *Hogarth* 1:269–72; as related to the civic humanist tradition, see Barrell, *Political Theory of Painting,* 27–33.

8. The relationship of Mandeville, the anti-Shaftesbury position, and Hogarth was pointed out in *Hogarth* 1:251–52, 335–36, 3:75–76.

9. John Toland, "A Word to the Honest Priests," in *An Appeal to Honest People against Wicked Priests* (1713), 38; see Stephen H. Daniel, *John Toland: His Methods, Manners, and Mind* (Kingston, 1984), 28–29.

10. Oscar Kenshur, *Dilemmas of Enlightenment: Studies in the Rhetoric and Logic of Ideology* (Berkeley, 1993), 67.

11. John Toland, *Christianity Not Mysterious,* ed. Peter A. Schouls (New York, 1984), xx–xxviii. For parallels and possible personal connections between Toland and Hogarth's father, see *Hogarth* 1:8, 345 n. 55.

12. Toland, *Christianity Not Mysterious,* xx.

13. In reacting against the stoic fraternity of civic humanists, Toland, and after him Hogarth, adapted as a counter the model of another fraternity, Freemasonry, which claimed to be democratic, capable of including members of the artisan classes as well as the gentry. As I have shown elsewhere, Hogarth had

close ties to Freemasonry, from the early 1720s (*Hogarth* 2:56–60, 147–48). Freemasonry does not play a part, however, in the other writers I discuss, and so I have not gone into it here.

14. Hogarth, *Analysis*, 22–26.

15. Like Toland, Anthony Collins, in *A Discourse of the Grounds and Reasons of the Christian Religion* (1724), started his argument by affirming "every man's natural right and duty to *think* for himself, and to *judge* upon such evidence as he can procure to himself, after he has done his best endeavours to get information." It follows that "*freely* to *profess* his opinions, and to endeavour, when he judges proper, to *convince* others also of their truth" is defined as "liberty" (emphasis added; Collins, *Discourse*, v, iv).

16. John Toland, "Clidophorus; or of the Exoteric and Esoteric Philosophy," in *Tetradymus* (1720); Shaftesbury, *An Essay on the Freedom of Wit and Humour* (1709), in *Characteristics* 1:45; Henry Fielding, *Tom Jones* 14.12. See David Berman, "Deism, Immortality, and the Art of Theological Lying," in *Deism, Masonry, and the Enlightenment*, ed. J. A. Leo Lemay (Newark, Del., 1987), 63 (see 61–78).

17. Stromberg, *Religious Liberalism*, 58. "Ridicule," wrote Woolston, "will cut the pate of an ecclesiastical numbskull, which calm and sedate reasoning will make no impression on" (*Mr. Woolston's Defense of His Discourses* [1729], 20).

18. Toland, "Clidophorus," 56–57.

19. Addison's distinction is in *Spectator* No. 315: "The Story should be such as an ordinary Reader may acquiesce in, whatever Natural, Moral or Political Truth may be discovered in it by Men of greater penetration" (3:146).

20. Toland, *Christianity Not Mysterious*, xxiii, xxviii. Cf. Samuel Clarke, of the teachings of Christ: "The *only Rule of Faith* therefore to every Christian, is *the Doctrine of Christ;* and that Doctrine, as applied to him by his own Understanding"—i.e., not by the clergy (*Scripture Doctrine of the Trinity* [1712], iii).

21. See Stromberg, *Religious Liberalism*, 71, 73; *Hogarth* 1:288–92.

22. *A Letter to the Archbishop of Canterbury, concerning Persecution for Religion and Freedom of Debate* (1732), by Hogarth's (and Fielding's) friend Thomas Cooke, was provoked by the case of Woolston, though Woolston is not named. Cooke, well known as a deist, argues "that Freedom of debate about Religion is not only consistent with Christianity, but recommended in the *New Testament*, as previously necessary before we can arrive at a certainty of Truth"; he attacks "the Wickedness of persecuting for religion, and the Folly and Baseness of attempting to lay any Restraint on the Minds of Men," an attack that can be read as a defense of liberty in moral matters (Cooke emphasizes both charity and love). He reads the Gospels "in their original Purity," against the perversions and self-serving interpretations of the clergy (6, 5). Cooke's tract coincides with the publication of Hogarth's *Harlot* (its writing is dated February 1732); he

cites Samuel Clarke against persecution (34–35), which could help to explain the presence of Clarke's portrait alongside Woolston's in *Harlot* 2. Hogarth had etched a frontispiece for Cooke's translation of Hesiod (1727/8), and, in the context of Cooke's pamphlet, and Hogarth's portraits of Woolston and Clarke, *A Harlot's Progress* can be interpreted as a plea for freedom from religious persecution.

23. It remained in the cheap set he commissioned from Giles King. For Hogarth's use of Woolston's *Discourses* in his planning of *The Pool of Bethesda* and its pendant, *The Good Samaritan,* see Hogarth, vol. 2, chap. 4; for Giles King, see 1:309–10; Ronald Paulson, *Hogarth's Graphic Works,* 3d ed. (London, 1989), 76. (Hereafter the latter work is cited as *Hogarth's Graphic Works.*)

24. Another example from much later in Hogarth's career: Werner Busch argues that *Beer Street / Gin Lane* (1751) presupposes not only contrasted scenes such as Brueghel's *Maigre Cuisine* and *Grasse Cuisine* but also tryptichs of the Last Judgment; that Hogarth has represented Heaven and Hell only, with the middle panel, the Last Judgment itself, omitted because artists and writers of Hogarth's time did not believe in the efficacy of rewards/punishments in the hereafter. He reads it, however, as merely a typical "Enlightenment" rendering (*Das sentimentalische Bild: Die Krise der Kunst im 18. Jahrhundert und die Geburt der Moderne* [Munich, 1993], 279–84, 288–94).

25. Cf. my different accounts in *Breaking and Remaking,* 149–55; and *Hogarth* 2:97–103.

26. See *Hogarth* 1:322–23.

27. However, in his *Discourse concerning Ridicule and Irony in Writing* (1729), which may have been influenced by Woolston's writings, Collins turns his attention to miracles—"the most extravagant, whimsical, absurd, and ridiculous Legends and Stories imaginable" (8).

28. George Vertue, *Notebooks* (Oxford, 1934–55), 3:58. Cf. Michael Godby's thesis that the origin of plate 3 was an emblem of Temperance ("The First Steps of Hogarth's *Harlot's Progress,*" *Art History* 10 [1987]: 23–37; and *Hogarth* 1:238). Apropos of plate 3, another of Collins's examples is "ABRAHAM offering up ISAAC, which was a type of CHRISTS being offer'd up on the cross" (64), a print of which she has hung on her own wall in plate 3 in plebeian imitation of her Jewish keeper's old master collection. Referring to priests as rabbis, Collins remarks that "therefore christianity is the allegorical sense of the Old Testament, and is not improperly call'd *mystical Judaism*" (92); good Christians should think of themselves as Jews. For the allusion to Woolston's Rabbi and *his* attitude toward Christianity, see *Hogarth* 1:288. Cf. also Toland, *Christianity Not Mysterious,* 136–38.

29. G. C. Lichtenberg, in *Ausführliche Erklärung der Hogarthischen Kupferstiche,* translated by Innes Herdan and Gustav Herdan as *The World of Hogarth: Lichtenberg's Commentaries on Hogarth's Engravings* (Boston, 1966), first

pointed this out (36). After a typically expansive series of speculations, he suggests, quite correctly, that it may imply that Macheath and Sacheverell are regarded by the Harlot as "calendar saints." That the image is of Christ is a possibility Lichtenberg considers and rejects; that it might be Mary is raised by John Ireland (*Hogarth Illustrated* [1791], 1:11). The idea that religion is being attacked is resisted by Lichtenberg; see chapter 10, below.

30. Such stories were reported in periodicals of circa 1710, at the time of the Sacheverell affair; see James Granger, *Biographical History of England* (1806), 6:129; pointed out to me by DeAnn DeLuna.

31. The biblical commentators emphasize the word "cousin," asking how Elizabeth, "who was one of the daughters of Aaron, *ver. 5,* and consequently of the tribe of Levi, could be cousin to Mary, who was of the house of David, and consequently of the tribe of Judah." But, the commentator proceeds to speculate, "*cousin* may be taken in a larger sense, as Paul calleth all the Jews his kinsmen." In short, there are two senses of "cousin" in plate 1. (Matthew Poole, *Commentary on the Holy Bible* [Peabody, Mass., n.d.], 3:190).

32. He has to have read Mandeville's *Modest Defence of Publick Stews* (1724): the value of prostitution to society is illustrated by the butcher who saves his meat from the flies by "very Judiciously cut[ting] off a fragment already blown, which serves to hang up for a cure; and thus, by sacrificing a Small Part, already Tainted, and not worth Keeping, he wisely secures the Safety of the rest" (xi–xii; cf. *Hogarth* 1:254 and 376 n. 51).

33. Cf. Goldsmith's use of the Magnificat in *The Vicar of Wakefield,* below, chap. 8.

34. Samuel Clarke, *Scripture Doctrine of the Trinity* (1712), i–ii.

35. Mandeville's chapter "Of Mysteries," in *Free Thoughts on Religion, the Church, and National Happiness,* 2d ed. (1729), focused on the Trinitarian mystery and came up with close to a deist position. Hogarth, in *Rake* 8, affixed the name of Athanasius to the wall of a madman's cell in Bedlam. William Whiston, whose name is also inscribed on the Bedlam wall, was notorious for his anti-Athanasian pamphlets. Given the presence of Rakewell and Sarah Young in the pose of Christ and Mary, Hogarth may be recalling with heavy irony the *absent* Rakewell senior (a weighty presence in plate 1, represented as a picture on the wall) to complete a parodic Trinity. Collins's *Discourse* was essentially an attack on Whiston, who attempted to salvage the validity of literal prophesy (listing all his virtues—"A great Mathematician, philosopher, and Divine," "A most Acute Person," "A good Christian," but concluding, "Deficient in Judgment"). This may also explain the reference to Whiston in Bedlam in *Rake* 8.

36. See *Hogarth's Graphic Works,* no. 43. For *The Lottery,* see no. 53.

37. In the *Analysis* Hogarth tells us that an inverted triangle serves to structure the grace of the Apollo Belvedere (90). Another parodic triangle appears in

the folded hands of the reader who is eying the young woman; but he is merely twiddling his thumbs in boredom.

38. Perhaps the closest graphic model was Watteau's *Italian Comedians* (1720; National Gallery, Washington), painted for Dr. Richard Mead in London and accessible to London artists, which shows Pierrot being presented to the audience by the other members of the commedia dell'arte troupe. The parallel to Rembrandt's etching *Christ Presented to the People* would have been evident to a sharp observer like Hogarth, as it was to Erwin Panofsky, even though a recent cataloger calls the resemblance "fortuitous." Watteau, a major influence on Hogarth's conversation pieces (see below, chap. 4), had painted scenes that replaced traditional religious with theatrical subjects, in some respects anticipating what Hogarth would call "modern moral subjects." (Panofsky, "Gilles or Pierrot?" *Gazette des Beaux-arts* 162 [1952]: 319–40; Margaret Morgan Grasselle and Pierre Rosenberg, *Watteau* [Washington, 1984], 441. The print, by Bernard Baron, was not published until 1733. See *Hogarth* 1:135–37.)

CHAPTER 2. Shaftesburian Disinterestedness

1. Jerome Stolnitz, *Aesthetics and the Philosophy of Art Criticism* (Boston, 1960), 34–35. Subsequently Stolnitz published an important series of essays on disinterestedness, the most significant for our purposes being "Of the Origins of Aesthetic Disinterestedness," *Journal of the History of Ideas* 22 (1961); reprinted in *Aesthetics: A Critical Anthology,* ed. G. Dickie and R. J. Sclafani (New York, 1977), 607: "If any one belief is the common property of modern thought, it is that a certain mode of attention is indispensable to and distinctive of the perception of beautiful things." See also, on Shaftesbury, "On the Significance of Lord Shaftesbury in Modern Aesthetic Theory," *Philological Quarterly* 2 (1961): esp. 98–99. For George Dickie's alternative reading, see his *Aesthetics: An Introduction* (Indianapolis, 1971); and idem, *Art and the Aesthetic* (Ithaca, 1974). For background on disinterestedness I am grateful to papers by Peter J. McCormick and Paul Guyer and to discussions with them at an NEH Institute in 1991 at the Johns Hopkins University. Guyer's essay has since been incorporated into his book *Kant and the Experience of Freedom: Essays on Aesthetics and Morality* (Cambridge, 1993).

2. Hogarth, *Analysis,* 42; Shaftesbury, *Characteristics* 2:21, 29–31. Theocles begins with the formulation "that our real good is pleasure"; and Philocles turns this into "Pleasure is our good" (29), and, many pages later, concludes "that beauty . . . and good with you, Theocles, I perceived, are still one and the same" (128). But by this time the connotation of "good" has changed from Theocles' sense of "virtuous" to Philocles' sense of "beneficial," and back to "virtuous."

3. W. K. Wimsatt Jr. and Cleanth Brooks, *Literary Criticism: A Short History*

(New York, 1957), 13–14. On Shaftesbury's homoeroticism, see Voitle, *Shaftesbury*, 242–44, 344–45.

4. To quote Richard Braverman's formulation of what he calls imagery expressing "the erotics of power": The imagery of empire versus republic in the Restoration took the form of a "masculine (meaning legitimate)" ruler "defined against forms of excess affiliated with the feminine Other" (an Almanzor vs. Lyndaraxa but also a Tarquin vs. Lucrece). Then in the post-1688 Whig myth, in what he calls "the civic mode, the terms of political-as-sexual difference were revised along fraternal lines" (*Plots and Counterplots: Sexual Politics and the Body Politic in English Literature, 1660–1730* [Cambridge, 1993], 187).

5. David Solkin, in *Painting for Money*, 14, 15, notes the significance of Fulvia's gender but does not see the connection between this literary prototype and Hogarth's subsequent centralizing of her in a theory (doubtless derived from Mandeville, among others) of aesthetic "pleasure."

6. Shaftesbury, "Freedom of Wit and Humour," in *Characteristics* 1:96; Hogarth, *Analysis*, 82. My discussion of Venus-Pleasure-Beauty is in *Breaking and Remaking*, 168–92; *Hogarth*, vol. 3, chap. 3.

7. See John Toland, *Pantheisticon* (1720; facsimile, New York, 1976), 65. Freemasonry focused on neither the civic humanist hero nor Christ but on a symbolic woman as a figure of Nature (in this respect overlapping with deist pantheists such as Toland), though excluding living women from the fraternity. My student Peter Mortensen has drawn my attention to Toland's unfinished *Critical History of the Celtic Religion*, in which he "speculated that the Druids had presided over an indigenous Anglo-Saxon and Celtic paganism centered on the worship of female symbols of nature." Margaret Jacob has argued that *Pantheisticon* "was probably used or intended to be used as a ritual for masonic meetings" (*Radical Enlightenment: Pantheistic Freemasons and Republicans* [London, 1981], 153).

8. Paul Monod, "Painters and Party Politics in England, 1714–1760," *Eighteenth-Century Studies* 26 (spring 1993): 390.

9. The fable of Swift's *Gulliver's Travels*, as Braverman has pointed out, includes Gulliver's enthusiasm for Laputa (*La Puta*, the whore): "The *femme fatale* who critiques pure reason as passion incarnate, she is the elusive feminine that cannot be represented, rationalized, or possessed" (*Plots and Counterplots*, 310).

10. One wonders if Hogarth intends the analogy: His Diana Multimammia is to Pope's Goddess Dulness as (moving from subscription ticket to plate 1) Hackabout is to Mother Needham.

11. To show how overdetermined a print such as *The Sleeping Congregation* can be, cf. the letter from a "Starer" in *Spectator* No. 20, who sits in a congregation and observes "one of the young Ladies" who "display'd the most beautiful

Bosom imaginable" (a fan is also mentioned). On the attraction of an exposed bosom, see also Addison's *Guardian* No. 100. As to the royal lion, Hogarth had used it (as well as the other royal supporter, the unicorn) in *Masquerade Ticket* (1727) to make a comment exclusively on royalty: They are shown lying on their backs using their tails in a masturbatory fashion.

12. See *Hogarth* 3:270–73.

13. Toland, *Christianity Not Mysterious*, 151–52.

14. For *The Good Samaritan*, see *Hogarth*, vol. 2, chap. 4, and fig. 39.

15. John Barrell has written on the subject of Shaftesbury's Anti-Venus, noting that his ideal of manliness rules out a woman as a subject of history painting, unless as an admonition, as in Hercules' temptation by Pleasure, but he sees no connection with Hogarth or Mandeville. Thus the fact that in the Choice of Hercules Shaftesbury "announced as the founding doctrine of civic criticism, 'the absolute opposition of pleasure to virtue,' " *should* also illuminate Hogarth's centering of the Venus de' Medici as not only pleasure but wantonness in the *Analysis*. Barrell cites only the response of poets and critics writing in the civic-humanist tradition: "the implicit, the covert, the hesitant form" of the descriptions of the Venus de' Medici by James Thomson, Joseph Spence, and Edward Wright began to shift the emphasis from "manly abstinence" to "virility" and so to "the pleasure of sexuality" as the crucial step that "establishes the relative autonomy of the civic discourse on the visual arts" from the political discourse. In its own terms Barrell's formulation is illuminating, but characteristically it prefers situations in which an issue is "both confirmed and put in question" to situations of confrontation in a historical period distinguished for the confrontational mode (in the 1750s focused on conflicting notions of a state academy of art, different electoral processes, and competing aesthetics). It ignores the possibility of a counterdiscourse that is *not* covert, hesitant, or "relative only."

Shaftesburian writers, according to Barrell, felt that Venus' sexuality could be neutralized by being placed in a narrative context. This is why the Venus de' Medici—its "absence of a narrative context"—so engrossed eighteenth-century visitors to the Tribuna in the Uffizi and, I am sure, led Hogarth to narrativize her in plate 1 of the *Analysis* by juxtaposing her with the Apollo Belvedere and a Hercules. In this case it should be noted (as Barrell does) that in *Polymetis* Spence had suggested the possibility of juxtaposing Venus with Mars in order to show that a civic-humanist Mars can be degraded by a woman if he lets down his guard. But by using the second edition (1755) of Spence's *Polymetis*, Barrell misses the fact that it first appeared in 1747 and served as one of the sources for Hogarth's revisionary account of Venus and other sculptures associated with civic humanism in the *Analysis*. Hogarth takes his hint from Spence, but he shows that far from neutralizing Venus' sexuality, the narrative context reveals her to be the center of a romantic triangle (Barrell, " 'The Dangerous Goddess': Masculinity, Prestige and the Aesthetic in early Eighteenth-Century Britain," in *The Birth of Pandora and the Division of Knowledge* [Philadelphia, 1992], 67).

16. Hogarth, *Analysis,* 66; Joseph Burke, introduction to Hogarth, *Analysis,* xlvii.

17. While he agrees with Shaftesbury (*Miscellaneous Reflections*) that "the same shapes and proportions which make beauty afford *advantage by adapting to activity and use,*" he takes his examples from an area Shaftesbury would have shunned (*Characteristics* 2:167).

18. See *Hogarth* 3:204–9, and pls. 46–48. As I argue in *Hogarth,* vol. 3, chap. 8, the choice of subject was very Woolstonian. For Woolston the Resurrection was the ultimate and climactic miracle.

19. See Susan Haskins, *Mary Magdalen: Myth and Metaphor* (New York, 1994); and Anne Hollander's review, *New Yorker,* Sept. 1994, 112–16.

20. Thomas Gordon, *The Trial of William Whiston* (1739); as quoted in Stromberg, *Religious Liberalism,* 49.

21. William Sherlock, *A Vindication of the Doctrine of the Holy and Ever Blessed Trinity* (1690), 238.

22. Sherlock, *Vindication,* quoting the author of *Brief Notes on the Creed of St. Athanasius* (1689), cited, Stromberg, *Religious Liberalism,* 38.

23. Luke Milbourne, *Mysteries in Religion Vindicated* (1692), 780.

24. The subject of the mystery of the Virgin Birth recalls, also, the *Harlot's Progress* (above, p. 17).

25. See *Hogarth's Graphic Works,* no. 152.

26. The figure of the milkmaid invokes the well-known vase-bearer in Raphael's Stanza of the Borgo Fire. Characteristically (as in his turnings of the sculptures in *Analysis,* plate 1), Hogarth has turned her to the front, but he has kept the emphatic serpentine lines of her skirt (though more in the unpublished than in the published state). Hogarth began *The Enraged Musician* by conflating the aesthetic and the sexual (as in *Satan, Sin, and Death* and *A Scene from "The Tempest"*): He included a romantic triangle of two little boys and a girl. In the published print he cancels this by turning one boy's head (also rendered less handsome) away from the girl. In the first version the girl could be interested in what she *sees* as well as what she *hears;* in the second only the sound is relevant and the focus is on this one sense (as in one of Jan Brueghel's paintings of the senses), and therefore the subject is simply aesthetic response.

27. See *Hogarth* 2:114–15. Since this study focuses primarily on print, in books and engravings, I have not gone into the question of the relation of Hogarth's paintings to his prints (in terms of color, texture, etc.). But for this important aspect, see the discussion in *Hogarth* 2:28–35, 149–50, 3:419–32, and passim.

28. Alexander Baumgarten, *Meditationes (Reflections on Poetry)*, trans. Karl Aschenbrenner and William B. Holther (Berkeley, 1954), 78. Baumgarten's *Aesthetica* was published in Latin in 1750 (pt. 2 in 1758). In the following passage, in the pairings as well as the general assumption about aesthetics and the body, I am indebted to Eagleton (*Ideology of the Aesthetic*, 13). Eagleton, who does not mention Hogarth, is drawing upon Baumgarten through Aschenbrenner and Holther.

29. For the response to Hogarth's *Analysis* in German, see *Hogarth* 3:149–50. There is no reason to think that Hogarth had read Baumgarten or the more popular disseminator of his ideas, Georg Friedrich Meier (*Anfangsgründe aller Schönen Wissenschaften* [Halle, 1748–50]).

30. In the conclusion of the *Analysis* "elegant wantonness" is reprised as "the true spirit of dancing," by which Hogarth means a "composed variety." The sexual game or play (in both senses of "play") is neither "pompous, unmeaning grand ballets" nor "the dances of barbarians . . . , composed of wild skiping, jumping, and turning round." The "composed" aspect of sexual desire, which makes it play (in both ludic and theatrical senses), is one of Hogarth's senses of disinterestedness: "serious dancing [is] even a contradiction in terms" (159–60).

31. In this respect Hogarth accepts Shaftesbury's equation of aesthetics and ethics in *The Moralists*. Philocles had answered Theocles that human desire is "natural"—Theocles is making himself "the accuser of Nature by condemning a natural enjoyment" (2:128); to which Theocles answers by distinguishing the "enjoyment" of woods, prospects, and bodies by animals, and the utilization of these as conduits to virtue by rational humans. The sheer "enjoyment," he tells us, is "beauty founded then in body only, and not in action, life, or operation" (131). Thus in Theocles' ascending scale of beauty (2:132 ff.), beyond "a natural beauty of figures" there is "one of actions."

32. W.J.T. Mitchell, "Metamorphoses of the Vortex: Hogarth, Turner, and Blake," in *Articulate Images: The Sister Arts from Hogarth to Tennyson*, ed. Richard Wendorf (Minneapolis, 1983), 132.

CHAPTER 3. Addison's Aesthetics of the Novel

1. See *Spectator* No. 83, 1:353–56; No. 555, 4:495–96.

2. Martin Price, *To the Palace of Wisdom: Studies in Order and Energy from Dryden to Blake* (New York, 1964), 362. On the disappearance of the Beautiful from eighteenth-century accounts of the Sublime, see Ferguson, *Solitude and the Sublime*, 45.

3. For Addison's reputation at the time, see, e.g., the words of Hogarth's friend Nicholas Amherst (later Caleb Danvers of *The Craftsman*), who called Addison "The greatest genius of the greatest age," who "No branch of human

knowledge left unknown" ("Upon the Death of Mr. Addison," in *Poems on Several Occasions* [1720], 32, 35). For Hogarth's reliance on the *Spectator* as a repository of knowledge and assumptions, see *Hogarth* 1:75–76.

4. Nevertheless, Addison employs the noun "Great" rather than the adjective "sublime" because Longinus's *Peri Hupsous* applied to rhetoric, a style of speaking that raised its audience in a peculiar way; whereas he needed the noun to designate the quality of oceans and mountains.

5. Addison's "liberty" is another case, compared with Anthony Collins's deist "liberty," of the overdetermination of that term for English writers of this period.

6. As Addison defines it, the "Pleasures of the Imagination" require a different sort of disinterestedness than Shaftesbury allowed: as between Shaftesbury's "more serious Employments" and "that Negligence and Remissness, which are apt to accompany our more sensual delights, but, like a gentle Exercise to the Faculties, awaken them from Sloth and Idleness, without putting them upon any Labour or Difficulty" (No. 411, 3:539).

7. For Sir Roger and the servant, see chapter 6, below.

8. In his tragedy *Cato* (1713) Addison couches the *Spectator* issues in terms of Roman versus barbarian culture centered on the Numidian prince Juba. Africa is represented by its spokesman, Syphax, as a body, its animal energy associated with heterosexuality on the level of a tiger hunt. If Rome "was founded on a Rape" (2.5.46), says Syphax, this vigor has been rarefied into the fraternalism of republican virtue. Or, as in the case of Sempronius, it erupts from this "virtue" in the attempted rape (in the guise of an African) of Cato's daughter Marcia. Addison is plainly on the side of Juba, who, like a reader of the *Spectator*, wants to Romanize himself and his countrymen, turning the "wilds of Africk" into Roman "Lords and Sov'reigns of the world": "Dost thou not see mankind fall down before them / And own the force of their superior virtue" (1.4.13–14). As Julie Ellison puts it, "In response to Syphax's celebration of 'Numidia's tawny sons' and 'glowing dames,' Juba defines the Roman mission as one which makes hunting yield to sociability—and this means homosociability" (Ellison, "Cato's Tears," *ELH*, forthcoming).

9. The Novel as new and surprising was already planted in Addison's essays on wit (Nos. 58 ff.): The similes of the sublime poets "who endeavour . . . to fill the Mind with great Conceptions" are contrasted with those of the wits who "divert it with such as are new and surprising" (No. 62, 1: 264)—"true Wit" being the "Resemblance and Congruity of Ideas" as opposed to the false wit of words only. But after establishing the relationship of true wit to taste and politeness, Addison devotes much more time to the bizarre varieties of false wit (as he does to the satiric dimension, officially condemned but unofficially utilized and reinvented by the *Spectator*).

10. Mandeville's anticipation of Hogarth's Beautiful/Novel associated the

"Wantonness of Fancy" with "a Luxuriousness of Pleasure" and both with sexual appetite, finding their source in "variety" (Mandeville, *Publick Stews,* ix, iii). For Locke, see *Essay concerning Human Understanding,* ed. Alexander C. Fraser (New York, 1959), 1:7; for the "pursuit of happiness," see *Essay* 2:xxi.

11. Hogarth also incorporates the Great into his unitary Beautiful (*Analysis,* chap. 6, pp. 46–47). Addison's triad was carried on by Akenside in his *Pleasures of Imagination* (1744), bk. 1, ll. 139–46; and Joseph Warton's *Adventurer* No. 80 (11 Aug. 1753), just a few months before Hogarth's *Analysis* was published. And, of course, it remained in the Picturesque theory of Gilpin, Price, and Payne Knight (below, chap. 9).

12. In this context, we might ask why Addison employed three categories rather than two, the Beautiful and the Great, the terms that actually caught on? One answer is that he felt he must find a category for an experience that fitted into neither of the conventional ones. But the resulting triad also recalls, in the general secularization (or polite-making) performed by the *Spectator,* the Trinity of Father, Son, and Holy Spirit. Throughout the *Spectator,* Addison employs a series of conventional dichotomies (judgment and wit, true and false wit, primary and secondary imaginations) in which he privileges the first term but then devotes more space and attention to the analysis of the second or negative term. Then, in the "Pleasures of the Imagination," he turns the dichotomy of Beautiful/Ugly into three terms—and, producing his own version of a trinitarian heresy, ends by focusing on the middle term, by which he encompasses and subordinates the other two.

13. Again, in *Spectator* No. 235: "There is nothing which lies more within the Province of a Spectator than Publick Shews and Diversions" (2:413); and see especially No. 370.

14. Aesthetics has been seen as merely Addison's recipe for filling the new leisure time of the "middle class," of which J. H. Plumb has made so much and Martha Woodmansee has written. We can accept the fact that on a trivial level the "Pleasures of the Imagination" are "a pedagogical project, a contribution . . . to the literature on leisure-time conduct" (Woodmansee, *The Author, Art, and the Market: Rereading the History of Aesthetics* [New York, 1994], 6, 87–88; Plumb, "The Commercialization of Leisure in Eighteenth-Century England," in *The Birth of a Consumer Society,* ed. Plumb, John Brewer, and Neil Mckendrick [Bloomington, Ind., 1982]).

15. See Ronald Paulson, "Life as Journey and as Theater: Two Eighteenth-Century Narrative Structures," *New Literary History* 8 (1976): 43–58, revised in *Popular and Polite Art in the Age of Hogarth and Fielding* (Notre Dame, 1979), chap. 2, sec. 2.

16. Another way to appear greater than you are, closely related to the social in the *Spectator,* is in the economic sphere and takes the form of credit. Thus the town was regulated by manners, and the City by credit, and both manners

and credit were structured by surface value, by the value at which something can be exchanged. The changes of this form of value, the problem of excessive surface, had to be managed. The *Spectator* attempted both to model and to mold the manners that regulated public surfaces. False credit, like false wit, was the excess of representation which allows a gentleman to "endure the Torment of Poverty, to avoid the Name of being less rich" (1:468). This was the economic side of the social problem of manners without virtue; the proper method of restoring public credit was to teach the gentleman to ground his credit on real wealth, and to invest disinterestedly in the proper correspondence between inside and outside. My thanks for the above to my student Scott Black.

17. *The Tatler,* ed. Donald F. Bond (Oxford, 1987), 1:437. For another Steele satire on imitation, see *Spectator* No. 88.

18. See Lennard Davis, *Factual Fictions: The Origins of the English Novel* (New York, 1983), 51, for a discussion of a "news/novels discourse"; and J. Paul Hunter, *Before Novels: The Cultural Contexts of Eighteenth-Century English Fiction* (New York, 1990), chap. 7. Hunter quotes John Dunton, "News, and new Things do the whole World bewitch," glossing this with just the distinction I am making between "intellectual curiosity and the desire to be *au courant,*" which he notes are "the fundamental motivations, respectively, for readers of science and journalism" (167).

19. See William Warner, "The Elevation of the Novel in England: Hegemony and Literary History," *ELH* 59 (1992): 577–96.

20. Locke, *Essay* 4.20.11, 10; 2:452, 450.

21. Cf. Collins's image of Wisdom, female and to be sought and seen (*Discourse,* xxi), which also recalls *Boys Peeping.*

22. John Toland, *Vindicius Liberius: or M. Toland's Defence of Himself against the Lower House of Convocation, and Others* (1702), 16–17. Theophilus Desaguliers, both Newtonian and Freemason, called Descartes' system a "philosophical novel" (*Course of Experimental Philosophy* [1734–44], vi). On the equation of "curiosity" and the "news," see *Spectator* No. 452.

23. Daniel, *John Toland,* 74.

24. Daniel Defoe, *Review* (1706), 3:6–7; see DeAnn DeLuna, "Defoe and the Invention of 'Journalism,'" forthcoming. On the "news," as the way to catch the nonscholarly and newly literate reader, but regarded by many with suspicion as subversive of public morals and distorted by political bias, see Peter M. Briggs, "What Angels Wouldn't Read: The Contested Standards of Newsworthiness in Eighteenth-Century British Journalism," forthcoming.

25. See *Hogarth,* vol. 1, chap. 8.

26. See Ronald Paulson, *Book and Painting: Shakespeare, Milton, and the Bible* (Knoxville, 1982), 87–98; and *Hogarth* 2:342–52; and for Sterne, see Melvyn New, *Sterne's Sermons* (Gainsville, Fla., 1995).

27. *Letters of Laurence Sterne,* ed. L. P. Curtis (Oxford, 1935), 219.

28. *Letters of Sterne*, 418. Another example is the enthronement sermon Sterne preached for Archbishop Thomas Herring, who followed the late Lancelot Blackburne, a notoriously negligent archbishop. Sterne chose for his text Genesis 4:7: "If thou doest well, shalt thou not be accepted? And if thou doest not well, sin lieth at the door"—a reference that was detected by his audience.

29. Arthur Cash, *Laurence Sterne: The Early and Middle Years* (London, 1975), 152.

30. Following from Watt, J. Paul Hunter refers to "the developing concern with contemporaneity, a wish to recognize the momentous in the momentary and to feel the power of all time in its most fleeting moment" (*Before Novels*, 168).

31. The quotations are from the anonymous *An Exact Relation of the Late Dreadful Tempest: or, a Faithful Account of the Most Remarkable Disasteers Which Hapned on That Occasion . . . Faithfully Collected by an Ingenious Hand, to Preserve the Memory of So Terrible a Judgment* (1704), 24, 3; cited in Hunter, *Before Novels*, 179.

32. But the sentence is supplemented by another: When "glutted with a succession of variety," the eye "finds relief in a certain degree of sameness," that is, "a composed variety," for "variety uncomposed, and without design, is confusion and deformity." By "confusion and deformity" Hogarth means Addison's Great, and in his chapter "Of Quantity" he makes the connection explicit: "Huge shapeless rocks have a pleasing kind of horror in them, and the wide ocean awes us with its vast contents; but when forms of beauty are presented to the eye in large quantities, the pleasure increases on the mind, and horror is soften'd into reverence" (46). "Beauty" "in large quantities" increases the "pleasure," "softens" (controls, delimits, closes) the "horror" of the Great.

33. See Nos. 412 and 413. Lee Andrew Elioseff points out that Addison's distinction between primary and secondary Pleasures of the Imagination in fact draws upon Aristotle's distinction between mimetic and nonmimetic arts, while his "imagination," a visual faculty only, both primary and secondary, fits with Locke's secondary qualities of matter (*The Cultural Milieu of Addison's Literary Criticism* [Austin, 1963], 163–64, and esp. 171 ff.).

34. *The Guardian*, ed. John Calhoun Stephens (Lexington, Ky., 1982), No. 23, p. 109. For a discussion of the controversy over pastoral, cf. Hoyt Trowbridge, "Pope, Gay, and *The Shepherd's Week*," *Modern Language Quarterly* 5 (1944): 79–89; and Annabel Patterson, *Pastoral and Ideology: Virgil to Valery* (Berkeley, 1987), 206–14.

35. *Hogarth*, vol. 3, chap. 13. Following tradition, I assumed the paintings in the exhibition signed "Hagarty" to be Hogarth's. This may have been an error. In correspondence, Bernd Krysmanski has suggested to me that "Hagarty" in fact refers to an Irish painter of animals and houses, James Hagarty (fl. 1762–83), who lived in Queen Street, Golden Square, not too far from Thornton's

quarters in Bow Street. The only evidence is Anthony Pasquin's reference to him as a "great humorist." He exhibited with the Free Society of Artists from 1767 to his death in 1783, but without any signs of humor. (See Anthony Pasquin, *An Authentic History of the Professors of Painting, Sculpture and Architecture, Who Have Practised in Ireland* [London, 1796]; cited in Walter G. Strickland, *A Dictionary of Irish Artists*, vol. 1 [London, 1913], 422 [see also 411– 23]; Algernon Graves, *The Society of Artists*, 109–10; Ulrich Thieme and Felix Becker, ed., *Allgemeines Lexikon der bildenden Künstler von der Antike bis zur Gegenwart*, vol. 15 [Leipzig, 1922], 451; Ellis Waterhouse, *The Dictionary of British Eighteenth-Century Painters in Oils and Crayons* [Woodbridge, England, 1981], 154.)

In general the names have been supposed to be those of "printers"; a few of the names (e.g., Adams and Mason) appear in Waterhouse's *Dictionary*, but most do not. "Van der Trout" is obviously a parodic name, suggesting Vander- bank, as Hagarty suggests Hogarth. If Hagarty did exhibit these works (a mere ten out of seventy-six works in the Great Room), it by no means follows that he masterminded, or helped Thornton to mastermind, the exhibition. Or that the signboards (as documented in the catalogue and supported by the newspaper accounts) can be construed as critical of Hogarth and his kind of art. The tradition for the Hagarty-Hogarth identification is not necessary to support the obvious centrality of Hogarth in the conception of the exhibition. The *Register* article (reprinted in the *St. James' Chronicle*) certainly does imply that Thornton *and* Hogarth were responsible for the idea, and the tradition goes back to John Nichols (*Genuine Works of William Hogarth* [1808–17], 1:345 ff., where the touching up of signs is mentioned). This invention could, in fact, derive from *Spectator* No. 122, in which Sir Roger directs a signpainter to change the "Sir Roger de Coverley's Head" into the "Saracen's Head" by adding "a Pair of Whiskers" (1:500).

36. Pope, in his *Guardian* essay (No. 40) parodying Philips, sees true pastoral as "an image of . . . the golden age. So that we are not to describe shepherds as shepherds at this day really are, but as they may be conceived then to have been; when the best of men followed the employment" (emphasis added). That is, shepherds are ideal not because the reality is being concealed to delude and please the reader, but because they represent an ideal of order in the past.

37. *The Poems of Ambrose Philips*, ed. M. G. Segar (Oxford, 1937), 31.

38. John Gay, *Poetry and Prose*, ed. Vinton A. Dearing (Oxford, 1974), 118.

39. *The What D'Ye Call It* makes the same point about the commonalty of the high and low as does *The Beggar's Opera* and focuses on tragedy as the high mode, with which it describes the situation of a fallen woman, discarded by her squire lover (which will reappear in the *Rake*), presented in the play-rehearsal structure that emphasizes the metaphor of life-as-theater to a greater extent

than does *The Beggar's Opera*. The subject is specifically the justices and other authorities who prey on the lower orders, in this case most vividly expressed in the whipping of a pregnant woman (cf. *Harlot* 4). Excepting its rustic environment, which becomes metropolitan in *The Beggar's Opera*, the world of *The What D'Ye Call It* is closer to that of the *Harlot;* although *The Beggar's Opera* is documentably Hogarth's formal model (as he proceeds from the pictorial structure of his *Beggar's Opera* paintings to that of the *Harlot*).

40. See Lennard Davis's discussion in *Factual Fiction* (above, n. 18).

CHAPTER 4. The Conversation Piece

1. Solkin, *Painting for Money;* Ronald Paulson, review of *Painting for Money, London Review of Books,* 4 Nov. 1993, 42–43; and an extended version of the latter in *Eighteenth-Century Life* (17 [1993]: 104–19), some of which is included in this section. Solkin, though a close follower of Barrell, does expose the less-than-utopian politics and discusses the actual practice of painting that underlay civic humanism. He also balances a long chapter on Shaftesbury with a short section on Mandeville's anti-Shaftesbury position, drawing attention to the crucial text, the dialogue on painting at the beginning of volume 2 of *The Fable of the Bees,* which defends Dutch realism against Italian (and Shaftesburian) abstraction, purity, and exclusivity. Solkin's account of Mandeville is an important concession, but he concludes that Mandeville was only an isolated phenomenon and, as he acknowledges, "the villain of our piece"; and while he reads Shaftesbury's texts subtly and sympathetically, he produces a caricature of Mandeville's. While acknowledging the schema of Shaftesbury versus Mandeville, he continues to privilege the "official line," regarding Mandeville as an isolated crank. Also recovered is the uncanonical figure of Hogarth, totally suppressed in Barrell's history. Any chapter on the conversation piece, of course, has no choice but to focus on Hogarth; but in his penultimate (climactic) chapter, Solkin arrives, almost parenthetically, at the conclusion that there *was* a surviving Hogarth tradition, though it comes as a surprise at this late point in his history to read that after the founding of the Royal Academy in 1768 "many artists were still prepared to continue the fight [Hogarth] had begun" (242), because this fight has nowhere been described prior to this sentence. Hogarth the theorist, however, still remains off limits, and this means ignoring *The Analysis of Beauty,* the one major text in the Mandevillian line, its importance obvious from the violent responses it evoked from the party advocating a state academy in the 1750s.

2. Solkin is utilizing the work on politeness of Pocock and Lawrence Klein (*Shaftesbury and the Culture of Politeness: Moral Discourse and Cultural Politics in Early Eighteenth-Century England* [Cambridge, 1994]). Solkin also draws heav-

ily on Jürgen Habermas's "public sphere" (*The Structural Transformation of the Public Sphere,* trans. Thomas Burger [Cambridge, Mass., 1992]).

3. The suggestion seems to be that Addison made the transition from civic humanist to polite discourse. As Klein has shown, Shaftesbury's whole oeuvre is an attempt to introduce politeness as a philosophical and civic discourse: beginning in *Sensus Communis* of 1709 and running through the rest of his works. The difference is between an elite and a more general discourse, between Shaftesbury's "senatorial" (Klein's word) and Addison's gentlemanly groupings. While accepting the fact that politeness was commonly defined as the art of pleasing in company, Klein argues that Shaftesbury replaced its associations of flattery and deference with the idea of critical expression and enquiry.

4. See Preface, n. 18, above.

5. This is a work we know Hogarth read, at least by the time he wrote his *Analysis,* where he reacts against its aesthetic doctrines (see *Hogarth* 3:72–73; and chap. 1, above).

6. Vertue, *Notebooks* (for 1729), 22:40; Solkin, *Painting for Money,* 84.

7. Solkin, *Painting for Money,* 89; Paulson, *Popular and Polite Art,* 26. While quoting from my discussion of the Hogarthian dog, Solkin makes no mention of the general argument concerning conversation pieces in my *Emblem and Expression* and in subsequent books and articles. Rereading the chapter on the conversation piece in *Emblem and Expression,* I see that I made the point about "conversation as social talk," "social intercourse," and "manners, in action and in word" (though "politeness" was not yet a fashionable term), but I added that "the gist of [the conversations] is that a formality of manners should be qualified by naturalness" (e.g., the dog or the child). The emphasis fell, correctly I still think, on the tradition (or discourse) of painting (*Emblem and Expression,* 128).

8. Cf. Fréderic Ogée, who draws attention to the various sacraments referred to within the context of a parodic Eucharist ("L'onction extrême: Une lecture de *A Midnight Modern Conversation* [1733] de William Hogarth," *Études anglaises* 44 [1992]: 56–65).

9. For these paintings, see *Hogarth* 1:209, 224–27 (fig. 93), 1:225–27 (fig. 92), 2:174, 262 (fig. 78), 2:174–77 (fig. 79), and in general, vol. 1, chap. 7.

10. For the importance of *The Beggar's Opera,* see *Hogarth,* vol. 1, chap. 5.

11. Solkin invokes Fielding as an advocate of politeness, but the quotations he cites are from a *Craftsman* essay published a year after Fielding severed relations with the journal. In *The Modern Husband* (1732) Fielding uses "polite" as a synonym for foppish: In the prologue he says that "His muse in schools ["seats of learning"] too unpolite was bred"; in 2.3 Bellamant chides his foppish son, "I would no more comply with a ridiculous fashion than with a vicious one; nor with that which makes a man look like a monkey, than that which

makes him act like any other beast." To which his son replies, "Lord, sir! you are grown strangely unpolite" (*Complete Works of Henry Fielding*, ed. W. E. Henley [London, 1903], 10:9, 28–29; also 42 and 77). Obviously Fielding implies some quality that transcends the term "politeness." Examples could be cited from Pope also: *Epistle to Burlington*, l. 150; *Epistle to Bathurst*, l. 386; and "virtues" vs. "decencies" in *Epistle to a Lady*, l. 164. A typical reference by Swift is in "Strephon and Chloe" (1734), ll. 271–72: "Some try to learn polite behaviour, / By reading books against their Saviour"; or in *An Argument against Abolishing Christianity* (1708), the "men of wit and pleasure" who "entail rottenness and politeness on their posterity." For a useful corrective to the school of politeness, see Claude Rawson's essay "Gentlemen and Dancing-Masters," in *Henry Fielding and the Augustan Ideal under Stress* (London, 1972), 3–34.

12. For Steele on the dangers of politeness, see, e.g. (contrasting virtue and politeness), *Spectator* No. 6.

13. Solkin, *Painting for Money*, 106–7.

14. For the paintings, their color and form, see chap. 2, n. 27, above.

15. See Hayman's *Lord Clive Receiving the Homage of the Nabob;* Solkin, *Painting for Money*, 196–97.

16. See *Hogarth* 1:259.

17. Solkin's words are: "up until the very end of the 1760s no writer on contemporary art, with the exception of Reynolds, was prepared to argue that classical history-painting offered a standard against which all the 'inferior' genres should be judged and found wanting" (255).

18. Marcia Pointon, *Hanging the Head: Portraiture and Social Formation in Eighteenth-Century England* (New Haven, 1993), 166.

19. Oliver Millar, *Later Georgian Pictures in the Collection of Her Majesty the Queen* (London, 1969), 1:149.

20. Pointon dates the picture 1764 because of the Telemachus costume, which was delivered in September of that year, when the prince would have been two. He looks older. Perhaps Zoffany wants to stress his manly maturity.

21. Jonathan Swift, *Battle of the Books*, in *A Tale of a Tub*, ed. Guthkelch and Smith, 2d ed. (Oxford, 1958), 215; see *Hogarth* 2:342–52.

22. For the story of the *Last Supper*, one painted in Calcutta and another on his return to England, see Lady Victoria Manners and G. C. Williamson, *John Zoffany, R.A.* (London, 1920), 100–2, 118–19. For *The Tribuna*, and for a general account of Zoffany, the range of his paintings, and his relationship to Hogarth, see my *Emblem and Expression*, chap. 9. I write there about the strong sexual reverberations of *The Tribuna* and other Zoffany conversation pieces; and the work of G. S. Rousseau and others on homosexual groups in the later eighteenth century has confirmed my speculations about homosexual as well as heterosexual references.

23. See Paulson, *Emblem and Expression*, 124–25.

24. Cf. Robert Rosenblum, *Transformations in Late Eighteenth-Century Art* (Princeton, 1967), 28–39; Ronald Paulson, "The Aesthetics of Mourning," in *Studies in Eighteenth-Century British Art and Aesthetics*, ed. Ralph Cohen (Berkeley, 1985), 148–81; and idem, *Breaking and Remaking*, chap. 5.

25. Lady Bradshaigh to Richardson, n.d., in *The Correspondence of Samuel Richardson*, ed. Anna Laetitia Barbauld (London, 1804), 282–83.

26. Solkin notes some modulations into "the pleasure of sexuality" in the 1760s in the history paintings of West, but sees this as part of the rise of sentimentality and makes no mention of Hogarth (183).

27. Although he calls West "a painter of the beautiful," Solkin sees no connection with Hogarth's theory of the Beautiful (*Painting for Money*, 183).

28. George Turnbull, *A Treatise on Ancient Painting* (1740), 71; Horace Walpole, annotations in the margins of catalogues of the 1760s exhibitions (Society of Artists and Free Society of Artists), cited in Solkin, *Painting for Money*, 184–85.

29. See *Hogarth* 2:108–13. Gavin Hamilton had portrayed *Andromache Weeping over the Body of Hector* in 1761 (following soon after Hogarth's Renaissance subject, *Sigismunda* of 1759), giving a classical and Poussiniste sanction to the subject of the grieving woman.

30. Solkin argues for the decorations of Vauxhall Gardens as another source for West's feminine imagery. The dating of the Vauxhall paintings of the loves of the gods remains questionable (they were hanging by 1761), but they could also have contributed.

31. For this and other examples, see Paulson, *Emblem and Expression*, chap. 11. While Solkin concludes his account of the *Air Pump* by acknowledging the influence of Hogarth, it is only by way of a figure perhaps borrowed from *The Reward of Cruelty* and the vague suggestion that Wright may have been echoing *A Midnight Modern Conversation*. As a conversation piece, Solkin sees the *Air Pump* as a showcase of luxury goods. But these items can also be seen either as the commodification that is the reality beneath the Shaftesbury man of taste (as collector) or as a bourgeois reaction against his oligarchic ideal. In fact, having laid out the revisionist civic humanist program in the *Air Pump*, Solkin is compelled by the visual evidence to add that Wright nevertheless "withheld ethical sanction from the social order he had produced on canvas, and from the fashionable world he addressed" ("ReWrighting Shaftesbury: The Air Pump and the Limits of Commercial Humanism," in Barrell, ed., *Painting and the Politics of Culture*, 99). My detailed account of Wright in *Emblem and Expression* is supplemented by that in *Breaking and Remaking*, chap. 5.

32. [R. Baker], *Observations . . .* (quoted in Solkin, *Painting for Money*, 300 n. 46).

33. W. Hazlitt, ed., *Criticism on Art and Sketches of the Picture Galleries of England* (London, 1856), 179.

34. Barrell, *Political Theory of Painting*, 320.

35. Allan Cunningham, *The Lives of the Most Eminent British Painters, Sculptors, and Architects*, vol. 1, 2d ed. (1830), 187–88.

CHAPTER 5. The "Great Creation"

1. *Champion*, 22 Jan. 1739/40; all quotations from the *Champion* are from the collected edition of 1740. An earlier version of the first part of this chapter appeared as "Henry Fielding and the Problem of Deism" in *The Margins of Orthodoxy: Heterodox Writing and Cultural Response, 1660–1750*, ed. Roger Lund (Cambridge, 1995), 240–70.

2. *The Welsh [Grub Street] Opera* 2.2. But this may be partly as a contrast and comparison with his mother (Prince Frederick with Queen Caroline), a supporter of religion who admired such controversial divines as Samuel Clarke.

3. In Fielding's *The Letter-Writers* of the same year, Commons is having his final fling before taking orders. His friend Rakel asks him if he has "the Impudence to pretend to a Call." Commons: "Ay, Sir; the usual Call: I have the Promise of a good Living. Lookee, captain, my Call of Piety is much the same as yours of Honour—You will fight, and I shall pray for the same Reasons I assure you" ([1731], 7).

4. *Joseph Andrews* 2.3. All quotations from this work are from Henry Fielding, *Joseph Andrews*, ed. Martin C. Battestin (Middletown, Conn., 1967). Aurélien Digeon presumed that Fielding was a deist until late in life and that his conversion explains the changes of perspective in *Amelia* (*Les romans de Fielding* [Paris, 1923], 260–62); and the Battestins believe that Fielding had a brush with deism in his youth but swiftly turned straight (Martin C. Battestin with Ruthe Battestin, *Henry Fielding: A Life* [London, 1989], 154–55).

5. The common ground with latitudinarians, as Margaret Jacob has put it, is the assumption that "rational argumentation and not faith is the final arbiter of Christian belief and dogma"—and in this limited sense, Fielding certainly qualifies as a latitudinarian. See Jacob, *The Newtonians and the English Revolution, 1789–1720* (Ithaca, 1976), 34. See also, on the association of deism and latitudinarianism (a charge often leveled at Bishop Benjamin Hoadly, Fielding's favorite contemporary clergyman), Roger L. Emerson, "Latitudinarianism and the English Deists," in *Deism, Masonry, and the Enlightenment*, ed. J. A. Leo Lemay (Newark, Del., 1987); John Redwood, *Reason, Ridicule, and Religion: The Age of Enlightenment in England, 1660–1750* (London, 1976), 175; Robert E. Sullivan, *John Toland and the Deist Controversy* (Cambridge, Mass., 1982), 35; Leslie Stephen, *History of English Thought in the Eighteenth Century* (1876; reprint, New York, 1962), 2:129.

6. James A. Work, "Henry Fielding, Christian Censor," in *The Age of Johnson: Essays Presented to Chauncey Brewster Tinker* (New Haven, 1949), 139–48;

334 Notes to Pages 99–101

Martin C. Battestin, *The Moral Basis of Fielding's Art: A Study of "Joseph Andrews"* (Middletown, Conn., 1959); Aubrey Williams, "Interpositions of Providence and the Design of Fielding's Novels," *South Atlantic Quarterly* 70 (1971): 265–86. See also Henry Knight Miller, *Essays on Fielding's "Miscellanies"* (Princeton, 1961), 76–83.

7. Thomas Cooke, *A Demonstration of the Will of God by the Light of Nature* (1733), introduction; cited by the Battestins, *Fielding*, 153, 156. This work, a collection of Cooke's periodical essays in *The Comedian,* is carefully couched in terms of Christianity, with none of Thomas Woolston's satiric thrust or obvious disrespect for the Fathers or for the New Testament itself. Cooke urges that instead of the institutional deity of the clergy and the biblical texts, man should "cast his Eye into the Book of *Nature,* which the bounteous Hand of *God* has opened to him" (*Demonstration,* xiii). *Comedian* No. 2 sets out "to prove that God, requires no more of us than *Nature* requires" (5); No. 4 concerns observance of the Sabbath "and some Cases in which we ought to break it" (14–17), concluding that one ought "not to offend God hereafter by neglecting to gather in his Harvest on the sabbath day when he cannot on another Day" (17); and subsequent papers are on the immortality of the soul and a future state (No. 5), on liberty, necessity, and the freedom of the will (No. 6), on the origin of evil (No. 7), and climactically on God, providence, and nature (No. 8).

8. See *Hogarth* 1:314.

9. For "contrast," see Fielding, *Tom Jones* 5.1; for an account of how an example—Settle's *Siege of Troy*—operated, see *Hogarth* 1:139–40.

10. Edward Young, preface to *Love of Fame,* 2d ed. (1728), sig. a, verso. Collins, however, cites Lucian's dialogues as a model in his *Discourse concerning Ridicule and Irony in Writing* (1729), connecting Lucian's impious dialogues with Erasmus's *Colloquies.* On Lucian, see Levi R. Lind, "Lucian and Fielding," *Classical Weekly* 29 (1936): 84–86; Christopher Robinson, *Lucian and His Influence in Europe* (Chapel Hill, 1979), 211–23; Miller, *Essays,* 366–86; Ronald Paulson, *The Fictions of Satire* (Baltimore, 1967), 31–42.

11. For Fielding's continuing utilization of the Lucianic persona, see Ronald Paulson, "The Lucianic Satirist," chap. 4 of *Satire and the Novel* (New Haven, 1967). Aristophanic comedy was the chief model for Lucian's dialogues, and the *Plutus* in particular for the *Dialogues of the Gods.* The one play by Aristophanes that Fielding chose to translate (with his friend William Young) was *Plutus* (published in 1742), which, beginning with a world in which rewards and punishments, wealth and virtue, do not correspond, supposes that the blind Plutus (god of wealth) has his sight returned. This rights the balance of rewards and punishments but incidentally has dire consequences. Fielding's preface ends with a quotation of Addison's précis of the play in which he emphasized the rewards-punishments theme (*Spectator* No. 464). (This *Spectator* was immediately preceded by an essay on the heavenly "golden balance" in which true

weights are measured—and was followed by Addison's creed of a Christian rationalist: a sequence that would have interested Fielding and, in many ways, corresponded to his own views.)

12. Unless the lost *Deborah; or, A Wife for You All* was a burlesque of the Old Testament story (or of Handel's *Deborah*).

13. Cooke, *Comedian* No. 1 (Apr. 1732), 4. For the prominence of this metaphor, see chap. 3, above.

14. Clive T. Probyn, *The Sociable Humanist: James Harris* (Oxford, 1991), 64, 62–63. The Battestins mention that Harris's mother was the daughter of the second earl, but do not mention the third, and instead of mentioning deism write that "it was Harris's keen mind and kind heart that drew Fielding to him" (*Fielding*, 310). The only serious attempt to recover Shaftesbury, primarily in terms of *Tom Jones,* is Lance St. John Butler's "Fielding and Shaftesbury Reconsidered: The Case of *Tom Jones,*" in *Henry Fielding: Justice Observed,* ed. K. G. Simpson (Totowa, N.J., 1985), 56–74.

15. Fielding, *Champion,* 22 Jan. 1739/40, 1:209. These *Champion* essays began with two on 22 and 24 January 1739/40, continuing with four more (the essays "defending" the clergy) on 29 March, and 5, 12, and 19 April 1740.

16. Swift, "A Digression on Madness," in *A Tale of a Tub* (1704), 173–74 (and so back to Rochester's "perfect joy of being well deceived" in "Artemesa to Chloe," l. 115). The passage also includes a sentence condemning "*Unmasking,* which I think, has never been allowed fair Usage, either in the *World* or the *Play-House.*" This sentence connects "Delusion" with the important strand of theatrical metaphor in Fielding's works.

17. Fielding's passage also invites comparison with Cooke's nonsatiric *Demonstration,* where he wrote of "that *Power* to which Man owes his Desire of Happyness, and his Aversion to Misery, which Power is *God.*" Cooke claims that obedience to "the rule of Right [vs. Christianity] advances our Happyness here; and consequently every Deviation from it is a Deviation from the Road which leads to Happyness" (xiii). The discussion of providence (8–11) concludes that Nature is "that *Power* to which Man owes his Desire of Happyness, and his Aversion to Misery, which Power is *God*": in short, nature, God, and happiness are one.

18. Shaftesbury, *Inquiry* 1.2.3, in *Characteristics* 1:279.

19. Shaftesbury, *An Essay on the Freedom of Wit and Humour* (1709), in *Characteristics* 1:45; Fielding, *Tom Jones* 14.12.

20. For Cooke too, beauty "is that which arises to the Mind in exact Proportion, and which gives that Pleasure which the Mind enjoys from Propriety of Action" (*Demonstration,* xii).

21. *Champion,* 19 Feb. 1739/40; 1:288.

22. Henry Fielding, *Miscellanies,* ed. H. K. Miller (Middletown, Conn., 1972) 225; Fielding, *Tom Jones* 1.2. Cf. Battestin's note to the latter (35), which

simply makes it a devotional commonplace; but this was Fielding's own personal concern. Another example is in *Tom Jones* 2.1, pp. 116–17. By contrast, Bishop Butler, among others, argued that if we are uncertain it is safer to assume the reality of future rewards and punishments. In his "Essay on the Characters of Men" (in *Miscellanies*, vol. 1, of 1743) Fielding redefines virtue as "Good Nature," which "disposes us to feel the Misfortunes and enjoy the Happiness of others; and consequently pushes us on to promote the latter, and prevent the former; and that"—he significantly adds—"without any abstract contemplation on the Beauty of Virtue, and without the Allurement or Terrors of Religion" (*Miscellanies* 1:158). He explains in his *Champion* essay on good nature (27 Mar. 1740), however, that good nature may need the support of one or both of these. In unusually tangled syntax, with ambiguous referents, he says that Christianity is necessary because it "hath taught us something beyond what the Religion of Nature and Philosophy [deism] could arrive at" (2:40). Once again, Christianity is a useful addendum because it keeps people happy, but to that is added the practical necessity of good nature to go beyond harmless benevolism to the rigorous judgment of good and evil, based on a belief in rewards and punishments in the afterlife.

23. These essays Battestin sees as simply a reflection of the low standing of the clergy at the time—"contempt of the clergy" being "a stock phrase of the time," words he quotes from an ecclesiastical history of 1885 (J. H. Overton, *Life in the English Church, 1660–1714* [1885], 302; quoted in the Battestins, *Fielding*, 130). But the key word of the deists was "priestcraft": John Toland, author of *Christianity Not Mysterious*, argued that a clergy maintained itself by focusing on the mysterious activity of God and arguing that clerics alone understood the mysteries of religion. Like Fielding, Toland distinguished bad priests from good—"an Order of Men not only useful and necessary, but likewise reputable and venerable" (he started a work called "Priesthood without Priestcraft"). See Toland, "A Word to the Honest Priests," in *An Appeal to Honest People against Wicked Priests* (1713); cited in Daniel, *John Toland*, 26.

24. The idea of bad clerics which Fielding expresses in the essays on the clergy is implicitly related to the bad stewards (lawyers, ministers, Walpole) of Opposition satire (see *Champion* for 12 Feb. 1739/40; cf. Howard Erskine-Hill, *The Social Milieu of Alexander Pope* [New Haven, 1975], 243–59).

25. *Champion* 2:120. Fielding's positive touchstones, based on the Gospels, are humility and charity, which allow him to emphasize the spirit versus the letter of the law. He quotes Luke 20:46, 47: "to beware of the Scribes which desire to walk in long Robes, and love Greetings in the Markets, and the highest Seats in the Synagogues, and the chief Rooms at Feasts, which devour Widows' Houses, and for Show make long Prayers" (2:49).

26. At Mr. B.'s advance Pamela faints, but she exposes her stratagem by the words of her text: "I sighed, and scream'd, and fainted away. And still he had his

Arms about my Neck"; on which Mr. B. comments, "As for *Pamela*, she has a lucky Knack at falling into Fits, when she pleases." Fielding's analysis of *Pamela* seen from one direction is libertine (Mr. B.'s analysis of Pamela's fainting fits), from another rationalist and deist. (See Samuel Richardson, *Pamela; or, Virtue Rewarded*, ed. T. C. Duncan Eaves and Ben D. Kimpel [Boston, 1971], 67, 68.)

27. See Henry Fielding, *Covent-Garden Journal*, 14 Mar. 1752; also idem, *Amelia* 3.5. Without being named, Mandeville is with Hobbes the villain of the attack in the *Champion* for 22 Jan. 1730/40. Cf. also Battestin's view (in *Providence of Wit*, 160) of Mandeville's lack of influence on Fielding.

28. Mandeville, *Fable of the Bees* 1:324, 42, 50, 51.

29. J. Paul Hunter's argument that Fielding is refuting Morgan is unconvincing; following Battestin, Hunter sees the Joseph-Abraham analogies as normative (*Occasional Form: Henry Fielding and the Chains of Circumstance* [Baltimore, 1975], 101–5; Battestin, *Moral Basis of Fielding's Art*, 30–43).

30. One wonders if Fielding's coachload of arguing and self-justifying and self-incriminating respectable folk is also a memory of Shaftesbury's "well-bred" men who "talk Philosophy in such a Circle of good Company . . . in [a] coach . . . in the Park" (*The Moralists*, in *Characteristics* 2:3).

31. See *Hogarth*, vol. 2, chap. 4.

32. Fielding, *Joseph Andrews* 1.13, p. 59.

33. Comparison of the sincere Muslim or Turk with the insincere Christian is also used by Fielding in *Jonathan Wild* (1743), attributed to Heartfree in his conversation with the orthodox Newgate Ordinary (4.1). Deist admiration for Mohammedanism was related to the smaller role it gave to church and clergy. The topos that Christians were morally inferior to non-Christians was, of course, deployed by latitudinarians as well as deists (one source for Fielding's usage was Hoadly's sermon "The Good Samaritan"). (See Isabel Rivers, *Reason, Grace, and Sentiment: A Study of the Language of Religion and Ethics in England, 1660–1780* [Cambridge, 1991], 8–12.)

34. Betty's charity proves to be lust, distinguished from Joseph's love of Fanny by Betty's willingness, once Joseph rejects her, to settle for the next man who comes along.

35. For a persuasive account of Joseph's development (as opposed to Adams's stasis), see Dick Taylor Jr., "Joseph as Hero in *Joseph Andrews*," *Tulane Studies in England* 7 (1957): 91–109.

36. For example: "View here the pourtrait of a faction's priest, / Who (spight of Proverbs) dares defile his nest; / And when he shou'd defend the Church's cause, / Barely deserts her, and arraigns her laws" (quoted in Redwood, *Reason, Ridicule, and Religion*, 175). Hoadly's mentor was Samuel Clarke, whose works he edited in 1738.

37. George Whitefield, "The Folly and Danger of Being Not Righteous Enough," sermon 1, in *Works* (London, 1835), 5:126.

38. Sullivan, *Toland*, 35. As Leslie Stephen has written, Hoadly was a "clergy-man who oppose[d] sacerdotal privileges"; one who "supported the political pretensions of the dissenters" and was therefore "the best-hated clergyman of the century amongst his own order" (*History of English Thought* 2:129). How Hoadly, essentially a political figure, fits into the deist argument is neatly summarized by Stromberg (*Religious Liberalism*, 132): Hoadly, he notes, though awarded the highest preferments in the church, in his works "seemed logically to leave no real place for the Church. His *Original and Institution of Civil Government* (1710) presented the Whig view that government is of human origin, not divine. . . . The end of government is the happiness of society; freedom of religion is essential to this happiness. Hoadly was consistent when, a few years later, in the famous Bangorian controversy, he defined the Church as invisible and wholly spiritual—in effect, as his critics noted, dissolving the Church of England as a society." Note the emphasis on "happiness" and on the social function of religion.

39. The motif goes back to Fielding's *Jonathan Wild* (1743), in the scene where Wild first sees Mrs. Heartfree; and runs throughout his work.

40. See his letter to James Harris, 24 Sept. 1742, in *Correspondence of Henry and Sarah Fielding*, ed. Martin C. Battestin and Clive T. Probyn (Oxford, 1993), 23–25.

41. Antoine Banier, *Mythology and Fables of the Ancients, Explain'd from History*, translation (1739–40). Fielding singles out Banier's volumes (repub-lished in 1748) for praise in the *Jacobite Journal*'s "Court of Criticism," and we know that he owned a copy himself. Fielding cites Banier by name only once in *Tom Jones* (12.1, p. 619), but Banier's approach is discernible in much of the historical analysis that is carried on. See Paulson, *Popular and Polite Art*, pt. 2, chap. 6.

42. See Homer Obed Brown, "*Tom Jones:* The 'Bastard' of History," *Bound-ary* 7 (1979): 201–33; *Hogarth* 2:360–63.

43. See Martin C. Battestin, "Tom Jones and 'His Egyptian Majesty': Field-ing's Parable of Government," *PMLA* 72 (1967): 68–77; Paulson, *Popular and Polite Art*, pt. 2, chap. 6.

44. Fielding frequently uses, and alludes to, the passage in Plato's *Phaedrus* (250d). But the passage in the *Phaedrus* does not have anything like the word "naked" or the erotic overtones of these passages; nor do its paraphrases by Cicero, Seneca, and Sir Philip Sidney—as "Orbilius" was quick to point out in his *Examen of the History of Tom Jones, a Foundling* ([1749]; in *Henry Fielding: The Critical Heritage*, ed. Ronald Paulson and Thomas Lockwood [London, 1969], 189). See also the reference in Fielding's "An Essay on the Knowledge of the Characters of Men," in *Miscellanies* 1:173.

45. Bernard Harrison, *Henry Fielding's "Tom Jones": The Novelist as Moral Philosopher* (London, 1975), 80–81.

46. See Paulson, *Popular and Polite Art,* chap. 5.

47. Hogarth must have had *Tom Jones* in mind in *The Analysis* when he wrote: "With what pleasure doth the mind follow, the well connected thread of a play or Novel which ever encreases as the Plot thickens, and ends, when that's disclos'd" (171, one of the rejected passages). At the opening of *The Masquerade* (1728), his earliest surviving publication, supposedly by "Lemuel Gulliver," Fielding had invoked "Curiosity": "From this [curiosity] we borrow hopes of greater / Discoveries of Madam Nature." The motive for Gulliver's four voyages and his fifth excursion, which is to see one of Heidegger's masquerades, is curiosity. It is, in the context of the masquerade, sexual curiosity, which is associated with Eve, as it will be by Hogarth twenty-five years later on the title page of the *Analysis of Beauty.*

48. George Lord Lyttelton, *Observations on the Conversion and Apostleship of St. Paul* (1748), in *The Works of George Lord Lyttelton* (1776), 2:3. By contrast, St. Paul was seen by deists as the first interfering priest. See Peter Annet, *Critical Examination of the Life of St. Paul* (London, 1823).

49. In *The True Patriot* (1745–56), Fielding had used Roman Catholicism to sum up all the worst in priestcraft, the determination "to extirpate Heresy by all Methods whatever" and "inevitably destroy [England's] Civil Liberties"—which he opposes to "the Temper of Protestants." And, in the dangerous situation of the '45 he also lumps "the most noble Party of Free-Thinkers, who has no Religion" with the Jacobites. See, e.g., Fielding, *Tom Jones* 9.6, pp. 516–17; see also 373; Henry Fielding, *True Patriot,* ed. W. B. Coley (Middletown, Conn., 1987), 124–25, 137. But the same reference to one bad clergyman as opposed to the order (in *Champion,* 23 Feb. 1740, 1:259) reappears in *True Patriot* No. 14, 28 Jan.–4 Feb. 1746, 207–8, where it is extended from clergymen to writers.

50. Henry Fielding, *Covent-Garden Journal,* ed. Bertrand Goldgar (Middleton, Conn., 1993), No. 29, 11 Apr. 1752, 423.

51. Henry Fielding, *Amelia,* ed. Martin C. Battestin (Middletown, Conn., 1983), 511–12. This was an orthodox view. Fielding could have found support in the sermons of Robert South, one of his favorite latitudinarian divines, which stated that "hope and fear are the two great handles, by which the will of man is to be taken hold of, when we would either draw it to duty or draw it off from sin" (*Sermons* [1834], 3:136).

52. Fielding, *Covent-Garden Journal* No. 6, 49: "There are certain Arcana Naturae, in disclosing which the Moderns have made great Progress; now whatever Merit there may be in such denudations of Nature, if I may so express myself, and however exquisite a Relish they may afford to *very* adult Persons of both sexes in their Closets, they are surely too speculative and mysterious for the Contemplation of the Young and Tender, into whose Hands Tarts and Pies are most likely to fall" (50). See also ibid., No. 9, p. 68 as an ironic but truth-

telling account; and 43, 49, on parents and children (cf. *"An Enquiry into the Causes of the Late Increase of Robbers" and Related Writings*, ed. Malvin R. Zirker [Middleton, Conn., 1988], 172).

53. Richardson constantly rewrites Hogarth's *Harlot's Progress*. I have noted the general "correction" of the *Harlot's* plot in *Pamela*—and in *Clarissa* such scenes as the death of Mother Sinclair, which conflates *Harlot* 5 and 6 (*Hogarth*, vol. 2, chap. 8). In the second edition of *Clarissa* Richardson has Lovelace fantasize an abduction and rape of Mrs. Howe, which is followed by his apprehension, trial, condemnation, and trip to Tyburn in a scene that echoes Hogarth's *Industry and Idleness* 11 of 1747; and this is closed by a reprieve from the king just like that of Charteris hailing back to *Harlot* 1 (Charteris being one model for Lovelace). My text for *Clarissa* is *The Clarissa Project*, ed. Florian Stuber and Margaret Anne Doody (New York, 1990), based on the third edition.

54. Charles Gildon, *The Life and Strange Surprising Adventures of Mr. D— De F—, of London, Hosier* (1719), in *Robinson Crusoe, Examin'd and Criticis'd*, ed. Paul Dottin (London, 1923), 88, 94, 106, 117.

55. Sarah Fielding's *Familiar Letters from the Characters in David Simple* had appeared in 1746, with some letters contributed by Fielding and an introduction with his comments on epistolary writing. This form was not, he wrote, "adapted to the Novel or Story-Writer; for what difference is there, whether a Tale is related this or any other way? And sure no one will contend, that the epistolary Style is in general the most proper to a Novelist, or that it hath been used by the best Writers of this Kind" (54). His models, he says, are Ovid's *Heroides* and Lyttelton's *Persian Letters*.

56. See *Tom Jones* 15.3, 16.5, 18.9.

57. See Frank Kermode, "Richardson and Fielding," *Cambridge Journal* 4 (1950): 106–14; Maurice Johnson, *Fielding's Art of Fiction* (Philadelphia, 1961), 100–104; Manuel Schonhorn, "Heroic Allusion in *Tom Jones:* Hamlet and the Temptations of Jesus," *Studies in the Novel* 6 (1974):218–27. Harrison also addresses Kermode's argument, from the perspective of Fielding's "moral philosophy" (*Henry Fielding's "Tom Jones"*).

CHAPTER 6. Aesthetics and Erotics

1. Volume 1 introduces Fanny's story with echoes of Hogarth's *Harlot*—she comes down from the country, is abandoned in London, and is picked up by a bawd; and volume 1 ends with a story similar to that implied in *Harlot* 2 (the story of the bawd Mrs. Jones, Mr. H, and the "low" country boy with whom she cheats on Mr. H). See *Hogarth* 3:85–88; the resemblance between Fanny and the Harlot was noticed by William Epstein, *John Cleland: Images of a Life* (New York, 1974), 94. Douglas Brooks-Davies connects Fanny with the iconography

of Venus (e.g., "Fanny Hill" equals *Mons Veneris*) in "The Mythology of Love: Venerean (and related) Iconography in Pope, Fielding, Cleland, and Sterne," *Sexuality in Eighteenth-Century Britain,* ed. Paul-Gabriel Boucé (Manchester, 1982), 184.

2. John Cleland, *Fanny Hill; or, Memoirs of a Woman of Pleasure,* ed. Peter Wagner (Harmondsworth, England, 1985), 39. Parenthetical references are to this text.

3. See Patrick J. Kearney, *A History of Erotic Literature* (London, 1982).

4. See Charles Johnston, *Chrysal* (1759), 4.2.17 ff.

5. Lynn Hunt shows the ultimate reduction of such a libertine ethos in the Marquis de Sade (*The Family Romance of the French Revolution* [Berkeley, 1992], 139).

6. Cleland and Fielding were connected in more ways than one: both wrote pamphlets on the Penlez case; in a response to Fielding's, Cleland expressed admiration for him and his Penlez pamphlet, and later (in the *Monthly Review*) expressed admiration for *Amelia* (see the Battestins, *Fielding,* 491 and n. 92).

7. See *Fanny Hill,* 82, 87, 91. *Spectator* No. 183, on fables, takes the Choice of Hercules between Virtue and Pleasure, adds a fable of pleasure and pain (Socrates in the *Phaedo*), and ends with Addison's own genealogical allegory of Pleasure and Pain. The paper is not really about the pleasure-pain issue but about rewards and punishments for virtue and vice, but it does once again define a middle area of mixed human beings (some painful, others pleasureful) between the pleasure of heaven and the pain of hell: as the Novel is between the Beautiful and the Great.

8. For a useful study of the views of women in the eighteenth century as sexual beings, see A. D. Harvey, *Sex in Georgian England* (London, 1994).

9. Cf. the discussion in *Hogarth* 3:88.

10. The penetration of the maidenhead, however, it has been argued by Forrest Tyler Stevens, is the one act of pleasure which designates permanence in the constant flux of pursuit: an act "which is, in and of itself, capable of retaining the permanence which doesn't exist in any other sexual act. Hence, its uniqueness guarantees its worth" (Stevens, "Sodomizing Fanny Hill," forthcoming).

11. These were published engravings, but there were also paintings that Fielding, being a close friend of Hogarth's, could have seen: *A Scene from "The Tempest"* and *Satan, Sin, and Death,* for example, of the late 1730s.

12. See chap. 2, above.

13. The last words are Angela J. Smallwood's: "Booth carries into Newgate an assumption about the intrinsic beauty of the female character" (*Fielding and the Woman Question* [New York, 1989], 163–64).

14. See Fielding, *Amelia* 9.6, p. 353; cf. explanation, 357–58; and then 360.

15. In this case cf. Hogarth's emphasis on Variety rather than Contrast. His

key term Variety comes from the aim of Addison's Novel "to vary Human Life, and to divert our Minds, for a while, with the Strangeness of its Appearance." Hogarth even gives Contrast a certain priority over variety: the eye can be "glutted with a succession of variety" and find "relief in a certain degree of sameness," which when "properly introduced, and contrasted with variety, adds to it more variety" (*Analysis*, 35). But Hogarth is subordinating contrast to, incorporating it within, a larger sense of variety.

16. Fielding, *The Wedding Day* 2.2; in Henley, ed., *Complete Works of Fielding* 12:85. Hogarth's particular fix on the metaphor of the chase was a commonplace of romantic comedies, which he could have remembered from (among countless others) Fielding's earliest play, *Love in Several Masques* (1728): Malvil says of Merital, "You are a sort of sportsmen, who are always hunting in a park of coquets, where your sport is so plenty that you start fresh game before you have run down the old" (8:18).

17. One might also ask how the physical flaw, including the image of Sophia imagined as stripped and raped, a more sinister version of the naked Virtue envisioned in the dedication, connects with the pain and scarring of Mary in *The Female Husband*—or indeed, implicitly, with Tom's beautiful adolescent body marked by the sinister Thwackum's whipping.

18. Smallwood, *Fielding and the Woman Question*, 159.

19. *Private Papers of James Boswell*, ed. Geoffry Scott and Frederick Pottle, 18 vols. (Mount Vernon, N.Y., 1928–34), 13:220.

20. It may be significant for the changing times that Hogarth, when he wrote his "Autobiographical Notes" in the 1760s, perhaps in the aftersight of the *Analysis* theory, though presumably he was reporting real walks through the streets of London, pictured himself as a flaneur: he sets up his dawdling around London, observing (as a reaction against copying from the ancients in Vanderbank's Academy) in a way that may first have caused him to link pleasure to pursuit and chase, as he does in these "Notes."

21. *Monthly Review* 38 (Mar.–Apr. 1768): 291; cited in Gardner Stout, ed., *Sentimental Journey* (Los Angeles, 1967), 24. My quotations are from Stout's text.

22. Wilkes to Churchill, 10 Apr. 1764 (BL, Add. MSS. 30878, fol. 44v); quoted in Cash, *Sterne*, 182.

23. Garrick, quoted in Cash, *Sterne*, 210; Sterne to Mrs. F [London, Apr. 1765], *Letters of Sterne*, 241; Sterne to Lady Warkworth, [23 Apr. 1765], ibid., 242–43. As Arthur Cash, Sterne's biographer, puts it: "Paradoxically, Sterne liked himself as a bawdy talker and writer, though he was unhappy with himself when his sexual urges became strong and explicit. The ribald joke in the drawing room probably made him feel that he had objectified his passions and set them at further distances." Cash emphasizes Sterne's aim "to banish sexual

desire, which continued to plague him." And he adds the fact that this "had no appreciable effect upon his popularity among the gentlemen and ladies who regularly bought his books and whose company he sought" (213).

24. We recall Jenny in *Tristram Shandy*, who when first introduced could be Tristram's lover, wife, child, or friend (*Tristram Shandy*, ed. James A. Work [New York, 1940], 48–49).

25. Cf. Stern to Stanhope: "Why do you banter me so about what I wrote to you? Tho' I told you, every morning I jump'd into Venus's lap (meaning thereby the sea) was you to infer from that, that I leap'd into the ladies beds afterwards?—The *body* guides you—the *mind* me" (*Letters of Sterne*, 394, emphasis added). Or to Hannah, about *Sentimental Journey*, he writes that if he were to "give up the Business of sentimental writing" he would "write to the Body": "—that is Hannah! what I am doing in writing to you—but you are a *good Body, &* that's worth half a Score *mean Souls*" (401).

26. Eve Sedgwick, *Between Men: English Literature and Male Homosocial Desire* (New York, 1985), chap. 4.

27. We might contrast Steele on Beautiful Women (*Spectator* No. 144). He remains specific, the emphasis remains on woman, and the paper consists of a series of characters of women (as later in Pope's *Epistle to a Lady*), built on binaries of art-nature, beauty-wit, and climaxing in Everatia, who is not beautiful but Beauty itself—which appears to have to do with her femininity rather than with aesthetics.

28. Sir Roger's continuing obsession with the Widow is evident in his response to Philips's *Distressed Mother*, about the widow Andromache (*Spectator* No. 335), and even in his death—heralded by his final experience of widows and of *the* Widow in No. 517, 4:340.

29. Much earlier, in *Spectator* No. 3, Addison feminized Credit into a figure as ambiguous and worrying as the Widow—withdrawing and shifting from enormous to diminutive—suggesting, as Barrell puts it, the "difficulty in seeing commerce except as a symptom or agent of corruption," both in the sense of effeminizing and of sexualizing (Barrell, *Birth of Pandora*, 67).

30. See Braverman, *Plots and Counterplots*, chap. 2. Sir Roger is associated with the Restoration (with Rochester and Etherege) (*Spectator* No. 2, 1:8; cf. Steele's attacks on Etherege's *Man of Mode* in Nos. 65, 75).

31. I should probably note here that the story of Sir Roger and his man servant in No. 107 is by Steele, servants being a Steele subject (cf. Nos. 88 and 96). The portrait gallery (No. 109) is also by Steele, one of whose subjects was painting.

32. Barrell, *Birth of Pandora*, 65.

33. Burke, *Philosophical Inquiries*, 113; Ferguson, *Solitude and the Sublime*, 50.

34. As I have pointed out elsewhere, *Tristram Shandy* is about unrelatedness

and demonstrates the unrelatedness of the world by focusing on the most apparently closed and related of groups, the family, in the most restricted of places, Shandy Hall and the bowling green ("a world in a small circle . . . of four *English* miles diameter" [*Tristram Shandy*, 11]). The emphasis falls on the conventions of society, on contracts, sermons, excommunications, Cyropedias, and other formalizations that prevent communication by choking the natural, primitive, intuitive, and sympathetic impulses, which appear only as isolated, exceptional moments such as the brief sympathies that pass between Walter and Toby. By contrast, *Sentimental Journey* is about just those isolated scenes of relatedness, but now they are the subject, the object of definition, and so are presented in a loose picaresque narrative where one would least expect to find relatedness, and Yorick is not among his family and friends but among strangers and foreigners in a state of war. (See Paulson, *Breaking and Remaking*, 221–22).

35. For the history of the evidence for Tristram's bastardy, see Melvyn New's annotation in his edition of *Tristram Shandy*, vol. 3 (Gainesville, Fla., 1984), 52–53.

36. See Cash, *Sterne*, 12–13; for Hogarth and Pitt, see *Hogarth* 3:246–51.

37. Jean André Rouquet, *Description de tableau . . . Finchley* (1750), 3; see below, chap. 10.

38. Wilkes to Jean-Baptiste Suard, 25 Mar. 1764, quoted by Joel Gold, "Tristram Shandy at the Ambassador's Chapel," *Philological Quarterly* 48 (1969): 421–24. William Cowper criticized Sterne's sermons ("though I admire Sterne as a man of genius, I can never admire him as a preacher") for their man-centered as opposed to Christ-centered philosophy (Cowper to Joseph Hill, 3 Apr. 1766, in *Correspondence*, ed. Thomas Wright [1904], 1:64–65). Sterne's friend Hall-Stevenson, who transplanted the Medmenham Monks to Yorkshire, may have been only a more open, less inhibited (by his cloth) freethinker and skeptic. His more than Sternean impudence was exposed in his *First Chapter of Prophecies of the Prophet Homer: With a Letter to the B[ishop] of G[loucester]* of 1766, which claimed, among other things, that Warburton was a cuckold.

39. Cf. Hogarth's *Invasion* prints of 1756 (*Hogarth's Graphic Works*, nos. 202–3) which contain these elements.

40. As we have seen before (with Hogarth and Fielding), the anti-Catholic emphasis is closely related to anti-Jacobitism. Slop's excommunication of Obadiah's knot was accompanied by Toby whistling the Protestant Williamite song "Lillibullero." We recall also that Trim, whose name is James Butler, is named for the Anglo-English Duke of Ormond; that Toby and Trim fought wars against the Catholics of the Continent; that Tristram was born on 5 November, the day the Gunpowder Plot was foiled and William III landed at Torbay; and that great-uncle Hammond Shandy was a soldier in Monmouth's rebellion against the Catholic James II.

CHAPTER 7. The Strange, Trivial, and Infantile

1. Solkin, *Painting for Money*, 136.

2. See *Hogarth's Graphic Works*, nos. 146–49.

3. The same contrast is evident in their adjacent paintings of the child Moses in the Foundling Hospital—one a bland rendition of the discovery of Moses in the bullrushes (Moses with all the expressiveness of a putto), the other a disquieting ("novel") portrayal of Moses as a young boy, a type of the "foundlings" of the 1740s, bewildered and torn between real and adoptive mothers, the latter an emblematic figure of Charity.

4. *Moses and Pharaoh's Daughter* was followed by *The March to Finchley,* which is plainly about "foundlings," both in the sense of the Foundling Hospital (where Hogarth contrived to have the painting hung) and of that "foundling" Tom Jones, both hero and novel, itself a "foundling" novel.

5. *Characteristics* 2:29.

6. Michael Levey, *From Rococo to Revolution* (New York, 1966), 121.

7. *The Life, Unpublished Letters, and Philosophical Regimen of Anthony, Earl of Shaftesbury,* ed. Benjamin Rand (London, 1900), 216–17.

8. John Locke, *Some Thoughts concerning Education* (1705 ed.), in *The Educational Writings of John Locke,* ed. James L. Axtell (Cambridge, 1968), 255, 273–74. See also Samuel F. Pickering Jr., *John Locke and Children's Books in Eighteenth-Century England* (Knoxville, 1981).

9. See above, p. 53.

10. Newbery's *A Little Lottery-Book for Children: Containing a "New" Method of "Playing" Them into a Knowledge of the Letters, Figures, Etc.* (1756) laid out the Lockean strategy for children's literature: "It would be much easier to teach Children to read were it possible to fix their Attention on the Letters, 'til they were become familiar; but the Infant Mind, ever charmed with new Objects, roves so precipitately from One Thing to another, that no adequate Idea can be formed, for the Impression fleets with the Object, and the Remembrance of it is no more." Thus to fix the letter in the child's mind it is necessary to have him look at a letter, then at a picture, read its name, and so on.

11. Isaac Kramnick, "Children's Literature and Bourgeois Ideology," in *Culture and Politics from Puritanism to the Enlightenment,* ed. Perez Zagorin (Berkeley, 1980), 203–40. The following account of *Goody Two-Shoes* first appeared as "The History of Little Goody Two-Shoes as a Children's Book," in *Literary Theory and Criticism: Festschrift Presented to René Wellek on His Eightieth Birthday,* ed. Joseph P. Strelka (Bern, 1982), 2:1075–92.

12. F. J. Harvey Darton, *Children's Books in England* 2d ed. (Cambridge, 1958); the first edition appeared in 1932.

13. Nicholas Tucker, *The Child and the Book: A Psychological and Literary Exploration* (Cambridge, 1981), 28–29.

14. For Locke's advocacy of the visual accompaniment, see *Thoughts concern-ing Education*, 164, 264–65. See also on this example, Paulson, *Popular and Polite Art*, 105–6.

15. Locke, *Thoughts concerning Education*, 275.

16. For *Goody Two-Shoes* I use the facsimile of the 1765 edition in the Garland Series, *Classics of Children's Literature 1621–1932* (New York, 1977). The informative preface is by Michael H. Platt. All page references are to this edition. For a recent study that dismisses both *Goody Two-Shoes* and the *Vicar* as showing "the same egregious faults," see Geoffrey Summerfield, *Fantasy and Reason: Children's Literature in the Eighteenth Century* (Athens, Ga., 1984), 93. Humphry Carpenter has noted the tendency of children's literature to de-mystify religious icons in "*Alice* and the Mockery of God," in *Secret Gardens: The Golden Age of Children's Literature* (London, 1985), 44–69.

17. John Bunyan, "Conclusion," in *Pilgrim's Progress* (1678).

18. The book is dedicated to the children, "inscribed by Their old Friend in St. Paul's Church-Yard," i.e., the publisher on the title page, John Newbery. The "Introduct-ion" is "By the Editor," and the appendix, a letter from the printer, is signed W.B. A few pages later (11) we read: "Why, do you suppose this is written by Mr. Newbery, Sir? This may come from another Hand. This is not the Book, Sir, mentioned in the Title, but the Introduction"—which means that the rest of the book may be by Newbery, but this part may be by another hand. For the sort of passage that sounds like Goldsmith, see 49.

19. Indeed, I am reminded, as perhaps *Two-Shoes's* readers were, of the fable of Patty and her pattins in Gay's *Trivia*.

20. For background on the aspect of reconstituting, see Paulson, *Breaking and Remaking*, chap. 1.

21. Words even serve in *Goody Two-Shoes* to quell the anger of quarreling couples, whom Two-Shoes instructs to recite the alphabet before embarking on a quarrel: "By this Means your Passions will be stifled," she says, "and Reason will have Time to take the Rule"—and thereafter, we are told, "they never could get their Passions to any considerable Height" (109). She invents a Swiftean "Considering Cap" with inscriptions (and hieroglyphics) on three sides and on the inside instructions for its use—all aimed at controlling the individual's tendency to lose control of himself and vent his frustration in some antisocial way.

22. For Locke's influential words on children's cruelty to animals, see *Thoughts concerning Education*, 225–28; and Pickering, *John Locke and Chil-dren's Books*, chap. 1, pp. 3–39.

23. See Locke, *Thoughts concerning Education*, 242–45; and Pickering, *John Locke and Children's Books*, chap. 2, 40–69.

24. On the subversive dog, see Paulson, *Popular and Polite Art*, 49–63; on the child, see Paulson, *Book and Painting*, 68–82.

CHAPTER 8. From Novel to Strange to "Sublime"

1. Henry Fielding, *Examples of the Interposition of Providence in the Detection and Punishment of Murder,* in Fielding, *Enquiry,* 180. For Hogarth's *Enthusiasm Delineated,* see *Hogarth* 3:251–63; and for *Credulity,* 3:362–68. The word "enthusiasm," for or expressed in art, goes back to Shaftesbury's *Sensus Communis.*

2. Arthur Friedman correctly identifies "Sperate miseri, cavete faelices" as from the last page of Burton's *Anatomy of Melancholy,* where the line is not identified and is presumably Burton's own Latin (see *Collected Works of Oliver Goldsmith,* ed. Friedman [Oxford, 1966], 4:13).

3. Cf. Sterne's "mirth," used to "endeavour to fence against the infirmities of ill health, and other evils of life" in the dedication to *Tristram Shandy,* vol. 1.

4. The essays in the *Bee* were essays Goldsmith took seriously. He used the "Introduction" as introduction to the *Essays of Oliver Goldsmith* (1765) and the essays "Happiness" and "Education" as, respectively, nos. 3 and 7 in the collection.

5. *Bee,* 6 Oct. 1759, in *Collected Works of Goldsmith* 1:354–55. All quotations from the *Bee* are from this edition.

6. The essay on the education of youth in the *Bee* is again purely practical, and while on one page Goldsmith prefers the story of the frugal Whittington (without his cat) to the fecklessness of Tom Jones and Joseph Andrews, on another he silently adopts Joseph's arguments for education in public schools rather than private tutoring (461, 459).

7. Beau Nash, another savior of others, though in his case at his own expense, also recalls the character of Two-Shoes. He is a mini-redeemer (for example of Miss S.——), relieving another's financial straits by spending all his own money, thus leaving himself in the same situation. The best way of getting repayment from Nash is to ask him for charity or a loan.

8. Although somewhat overstated, Robert Hopkins's thesis that Primrose was a sort of Swiftean author draws attention to the anomalies of his self-presentation (*The True Genius of Oliver Goldsmith* [Baltimore, 1969], chap. 5).

9. The story of Asem and the reverie in the Boar's Head were reprinted in Goldsmith's *Essays* as, respectively, nos. 16 and 19.

10. In the case of the Cock Lane Ghost, the Methodists, who believed in "ghosts," had enthusiastically taken up the cause. Hogarth uses this to connect his satire on religion in *Enthusiasm Delineated* to the Cock Lane affair; Goldsmith, though he makes no reference to the Methodists, makes a more general point: "even pious and orthodox divines themselves have been known to give credit to the strangest falsehoods of this kind," alluding to the "worthy Clergyman" mentioned in the *St. James's Chronicle* for 2–4 Feb. 1762 (4:438 and n. 2). For Goldsmith on witches, see his *Bee,* 24 Nov. 1759, in *Collected Works of Goldsmith* 1:496.

11. Battestin, *Providence of Wit*, chap. 7; Thomas Preston, "The Uses of Adversity: Worldly Detachment and Heavenly Treasure in *The Vicar of Wakefield*," *Studies in Philology* 81 (1984): 229–51.

12. These pages on Goldsmith's use of the metaphors of pilgrimage and theater are adapted from my essay, referred to above, chap. 3, n. 15.

13. Battestin, *Providence of Wit*, 196 ff.

14. K. Eichenberger, *Oliver Goldsmith, das Kömische in den Werken seiner Reifeperiode* (Bern, 1954), 78; see also Sven Backman, *This Singular Tale: A Study of "The Vicar of Wakefield" and Its Literary Background* (Lund, 1971), 94 and 131 n. 33.

15. The primrose is also used by Goldsmith in *The Deserted Village* to suggest rural innocence and simplicity; but even here it is "Sweet as the primrose peeps beneath the thorn" (*Collected Works of Goldsmith* 4:299).

16. Nicholas Rowe, *Fair Penitent*, ed. Malcolm Goldstein (Lincoln, Neb., 1969), 5.

17. James Lehman, "*The Vicar of Wakefield:* Goldsmith's Sublime, Oriental Job," *ELH* 46 (1979): 97–121.

18. For another example, in the exchange with Burchell, Dr. Primrose cites, with approval for the popular-ballad side of the argument, Pope's "An honest man is the noblest work of God." He is arguing against "wit and understanding" (surely Popean qualities) as opposed to "integrity"; the philosopher vs. the "ignorant peasant"—the one with "faults," the other without. The terms are jumbled and contradictory, and it would appear that Burchell's reply is intended as a corrective: for he opposes "the low mechanic, who laboriously plods on through life, without censure or applause," exemplified by "the tame correct paintings of the Flemish school," to "the erroneous, but sublime animations of the Roman pencil" (4:79).

19. "Starts" alludes to Garrick's famous style, in particular to his playing of Hamlet when he saw the ghost—represented by Fielding in *Tom Jones.*

20. The lines are elegy, but so were the lines on the mad dog, and more pertinently they parallel the living epitaph Dr. Primrose composed and displayed on the wall for Mrs. Primrose back in chapter 2, which was equally odd, though in the comic mode of the earlier chapters. This story emerges when Dr. Primrose tells us that William Whiston, whose stand on monogamy he admires, "had engraved upon his wife's tomb that she was the *only* wife of William Whiston." Dr. Primrose therefore writes "a similar epitaph" for his own wife, "though still living,"

> in which I extoled her prudence, and obedience till death; and having got it copied fair, with an elegant frame, it was placed over the chimney-piece, where it answered several very useful purposes. It admonished my wife of her

duty to me, and my fidelity to her; it inspired her with a passion for fame, and constantly put her in mind of her end. (4:22)

Both Primrose parents impose epitaphs on a living person, bodily conveying the inscription from the dead to the living, while making it prescriptive, admonitory, and, in an emphatic way, predictive, while couched in the retrospective tense. It anticipates the predictive quality of the popular ballads and songs (the stories of the giant and dwarf, of the mad dog, and so on) which both interrupt and convey the narrative, including Olivia's. It also regards the object of the epitaph as a possession, in another Primrosian assertion comically incongruous with the manifest dominance of both wife and daughter—the former (as a Deborah) dominant over his better judgment, the latter dominant over his exaggerated sense of "family."

CHAPTER 9. From Novel to Picturesque

1. Gilpin is also, however, capable of strong statements in favor of nature: "But all objects are best as nature made them. Art cannot mend them. Where Art interferes, picturesque beauty vanishes"; and "The more refined our taste grows from the *study of nature,* the more insipid are the *works of art.*" Of course, Gilpin himself regards nature through the eyes of art (e.g., a Salvator Rosa); and yet the principles of art by which nature is transformed for the artist, or observer, are based on the natural—roughness, irregularity, and accident. See Gilpin, *Remarks on Forest Scenery,* 2d ed. (1808), 2:273–74 (the first edition appeared in 1792); and idem, "Essay on Picturesque Travel," in *Three Essays: On Picturesque Beauty; on Picturesque Travel; and on Sketching Landscape: To Which Is Added a Poem, on Landscape Painting,* 2d ed. (1794), 57, 6 (the first edition appeared in 1791).

2. See William Gilpin, *Essay upon Prints* (1768), 168–77, on Hogarth in general, and 216–34 on *A Rake's Progress.* For the story about Gilpin, Hogarth, and *Paul before Felix,* see Carl P. Barbier, *William Gilpin* (Oxford, 1963), 24.

3. Gilpin, *Three Essays,* 4.

4. Gilpin had among his papers a manuscript page by Hogarth on his Line of Beauty: *Hogarth* 3:462 n. 74.

5. The gardener had already been asked to help nature along, as when at Stowe he constructed and contrasted a Temple of Ancient Virtue, a perfect Palladian structure, and a ruinous Temple of Modern Virtue.

6. William Gilpin, *Dialogue upon the Gardens . . . at Stowe* (1748), 5. The proto-Picturesque sketched by Gilpin in this work is evident in his utilization of such terms as "curiosity" (2), "Novelty," "varies," and "New" (22).

7. Ferguson, *Solitude and the Sublime,* 134–35.

8. Uvedale Price, *An Essay on the Picturesque* (1794), 5–9, 22–23, 29.

9. Hogarth would have associated "broken and rugged forms" not with the Novel or Picturesque but with Burke's Sublime: See his *Tailpiece* (*Hogarth* 3:422). Cf. Burke's Beautiful: "Most people must have observed the sort of sense they have had, on being swiftly drawn in an easy coach, on a smooth turf, with gradual ascents and declivities" (Burke, *Philosophical Enquiry*, 155).

10. Or "ruined"—and the ruin is implicitly, given the human examples of Marius and Satan (perhaps significantly, rebels), accomplished by the effects of passion (Price, *Essay*, 71). Cf. Burke's example of Satan (*Philosophical Enquiry*, 62).

11. See Paulson, *Breaking and Remaking*, chap. 6.

12. Uvedale Price, *Essay on the Picturesque* (1796 ed.), 378; cited in Sidney K. Robinson, *Inquiry into the Picturesque* (Chicago, 1991), 74; on picturesque politics, see 73–93. Brown and Price's distrust of the Beautiful was also of the elevated prospect. The civic humanist rejected the low "private view" and detailed foregrounds that were taken to imply an absorption in the particular and concrete private interests that ignore the public good. The low was precisely the point of view taken by the theorists of the Picturesque, as by Hogarth. (See John Barrell, *The Idea of Landscape and the Sense of Place, 1730–1840* [Cambridge, 1972], chap. 1.)

13. For Turner's adaptation of Hogarth's Line in his vortex, his utilization of Hogarth's fringe of history on a sublime landscape that reduces it to ironic meaninglessness, and the prominent (often obtrusive) verbal element of his paintings, see Paulson, *Literary Landscape* (New Haven, 1982), chap. 6; and W.J.T. Mitchell, "Metamorphoses of the Vortex: Hogarth, Turner, and Blake," in *Articulate Images: The Sister Arts from Hogarth to Tennyson,* ed. Richard Wendorf (Minneapolis, 1983), 125–68.

14. See Paulson, *Rowlandson*, 13–18.

15. Rowlandson's drawings for William Combe's satiric poems on Dr. Syntax began to appear in 1809 and were published as three *Tours of Doctor Syntax in Search of the Picturesque* in 1812, 1820, and 1821.

16. On Rowlandson and the Picturesque, and on the Dr. Syntax drawings, see Paulson, *Rowlandson*, 38–45 and 87–89, respectively.

17. Suggested by Frank Davis, "A Break with Tradition," *Country Life* 22 (Nov. 1979): 1890.

18. The simplest example is the circle of male heads at the bottom looking up at the woman—as in the drawing, *The Dancer* (Yale Center for British Art, Mellon Collection, reproduced in Paulson, *Rowlandson*), or, the explicit version, the etching *The Congregation* (in *The Amorous Illustrations of Thomas Rowlandson* [New York, 1969], no. 24). Then there is the lone nude, observed only by the viewer outside the print (mute sculptures take the spectator's place): *Lonesome Pleasures,* in ibid., no. 29; as well as old men looking at the nude (*The*

Inspection or *Susannah and the Elders,* etchings, in ibid., nos. 25, 23); and the nude with one spectator (*The Curious Parson,* etching, in ibid., no. 22).

19. For a cuckolded spectator with thoughts of revenge, see *The Revenge* or *The Observers,* etchings, in *Amorous Illustrations of Rowlandson,* nos. 9, 18; for a preoccupied husband, *not* watching, see *The Old Husband* or *The Star Gazer,* nos. 1, 8.

20. I discuss many of Rowlandson's works of this sort in "The Artist, the Beautiful Girl, and the Crowd: The Case of Thomas Rowlandson," in *Georgia Review* 31 (1977): 121–59; and *Representations of Revolution,* chap. 5.

21. For his constructing Sarah Siddons's likeness out of a sequence of "nose" shapes (which derive from both the drawing manuals of the academy and his first response to Mrs. Siddons—"Damn the nose—there's no end to it"), and his paralleling the form of the musical Mrs. Thicknesse and that of her cello, that of the Duke of Bedford with that of a vase, and that of Lord Ligonier with that of his horse, see Paulson, *Emblem and Expression,* chap. 12.

22. See Paulson, *Breaking and Remaking,* 172–74.

23. In practice, only Henry Fuseli can be called a sublime artist in the Burkean sense. He puts all of his energy into dramatizing fields of force and power. His sexually explicit drawings, for example, are of women exerting power and inflicting pain on men. Though these "symplegmas," as he called them, fit into his obsessive drawings of women binding and often murdering their men, they may of course be part of a scenario dictated by the desires of the men. In terms of his own choice of a subject, *as* artist, Fuseli is dictating some such scenario in which his power over the women involves this sadomasochistic fantasy. In any case, he is operating within the Burkean-Sadean pornographic Sublime.

24. By a poetic coincidence, Sterne's daughter Lydia (who herself, returning from Italy a surprisingly beautiful young woman, replaced Eliza in Sterne's affections) met the Marquis de Sade and later, enjoying one of his *fêtes cham-pêtres,* reported Sade as saying something (alas lost to us) which prompted Sterne to write in reply: "I am out of al patience with the answer the Marquis made the Abbé [his uncle]; 'twas truly coarse, and I wonder he bore it with any christian patience" (*Letters of Sterne,* 301).

CHAPTER 10. The Novelizing of Hogarth

1. This chapter originally appeared as "The Harlot, Her Father, and the Parson: Representing and Interpreting Hogarth in the Eighteenth Century," in *Icons Texts Iconotexts,* ed. Peter Wagner, forthcoming.

2. John Trusler, *Hogarth Moralized: Being a Complete Edition of Hogarth's Works* (1768); this work was printed for Jane Hogarth. Trusler's title page reads: "Pointing out the many Beauties that may have hitherto escaped Notice; and A

Comment on their Moral Tendency. Calculated to improve the Minds of Youth, and, convey Instruction, under the Mask of Entertainment. Now First Published, With the Approbation of Jane Hogarth, Widow of the late Mr. Hogarth." The work was sold, inter alia, by "Mrs. Hogarth, at her House in Leicester-Fields." The small copies were by Corbauld and Dent. Ireland's commentary was written to accompany Boydell's Hogarth folios, and Lichtenberg's was accompanied by E. Riepenhausen's engravings after Hogarth.

3. Hogarth's intention was not, however, detected by Trusler, who remarks in the "Advertisement," which follows the title page: "The author of these sheets hopes to stand excused in his omission of the print of the Times, it being merely a temporary publication, now out of date; and, of [t]hose of BEFORE, and, AFTER, they being of too ludicrous [he means obscene] a nature to have a place in this work."

4. Hogarth's own commentary—though it survives in a very fragmentary form—recalls Rouquet's and points toward Trusler's. See "Autobiographical Notes" in Burke's edition of Hogarth, *Analysis*.

5. See *Hogarth* 3:251–54.

6. G. C. Lichtenberg, *Aüsfuhrliche Erklärung der Hogarthischen Kupferstiche*, vol 3. of *Georg Christoph Lichtenberg Schriften und Briefe*, ed. Franz H. Mautner (Frankfurt am Main, 1983), 15; translated as Herdan and Herdan, *World of Hogarth*, 86; Rouquet, *Description du tableau . . . Finchley*, 3. Cf. Samuel Johnson, who in his *Proposals for an Edition . . . of William Shakespeare* (1756) had referred to the need for commentary on "any accidental or minute particularity, which cannot be supplied by common understanding, or common observation" (*Yale Edition of the Works of Samuel Johnson*, vol. 7, ed. Arthur Sherbo [New Haven, 1968], 57).

7. John Ireland tells us that Hogarth assisted Rouquet and that Trusler got information from Jane Hogarth (*Hogarth Illustrated* 1:xii, xiii).

8. Jean André Rouquet, *Lettres de Monsieur * * à un de ses amis à Paris* (London, 1747), 3–4. All translations from Rouquet in the current volume are my own.

9. The "poor goose [is] almost strangled by the address label round its neck (in a way, like the poor parson on horseback through his)." Lichtenberg acknowledges that the cousin has not shown up: "Where now is little Pandemos [his Greek *Everyman*, for the Harlot] to go? For in Thames Street, one of the most roaring and crowded thoroughfares in London, live lofing Cosens by the thousand who are only too willing to accept unlabelled geese with their heart in their mouth. The poor animal is addressed, just like you, my good little Mary, and like your poor Yorkshire travelling companions in the cart who are going on farther and who will not lack lofing Cosens, either!" (Lichtenberg, *World of Hogarth*, 15). But for another sense of "cousin," see the interpretation in chapter 1, above.

10. Cf. Rouquet, who mentioned that this ecclesiastic, on a white horse, has come to seek his fortune in London. "He reads the address of a letter which is a recommendation to a bishop. The poor condition of his horse, and of his general figure, indicates his poverty" (*Lettres,* 3).

11. Richardson's remark about his novel as preferable to the sermon preached from a pulpit is also apposite as a key to a way of thinking which he shared with Hogarth but which no longer registered on Trusler: He refers to the "general depravity, when even the pulpit has lost a great part of its weight, and *the clergy are considered as a body of interested men*"; it is against this that he employs the form of *Pamela* and *Clarissa* ("Postscript" to *Clarissa,* emphasis added).

12. The *Bemerkung* is based on Rouquet's remark (3), "Cet ecclésiastique monté sur un cheval blanc, comme ils affectent ici de l'être" (this clergyman mounted on a white horse, which they affect in this country). Lichtenberg assumes that Hogarth, while shading in the horse's body to gray, told the credulous Rouquet it was white, and so corrects Rouquet's *cheval blanc* with the German *Schimmel:* "die englischen Geistlichen ritten gewöhnlich Schimmel," adding his own words: "Also *Schwarz* und *Weiss*" (i.e., a black-dressed clergyman on a white horse). *Schimmel* is both white horse and mold; therefore a *gray* horse. If the witticism *were* Hogarth's it might also explain the black-white checkerboard of the Bell Tavern sign. But it is of course Lichtenberg's and perishes in translation. "Gray" is Herdan's translation of Lichtenberg's *Schimmel.* Herdan, who evidently did not check the quotation from Rouquet, misplaces his quotation marks, suggesting that the second sentence ("Therefore *black* and *white*") is Rouquet's also. (Lichtenberg, *World of Hogarth,* 5 n.; Rouquet, *Lettres,* 3; Lichtenberg, *Ausführliche Erklärung,* 79 n.)

13. See Fielding, *Covent-Garden Journal* No. 57, 1 Aug. 1752; and *Jacobite's Journal* No. 32, 9 July 1748 (see also No. 31). See also Fielding's *Miscellanies,* vol. 2, ed. Bertrand A. Goldgar (Middletown, Conn., 1993), 192.

14. Fielding, *Rape upon Rape* 2.5, in Henley, ed., *Complete Works of Fielding* 9:100–102. The detail is also significant for the question of Fielding's attitude toward the clergy prior to his *Champion* essays defending them.

15. See *Hogarth,* vol. 1, chap. 8.

16. Lichtenberg got only as far as the *Harlot* and the *Rake, The Times of the Day, Marriage A-la-mode, Industry and Idleness,* and a few of the single plates. See Frederick Burwick, "The Hermeneutics of Lichtenberg's Interpretation of Hogarth," *Lessing Yearbook* 19 (1987): 165–89. Burwick draws attention to the influence of David Hartley's associationism on Lichtenberg—which supplements and helps to explain the influence of Sterne. He also distinguishes between Lichtenberg's Hogarthian discourses in the version published in the *Göttingen Taschenkalender* of 1784 and in the *Ausführliche Erklärung* of the 1790s.

17. On the German appreciation of *Tristram Shandy,* known by Sterne

during his own lifetime, see Bernard Fabrian, "Tristram Shandy and Parson Yorick among Some German Greats," in *The Winged Skull: Papers from the Laurence Sterne Bicentenary Conference*, ed. Arthur H. Cash and John M. Stedmond (London, 1971), 194–209.

18. These facts were gleaned presumably from Nichols's *Biographical Anecdotes*, from which he also learned the facts of Colonel Charteris and Mother Needham; more frequently, however, he cites John Ireland, whose speculative approach is closer to his own approach to Hogarth.

19. Sterne, *Tristram Shandy*, vol. 1, chap. 12, p. 31.

20. See above, chap. 1.

21. This should be contrasted with my own earlier hypothesis about the detail of the Harlot's paternity (*Hogarth* 1:328–29), that Hogarth wished to suggest that the Harlot was rejecting a definition of the self conferred by her family.

22. *Grub-Street Journal*, 24 Sept. 1730; *Hogarth* 1:250–51.

23. For some reason Trusler interprets the Harlot's servant—the one sympathetic figure in the series—as bad: he believes it is she who is deriding the Harlot, while in the next plate, which he reads as criticism of all the characters except the child, who is sensibly cooking meat for his supper, he ignores the servant's protective gesture.

24. Instead Lichtenberg displaces the theme to her servant, reading the servant's "fancy stockings" and "embroidered shoes" as "the acquired property of the woman who, in order to impress town and Court had, in the appearance of her legs at least, to try to imitate them" (50). Trusler identifies a general theme of affectation in his analysis of *Harlot*, plate 6, which he calls the annex to the tragedy, in "the folly of mankind, in making expensive funerals, particularly, of those, who cannot afford it; but, such," he adds, "is the general pride of the world, as to be, always, aiming at something above them; the poor apeing, as it were, the vanities of the rich" (12). His evidence is one whore viewing another "tricking herself out before the glass." He generalizes the aping, as is his custom, not as affectation but as *Vanitas*.

25. Ireland, *Hogarth Illustrated* 1:6. Ireland makes no mention of Lichtenberg, though his commentary, perhaps coincidentally, recalls Lichtenberg's in its playful treatment of detail. If he read German, he could have read Lichtenberg's text of 1784 in the *Göttingen Taschenkalender*. Volume 1 covers the plates of the 1730s and 1740s. Volume 2 continues with the *Stages of Cruelty* and subsequent prints, plus a few earlier ones (*Four Groups of Heads, Sarah Malcolm*, the *Beggar's Opera* painting, etc.). A third volume, issued seven years later, publishes for the first time Hogarth's manuscripts.

26. Sir Joshua Reynolds, *Discourses*, ed. Robert W. Wark (New Haven, 1959), 51.

27. Rouquet, *Description du tableau . . . Finchley*, 2.

28. See *Hogarth,* vol. 1, chap. 8, "Hogarth and the Rise of the Novel."

29. See Hogarth, "Autobiographical Notes," 209–11, 214–15.

30. In 1791 Ireland, in some ways the most astute of the early commentators, starts his account of the *Harlot* with the context of history paintings and, taking his cue from its subscription ticket, sees it as a modernizing, naturalizing, even "biographizing" of that genre whose aim "has been to emblazon some signal exploit of an exalted and distinguished character"; and he returns from time to time to the subject of greatness and false greatness (associated with Fielding's works of the 1730s). He calls Hogarth "the biographical dramatist of domestic life"—as contrasted to the lives of monarchs and heroes—and relates him to the dramatist George Lillo as a portrayer of "scenes of humble life" (1:2). He refers to the *Rake's Progress* as telling another "little domestic story" (1:24). He suggests that this domestic drama has a thematic (or satiric), but not a formal, relationship to epic: the characters criticize high life, but in the dramatic form of Lillo.

31. *The Gentleman's Magazine* review of *Shakespeare Illustrated* (23 [1753]: 250) categorized it under "entertainment" (as distinct from divinity, morality, history, poetry, etc.), which would have included novels. I want to thank Jonathan Brody Kramnick for drawing my attention to the example and significance of Lennox's *Shakespeare Illustrated* in his essay "Reading Shakespeare's Novels: Literary History and Cultural Politics in the Lennox-Johnson debate," *Modern Language Quarterly* 55 (1994): 429–53.

32. Fielding, *Covent-Garden Journal,* 161.

33. Charlotte Lennox, *Shakespeare Illustrated: Or, The Novels and Histories on Which the Plays of Shakespeare Are Founded . . . by the Author of the Female Quixote* (1753), 1:245.

34. The question of whether Johnson wrote the *Gentleman's Magazine* reviews of Hogarth's *Analysis* remains unsettled. See *Hogarth* 3:141 and n.; and for a general assessment of the Hogarth-Johnson relationship, 263–68.

35. *Rasselas,* in *Rasselas and Other Tales,* ed. Gwin J. Kolb, in *The Yale Edition of the Works of Samuel Johnson,* vol. 16 (New Haven, 1990), 14.

36. "Preface" (1765), in *Johnson on Shakespeare,* ed. Arthur Sherbo, in *Yale Edition of the Works of Johnson,* vol. 7 (New Haven, 1968), 66.

37. Samuel Johnson, *Lives of the English Poets,* ed. G. B. Hill (Oxford, 1905), 1:178.

38. These remarks are scattered through the "Preface" to Johnson's *Shakespeare.*

Acknowledgments

For most useful and sympathetic readings, which clarified my thought in important ways, I want to thank Michael McKeon and Peter Sacks; for other suggestions and corrections, Joan Dayan, DeAnn DeLuna, Jackson I. Cope, and Ann Stiller; for exchange of ideas in the early stages, Frances Ferguson and the NEH Summer Institute in Aesthetics we directed in 1990 (especially the paper of Paul Guyer and talks with Peter J. McCormick); for mutual exchanges on deism, the symposium on heterodoxy led by Roger Lund at Syracuse in 1992; for particular supporting research and cross-fertilizations, my graduate students Andres Virkus, Peter Mortensen, and Scott Black; for expert copyediting, Miriam Kleiger; and for indexing, Gordon L. Brumm.

Index

Library of Congress Cataloging-in-Publication Data

Paulson, Ronald
    The beautiful, novel, and strange : aesthetics and heterodoxy / Ronald Paulson.
        p.   cm.
    Includes bibliographical references and index.
    ISBN 0-8018-5171-8 (hc : alk. paper)
        1. English fiction—18th century—History and criticism. 2. Art and literature—Great
Britian—History—18th century. 3. Aesthetics, British—18th century. 4. Literature and
society—Great Britain—History—18th century. 5. Fiction—Technique.
I. Title
PR858.A74P38   1996
700'.94109033—dc20   95-18983